april 28, 1980.

Reading & Vocabulary

Reader's Choice

Reader's Choice

A Reading Skills Textbook for
Students of English as a Second Language

E. Margaret Baudoin, Ellen S. Bober,
Mark A. Clarke, Barbara K. Dobson, Sandra Silberstein

Under the Auspices of the English Language Institute at the University of Michigan

Ann Arbor   The University of Michigan Press

Copyright © by The University of Michigan 1977
All rights reserved
ISBN 0-472-08100-4
Library of Congress Catalog Card No. 76-49148
Published in the United States of America by
The University of Michigan Press and simultaneously
in Rexdale, Canada, by John Wiley & Sons Canada, Limited
Manufactured in the United States of America

79   80   10   9   8   7   6

Grateful acknowledgment is made to the following publishers, newspapers, magazines, and authors for permission to reprint copyrighted materials:

American Automobile Association for material adapted from Kentucky-Tennessee road map. Basic map reproduced by permission of the American Automobile Association, copyright owner.

Ann Arbor News for "Pockety Women Unite?" by Jane Myers, Staff Reporter, *Ann Arbor News*, September 22, 1975.

Beacon Press for adapted excerpts from *Deception Detection* by Jeffrey Schrank. Copyright © 1975 by Jeffrey Schrank. Reprinted by permission of Beacon Press.

Christian Science Publishing Society for adapted version of *"Non Smokers Lib.* Shout heard 'round the world 'Don't puff on me'," by Clayton Jones, July 3, 1975. Reprinted by permission from the *Christian Science Monitor.* Copyright © 1975 by The Christian Science Publishing Society. All rights reserved.

William Collins and World Publishing Company, Inc., with permission from *Webster's New World Dictionary* for material from the College Edition, copyright © 1966 by The World Publishing Company.

Thomas Y. Crowell Company, Inc., for material adapted from *Cheaper by the Dozen* by Frank B. Gilbreth, Jr., and Ernestine Gilbreth Carey, copyright © 1963, 1948. Reprinted by permission of Thomas Y. Crowell Company, Inc., publisher.

Detroit Free Press for material from "The Calendar," *Detroit Free Press*, Sunday Edition, April 4, 1976.

Farrar, Straus and Giroux, Inc., and Brandt and Brandt for material from "The Lottery" by Shirley Jackson, copyright © 1948, 1949 by Shirley Jackson, copyright renewed 1976 by Laurence Hyman, Barry Hyman, Mrs. Sarah Webster, and Mrs. Joanne Schnurer. "The Lottery" originally appeared in *The New Yorker*. Reprinted with the permission of Farrar, Straus and Giroux, Inc.

Features and News Service for adapted version of "How Do You Handle Everday Stress?" by Dr. Syvil Marquit and Marilyn Lane.

Harper's Magazine Company for "The Odds for Long Life" by Robert Collins. Copyright © 1973 by *Harper's* Magazine. Reprinted from the May 1973 issue by special permission.

Houghton Mifflin Company for material from *The American Heritage Dictionary of the English Language*. Copyright © 1969, 1970, 1971, 1973, 1975, 1976, Houghton Mifflin Company. Reprinted by permission from *The American Heritage Dictionary of the English Language*.

Houghton Mifflin Company and William Collins Sons and Company Ltd., for material adapted from *In the Shadow of Man* by Jane van Lawick-Goodall. Copyright © 1971 by Hugo and Jane van Lawick-Goodall. Reprinted by permission of Houghton Mifflin Company.

King Features Syndicate, Inc., for comics from "*The Lockhorns*," "*Laff-A-Day*," and "*Trudy*." Copyright © King Features Syndicate, Inc., 1970.

Ladies' Home Journal for "Why We Laugh" by Janet Spencer, *Ladies' Home Journal*. November 1974.

Harold Matson Company, Inc., for "The Chaser" by John Collier. Copyright © 1941, 1968 by John Collier, reprinted by permission of Harold Matson Company, Inc. "The Chaser" originally appeared in *The New Yorker*.

Michigan Daily for selected advertisements from the classified section, *Michigan Daily*, November 19, 1976.

Harry Miles Muheim for "The Dusty Drawer" by Harry Miles Muheim. Copyright © 1969 by Harry Miles Muheim. Published in *Alfred Hitchcock Presents a Month of Mystery*, copyright © 1969 by Random House, Inc. Reprinted by permission of the author.

New York Times Company for "Japanese Style in Decision-Making" by Yoshio Terasawa, *New York Times*, May 12, 1974. Copyright © 1974 by The New York Times Company. Reprinted by permission.

Newspaper Enterprise Association, Inc., for material from *The World Almanac and Book of Facts*, 1974 edition; Copyright © Newspaper Enterprise Association, New York, 1973.

Newsweek, Inc., for adaptations of the following articles: "Sonar for the Blind" by Matt Clark and Susan Agrest, copyright © 1975 by Newsweek, Inc.; "Graveyard of the Atlantic," copyright © 1974 by Newsweek, Inc.; and "Conjugal Prep," copyright © 1975 by Newsweek, Inc. All rights reserved. Reprinted by permission.

W. W. Norton and Company, Inc., and The Bodley Head for material reprinted from *The City* by John V. Lindsay, by permission of W. W. Norton and Company, Inc. Copyright © 1969, 1970 by W. W. Norton and Company, Inc.

Overseas Development Council for material from "The Sacred Rac" by Patricia Hughes, *Focusing on Global Poverty and Development* by Jayne C. Millar (Washington, D.C.: Overseas Development Council, 1974), pp. 357-58. Reprinted by permission.

Random House, Inc., and William Morris Agency, Inc., for material adapted from *Iberia: Spanish Travels and Reflections* by James A. Michener. Copyright © 1968 by Random House, Inc. Copyright © 1968 by Marjay Productions, Inc. Reprinted by permission of Random House, Inc. Reprinted by permission of William Morris Agency, Inc., on behalf of the author.

Random House, Inc., for an adaptation of "The Midnight Visitor" from *Mystery and More Mystery* by Robert Arthur. Copyright © 1939, 1967 by Robert Arthur. Reprinted by permission of Random House, Inc.

Random House, Inc., for an adaptation from *Future Shock* by Alvin Toffler. Copyright © 1970 by Alvin Toffler. Reprinted by permission of Random House, Inc. Originally appeared in *Playboy* Magazine in a slightly different form.

Sterling Publishing Company, Inc., and Guinness Superlatives Ltd., for material from *The Guinness Book of World Records*, copyright © 1975 by Sterling Publishing Company, Inc., N.Y. 10016.

May Swenson for the following poems: "By Morning," "Living Tenderly," and "Southbound on the Freeway," by May Swenson. Used by permission of the author from *Poems to Solve*, copyright © 1966 by May Swenson.

U.S. News and World Report, Inc., for "Crowded Earth—Billions More Coming," *U.S. News and World Report*, October 21, 1974. Copyright © 1974 by U.S. News and World Report, Inc.

Viking Press, Inc., and Granada Publishing Ltd., for adapted excerpts from *My Family and Other Animals* by Gerald Durrell. Copyright © 1956 by Gerald M. Durrell. Reprinted by permission of The Viking Press and Granada Publishing Ltd.

Acknowledgments

The successful completion of *Reader's Choice* is the result of the cooperation, confidence, and endurance of many people. The authors greatly appreciate the contributions of the individuals listed below. It is impossible to overestimate the importance of their efforts in helping us meet deadlines, their insights during classroom testing, and their encouragement through critique and re-write sessions.

Heartfelt thanks, therefore to:

H. Douglas Brown, director of the English Language Institute (ELI), University of Michigan, whose assistance ranged from personal and professional advice to administrative and financial support. Professor Brown has consistently encouraged creativity and innovation at the ELI. His continued support of *Reader's Choice* ensured its successful completion.

Eleanor Foster, ELI administrative assistant and her capable secretarial and production staff: Elaine Allen, Ginny Barnett, Shelly Cole, Gail Curtis, Lynne Davis, Sue Feldstein, Martha Graham, Donna Head, Barbara Kerwin, Debbie Milly, Lisa Neff, Cathy Pappas, and Louisa Plyler.

George E. Luther and Roderick D. Fraser, ELI administrators, whose efforts made possible financial support and the classroom testing of *Reader's Choice*.

David P. Harris, director of the American Language Institute, Georgetown University; ELI authors Joan Morley and Mary Lawrence; Betsy Soden, ELI lecturer and reading coordinator; Carlos A. Yorio, professor of Linguistics, Toronto University—colleagues in English as a second language (ESL) whose critiques of early drafts proved invaluable.

ESL teachers whose patient and skillful use of the materials through numerous stages of development made detailed revisions and improvements possible—Honor Griffith and Lynne Kurylo of the University of Toronto; Betsy Berriman, Cristin Carpenter, Eve Daniels, Susan Dycus, Adelaide Heyde, Wayne Lord, Michele McCullough, Nancy Morrison, Syd Rand, and John Schafer of the English Language Institute.

And finally, thank you to Mario, Patricia, Tom, and Doug, friends and family for their patience and support; our parents and children, for whose pride and enthusiasm we are grateful; our students, whose insightful suggestions made revisions possible; and all the teachers and staff of the English Language Institute for providing an atmosphere which nurtures innovative teaching and creative materials development.

The authors wish to gratefully acknowledge grants from the English Language Institute and *Language Learning* which provided funds for released time for several of the authors, and for secretarial and production assistance.

Contents

Contents

Unit 11

Unit 12

Unit 13

Unit 14

Unit 15

Introduction

To Students and Teachers

Reader's Choice is a reading skills textbook for students of English as a second language (ESL). The authors of *Reader's Choice* believe that reading is an active, problem-solving process. This book is based on the theory that proficient reading requires the coordination of a number of skills. Proficient reading depends on the reader's ability to select the proper skill or skills to solve each reading problem. Efficient readers determine beforehand why they are reading a particular selection and they decide which strategies and skills they will use to achieve their goals. They develop expectations about the kinds of information they will find in a passage and read to determine if their expectations are correct. The exercises and readings in *Reader's Choice* will help students to become independent, efficient readers.

When you look at the Contents page you will notice that there are three kinds of units in *Reader's Choice*. The odd-numbered units (1 through 11) contain skills exercises. These exercises give students intensive practice in developing their ability to obtain the maximum amount of information from a reading selection using the minimum number of language clues. The even-numbered units (2 through 12) contain reading selections which give students the opportunity to use the skills they have learned. Finally, Units 13, 14, and 15 consist of longer, more complex reading selections.

Basic language and reading skills are introduced in early units and reinforced throughout the book. The large number of exercises presented gives students repeated practice in these skills. Students should not be discouraged if they do not finish each exercise, if they have trouble answering specific questions, or if they do not understand everything in a particular reading. The purpose of the tasks in *Reader's Choice* is to help students improve their problem-solving skills. For this reason, the process of attempting to answer a question is often as important as the answer itself.

Reader's Choice contains exercises which give students practice in both language and reading skills. In this Introduction we will first provide a description of language skills exercises followed by a description of the reading skills work contained in the book.

LANGUAGE SKILLS EXERCISES

WORD STUDY EXERCISES

Upon encountering an unfamiliar vocabulary item in a passage there are several strategies readers can use to determine the message of the author. First, they can continue reading, realizing that often a single word will not prevent understanding of the general meaning of a selection. If further reading does not solve the problem, readers can use one or more of three basic skills to arrive at an understanding of the unfamiliar word. They can use context clues to see if surrounding words and grammatical structures provide information about the unknown word. They can use word analysis to see if understanding the parts of the word leads to an understanding of the word. Or, they can use a dictionary to find an appropriate definition. *Reader's Choice* contains numerous exercises which provide practice in these three skills.

Word Study: Vocabulary from Context
Guessing the meaning of an unfamiliar word from context clues involves using the following kinds of information:
- (*a*) knowledge of the topic about which you are reading
- (*b*) knowledge of the meanings of the other words in the sentence (or paragraph) in which the word occurs

(*c*) knowledge of the grammatical structure of the sentences in which the word occurs
Exercises which provide practice in this skill are called Vocabulary from Context exercises.

When these exercises appear in skills units, their purpose is to provide students with practice in guessing the meaning of unfamiliar words using context clues. Students should not try to learn the meanings of the vocabulary items in these exercises. However, the Vocabulary from Context exercises which appear with reading selections have a different purpose. Generally these exercises should be done before a reading selection is begun and used as an introduction to the reading. The vocabulary items have been chosen for three reasons:

(*a*) because they are fairly common, and therefore useful for students to learn
(*b*) because they are important for an understanding of the passage
(*c*) because their meanings are not easily available from the context in the selection

Word Study: Stems and Affixes

Another way to discover the meanings of unfamiliar vocabulary items is to use word analysis, that is, to use knowledge of the meanings of the parts of a word. Many English words have been formed by combining parts of older English, Greek, and Latin words. For instance, the word bicycle is formed from the parts *bi*, meaning two, and *cycle*, meaning round or wheel. Often knowledge of the meanings of these word parts can help the reader to guess the meaning of an unfamiliar word. Exercises providing practice in this skill occur at regular intervals throughout the book. The Appendix lists all of the stems and affixes which appear in *Reader's Choice*.

Word Study: Dictionary Usage

Sometimes the meaning of a single word is essential to an understanding of the total meaning of a selection. If context clues and word analysis do not provide enough information, it will be necessary to use a dictionary. We believe that advanced ESL students should use an English/English dictionary. The Word Study: Dictionary Usage exercises in the skills units provide students with a review of the information available from dictionaries, and practice in using a dictionary to obtain that information. The Dictionary Study exercises which accompany some of the reading selections require students to use the context of an unfamiliar vocabulary item to find an appropriate definition of these items from the dictionary entries provided.

SENTENCE STUDY EXERCISES

Sometimes comprehension of an entire passage requires the understanding of a single sentence. Sentence Study exercises give students practice in analyzing the structure of sentences to determine the relationships of ideas within a sentence. Students are presented with a complicated sentence followed by tasks which require them to analyze the sentence for its meaning. Often the student is required to use the available information to draw inferences about the author's message.

PARAGRAPH READING AND PARAGRAPH ANALYSIS EXERCISES

These exercises give students practice in understanding how the arrangement of ideas affects the overall meaning of a passage. Some of the paragraph exercises are designed to provide practice in discovering an author's general message. Students are required to determine the main idea of a passage: that is, the idea which is the most important, around which the paragraph is organized. Other paragraph exercises are meant to provide practice in careful, detailed reading. Students are required not only to find the main idea of a passage, but also to guess vocabulary meanings of words from context, to answer questions about specific details in the paragraph, and to draw conclusions based on their understanding of the passage.

NONPROSE READING

Throughout *Reader's Choice* students are presented with nonprose selections (such as a menu, train schedule, road map, etc.) so that they can practice using their skills to read material which is not arranged in sentences and paragraphs. It is important to remember that the same problem-solving skills are used to read both prose and nonprose material.

READING SKILLS EXERCISES

Students will need to use all of their language skills in order to understand the reading selections in *Reader's Choice*. The book contains many types of selections on a wide variety of topics. These selections provide practice in using different reading strategies to extract the message of the writer. They also give students practice in four basic reading skills: skimming, scanning, reading for thorough comprehension, and critical reading.

SKIMMING

Skimming is quick reading for the general idea(s) of a passage. This kind of rapid reading is appropriate when trying to decide if careful reading would be desirable or when there is not time to read something carefully.

SCANNING

Like skimming, scanning is also quick reading. However, in this case the search is more focused. To scan is to read quickly in order to locate specific information. When you read to find a particular date, name, or number you are scanning.

READING FOR THOROUGH COMPREHENSION

Reading for thorough comprehension is careful reading in order to understand the total meaning of the passage. At this level of comprehension the reader is able to summarize the author's ideas but has not yet made a critical evaluation of those ideas.

CRITICAL READING

Critical reading demands that readers make judgments about what they read. This kind of reading requires posing and answering questions such as *Does my own experience support that of the author? Do I share the author's point of view? Am I convinced by the author's arguments and evidence?*
Systematic use of the exercises and readings in *Reader's Choice* will give students practice in the basic language and reading skills necessary to become proficient readers. Additional suggestions for the use of *Reader's Choice* in a classroom setting are included in the section To the Teacher.

To the Teacher

It is impossible to outline one best way to use a textbook; there are as many ways to use *Reader's Choice* as there are creative teachers. However, based on the experiences of teachers and students who have worked with *Reader's Choice*, we provide the following suggestions to facilitate classroom use. First, we outline general guidelines for the teaching of reading in a skills-based program; second, we provide hints for teaching specific exercises and readings in the book; and finally, we suggest a sample lesson plan.

GENERAL GUIDELINES

The ultimate goal of *Reader's Choice* is to produce independent readers who are able to determine their own goals for a reading task, then use the appropriate skills and strategies to reach those goals. For this reason, we believe the best learning environment is one in which all individuals—students and teachers—participate in the process of setting and achieving goals. A certain portion of class time is therefore profitably spent in discussing reading tasks before they are begun. When confronted with a specific passage, students should become accustomed to the practice of skimming it quickly, taking note of titles and subheadings, pictures, graphs, etc., in an attempt to determine the most efficient approach to the task. In the process, they should develop expectations about the content of the passage and the amount of time and effort needed to accomplish their goals. In this type of setting students are encouraged to offer their opinions and ask for advice, to teach each other and to learn from their errors.

Reader's Choice was written to encourage maximum flexibility in classroom use. Because of the large variety of exercises and reading selections, the teacher can plan several tasks for each class and hold in reserve a number of appropriate exercises to use as the situation demands. In addition, the exercises have been developed to make possible variety in classroom dynamics. The teacher should encourage the independence of students by providing opportunities for work in small groups or pairs. Small group work in which students self-correct homework assignments has also been successful.

Exercises do not have to be done in the order in which they are presented. In fact, we suggest interspersing skills work with reading selections. One way to vary reading tasks is to plan lessons around pairs of units, alternating skills exercises with the reading selections. In the process, the teacher can show students how focused skills work transfers to the reading of longer passages. For example, Sentence Study exercises provide intensive practice in analyzing grammatical structures to understand sentences; this same skill should be used by students in working through reading selections. The teacher can pull sentences from readings for intensive classroom analysis, thereby encouraging students to do the same on their own.

In a skills-based curriculum, it is important to *teach, then test*. Skills work should be thoroughly introduced, modeled, and practiced before students are expected to perform on their own. Although we advocate rapid-paced, demanding class sessions, we believe it is extremely important to provide students with a thorough introduction to each new exercise. At least for the first example of each type of exercise, some oral work is necessary. The teacher can demonstrate the skill using the example item, and work through the first few items with the class as a whole. Students can then work individually or in small groups as they practice the skill.

SPECIFIC SUGGESTIONS

Reader's Choice has been organized so that specific skills can be practiced before students use those skills to attack reading selections. Although exercises and readings are generally graded according to difficulty, it is not necessary to use the material in the order in which it is presented. Teachers are encouraged:

(*a*) to intersperse skills work with reading selections

(*b*) to skip exercises which are too easy or irrelevant to students' interests

(*c*) to do several exercises of a specific type at one time if students require intensive practice in that skill

(*d*) to jump from unit to unit, selecting reading passages which satisfy students' interests and needs

(*e*) to sequence longer readings as appropriate for their students either by interspersing them among other readings and skills work, or by presenting them at the end of the course

LANGUAGE SKILLS EXERCISES

Nonprose Reading

For students who expect to read only prose material, teachers can point out that nonprose reading provides more than an enjoyable change of pace. These exercises provide legitimate skill work. The same problem-solving skills can be used for both prose and nonprose material. Just as one can skim a textbook for general ideas, it is possible to skim a menu for a general idea of the type of food offered, the price range of the restaurant, etc. Students may claim that they can't skim or scan; working with nonprose items shows them that they can.

Nonprose exercises are good for breaking the ice with new students, for beginning or ending class sessions, for role playing, or for those Monday blues and Friday blahs. Because they are short, rapid-paced exercises, they can be kept in reserve to provide variety, or to fill a time gap at the end of class.

The Menu, Newspaper Advertisements, Train Schedule, and Road Map exercises present students with realistic language problems which they might encounter in an English-speaking country. The teacher can set up simulations to achieve a realistic atmosphere. The Questionnaire exercise is intended to provide practice in filling out forms. Since the focus is on following directions, students usually work individually.

In the Poetry exercise, students' problem-solving skills are challenged by the economy of poetic writing. Poetry is especially good for reinforcing vocabulary from context skills, for comprehending through syntax clues, and for drawing inferences.

Word Study

These exercises can be profitably done in class either in rapid-paced group work or by alternating individual work with class discussion. Like nonprose work, Word Study exercises can be used to fill unexpected time gaps.

Context Clues exercises appear frequently throughout the book, both in skills units and with reading selections. Students should learn to be content with a general meaning of a word and to recognize situations in which it is not necessary to know a word's meaning. In skills units, these exercises should be done in class to ensure that students do not look for exact definitions in the dictionary. When Vocabulary from Context exercises appear with reading selections, they are intended as tools for learning new vocabulary items and often for introducing ideas to be en-countered in the reading. In this case they can be done at home as well as in class.

Stems and Affixes exercises appear in five units and must be done in the order in which they are presented. The exercises are cumulative: each exercise makes use of word parts presented in previous units. All stems and affixes taught in *Reader's Choice* are listed in the Appendix with their definitions. These exercises serve as an important foundation in vocabulary skills work for students whose native language does not contain a large number of words derived from Latin or Greek. Students should focus on learning word parts, not the words presented in the exercises. During the introduction to each exercise students should be encouraged to volunteer examples of words containing the stems and affixes presented. Exercise 1 can be done as homework, exercise 2 can be done as a quiz.

Dictionary Study exercises provide review of information available in English/English dictionaries. Exercise 1 in Dictionary Usage in Unit 1 requires a substantial amount of class discussion to introduce information necessary for dictionary work. Students should view the dictionary as the last resort when attempting to understand an unfamiliar word.

Sentence Study

Students should not be concerned about unfamiliar vocabulary in these exercises; grammatical clues will provide enough information to allow them to complete the tasks. In addition questions are syntax based; errors indicate structures which students have trouble reading, thus providing the teacher with a diagnostic tool for grammar instruction.

Paragraph Reading and Paragraph Analysis

Main Idea paragraphs should be read once, and questions answered without referring to the text. If the exercises are done in class, they are good for timed readings. If the exercises are done at home, students can be asked to come to class prepared to defend their answers in group discussion. One way to stimulate discussion is to ask students to identify incorrect choices as too broad, too narrow, or false.

Restatement and Inference and Paragraph Analysis exercises are short enough to allow sentence-by-sentence analysis. These exercises give intensive practice in syntax and vocabulary work. In the Paragraph Analysis exercises the lines are numbered to facilitate discussion.

READING SELECTIONS

Teachers have found it valuable to introduce readings in terms of ideas, vocabulary, and syntax before students are asked to work on their own. Several types of classroom dynamics have been successful with reading selections:

1. In class—teacher reads entire selection orally; or teacher reads part, students finish selection individually; or students read selection individually (perhaps under time constraint).
2. In class and at home—part of selection is read in class, followed by discussion; students finish reading at home.
3. At home—students read entire selection at home.

Comprehension questions are usually discussed in class with the class as a whole, in small groups, or in pairs. The paragraphs in the selections are numbered to facilitate discussion.

The teacher can pull out difficult vocabulary and/or sentences for intensive analysis and discussion.

Readings represent a variety of topics and styles. The exercises have been written to focus on the most obvious characteristics of each reading.

(*a*) Fiction and personal experience narratives are to be read for enjoyment. Teachers often find it useful to read these to students, emphasizing humorous parts.

(*b*) Well-organized readings with many facts and figures are appropriate for scanning and skimming. This type of reading can also be used in composition work as a model of organizational techniques.

(*c*) If the reading is an editorial, essay, or other form of personal opinion, students should read critically to determine if they agree with the author. Students are encouraged to identify excerpts which reveal the author's bias or which can be used to challenge the validity of the author's argument.

(*d*) Satire should be read both for enjoyment and for analysis of the author's comment on human affairs.

LONGER READINGS

These readings can be presented in basically the same manner as other selections in the book. Longer readings can be read either at the end of the course, or at different points throughout the semester. The schedule for working with longer readings is roughly as follows:

(*a*) Readings are introduced by vocabulary exercises, discussion of the topic, reading and discussion of selected paragraphs.

(*b*) Students read the selection at home and answer the comprehension questions. Students are allowed at least two days to complete the assignment.

(*c*) In-class discussion of comprehension questions proceeds with students referring to the passage to support their answers.

(*d*) The vocabulary review can be done either at home or in class.

(*e*) Vocabulary questions raised on the off day between the assignment and the due day may be resolved with items from Vocabulary from Context exercises 2 and 3 and Figurative Language and Idioms exercises.

"The Dusty Drawer" is a suspense story whose success as a teaching tool depends on students understanding the conflict between the two main characters. Teachers have found that a preliminary reading and discussion of the first eleven paragraphs serves as an introduction to the most important elements of the story. The discussion questions can be integrated into the discussion of comprehension questions.

"In the Shadow of Man" is well organized and may, therefore, be skimmed. Teachers can ask students to read the first and last sentences of the paragraphs, then paraphrase the general position of the author. Discussion of some Discussion-Composition items can serve as an effective introduction to the reading. In addition, some questions lead discussion away from the passage and might, therefore, lead to further reading on the topic. Some teachers may want to show the film, *Miss Jane Goodall and the Wild Chimpanzees* (National Geographic Society; Encyclopedia Britannica Educational Films) in conjunction with this reading. Teachers should be aware that this selection raises the subject of evolution, a sensitive topic for students whose religious or personal beliefs deny evolutionary theory.

"The 800th Lifetime" requires a careful introduction because of the challenging syntax and the colloquial vocabulary. In addition, the author assumes that the reader is familiar with many of the phenomena described. For this reason, the teacher may want to spend some time discussing certain cultural and social phenomena in the United States to help students develop appropriate expectations. Because students may be personally familiar with cultural shock, they can be asked to read the article for the parallels between culture shock and future shock. As with "In the Shadow of Man," discussion questions can lead the class to other topics and readings.

ANSWER KEY

Because the exercises in *Reader's Choice* are designed to provide students with the opportunity to practice and improve their reading skills, the processes involved in arriving at an answer are often more important than the answer itself. It is expected that students will not use the Answer Key until they have completed the exercises and are prepared to defend their answers. If a student's answer does not agree with the Key, it is important for the student to return to the exercise to discover the source of the error. In a classroom setting, students should view the Answer Key as a last resort, to be used only when they cannot agree on an answer. The Answer Key also makes it possible for students engaged in independent study to use *Reader's Choice*.

SAMPLE LESSON PLAN

The following lesson plan is meant only as an example of how goals might be translated into practice. We do not imply that a particular presentation is the only one possible for a given reading activity, nor that the exercises presented here are the only activities possible to achieve our goals. The lesson plan demonstrates how skills work can be interspersed with reading selections.

It is assumed that the lessons described here would be presented after students have worked together for several weeks. This is important for two reasons. First, we hope that a nonthreatening atmosphere has been established in which people feel free to volunteer opinions and make guesses. Second, we assume that by now students recognize the importance of a skills-based reading program and that they are working to improve those skills using a variety of readings and exercises.

Although these lessons are planned for fifty-minute, daily, ESL reading classes, slight modification would make them appropriate for a number of other situations. Approximate time limits for each activity are indicated. The exercises and readings are taken from Units 7 and 8.

Monday
Nonprose Reading: Poetry (20 minutes)
(a) The teacher points out that each poem is a puzzle; that students will have to use their reading skills to solve each one.
(b) The teacher reads the first poem aloud; students follow in their books.
(c) Discussion focuses on getting information from vocabulary and syntax clues and drawing inferences.
(d) If the students can't guess the subject of the poem, the class should do the Comprehension Clues exercise.
(e) The last two poems can be handled in the same manner or students can work individually with discussion following.

Reading Selection: Magazine Article ("Why We Laugh") (30 minutes)

Introduction:

(a) Discussion: Why do we laugh? Is laughter culturally conditioned? Do students think English jokes are funny?

(b) Vocabulary: Vocabulary from Context exercises 1 and 2; students work as a class or individually, with discussion following.

(c) Skimming: the teacher skims the article aloud, reading first (and sometimes second and last) sentences of each paragraph.

(d) Discussion: What is the main idea of the author? What type of article is it? Is the author an expert? Who are the experts she quotes?

Homework: Read "Why We Laugh"; do Comprehension exercises 1 and 2.

Tuesday

"Why We Laugh" (35 minutes)

(a) Work through Comprehension and Critical Reading exercises as a class, in small groups or in pairs. Students should defend answers with portions of the text; emphasis is on convincing others or being convinced on the basis of the reading.

(b) Pull out, analyze, and discuss structure problems, difficult vocabulary.

(c) Wrap-up discussion proceeds from Critical Reading and Discussion questions.

Stems and Affixes (15 minutes)

(a) Introduction: students volunteer examples of words containing stems and affixes presented in the exercise.

(b) Class does exercise 1 orally as a group, if time permits.

Homework: Finish Stems and Affixes exercises.

Wednesday

Stems and Affixes (15 minutes)

(a) Go over as a class; students volunteer and defend answers.

(b) The Appendix can be used if a dispute arises concerning one of the stems or affixes presented in previous units.

(c) Work is fast paced and skills focused. Students concentrate on learning word parts, not the words.

Sentence Study: Restatement and Inference (35 minutes)

(a) The first one or two items are done orally. The teacher reads the sentence and the choices aloud and students mark answers in the book.

(b) Discussion follows. Students must defend answers using grammatical analysis of sentences.

(c) Students complete the exercise individually after which answers are discussed.

Word Study: Context Clues (if time permits)

(a) Group or individual work.

(b) Students arrive at a definition, synonym, or description of each word, then defend their answers by referring to the syntax and other vocabulary items in the sentence.

Thursday

Reading Selection: Narrative ("An Attack on the Family") (40 minutes)

(a) Vocabulary from Context: students work as a class or individually with discussion following.

(b) The teacher reads story aloud, students follow in their books.

(*c*) Students take ten minutes to answer Comprehension questions individually.

(*d*) Discussion follows. Students will have to examine the text carefully to answer the questions.

Paragraph Analysis: Reading for Full Understanding (10 minutes)

(*a*) The teacher reads the Example paragraph aloud. Students mark answers in their books.

(*b*) The class discusses the answers using the Explanation on pages 118-19.

Homework: Finish Paragraph Analysis exercise.

Friday

Paragraph Analysis (25 minutes)

(*a*) Discussion of the homework: students must use excerpts from the paragraphs to defend their answers or to refute the choices of other students.

(*b*) Grammatical analysis can be used to develop convincing arguments supporting the correct answers. Context clues often furnish the definition of unfamiliar words.

Reading Selection: Narrative ("The Lottery") (25 minutes)

Introduction:

(*a*) Discussion of lotteries in general, lotteries in the students' countries.

(*b*) Vocabulary from Context exercise 1: students work as a class or individually with discussion following.

(*c*) The teacher reads the first nine paragraphs, discusses content, vocabulary, syntax with students. Most of Vocabulary from Context exercises 2 and 3 can be covered during this discussion.

Homework: Read "The Lottery"; do Comprehension exercises for Monday.

This lesson plan represents a skills approach to the teaching of ESL reading. Students are required to do more than merely read passages and answer questions. The type of reading that the students are asked to do varies from task to task. They skim "Why We Laugh" to determine the main idea, then scan to find the answers to some of the Comprehension questions. Sentence Study exercises require close grammatical analysis, just as Stems and Affixes exercises require analysis of word parts. "Why We Laugh" and "The Lottery" both require critical reading. The vocabulary and syntax work is presented as a tool for comprehension, appropriate for helping students solve persistent reading problems.

Within a single week, a great variety of activities is presented. In the course of any single lesson, the tempo and tasks change several times. In the course of the week, virtually all language and reading skills are reinforced in a variety of contexts and with a variety of materials. This variety has important implications for the nature of the class and for the role of the teacher.

The classroom dynamics change to fit the task. The poetry and the discussion sessions are class activities, the teacher encouraging students to volunteer answers and opinions. The vocabulary and structure exercises on Tuesday and Wednesday, as well as the paragraph work on Thursday and Friday might be organized as workshop sessions, giving students the chance to work at their own pace and providing the teacher the opportunity to assist individuals.

The role of the teacher also changes from activity to activity. During vocabulary and structure work, the teacher teaches, providing help and encouragement as students work to solve language problems. The teacher is a facilitator during the poetry and short passage readings, intervening only in the event that linguistic expertise is needed to keep the discussion going. In discussions of how readings relate to the "real world," the teacher is primarily a participant on equal terms with the students in exploring mutually interesting topics. Of course, the role and behavior of the teacher can change a number of times in the course of a class session to suit the situation. It is hoped, however, that as the semester progresses, the teacher as teacher will gradually be replaced by the teacher as facilitator and participant.

Another important feature of this lesson plan is the opportunity provided to encourage students to choose their own reading strategies and to apply the skills dictated by the strategy chosen. It should be noted that "Why We Laugh" and "The Lottery" are introduced by the teacher through vocabulary work and discussion, followed by skimming and scanning. This type of introduction gives students the opportunity to develop expectations about the selection and, guided by their expectations, to read more effectively. It is hoped that this procedure will be repeated when students encounter similar readings in the future. Often the teacher will want to simulate a "real life" situation by giving the students a task and asking them how they would approach it. The approach to a newspaper editorial, for example, might be quite different depending on whether the selection is read for pleasure or for a university political science course.

Throughout the semester, students are taught to shift gears, to vary their reading strategies according to their goals for the selection at hand. As they become more proficient readers, we expect them to determine for themselves what they read, why they read it, and how they read it.

Special Sandwiches

CHEESEBURGER SPECIAL 1.40
CLUBHOUSE, 3 Decker on Toast 1.95
SIRLOIN BURGER ON TOASTED BUN . . 1.25
REUBEN SANDWICH 1.85
FRENCH DIP 1.95
HAM AND CHEESE DELIGHT 1.85

Served With Cole Slaw And Potato Chips

Beverages

Pot of Hot Tea 30
Milk 25
Hot Chocolate 30
Iced Tea 30
Pot of Sanka 25
Chocolate Milk 25
Soft Drinks 25

Hot Sandwiches

HOT BEEF 1.65
HOT TURKEY 1.65
HOT MEAT LOAF 1.45

Served With Mashed Potatoes And Gravy

ITALIAN SPAGHETTI 1.90
With Meat Balls, Extra 50
Tasty Meat Sauce, Roma Cheese And Tossed Salad

WEIGHT WATCHERS' SPECIAL, Hamburger Pat-
tie, Sliced Tomato, Cottage Cheese, and Fruit 1.70

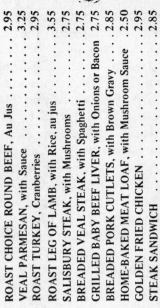

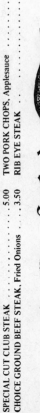

Special Daily Frono Dinners

ROAST CHOICE ROUND BEEF, Au Jus 2.95
VEAL PARMESAN, with Sauce 3.25
ROAST TURKEY, Cranberries 2.95
ROAST LEG OF LAMB, with Rice, au jus 3.55
SALISBURY STEAK, with Mushrooms 2.75
BREADED VEAL STEAK, with Spaghetti 2.75
GRILLED BABY BEEF LIVER, with Onions or Bacon . 2.75
BREADED PORK CUTLETS, with Brown Gravy 2.85
HOME-BAKED MEAT LOAF, with Mushroom Sauce . . 2.50
GOLDEN FRIED CHICKEN 2.95
STEAK SANDWICH 2.85
PORK CHOP SANDWICH 1.95

Above Served With Salad And Potatoes

Salads

GREEK SALAD BOWL,
    Our Special Dressing 2.10
FRESH SHRIMP SALAD BOWL 2.25
JULIENNE SALAD BOWL 1.90
TURKEY SALAD BOWL 1.90
COTTAGE CHEESE AND FRUIT 1.25
COMBINATION SALAD 1.25
    Choice Of Dressing

Side Orders

TOSSED SALAD 70
COLE SLAW 55
COTTAGE CHEESE 60
SMALL GREEK SALAD 1.50
APPLESAUCE 50
FRUIT CUP 50
FRENCH FRIES 50
ONION RINGS 80

Desserts

Pecan Pie 65
Homemade Pie 55
Pie a La Mode 80
Ice Cream 45
Cheese Cake 75
Rice Pudding 45
Sundae 75

Cocktails

BEFORE DINNER COCKTAILS

Highball 85
Manhattan 1.15
Martini 1.15
Martini, Extra Dry 1.25
Old Fashioned 1.15
Whiskey Sour 1.15
Gimlet 1.25
Bacardi 1.15
Tom Collins 1.15
Gibson 1.15
Bloody Mary 1.10
Marguerita 1.35

AFTER DINNER COCKTAILS

Brandy, Bar 1.00
Stinger 1.35
Grasshopper 1.35
B & B 1.35
Alexander 1.35
Angel Tip 1.10
Black Russian 1.50
Side Car 1.35
Galiano 1.50
Pink Lady 1.50

FOR YOUR LATE
BREAKFAST PLEASURE . . .

TWO FRESH EGGS, Any Style 95
    With Toast & Jelly
    With Fried Ham, Bacon
    or Sausage 1.55
FLUFFY PANCAKES,
    With Syrup & Butter 80
    With Fried Ham, Bacon
    or Sausage 1.40
ONE EGG 75

Omelettes

HAM 1.50
HAM AND CHEESE 1.65
MUSHROOM AND CHEESE . . . 1.65
WESTERN 1.65
PLAIN CHEESE 1.35

Served With Toast And Jelly

Steaks & Chops

COOKED THE WAY YOU LIKE IT

CHOICE OF: Cup of Soup of the Day, Chilled Tomato Juice, or Grapefruit Juice

N.Y. STRIP SIRLOIN STEAK 5.25
SPECIAL CUT CLUB STEAK 3.85
CHOICE GROUND BEEF STEAK, Fried Onions 4.75

MINUTE STEAK, Mushrooms 6.00
TWO PORK CHOPS, Applesauce 5.00
RIB EYE STEAK 3.50

SHRIMP COCKTAIL 1.75

Seafood

RAINBOW TROUT 3.50
BROILED FRESH RED SNAPPER 3.95
GOLDEN FRIED DEEP SEA SCALLOPS 2.75
GOLDEN FRIED FRESH SHRIMP 2.75

GRILLED HALIBUT STEAK 3.50
ASSORTED SEAFOOD PLATTER 3.50
BREADED OCEAN PERCH 3.25
FISH & CHIPS 3.50
HALF DOZ. GOLDEN FRIED JUMBO OYSTERS . 3.00

Above Served With Chef's Salad,
Potatoes, And Assorted Bread Basket

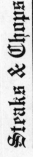

Main Sandwiches

CRISP BACON, LETTUCE, TOMATO 1.10
SLICED TURKEY AND TOMATO 1.25
FISH SANDWICH 85
WESTERN ON TOAST 95
TURKEY SALAD, On Toast 1.05
TUNA SALAD, on Toast 1.05
CORNED BEEF 1.35

ROAST BEEF SANDWICH 1.25
GRILLED HAM AND CHEESE 1.10
GRILLED CHEESE 75
CANADIAN BACON on Bun 1.00
HAMBURGER 95
HAMBURGER DELUX 1.20
CHEESEBURGER 1.10
GRILLED CORNED BEEF AND CHEESE . 1.45

Menu courtesy of Manikas Sirloin House, Ann Arbor, Michigan.

NONPROSE READING: Menu

Nonprose writing consists of disconnected words and numbers instead of the sentences and paragraphs you usually learn to read. Each time you need information from a train schedule, a graph, a menu, or the like, you must read nonprose material. This exercise and similar exercises which begin subsequent units will help you practice the problem-solving skills that you will need in order to read nonprose material.

On the opposite page is a menu such as you might find in a restaurant in the United States. Look at it quickly, then scan the menu to answer the questions in exercise 1. Do not go on to exercise 2 until you have checked your answers to exercise 1.

Exercise 1

1. If you wanted something alcoholic to drink before dinner, in which section would you find it? _Cocktails (after dinner)_

2. In which section would you find something nonalcoholic to drink? _Beverages_

3. In which section would you find something sweet to eat after dinner? _Desserts_

4. Which special meal is provided for people who are trying to lose weight? _Hamburger Pattie_

5. If you didn't want to eat pork, list some entries you would avoid. _cup of soup of the day, grilled tomato juice or grapefruit juice_

6. Do we know if this restaurant serves Coca-Cola? _YES NO_

7. How much does a Reuben sandwich and an order of French fries cost? _1.85   .50_

8. Under which section would you find a small salad to eat with a rib eye steak? _side orders_

9. If you wanted eggs, under which sections would you look? _omelet breakfast_

10. How much does two eggs with bacon cost? _1.55_

11. Is tipping permitted in this restaurant? _I don't know_

Stop! Do not go on without discussing your answers.

Exercise 2
Indicate if each statement is true (T) or false (F).

1. _F_ The cheapest item on the menu containing fish is fish and chips.

2. _F_ The grilled baby beef liver dinner is always served with bacon.

3. 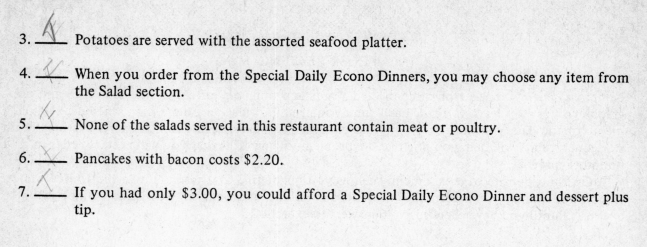 Potatoes are served with the assorted seafood platter.

4. ____ When you order from the Special Daily Econo Dinners, you may choose any item from the Salad section.

5. ____ None of the salads served in this restaurant contain meat or poultry.

6. ____ Pancakes with bacon costs $2.20.

7. ____ If you had only $3.00, you could afford a Special Daily Econo Dinner and dessert plus tip.

WORD STUDY: Context Clues

Efficient reading requires the use of various problem-solving skills. For example, it is impossible for you to know the exact meaning of every word you read, but by developing your guessing ability, you will be able to understand enough to arrive at the total meaning of a sentence, paragraph, or essay. These exercises are designed to help you improve your ability to guess the meaning of unfamiliar words by using context clues. (Context refers to the sentence and paragraph in which a word occurs.) In using the context to decide the meaning of a word you have to use your knowledge of grammar and your understanding of the author's ideas. Although there is no formula which you can memorize to improve your ability to guess the meaning of unfamiliar words, you should keep the following points in mind:

1. Use the meanings of the other words in the sentence (or paragraph) and the meaning of the sentence as a whole to reduce the number of possible meanings.
2. Use grammar and punctuation clues which point to the relationships among the various parts of the sentence.
3. Be content with a general idea about the unfamiliar word; the exact definition or synonym is not always necessary.
4. Learn to recognize situations in which it is not necessary to know the meaning of the word.

Exercise 1

Each of the sentences in this exercise contains a blank in order to encourage you to look only at the context provided as you attempt to determine the possible meanings of the missing word. Read each sentence quickly and supply a word for each blank. There is no single correct answer. You are to use context clues to help you provide a word which is appropriate in terms of grammar and meaning.

1. I removed the _____ book _____ from the shelf and began to read.

2. Harvey is a thief; he would _____ rob _____ the gold from his grandmother's teeth and not feel guilty.

3. Our uncle was a _____ nomad _____, an incurable wanderer who never could stay in one place.

4. Unlike his brother, who is truly a handsome person, Hogartty is quite _____ ugly _____.

5. The Asian _____ ape _____, like other apes, is specially adapted for life in trees.

6. But surely everyone knows that if you step on an egg, it will _____ break _____.

7. Tom got a new _____ car _____ for his birthday. It is a sports model, red, with white interior and bucket seats.

Explanation:

1. I removed the _____ from the shelf and began to read.

   book
   magazine
   paper
   newspaper

   The number of things that can be taken from a shelf and read is so few that the word *book* probably jumped into your mind at once. Here, the association between the object and the purpose for which it is used is so close that you have very little difficulty guessing the right word.

2. Harvey is a thief; he would _____ the gold from his grandmother's teeth and not feel guilty.

   steal
   take
   rob

   Harvey is a thief. A thief steals. The semicolon (;) indicates that the sentence which follows contains an explanation of the first statement. Further, you know that the definition of *thief* is: a person who steals.

3. Our uncle was a _____, an incurable wanderer who never could stay in one place.

   nomad
   roamer
   traveler
   drifter

   The comma (,) following the blank indicates a phrase in apposition, that is, a word or group of words which could be used as a synonym of the unfamiliar word. The words at the left are all synonyms of wanderer.

4. Unlike his brother, who is truly a handsome person, Hogartty is quite _____.

   ugly
   homely
   plain

   Hogartty is the opposite of his brother, and since his brother is handsome, Hogartty must be ugly. The word *unlike* signals the relationship between Hogartty and his brother.

5. The Asian _____, like other apes, is specially adapted for life in trees.

   gibbon
   monkey
   chimp
   ape

   You probably didn't write *gibbon*, which is the word the author used. Most native speakers wouldn't be familiar with this word either. But since you know that the word is the name of a type of ape, you don't need to know anything else. This is an example of how context can teach you the meaning of unfamiliar words.

6. But surely everyone knows that if you step on an egg, it will _____.

   break

   You recognized the cause and effect relationship in this sentence. There is only one thing that can happen to an egg when it is stepped on.

7. Tom got a new _____ for his birthday. It is a sports model, red, with white interior and bucket seats.

   car

   The description in the second sentence gave you all the information you needed to guess the word *car*.

4

Exercise 2

In the following exercise, do NOT try to learn the italicized words. Concentrate on developing your ability to guess the meaning of unfamiliar words using context clues. Read each sentence carefully, and write a definition, synonym, or description of the italicized word on the line provided.

1. _sith slighted jumped_   We watched as the cat came quietly through the grass toward the bird. When it was just a few feet from the victim, it gathered its legs under itself, and *pounced.*

2. _to mold, to mildew, to rot_   What could John expect? He had left his wet swimming trunks in the dark closet for over a week. Of course they had begun to *mildew.*

3. _a type of bird._   In spite of the fact that the beautiful *egret* is in danger of dying out completely, many clothing manufacturers still offer handsome prices for their long, elegant tail feathers, which are used as decorations on ladies' hats.

4. _to protest, to talk loudly / to attack verbally, against_   When he learned that the club was planning to admit women, the colonel began to *inveigh against* all forms of liberalism; his shouting attack began with universal voting and ended with a protest against the volunteer army.

5. _To slide_   The snake *slithered* through the grass.

6. _to hit_   The man thought that the children were defenseless, so he walked boldly up to the oldest and demanded money. Imagine his surprise when they began to *pelt* him with rocks.

7. _____   Experts in *kinesics*, in their study of body motion as related to speech, hope to discover new methods of communication.

8. _sociable, friendly_   Unlike her *gregarious* sister, Jane is a shy, unsociable person who does not like to go to parties or to make new friends.

9. _extremely hungry_   After a day of hunting, Harold is *ravenous.* Yesterday, for example, he ate two bowls of soup, salad, a large chicken, and a piece of chocolate cake before he was finally satisfied.

10. _____   After the accident, the ship went down so fast that we weren't able to *salvage* any of our personal belongings.

WORD STUDY: Dictionary Usage

The dictionary is a source of many kinds of information about words. Look at this sample entry carefully; notice how much information the dictionary presents under the word *prefix*.

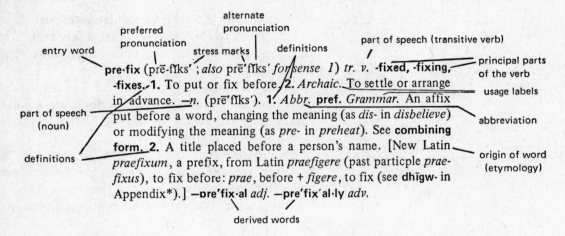

Your dictionary may use a different system of abbreviations or different pronunciation symbols. It is important for you to become familiar with your English dictionary and with the symbols that it uses. Look up *prefix* in your dictionary, and compare the entry to the sample entry. Discuss the differences that you find.

Exercise 1

Use the sample entry above, the dictionary page* (opposite), and your own dictionary to discuss this exercise.

1. When the dictionary gives more than one spelling or pronunciation of a word, which is preferred?

2. How many syllables are in *prefix*? What symbol does this dictionary use to separate the syllables? Which syllable is accented in the preferred pronunciation of the verb *prefix*?

3. Why would you need to know where a word is divided into syllables?

4. Where is the pronunciation guide on page 7? Where is it in your dictionary? What is the key word in the pronunciation guide on page 7 which shows you how to pronounce the *e* in the preferred pronunciation of *prefix*?

5. What are *derived words*?

6. What is the meaning of the Latin root from which *pre* has developed?

7. Dictionary entries sometimes include usage labels such as *archaic, obsolete, slang, colloquial, poetic, regional,* and *informal.* Why are these labels useful?

---

*Copyright © 1969, 1970, 1971, 1973, 1975, 1976, Houghton Mifflin Company. Reprinted by permission from *The American Heritage Dictionary of the English Language.*

in the margin or between lines of a text or manuscript. **2.** An expanded version of such notes; a glossary. **3.** A purposefully misleading interpretation or explanation. **4.** An extensive commentary, often accompanying a text or publication. —*v.* **glossed, glossing, glosses.** —*tr.* **1.** To provide (a text) with glosses. **2.** To give a false interpretation to. —*intr.* To make glosses. [Middle English *glose,* from Old French, from Medieval Latin *glōsa,* from Latin *glōssa,* word that needs explanation, from Greek *glōssa,* tongue, language. See **glōgh-** in Appendix.*] —**gloss'er** *n.*

gloss. glossary.

glos·sal (glôs'əl, glŏs'-) *adj.* Of or pertaining to the tongue. [From Greek *glōssa,* tongue. See **gloss** (explanation).]

glos·sa·ry (glôs'ə-rē, glŏs'-) *n., pl.* **-ries.** *Abbr.* **gloss.** A collection of glosses, such as a vocabulary of specialized terms with accompanying definitions. [Latin *glossārium,* from *glōssa,* GLOSS (explanation).] —**glos·sar'i·al** (glô-sâr'ē-əl, glŏ-) *adj.* —**glos·sar'i·al·ly** *adv.* —**glos'sa·rist** *n.*

glos·sog·ra·phy (glô-sŏg'rə-fē, glŏ-) *n.* The writing and compilation of glosses or glossaries. [Greek *glōssa,* tongue, language, GLOSS (explanation) + -GRAPHY.] —**glos·sog'ra·pher** *n.*

glos·so·la·li·a (glôs'ō-lā'lē-ə, glŏs'-) *n.* **1.** Fabricated nonmeaningful speech, especially as associated with certain schizophrenic syndromes. **2.** The **gift of tongues** *(see).* [New Latin *glossolalia,* from (New Testament) Greek *glōssais lalein,* "to speak with tongues" : *glossa,* tongue (see **glōgh-** in Appendix*) + *lalein,* to talk, babble (see **la-** in Appendix*).]

glos·sol·o·gy (glô-sŏl'ə-jē, glŏ-) *n. Obsolete.* Linguistics. [Greek *glōssa,* tongue, language, GLOSS (explanation) + -LOGY.] —**glos·sol'o·gist** *n.*

gloss·y (glôs'ē, glŏs'ē) *adj.* **-ier, -iest.** **1.** Having a smooth, shiny, lustrous surface. **2.** Superficially attractive; specious. —*n., pl.* **glossies.** *Photography.* A print on smooth, shiny paper. Also called "glossy print." —**gloss'i·ly** *adv.* —**gloss'i·ness** *n.*

glost (glôst, glŏst) *n.* **1.** A lead glaze used for pottery. **2.** Glazed pottery. [Variation of GLOSS (sheen).]

glot·tal (glŏt'l) *adj.* **1.** Of or relating to the glottis. **2.** *Phonetics.* Articulated in the glottis. [From GLOTTIS.]

glottal stop. *Phonetics.* A speech sound produced by a momentary complete closure of the glottis, followed by an explosive release.

glot·tis (glŏt'ĭs) *n., pl.* **-tises** or **glottides** (glŏt'ə-dēz') **1.** The space between the vocal cords at the upper part of the larynx. **2.** The vocal structures of the larynx. [New Latin, from Greek *glōttis,* from *glōtta, glōssa,* tongue, language. See **glōgh-** in Appendix.*]

Glouces·ter (glôs'tər, glŏs'-). **1.** Also **Glouces·ter·shire** (-shĭr, -shər). *Abbr.* **Glos.** A county of south-central England, 1,257 square miles in area. Population, 1,034,000. **2.** The county seat of this county. Population, 72,000. **3.** A city, resort center, and fishing port of Massachusetts, 27 miles northeast of Boston. Population, 26,000.

glove (glŭv) *n.* **1. a.** A fitted covering for the hand, usually made of leather, wool, or cloth, having a separate sheath for each finger and the thumb. **b.** A gauntlet. **2. a.** *Baseball.* An oversized padded leather covering for the hand, used in catching balls; especially, one with more finger sheathes than the catcher's or first baseman's mitt. **b.** A **boxing glove** *(see).* —**hand in glove.** In a close or harmonious relationship. —*tr.v.* **gloved, gloving, gloves.** **1.** To furnish with gloves. **2.** To cover with or as if with a glove. [Middle English *glove,* Old English *glōf.* See **lep-²** in Appendix.*]

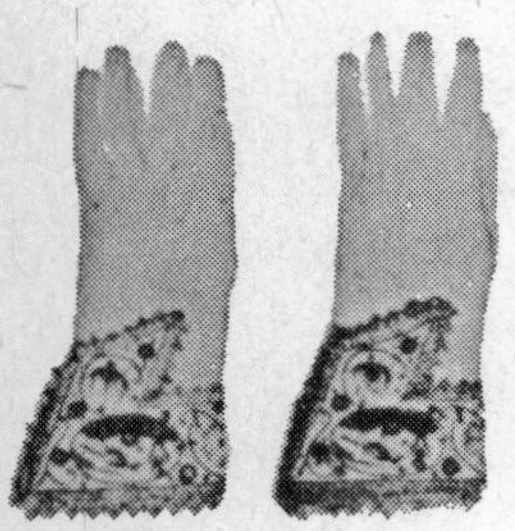

glove
Pair of 17th-century English leather gloves with embroidered cuffs

glove compartment. A small storage container in the dashboard of an automobile.

glov·er (glŭv'ər) *n.* One who makes or sells gloves.

glow (glō) *intr.v.* **glowed, glowing, glows.** **1.** To shine brightly and steadily, especially without a flame: *"a red bed of embers glowing in the furnace"* (Richard Wright). **2.** To have a bright, warm color, usually reddish. **3. a.** To have a healthful, ruddy coloration. **b.** To flush; to blush. **4.** To be exuberant or radiant, as with pride. —*n.* **1.** A light produced by a body heated to luminosity; incandescence. **2.** Brilliance or warmth of color, especially redness: *"the evening glow of the city streets when the sun has gone behind the tallest houses"* (Sean O'Faolain). **3.** A sensation of physical warmth. **4.** A warm feeling of passion or emotion; ardor. —See Synonyms at **blaze.** [Middle English *glowen,* Old English *glōwan.* See **ghel-²** in Appendix.*]

glow·er (glou'ər) *intr.v.* **-ered, -ering, -ers.** To look or stare angrily or sullenly; to frown. —*n.* An angry, sullen, or threatening stare. [Middle English *glo(u)ren,* to shine, stare, probably from Scandinavian, akin to Norwegian dialectal *glora.* See **ghel-²** in Appendix.*] —**glow'er·ing·ly** *adv.*

glow·ing (glō'ĭng) *adj.* **1.** Incandescent; luminous. **2.** Characterized by rich, warm coloration; especially, having a ruddy, healthy complexion. **3.** Ardently enthusiastic or favorable.

glow plug. A small heating element in a diesel engine cylinder used to facilitate starting.

glow·worm (glō'wûrm') *n.* A firefly; especially, the luminous larva or wingless, grublike female of a firefly.

gloxinia
Sinningia speciosa

glox·in·i·a (glŏk-sĭn'ē-ə) *n.* Any of several tropical South American plants of the genus *Sinningia;* especially, *S. speciosa,* cultivated as a house plant for its showy, variously colored flowers. [New Latin, after Benjamin Peter *Gloxin,* 18th-century German botanist and physician.]

gloze (glōz) *v.* **glozed, glozing, glozes.** —*tr.* To minimize or underplay; to gloss. Used with *over.* —*intr. Archaic.* To use flattery or cajolery. [Middle English *glosen,* to gloss, falsify, flatter, from Old French *glosser,* from *glose,* GLOSS (explanation).]

Gluck (glo͝ok), **Christoph Willibald.** 1714–1787. German composer of operas.

glu·cose (glo͞o'kōs') *n.* **1.** A sugar, **dextrose** *(see).* **2.** A colorless to yellowish syrupy mixture of dextrose, maltose, and dextrins with about 20 per cent water, used in confectionery, alcoholic fermentation, tanning, and treating tobacco. [French, from Greek *gleukos,* sweet new wine, must. See **dlku-** in Appendix.*]

glu·co·side (glo͞o'kə-sīd') *n.* A **glycoside** *(see),* the sugar component of which is glucose. —**glu'co·sid'ic** (-sĭd'ĭk) *adj.*

glue (glo͞o) *n.* **1.** An adhesive substance or solution; a viscous substance used to join or bond. **2.** An adhesive obtained by boiling animal **collagen** *(see)* and drying the residue. In this sense, also called "animal glue." —*tr.v.* **glued, gluing, glues.** To stick or fasten together with or as if with glue. [Middle English *gleu,* glue, birdlime, gum, from Old French *glu,* from Late Latin *glūs* (stem *glūt-*), from Latin *glūten.* See **gel-¹** in Appendix.*]

glum (glŭm) *adj.* **glummer, glummest.** **1.** In low spirits; dejected. **2.** Gloomy; dismal. [From Middle English *glomen, gloumen,* to look sullen, GLOOM.] —**glum'ly** *adv.* —**glum'ness** *n.*

Synonyms: *glum, gloomy, morose, dour, saturnine.* These adjectives mean having a cheerless or repugnant aspect or disposition. *Glum* implies dejection and silence, and more often than the other terms refers to a mood or temporary condition rather than to a person's characteristic state. *Gloomy* differs little except in being more applicable to a person given to somberness or depression by nature. *Morose* implies sourness of temper and a tendency to be uncommunicative. *Dour* especially suggests a grim or humorless exterior and sometimes an unyielding nature. *Saturnine* suggests severity of aspect, extreme gravity of nature, and often a tendency to be bitter or sardonic.

glu·ma·ceous (glo͞o-mā'shəs) *adj.* Having or resembling a glume or glumes.

glume (glo͞om) *n. Botany.* A chaffy basal bract on the spikelet of a grass. [New Latin *gluma,* from Latin *glūma,* husk. See **gleubh-** in Appendix.*]

glut (glŭt) *v.* **glutted, glutting, gluts.** —*tr.* **1.** To fill beyond capacity; satiate. **2.** To flood (a market) with an excess of goods so that supply exceeds demand. —*intr.* To eat excessively. —See Synonyms at **satiate.** —*n.* **1.** An oversupply. **2.** The act or process of glutting. [Middle English *glotten, glouten,* probably from Old French *gloutir,* to swallow, from Latin *gluttīre.* See **gwel-⁵** in Appendix.*]

glu·tam·ic acid (glo͞o-tăm'ĭk) *n.* An amino acid present in all complete proteins, found widely in plant and animal tissue, and having a salt, sodium glutamate, that is used as a flavor-intensifying seasoning. [GLUT(EN) + AM(IDE) + -IC.]

glu·ta·mine (glo͞o'tə-mēn', -mĭn) *n.* A white crystalline amino acid, $C_5H_{10}N_2O_3$, occurring in plant and animal tissue and produced commercially for use in medicine and biochemical research. [GLUT(EN) + AMINE.]

glu·ten (glo͞ot'n) *n.* A mixture of plant proteins occurring in cereal grains, chiefly corn and wheat, and used as an adhesive and as a flour substitute. [Latin *glūten,* glue. See **gel-¹** in Appendix.*] —**glu'te·nous** *adj.*

gluten bread. Bread made from flour with a high gluten content and low starch content.

glu·te·us (glo͞o'tē-əs, glo͞o-tē'-) *n., pl.* **-tei** (-tē-ī', -tē'ī'). Any of three large muscles of the buttocks: **a.** *gluteus maximus,* which extends the thigh; **b.** *gluteus medius,* which rotates and abducts the thigh; **c.** *gluteus minimus,* which abducts the thigh. [New Latin, from Greek *gloutos,* buttock. See **gel-¹** in Appendix.*] —**glu'te·al** *adj.*

glu·ti·nous (glo͞ot'n-əs) *adj.* Resembling or of the nature of glue; sticky; adhesive. [Latin *glūtinōsus,* from *glūten,* glue. See **gel-¹** in Appendix.*] —**glu'ti·nous·ly** *adv.* —**glu'ti·nous·ness, glu'ti·nos'i·ty** (-ŏs'ə-tē) *n.*

glut·ton¹ (glŭt'n) *n.* **1.** One that eats or consumes immoderately. **2.** One that has inordinate capacity to receive or withstand something: *a glutton for punishment.* [Middle English *glotoun,* from Old French *gluton, gloton,* from Latin *gluttō.* See **gwel-⁵** in Appendix.*] —**glut'ton·ous** *adj.* —**glut'ton·ous·ly** *adv.*

glut·ton² (glŭt'n) *n.* A mammal, the **wolverine** *(see).* [From GLUTTON (eater), translation of German *Vielfrass,* "great eater."]

glut·ton·y (glŭt'n-ē) *n.* Excess in eating or drinking.

glyc·er·ic acid (glĭ-sĕr'ĭk, glĭs'ər-). A syrupy, colorless compound, $C_3H_6O_4$. [From GLYCERIN.]

glyc·er·ide (glĭs'ə-rīd') *n.* An ester of glycerol and fatty acids. [GLYCER(IN) + -IDE.]

glyc·er·in (glĭs'ər-ĭn) *n.* Glycerol. [French, from Greek *glukeros,* sweet. See **dlku-** in Appendix.*]

glyc·er·ol (glĭs'ə-rôl', -rōl', -rŏl') *n.* A syrupy, sweet, colorless or yellowish liquid, $C_3H_8O_3$, obtained from fats and oils as a by-product of the manufacture of soaps and fatty acids, and used as a solvent, antifreeze and antifrost fluid, plasticizer, and sweetener, and in the manufacture of dynamite, cosmetics, liquid soaps, inks, and lubricants. [GLYCER(IN) + -OL.]

glyc·er·yl (glĭs'ər-əl) *n.* The trivalent glycerol radical CH_2CHCH_2. [GLYCER(IN) + -YL.]

gly·cin (glī'sĭn) *n.* Also **gly·cine** (-sēn', -sĭn). A poisonous compound, $C_8H_9NO_3$, used as a photographic developer. [From GLYCINE.]

gly·cine (glī'sēn', -sən) *n.* **1.** A white, very sweet crystalline amino acid, $C_2H_5NO_2$, the principal amino acid occurring in sugar cane, derived by alkaline hydrolysis of gelatin, and used in biochemical research and medicine. **2.** Variant of **glycin.** [GLYC(O)- + -INE.]

Exercise 2

In this exercise you will scan a page of a dictionary (on page 7) to find answers to specific questions. Read each question, find the answer as quickly as possible, then write it in the space provided. These questions will introduce you to several kinds of information to be found in a dictionary.

1. Would you find the word *glory* on this page? _____ NO _____

2. How many syllables are there in *glossolalia*? _____ 5 _____

3. Which syllable is stressed in the word *glutamic*? _____ 2 _____

4. What are the key words that tell you how to pronounce the *o* in the preferred pronunciation of *glycerol*? _____

5. What is the preferred spelling of the plural of *glottis*? _____

6. What is the past tense of *to glue*? _____

7. What is the adverb derived from *glower*? _____

8. What word must you look up to find *glossographer*? _____

9. For whom was *gloxinia* named? _____

10. From what two languages has *glucose* developed? _____

11. Is the intransitive verb *gloze* commonly used today? _____

12. How many synonyms are listed for the word *glum*? Why are these words defined here? _____
_____

13. When was Christoph Willibald Gluck born? _____

14. What is the population of Gloucester, Massachusetts? _____

15. List the different kinds of information you can find in a dictionary. _____
_____
_____
_____

WORD STUDY: Stems and Affixes

Using context clues is one way to discover the meaning of an unfamiliar word. Another way is word analysis, that is, looking at the meanings of parts of words. Many English words have been formed by combining parts of older English, Greek, and Latin words. If you know the meanings of some of these word parts, you can often guess the meaning of an unfamiliar English word.

For example, *report* is formed from *re*, which means back, and *port* which means carry. *Scientist* is derived from *sci*, which means know, and *ist*, which means one who. *Port* and *sci* are called stems. A stem is the basic part on which groups of related words are built. *Re* and *ist* are called affixes, that is, word parts which are attached to stems. Affixes like *re*, which are attached to the beginning of stems are called prefixes. Affixes attached to the end, like *ist*, are called suffixes. Generally, prefixes change the meaning of a word and suffixes change its part of speech. Here is an example:

Stem:	pay (verb)	honest (adjective)
Prefix:	*re*pay (verb)	*dis*honest (adjective)
Suffix:	repay*ment* (noun)	dishonest*ly* (adverb)

Word analysis is not always enough to give you the precise definition of a word you encounter in a reading passage, but often it will help you to understand the general meaning of the word so that you can continue reading without stopping to use a dictionary.

Below is a list of some commonly occurring stems and affixes. Study their meanings. Your teacher may ask you to give examples of words you know which are derived from these stems and affixes. Then do the exercises which follow. Some questions require the use of a dictionary.

Prefixes:	
com-, con-, col-, cor-, co-	together, with
in-, im-	in, into, on
in-, im-, il-, ir-	not
micro-	small
pre-	before
re-, retro-	backward, back, behind

Stems:	
-audi-, -audit-	hear
-chron-	time
-dic-, -dict-	say, speak
-graph-, -gram-	write, writing
-log-, -ology-	speech, word, study
-metr-, -meter-	measure
-phon-	sound
-scop-	see, look at
-scope-	instrument for seeing or observing
-scrib-, -script-	write
-spect-	look at

(Suffixes *on page 10*)

Suffixes:

-er, -or   one who

-tion, -ation   condition, the act of

Exercise 1

1. In each item, select the best definition of the italicized word.

    a. *In retrospect*, we would have been wise to leave our money in the bank.

          ___ 1. Many years ago   ___ 3. In fact
          ___ 2. Looking around   ✓ 4. Looking back

    b. He lost his *spectacles*.

          ✓ 1. glasses   ___ 3. pants
          ___ 2. gloves   ___ 4. shoes

    c. He drew *concentric* circles.

          ___ 1. OO   ___ 3. OO
          ✓ 2. ◎   ___ 4. ⊙⊙

    d. He *inspected* their work.

          ___ 1. spoke highly of   ✓ 3. examined closely
          ___ 2. did not examine   ___ 4. did not like

2. In the word *inspected*, what is the meaning of the prefix *in*? _____

3. List three words familiar to you which contain *in* where it means *not*.
   INDISCRIMINATION, INCULT, INCAPABLE

4. Is *scribble* derived from *scrib*? (Use your dictionary.) _____
What does scribble mean? _____

5. Is *coloration* derived from *col*? (Use your dictionary.) _____

6. Using what you know about stems and affixes, define the italicized word in the following sentence:
Some scholars have been able to read the *inscriptions* on the walls of ancient temples.
   IN into   scrip - write

7. Use word analysis to explain what *predict* means.
   pre - before   dict - speak

8. In current usage, the prefix *co* is frequently used to form new words (for example, *co* + editors becomes coeditors). Give another example of a word which uses *co* in this way.
   cooperation

9. *Spir* is a root which means breathe. Look up *conspirators* in your dictionary, and explain how the meaning of the word developed from the meanings of the stem and affixes from which it is derived. _____

_____

_____

Exercise 2

Following is a list of words containing some of the stems and affixes introduced in this unit. Definitions of these words appear on the right. These words are probably unfamiliar to you. It is NOT the purpose of this exercise to teach you the definitions of all these words. Instead, the exercise is designed to serve as a review of the stems and affixes defined in this section and as a way for you to practice using the technique of word analysis to guess the meanings of unfamiliar words.

Put the letter of the appropriate definition next to each word.

1. __b__ microscope
2. __c__ audition
3. __d__ phonoscope
4. __e__ audiometer
5. __a__ audiology

a. the science of hearing
b. an instrument used to make small objects large enough to see and study
c. the act or sense of hearing
d. an instrument which tests the quality of strings for musical instruments
e. an instrument for measuring hearing

Stop. Check your answers before going on to the next part.

6. __d__ gramophone
7. __e__ chronometer
8. __b__ micrometer
9. __a__ micrograph
10. __c__ chronology

a. an instrument for doing extremely small writing
b. an instrument for measuring small distances
c. the science of dating events accurately and arranging them in order of occurrance
d. phonograph; an instrument that records or reproduces sound
e. an instrument for measuring time very accurately

11. __b__ chronoscope
12. __a__ phonogram
13. __e__ microphone
14. __c__ phonology
15. __d__ micrology

a. the sign or symbol representing a sound or word
b. an instrument to measure small periods of time
c. the study of speech sounds
d. the study of unimportant matters
e. an instrument used to make weak sounds louder

16. __d__ audiphone
17. __c__ chronic
18. __a__ audiogram
19. __e__ phonometer
20. __b__ chronicler

a. a graph showing the percentage of hearing loss in a particular ear
b. a historian
c. long-lasting; constant; habitual
d. a device to help the partially-deaf hear
e. an instrument used to measure the intensity and vibration frequency of sound

11

SCANNING

To scan is to read quickly in order to locate specific information. The steps involved in scanning are the following:

1. Decide exactly what information you are looking for, and think about the form it may take. For example, if you want to know when something happened, you would look for a date. If you want to find out who did something, you would look for a name.
2. Next, decide where you need to look to find the information you want. You probably would not look for sports scores on the front page of the newspaper, nor look under the letter *S* for the telephone number of Sam Potter.
3. Move your eyes as quickly as possible down the page until you find the information you need. Read it carefully.
4. When you find what you need, do not read further.

The four exercises in this section are designed to give you practice in the various skills necessary for scanning.

Exercise 1

The index on page 13 is from the *World Almanac*, a general reference text which provides a variety of information on a large number of topics.

Scan to find the answers to the following questions.

1. If you wanted to learn about world religions, where might you begin your search?

2. Where could you find information on the current population of your country?

3. Where would you look to find information on the Chinese Lunar Calendar?

4. Where would you look to find a map of Africa?

QUICK REFERENCE INDEX

The World Almanac and Book of Facts, 1974 edition; Copyright © Newspaper Enterprise Association, New York, 1973.

Exercise 2
The chart on page 15 was also taken from the *World Almanac*.

Scan to find the answers to the following questions.

1. What is the name of the highest waterfall listed here?

2. What is the name of the highest single-leap waterfall listed here?

3. What is the height of the shortest waterfall listed here?

4. What is the height of Catarata de Candelas in Columbia? What is the name of the river which feeds it?

5. How many waterfalls are listed for Japan?

6. How many of California's waterfalls run full force throughout the year?

7. How many waterfalls are listed for Colorado?

Famous Waterfalls

Source: National Geographic Society, Washington, D. C.

Height=total drop in one or more leaps. †=falls of more than one leap; *=falls that diminish greatly seasonally; **=falls that reduce to a trickle or are dry for part of each year. If river names not shown, they are same as the falls. R.=river; L.=lake; (C)=cascade-type. See notes following list.

Name and Location	Ft.	Name and Location	Ft.	Name and Location	Ft.
AFRICA		**Norway—**		**Twin, Snake R	125
Angola		† Eastern Mardalsfoss	1,696	**Kentucky**	
Duque de Braganca,		Highest fall	974	Cumberland	68
Lucala R	344	Western Mardalsfoss	1,535	**Maryland**	
Ruacana, Cunene R	406	(Both on L. Eikesdal)		Great, Potomac R. (C)	90
Ethiopia		Skjeggedal	525	**Minnesota**	
Baratieri, Ganale		Skykkje, Skykkjua R	820	**Minnehaha	54
Dorya R	459	Vettis, Morkedöla R	1,214	**Montana**	
Dal Verme, Ganale		Highest fall	889	Missouri	75
Dorya R	98	Vöring, Bjoreia R	597	**New Jersey**	
Fincha	508	**Sweden**		**Passaic	70
*Tesissat, Blue Nile R	140	† Handöl, Handöl Cr.	345	**New York**	
Lesotho		† *Stora Sjöfallet, Lule R	130	Taughannock	215
Maletsunyane	630	Tannforsen, Are R	120	**Oregon**	
Rhodesia-Zambia		**Switzerland**		† Multnomah	620
*Victoria, Zambezi R	355	† Giétroz (Glacier) (C)	1,640	Highest fall	542
South Africa		† Diesbach	394	**Tennessee**	
*Aughrabies, Orange R	400	† Giessbach	1,312	Fall Creek	256
Howick, Umgeni R	311	Handegg, Aare R	151	Rock House Creek	125
† Tugela (5 falls)	3,110	Iffigen	394	**Washington**	
Highest fall	1,350	Pissevache, La Salanfe R	213	Fairy Falls	700
Tanzania-Zambia		† Reichenbach	656	Mt. Rainier Nat. Pk.	
*Kalambo	726	Rhine	65	Narada, Paradise R	168
Uganda		† Simmen, Simme R	459	Sluiskin, Paradise R	300
Murchison, Victoria		Stäuber	590	Palouse	198
Nile R	140	Staubbach	984	Snoqualmie	270
Zambia		† Trümmelbach	1,312	**Wisconsin**	
Chirombo, Ieisa R	880	**NORTH AMERICA**		Manitou, Black R	165
ASIA		**Canada**		**Wyoming**	
India—Cauvery	330	British Columbia		Yellowstone Pk. Tower	132
† **Gersoppa (Jog),		†Takakkaw (Daly Glacier)	1,650	Yellowstone (upper)	109
Sharavati R	830	Highest fall	1,200	Yellowstone (lower)	308
Japan		Della Falls	1,443	**Mexico—**El Salto	218
**Kegon, L. Chuzenji	330	Panther, Nigel Cr.	600	**Juanacatlán. Rio	
Yudaki, L. Yuno	335	Labrador		Grande de Santiago	66
AUSTRALASIA		Churchill Falls, Churchill R	245	**SOUTH AMERICA**	
Australia		Mackenzie District		**Argentina—Brazil**	
New South Wales		Virginia, S. Nahanni R	315	† Iguazú	237
† Wentworth	518	Quebec		**Brazil—**Glass	1,325
Highest fall	360	Montmorency	274	Herval	400
Wollomombi	1,100	**Canada—United States**		Paulo Afonso, São Fran-	
Queensland		Niagara: American	193	cisco R	275
Coomera	210	Horseshoe	186	Patos-Maribondo, Río	
Tully	450	**United States**		Grande	115
New Zealand		California		Urubupunga, Alto	
*Bowen (from Glaciers)	540	Feather, Fall R	640	Parana R	40
Helena	890	Yosemite National Park		**Brazil-Paraguay**	
Stirling	505	Bridalveil	620	Sete Quedas, or Guaira	
† Sutherland, Arthur R	1,904	Illilouette	370	Alto Paraná R	130
EUROPE		Nevada	594	**Colombia—**Tequendama,	
Austria—Upper Gastein	207	**Ribbon	1,612	Bogotá R	427
Lower Gastein	280	Silver Strand	1,170	Catarata de Candelas,	
(Both on Ache R.)		Vernal	317	Cusiana R	984
† Golling, Schwarzbach R	200	†Yosemite	2,425	**Ecuador**	
Krimml (Krimmler)	1,250	*Yosemite (upper)	1,430	Agoyan, Pastaza R	200
France—† Gavarnie (C)	1,385	*Yosemite (lower)	320	**Guyana**	
Great Britain—Wales		*Yosemite (middle)	675	Kaieteur, Potaro R.	741
Pistyll Cain, Afon Gain R	150	Colorado		King George VI, Utshi R	1,600
Pistyll Rhaiadr	240	Seven	266	† Marina, Ipobe R	500
Scotland		Georgia		Highest fall	300
Glomach	370	† Tallulah	251	**Peru**	
Iceland—Detti, Jokul R	144	Hawaii		Sewerd, Cutibirene R	877
Gull, Hvita R	101	Akaka	442	**Venezuela—**† Angel	3,212
Italy—Toce (C)	470	Idaho		Highest fall	2,648
		Henry's Fork (upper)	96	Cuquenán	2,000
		Henry's Fork (lower)	70		
		**Shoshone, Snake R	195		

The earth has thousands of waterfalls, some of considerable magnitude. Their importance is determined not only by height but volume of flow, steadiness of flow, crest width, whether the water drops sheerly or over a sloping surface, and one leap or a succession of leaps. A series of low falls flowing over a considerable distance is known as a cascade.

Sete Quedas or Guaira is the world's greatest waterfall when its mean annual flow (estimated at 470,000 cusecs, cubic feet per second) is combined with height. A greater volume of water passes over Stanley Falls, though not one of its seven cataracts, spread over nearly 60 miles of the Congo River, exceeds 10 feet.

Estimated mean annual flow, in cusecs, of other major waterfalls are: Niagara, 212,200; Paulo Afonso, 100,000; Urubupunga, 97,000; Iguazú, 61,600; Patos-Maribondo, 53,000; Victoria, 38,400; Churchill, Labrador, 40,000; and Kaieteur, 23,400.

The World Almanac and Book of Facts, 1974 edition; Copyright © Newspaper Enterprise Association, New York, 1973.

Exercise 3

The calendar on page 17 is typical of the list of social events provided by many newspapers in the United States.

Scan to find the answers to the following questions.

1. Under which section(s) would you look if you wanted to go to a play?

2. Under which section(s) would you look if you wanted to spend an evening eating, drinking, and dancing?

3. When do the Detroit Pistons play basketball this week?

4. Is Lou Rawls singing at a Detroit area night club this week?

5. Is there a pop concert Thursday night?

6. Could you attend a classical music concert Saturday night?

7. What is the topic of Seymour Hersh's lecture Wednesday morning?

Detroit Free Press
The Calendar

James Tatum and his trio play reverent jazz Thursday night in the Hamtramck Public Library.

Journalist Seymour Hersh speaks at Detroit Town Hall Wednesday at the Fisher.

Lou Rawls sings at db's Club in the Hyatt Regency, Dearborn's newest hotel.

Theater

SAME TIME, NEXT YEAR—Comedy-romance. 7 tonight; 8:30 p.m. Mon.-Sat.; matinee at 2 p.m. Wed. and Sat. Fisher Theatre, Second at Grand Blvd.

GODSPELL—The story of Jesus in rock at 2 and 7:30 p.m. today; 8:30 p.m. Tues.-Fri.; 2 and 8:30 p.m. Sat. Music Hall, 350 Madison, downtown.

HILBERRY THEATRE, Cass at Hancock:
● **"As You Like It,"** delightful Shakespeare at 2:30 p.m. Wed. and 8:30 p.m. Thur.
● **"The Miser,"** Moliere folderol at 2:30 p.m. Thur. and 8:30 p.m. Fri.-Sat.

THE ME NOBODY KNOWS—U-D-Marygrove production once only, 8:30 p.m. Tues. at Northwest Activities Center, Meyers at Curtis.

OAKLAND UNIVERSITY, University Drive east of I-75, Rochester:
● **"An Italian Straw Hat"**—Lots of people run through flapping doors and joyous misunderstandings. 8:15 p.m. Thur.-Sat. and 2 and 6:30 p.m. Sun. Studio Theatre.
● **"An Italian Straw Hat"**—Lots of people run through flapping doors and joyous misunderstandings. 8:15 p.m. Thur.-Sat. and 2 and 8:30 p.m. Sun. Studio Theatre.

Children's Theater

THE MIDNIGHT RIDE OF PAUL REVERE follows the famed horseman through every Middlesex village and town, 10 a.m. and 1 p.m. Mon.-Fri.; 11 a.m. and 2 p.m. Sat. Detroit Institute of Arts, 5200 Woodward.

THE SIGNIFYING MONKEY is fun in the jungle. 10 a.m. and 1:30 p.m. Mon.-Fri. Langston Hughes Theatre, Livernois at Davison.

Community Theater

GEORGE WASHINGTON SLEPT HERE is not Bicentennial, despite the title. By the Ibex Club at 8:30 p.m. Fri.-Sat. Grosse Pointe War Memorial, 32 Lake Shore, Grosse Pointe Farms.

ONCE UPON A MATTRESS, a grown-up fairy tale by the Southfield Civic Theatre at 2 p.m. today. Civic Center, 26000 Evergreen, Southfield.

THE TIME OF YOUR LIFE—Saroyan by Red Door Players, 2 p.m. today. Unitarian Church, Forest at Cass.

Nightlife

HYATT REGENCY HOTEL—Lou Rawls changes the singing mood at the new db's Club. Strutters Ball plays for dancing. Tues.-Sat., Michigan at Southfield, Dearborn.

TOP HAT—Bob Taylor sings show, classic and pop songs Mon.-Sat. 73 E. University, Windsor.

BLOOMFIELD CANOPY—Elaine Philpot with music from '20s-'70s Tues.-Sat. 6560 Orchard Lake Rd., West Bloomfield.

ROOSTERTAIL turns comic. **Marv Welch** loose with the American Scene in the Palm River Club Tues.-Sun. 100 Marquette at the river.

HOTEL PONTCHARTRAIN introduces **Laurie Seaman** and Celebration Roadshow to downtown at the Top. Two Washington Blvd.

GINO'S SURF—Chicago singer **Deanna Guest** sings and **Lyla** and **Bahia** dance Tues.-Sun. 37400 E. Jefferson, Mt. Clemens.

GOLDEN COACH—**Terry Moretti** and the Las Vegas '76 revue Tues.-Sun. Him and I play bluegrass Mon. 30450 Van Dyke, Warren.

PALOMBO'S has **Donna Marie** and Motion Mon.-Sat. 20401 W. Eight Mile.

MONEY TREE—Guitarist **Mickey Stein** 7-10 p.m. Mon.-Tues.; **Pat Tolias, Monica Stoval** and **Kathy Caesar** Thur.-Fri. when the French restaurant stays open late for the theater crowd. 33 W. Fort, downtown.

WARREN HOLIDAY INN—**Michael Strika** and guitar entertain Tues.-Sat. 32035 Van Dyke.

ROMAN TERRACE—**Gary Primo** Duo, he's the piano, Mon.-Sat. Orchard Lake at Twelve Mile, Farmington Hills.

DEARBORN INN—**Dennis Day** plays piano Tues.-Thur. and Sun. **Mack Ferguson** provides dance music Sat. Oakwood Blvd. south of Michigan Ave.

THE OLD PLACE—Dancing and entertainment Wed.-Sat. **Sherry Johnson**, piano, **Mark Van Haaken**, guitar. 15301 E. Jefferson.

DETROIT TONIGHT TOURS—Visit night places in a British double-decker bus. 961-5180.

Classical Music & Dance

DETROIT SYMPHONY—**Aldo Ceccato** and the Trio di Trieste, 8:30 p.m. Thur. and Sat. and in an NBD Coffee Concert at 9:30 a.m. Fri. Ford Aud., Jefferson at Woodward, downtown.

MISCHA LEFKOWITZ, violin, as part of the Kolego Concert Series at 3 p.m. today at Detroit Institute of Arts, 5200 Woodward.

BRUNCH WITH BACH and harpsichordist **Evelyne Scheyer** at 10 and 11:15 a.m. today. Detroit Institute of Arts, 5200 Woodward.

OAKWAY SYMPHONY, **Francesco Di Blasi**, conducting, and Dance Detroit in a Gershwin spectacular at 8 p.m. Sat. Redford Theatre, Lahser at Grand River.

THE ELIJAH, Mendelssohn's dramatic oratorio by WSU Symphonic Choir and Temple Beth El Choir. Free at 8 p.m. Fri. Temple Beth El, Fourteen Mile at Telegraph, Bloomfield Township.

WARREN COMMUNITY BAND CONCERT at 3:30 p.m. today. Van Dyke Lincoln High, Nine Mile at Federal, Warren.

Discotheque

SUBWAY sometimes has live music but usually doesn't. Shelby Hotel, 525 W. Lafayette, downtown.

SINDROME—Disco all week, instructions Mon. Telegraph at Ford Road, Dearborn Heights.

PERFECT BLEND—Nightly after 9 p.m. South side of Northwestern at Ten Mile, Southfield.

CLAM SHOP UPSTAIRS Thur.-Fri. Grand Blvd. west of Woodward.

THE LANDING nightly from 6 p.m. to 2 a.m. Southfield at Ten Mile, Southfield.

Pop Concerts

GEORGE CARLIN discusses the world's funnies at 8 and 11 p.m. Fri. Royal Oak Theatre, Fourth at Washington.

AIRTIGHT rocks for Jazz Development Workshop at 8:15 and 10:15 p.m. Mon.-Wed. Langston Hughes Theatre, Livernois at Davison.

Jazz, Folk & Rock

GABOR SZABO, jazz guitarist, Tues.-next Sun. **Sonny Fortune, sax,** closes tonight. Baker's Keyboard Lounge, Livernois at Eight Mile.

LITTLE SONNY blows authentic harmonica blues out of the Depression in Greensboro, Ala. Tues.-Sun. at the Raven Gallery, Greenfield at Twelve Mile, Southfield.

JUDY ROBERTS, electronic jazz piano, Wed.-Sat. at Inn Between, Huron at Elizabeth Lake Road, Pontiac.

BOBBY LAUREL'S smooth Suburban Renewal plays Thur.-Sat. in the Gazebo, Mound at Thirteen Mile, Warren.

SHADES OF GREY rocks Tues.-Sun. at Belanger House, Main at Twelve Mile, Royal Oak.

COPELAND BLUES BAND Thur.-Sat. at That Gnu Joint, Cass at Palmer.

EDDY KAY, folk, rock and comedy, Fri.-Sat. Colonial Lounge, Farmington Road at Seven Mile, Livonia.

CONNIE GRAHAM and band sing pops Wed.-Sat. at Bobbies, Telegraph between Twelve and Thirteen Mile roads, Bingham Farms.

JIM FREEMAN joshes the girls and sings Wed.-Sat. Dirty Helen's, Cass at Bagley, downtown.

GREG HOWARD leads Fourth Edition and **Karen Johnson** in Top 40 stuff Mon.-Sat. **AMIRA AMIR** lectures on the mystic art of the belly dance Fri.-Sat. Playboy Club, James Couzens at Eight Mile.

MIDTOWN FOLK—**Bruce Hambright** Mon.-Wed. and **Fresh Air** Thur.-Sat. Midtown Cafe, 139 S. Woodward, Birmingham.

PHIL ESSER sings solo folk Mon.-Tues. **Ron Coden** does the rest of the week at his club, the Railroad Crossing, 6640 E. Eight Mile.

FEATHER CANYON rolls along Mon.-Tues., followed by Travis West-next Sun. Wagon Wheel, Rochester at Big Beaver, Troy.

RIOT rocks Wed.-Sat. at the Library, 37235 Groesbeck, Mt. Clemens.

JOHN AMORE puts his high-energy songs to work Tues.-Sat. Old-time rocker **Del Shannon** closes tonight. Golden Spur, 14315 Northline, Southgate.

TIM HAZEL in a western mood, Mon.-Sat. Dearborn Towne House, Telegraph south of Michigan Ave.

GEORGE YOUNG heads the instrumental, vocal and comedy show Wed.-Sun. at Bimbo's beer emporium, 22041 Michigan Ave., Dearborn.

Fun Stuff

ICE SHOW—200 skaters in a flag-waving mood. 2 and 7 p.m. Sat.-next Sun. Oak Park Ice Arena, 13950 Oak Park Blvd.

BICENTENNIAL AUCTION for mentally handicapped. 7-11 p.m. Fri. Wing Lake Development Center, 6490 Wing Lake Rd., Bloomfield Hills.

BLUE ENGELS, Humperdinck fans, throw a diabetes research benefit fashion show-dinner at 7:30 p.m. Tues. Salvatore's Italian Villa, Middlebelt between Warren and Ford Roads, Garden City.

Films/Lectures

FAMILY FILM FESTIVAL, comedy, classics and selected short subjects, 9 a.m.-3 p.m. today. Howard Johnson's, West Grand Blvd. at Third, downtown.

DETROIT INSTITUTE OF ARTS, 5200 Woodward:
● **George Pierrot**—Stan Midgley takes a Bicentennial tour of the U.S. at 3 p.m. today.
● **"Basic Training,"** a documentary about Ft. Knox. 7 tonight.
● **"Blonde Venus"**—Josef von Sternberg made Marlene Dietrich wear an ape suit and sing "Hot Voodoo" in 1932. 2 p.m. Wed.-Fri.
● **"Distant Thunder,"** a Bengal doctor and wife are caught up in a corrupt system. 7 and 9:30 p.m. Fri.
● **"My Night at Maud's"** is French and why not? 7 and 9:30 p.m. Sat.

THE EVIL WEED, a slapstick movie by the man who brought you Sha Na Na. 8 and 10 p.m. Fri.-Sat. Cass City Cinema, Unitarian Church, Cass at Forest.

SITDOWN AT DODGE and **"I Am Somebody,"** films about union ordeals at 7:30 p.m. Sun. Trinity Church, 13100 Woodward, Highland Park.

VEGETABLE GARDENING, a free lecture to help you raise a bumper crop by **Gerald Drahelm** of MSU. 5 p.m. today. Detroit Science Center, 52 E. Forest.

SIX WIVES OF HENRY VIII is runnning at 10 a.m. and 7 p.m. Fri. in Macomb County Service Center, Groesbeck at Elizabeth, Mt. Clemens.

SEYMOUR HERSH, Pulitzer Prize-winning journalist, speaks at Detroit Town Hall at 11 a.m. Wed. Fisher Theatre, Second at Grand Blvd.

Sports

RED WINGS meet Pittsburgh in the Wings' last hockey game of their season tonight at 7 on Olympia ice, 5920 Grand River.

PISTONS play three home basketball games—Philadelphia at 7 tonight; Milwaukee at 7:35 p.m. Wed. and Atlanta, to finish the season, at 8:05 p.m. Fri. Cobo Arena, downtown.

THOROUGHBREDS race at 3:20 p.m. Mon.-Fri. and 2:20 p.m. Sat. Hazel Park, Dequindre at Ten Mile.

NORTH AMERICAN SPEED SKATING qualifying tryouts after 1:30 p.m. today. Further information at 284-1124. Yack Recreation Center, 3131 Third, Wyandotte.

HARNESS RACES:
● **Northville Downs**, Mon.-Sat. Post time, 8:15 p.m. W. Seven Mile at Sheldon, Northville.
● **Windsor Raceway**, 8 p.m. Tues.-Sat. and 1:30 p.m. Sun. Windsor, Ont.

Exhibits

OUTDOOR LIVING SHOW noon-6 p.m. today, 9:30 a.m.-9 p.m. the rest of the week. Pontiac Mall, Telegraph north of Elizabeth Lake Road.

BOAT SHOW, campers and equipment 5-10 p.m. Thur.-Fri. and noon-10 p.m. next Sat.-Sun. Yack Arena, 3131 Third St., Wyandotte.

BEHOLD YOUR BODY, an exhibit to acquaint you with yourself. 9 a.m.-5 p.m. Mon.-Fri. and noon-5 p.m. Sun. Detroit Science Center, 52 E. Forest.

SPRING ARTS AND CRAFTS show and sale from 11 a.m.-9 p.m. Fri.-Sat. Plymouth Cultural Center, 525 Farmer St.

compiled by
CHUCK THURSTON

Adapted from "The Calendar," *Detroit Free Press*, Sunday Edition, April 4, 1976.

Exercise 4

The *Guinness Book of World Records* collects statistics on a large variety of unusual games, stunts, and contests. The excerpt on page 19 gives you an example of the type of information recorded in the book.*

Scan to find the answers to the following questions.

1. What is the fastest time recorded for smashing a piano into 9-inch pieces?

2. What is the fastest recorded time for tap dancing?

3. Do you think you could break the world handshaking record?

4. How long would you have to sit on a pole in order to set a new world record?

5. If you wanted to set a record for balancing on one foot, what record would you have to beat? What rules would you have to observe?

6. How many coins would you need to better the current coin balancing record?

*From the *Guinness Book of World Records*, copyright © 1975 by Sterling Publishing Company, Inc., N.Y. 10016.

STUNTS AND MISCELLANEOUS ENDEAVORS

Apple Peeling. The longest single unbroken apple peel on record is one of 130 feet 8½ inches peeled by Frank Freer (U.S.) in 8 hours at Wolcott, N.Y., on October 17, 1971. The apple was 15 inches in circumference.

Apple Picking. The greatest recorded performance is 270 U.S. bushels picked in 8 hours by Harold Oaks, 22, at his father's orchard, Hood River, Oregon, on September 30, 1972.

Baby Carriage Pushing. The greatest distance covered in 24 hours in pushing a perambulator is 319 miles on a track by a 60-man team from the White Horse Sports and Social Club, Stony Stratford, England, on May 19–20, 1973. A team of 10 with an adult "baby" from "Flore Moderns" covered 226.1 miles at Flore, Northamptonshire, England, in 24 hours on June 28–29, 1975.

Balancing on One Foot. The longest recorded duration for continuous balancing on one foot is 8 hours 5 minutes by Alan Maki at Beverly Hills Junior High School, Upper Darby, Pennsylvania, on March 3, 1975. The disengaged foot may not be rested on the standing foot nor may any sticks be used for support or balance.

Gordon Clark and John Wheeler of Corsham, England, went 12 hours 15 minutes on October 6, 1973. They took a 5-minute rest break every hour.

Balloon Racing. The largest balloon release on record has been one of 100,000 helium balloons at the opening of "Transpo 72" at Dulles Airport, Washington, D.C., on May 27, 1972. The longest reported toy balloon flight is one of 9,000 miles from Atherton, California (released by Jane Dorst on May 21, 1972) and found on June 10, 1972, at Pietermaritzburg, South Africa.

Ball Punching. Ron Reunalf (Australia) equaled his own world duration ball-punching record of 125 hours 20 minutes at 10:20 p.m. on December 31, 1955, at the Esplanade, Southport, Northern Territory, Australia.

Band, One-Man. The greatest number of musical instruments played in a single tune is 49 by Werner Hirzel (b. 1919) (known as Schnickelgruber), who performed on ABC-TV with the David Frost Show on April 5, 1974.

Don Davis of Hollywood, California, is the only one-man band able to play 4 melody and 2 percussion instruments simultaneously. For a rendition of Beethoven's Fifth Symphony, he utilizes an 8-prong pendular perpendicular piano pounder and a semi-circular chromatic radially operated centrifugally sliding left-handed glockenspiel.

Barrel Jumping. The greatest number of barrels jumped by a skater is 17 (total length 28 feet 8 inches) by Kenneth LeBel at the Grossinger Country Club, Liberty, New York, on January 9, 1965. Roger Wood leaped 29 feet 2 inches on December 14, 1972.

Bed of Nails. The duration record for non-stop lying on a bed of nails (needle-sharp 6-inch nails, 2 inches apart) is 25 hours 20 minutes by Vernon E. Craig (Komar, the Hindu *fakir*) at Wooster, Ohio, July 22–23, 1971. The greatest live weight borne on a bed of nails is also by Komar with 4 persons aggregating 1,142 lbs. standing on him on the Mike Douglas Show on TV in Philadelphia on March 26, 1974. Barrie Walls (El Hakim), 37, endured 26 hours 37 minutes with brief rests at Sophia Garden, Cardiff, Wales, January 16–17, 1975. The feminine record (with 5-minute rests per hour) is 25 hours 30 minutes by Ruth Marie Porter, 18, at Springfield, Virginia, on February 13–14, 1975.

Much longer durations are claimed by unwitnessed *fakirs*—the most extreme case being *Silki* who claimed 111 days in São Paulo, Brazil, ending on August 24, 1969.

Coal Carrying. The record time for the annual "World Coal Carrying Championship" over the uphill, 1,080-yard course at Ossett cum Gawthorpe, Yorkshire, England, with a 112-lb. sack is 4 minutes 36 seconds by Tony Nicholson, 26, on April 3, 1972.

The non-stop distance record is 14 miles from Perranporth to and around Camborne, Cornwall, England, by E. John Rapson in 3 hours 40 minutes on April 4, 1953.

Coin Balancing. The greatest recorded feat of coin balancing is the stacking of 126 coins on top of a silver U.S. dollar on edge by Alex Chervinsky, 65, of Lock Haven, Pennsylvania, on September 16, 1971, after 23 years' practice.

Contest Winnings. The largest recorded individual prize won was $307,500 by Herbert J. Idle, 55, of Chicago in an encyclopedia contest run by Unicorn Press, Inc., on August 20, 1953.

Crawling. The longest crawl (at least one knee always on the ground) is 7 miles 803 yards by Kevin Goodhew and Simon Holmes of Preston Minor High School, Wembley Park, London, in 6 hours 26 minutes on May 10, 1975.

Dance Band. The most protracted session is one of 321 hours (13 days 9 hours) by the Black Brothers of Bonn, West Germany, ending on January 2, 1969. Never less than a quartet were in action during the marathon.

Dancing, Modern. The longest recorded dancing marathon (50 minutes per hour) in modern style is 114 hours 12½ minutes by Albert Harding at the Inn Cognitos, Middlesbrough, England, on May 17–22, 1975.

Dancing, Tap. The fastest *rate* ever measured for any tap dancer has been 1,440 taps per minute (24 per second) by Roy Castle on the BBC-TV *Record Breakers* program on January 14, 1973.

Dancing the Twist. The duration record for the twist is 102 hours 28 minutes 37 seconds by Roger Guy English at La Jolla, California, on July 11–16, 1973.

Grave Digging. It is recorded that Johann Heinrich Karl Thieme, sexton of Aldenburg, Germany, dug 23,311 graves during a 50-year career. In 1826, his understudy dug *his* grave.

Guitar Playing. The longest recorded solo guitar playing marathon is one of 110¼ hours by Dennis Blakey at radio station WQYK, Tampa, Florida, from July 29 to August 3, 1973.

Hairdressing. The world record for non-stop styling, cutting and setting hair is 120 hours 3 minutes by Louis Sanft of Fall River, Massachusetts, June 4–9, 1975.

The most expensive men's hairdresser is Tristan of Hollywood, who charges any "client" $100 on a first visit. This consists of a "consultation" followed by "remedial grooming."

Handshaking. The world record for handshaking was set by President Theodore Roosevelt (1858–1919), who shook hands with 8,513 people at a New Year's Day White House Presentation in Washington, D.C., on January 1, 1907. Outside public life the record has become meaningless because aspirants merely arrange circular queues and shake the same hands repetitively.

Handwriting. The longest recorded handwriting marathon was one of 88 hours by Sara Morris of Dudley College of Education, Hereford and Dorcester, England, on June 6–9, 1975. Her highly legible writing was mostly from the Bible.

Hiking. The longest recorded hike is one of 18,500 miles through 14 countries from Singapore to London by David Kwan, aged 22, which occupied 81 weeks from May 4, 1957, or an average of 32 miles a day.

Hoop Rolling. In 1968 it was reported that Zolilio Diaz (Spain) had rolled a hoop 600 miles from Mieres to Madrid and back in 18 days.

House of Cards. The greatest number of stories achieved in building houses of cards is 39 in the case of a tower using 1,240 cards by John Wilson, 15, of Port Credit, Ontario, Canada. The highest house with alternate 8- and 6-card stories is 30, achieved by Julian Bardo in St. John's College, Cambridge, England, on June 14, 1974. He used 4 packs and a plumb-line.

Joe E. Whitlam of Deborah Scaffolding Ltd., Barnsley, South Yorkshire, England, by exercise of professional skill, built a structure of 73 stories to a height of 13 feet 10½ inches with 1,440 cards, July 4–5, 1974. Added strength was given to the structure by bending some cards into angle supports. The highest claim authenticated by affidavit for a 7- or 8-card-per-story house is 27 stories by Joe Whitlam of Barnsley, Yorkshire, England, on February 28, 1972.

Needle Threading. The record number of strands of cotton threaded through a number 13 needle (eye ½ of an inch by $\frac{1}{16}$ of an inch) in 2 hours is 3,795 by Brenda Robinson of the College of Further Education, Chippenham, Wiltshire, England, on March 20, 1971.

Pancake Tossing. Mrs. Sally Cutter, tossed a pancake 5,010 times in 65 minutes at the Island Club, Limassol, Cyprus, on February 26, 1974.

Paper Airplanes. A paper airplane was reported to have been flown 1,126 yards by Greg Ruddue, 11, at San Geronimo Valley Elementary School, California, on May 31, 1973.

Paper Chains. The longest recorded paper link chain made in under 24 hours has been one of 8 miles 897 yards by children at the Thorpe-le-Soken Centre, Essex, England, May 24–25, 1975. They used 125,000 staples.

Piano Playing. The longest piano-playing marathon has been one of 1,091 hours (45 days 11 hours) playing 22 hours every day from October 11 to November 24, 1970, by James Crowley, Jr., 30, in Scranton, Pennsylvania.

The women's world record is 133 hours (5 days 13 hours) by Mrs. Marie Ashton, aged 40, in a theatre at Blyth, Northumberland, England, on August 18–23, 1958.

Piano Smashing. The record time for demolishing an upright piano and passing the entire wreckage through a circle 9 inches in diameter is 2 minutes 26 seconds by six men representing Ireland led by Johnny Leydon of Sligo, at Merton, Surrey, England, on September 7, 1968.

Dave Gibbons, Les Hollis and "Ginger" O'Regan smashed a piano with bare hands in 14 minutes in Guernsey, Channel Islands, on July 20, 1974.

Pipe Smoking. The duration record for keeping a pipe (3.3 grams of tobacco) continuously alight with only an initial match is 253 minutes 28 seconds by Yrjö Pentikäinen of Kuopio, Finland, on March 15–16, 1968.

Pole Sitting. There being no international rules, the "standards of living" atop poles vary widely. The record squat is 273 days by Rick Weeks, 43, from March 9 to December 7, 1974, in a camper atop a 32-foot-high pole in Augusta, Georgia.

Modern records do not, however, compare with that of St. Daniel (409–493 A.D.), called Stylites (Greek, *stylos*=pillar), a monk who spent 33 years 3 months on a stone pillar in Syria. This is probably the earliest example of record setting.

*instead
is stated*

the writer's general message

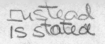

PARAGRAPH READING: Main Idea

In this exercise, you will practice finding the main idea of a paragraph. Being able to determine the main idea of a passage is one of the most useful reading skills you can develop. It is a skill you can apply to any kind of reading. For example, when you read for enjoyment or to obtain general information, it is probably not important to remember all the details of a selection. Instead, you want to quickly discover the writer's general message—the main idea of the passage.

For other kinds of reading, such as reading textbooks or articles in your own field, you need both to determine the author's main ideas and to understand the way he develops them. A good way to increase your understanding of this kind of passage is to read it once quickly to find the author's main ideas and then to read it again looking for the details used to support them.

The main idea of a passage is the most important message presented by the author; it is the thought which is present from the beginning to the end of the passage. In a well-written paragraph, most of the sentences support, describe, or explain the main idea of that paragraph. The main idea is sometimes stated in the first or last sentence of the paragraph. Sometimes it is only implied.

In order to determine the main idea of a paragraph, you should ask yourself what idea is common to most of the sentences in the paragraph: What is the idea that relates these sentences to each other? What opinion do they all support? What idea do they all explain or describe?

Read the following paragraphs quickly. Concentrate on discovering the author's main idea. Remember, don't worry about the details in the paragraphs. You only want to determine the author's general message. After each of the paragraphs, indicate the statement which best expresses the writer's main idea. Do not look back at the paragraphs. Study the example paragraph carefully before you begin.

Example:

By the time the first European travelers on the American continent began to record some of their observations about Indians, the Cherokee people had developed an advanced culture that probably was exceeded only by the civilized tribes of the Southwest: Mayan and Aztec groups. The social structures of the Cherokee people consisted of a form of clan kinship in which there were seven recognized clans. All members of a clan were considered blood brothers and sisters and were bound by honor to defend any member of that clan from wrong. Each clan, the Bird, Paint, Deer, Wolf, Blue, Long Hair, and Wild Potato was represented in the civil council by a counselor or counselors. The chief of the tribe was selected from one of these clans and did not inherit his office from his kinsmen. Actually, there were two chiefs, a Peace chief and War chief. The Peace chief served when the tribe was at peace, but the minute war was declared, the War chief was in command.*

Select the statement which best expresses the main idea of the paragraph.

_____ a. The Cherokee chief was different in war time than in peace time.

✓ b. Before the arrival of the Europeans the Cherokees had developed a well-organized society.

_____ c. The Mayans and the Aztecs were part of the Cherokee tribe.

_____ d. Several Indian cultures had developed advanced civilizations before Europeans arrived.

---

*From Tim B. Underwood, *The Story of the Cherokee People* (S.B. Newman Printing Co., 1961), p. 13.

Explanation:

_____ a. This is not the main idea. Rather, it is one of several examples the author uses to support his statement that the Cherokee people had developed an advanced culture.

__✓__ b. This statement expresses the main idea of the paragraph. All other sentences in the paragraph are examples which support the idea that the Cherokees had developed an advanced culture by the time Europeans arrived on the continent.

_____ c. This statement is false, so it cannot be the main idea.

_____ d. This statement is too general. The paragraph describes the social structure of the Cherokee people only. Although the author names other advanced Indian cultures, he does this only to strengthen his argument that the Cherokees had developed an advanced culture.

Paragraph 1

The first invention of mankind was the wheel. Although no wheel forms are found in nature, undoubtedly the earliest "wheels" were smooth logs which were used for moving weights over the earth's surface. No one recorded who he was or when it happened, but when the "first inventor" placed a wheel on an axle, mankind began to roll from one place to another. Records of this type of wheel have been found among Egyptian relics dating back to 2,000 B.C. and earlier Chinese civilizations are credited with independent invention of the same mechanism. The wheel so fascinated the mind of man that he has spent centuries building machines around it; yet in over 4,000 years he has not changed its basic design. All about us we see the spinning shafts, gears, flywheels, pulleys, and rotors which are the descendents of the first wheel. The roaring propeller of an aircraft engine, the whirling wheel of a giant steam turbine, and the hairspring of a tiny watch are examples of the rotary motion which characterizes our mechanical world. It is hard to conceive of continuous motion without the wheel.*

Select the statement which best expresses the main idea of the paragraph.

_____ a. The wheel is used today in industry and transportation.

_____ b. One of mankind's first inventions, the wheel, has remained important for 4,000 years.

_____ c. Man has changed the basic design of the wheel to meet the needs of his industrial society.

_____ d. Although we don't know exactly who invented the wheel, it is evident that the Egyptians and Chinese used it about 4,000 years ago.

---

*From William P. Brotherton, *The Evolution of Speed* (Ryan Aeronautical Co., 1957), p. 2.

Paragraph 2

At the University of Kansas art museum, investigators tested the effects of different colored walls on two groups of visitors to an exhibit of paintings. For the first group the room was painted white; for the second, dark brown. Movement of each group was followed by an electrical system under the carpet. The experiment revealed that those who entered the dark brown room walked more quickly, covered more area, and spent less time in the room than the people in the white environment. Dark brown stimulated more activity, but the activity ended sooner. Not only the choice of colors but also the general appearance of a room communicates and influences those inside. Another experiment presented subjects with photographs of faces that were to be rated in terms of energy and well-being. Three groups of subjects were used; each was shown the same photos, but each group was in a different kind of room. One group was in an "ugly" room that resembled a messy storeroom. Another group was in an average room—a nice office. The third group was in a tastefully designed living room with carpeting and drapes. Results showed that the subjects in the beautiful room tended to give higher ratings to the faces than did those in the ugly room. Other studies suggest that students do better on tests taken in comfortable, attractive rooms than in ordinary-looking or ugly rooms.*

Select the statement which best expresses the main idea of the paragraph.

_____ a. People in beautiful rooms tend to give higher ratings to photographs of faces than people in ugly rooms.

_____ b. The color and general appearance of a room influence the behavior and attitudes of the people in it.

_____ c. The University of Kansas has studied the effects of the color of a room on people's behavior.

_____ d. Beautifully decorated, light-colored rooms make people more comfortable than ugly, dark rooms.

---

*From Jeffrey Schrank, *Deception Detection* (Boston: Beacon Press, 1975), p. 53.

hw. nby 14.

Paragraph 3

Teaching is supposed to be a professional activity requiring long and complicated training as well as official certification. The act of teaching is looked upon as a flow of knowledge from a higher source to an empty container. The student's role is one of receiving information; the teacher's role is one of sending it. There is a clear distinction assumed between one who is supposed to know (and therefore not capable of being wrong) and another, usually younger person who is supposed not to know. However, teaching need not be the province of a special group of people nor need it be looked upon as a technical skill. Teaching can be more like guiding and assisting than forcing information into a supposedly empty head. If you have a certain skill you should be able to share it with someone. You do not have to get certified to convey what you know to someone else or to help them in their attempt to teach themselves. All of us, from the very youngest children to the oldest members of our cultures should come to realize our own potential as teachers. We can share what we know, however little it might be, with someone who has need of that knowledge or skill.*

Select the statement which best expresses the main idea of the paragraph.

_____ a. The author believes that it is not difficult to be a good teacher.

_____ b. The author believes that every person has the potential to be a teacher.

_____ c. The author believes that teaching is a professional activity requiring special training.

_____ d. The author believes that teaching is the flow of knowledge from a higher source to an empty container.

---

*From Herbert Kohl, *Reading: How To* (New York: Bantam Books, 1973), p. 1.

Paragraph 4

Albert Einstein once attributed the creativity of a famous scientist to the fact that he "never went to school, and therefore preserved the rare gift of thinking freely." There is undoubtedly truth in Einstein's observation; many artists and geniuses seem to view their schooling as a disadvantage. But such a truth is not a criticism of schools. It is the function of schools to civilize, not to train explorers. The explorer is always a lonely individual whether his or her pioneering be in art, music, science, or technology. The creative explorer of unmapped lands shares with the genius what William James described as the "faculty of perceiving in an unhabitual way." Insofar as schools teach perceptual patterns they tend to destroy creativity and genius. But if schools could somehow exist solely to cultivate genius, then society would break down. For the social order demands unity and widespread agreement, both traits that are destructive to creativity. There will always be conflict between the demands of society and the impulses of creativity and genius.*

Select the statement which best expresses the main idea of the paragraph.

_____ a. Albert Einstein and other geniuses and artists have said that schools limit creativity and genius.

_____ b. Schools should be designed to encourage creativity.

_____ c. Explorers can be compared to geniuses because both groups look at the world differently from the way most people do.

_____ d. Schools can never satisfy the needs of both geniuses and society as a whole.

---

*From Jeffrey Schrank, *Deception Detection* (Boston: Beacon Press, 1975), p. 100.

Paragraph 5

Perhaps the most startling theory to come out of kinesics, the study of body movement, was suggested by Professor Ray Birdwhistell. He believes that physical appearance is often culturally programmed. In other words, we learn our looks—we are not born with them. A baby has generally unformed facial features. A baby, according to Birdwhistell, learns where to set the eyebrows by looking at those around—family and friends. This helps explain why the people of some regions of the United States look so much alike. New Englanders or Southerners have certain common facial characteristics that cannot be explained by genetics. The exact shape of the mouth is not set at birth, it is learned after. In fact, the final mouth shape is not formed until well after permanent teeth are set. For many, this can be well into adolescence. A husband and wife together for a long time often come to look somewhat alike. We learn our looks from those around us. This is perhaps why in a single country there are areas where people smile more than those in other areas. In the United States, for example, the South is the part of the country where the people smile most frequently. In New England they smile less, and in the western part of New York state still less. Many Southerners find cities such as New York cold and unfriendly, partly because people on Madison Avenue smile less than people on Peachtree Street in Atlanta, Georgia. People in densely populated urban areas also tend to smile and greet each other in public less than do people in rural areas and small towns.*

Select the statement which best expresses the main idea of the paragraph.

_____ a. Ray Birdwhistell can tell what region of the United States a person is from by how much he or she smiles.

_____ b. Ray Birdwhistell is a leader in the field of kinesics.

_____ c. Ray Birdwhistell says that our physical appearance is influenced by the appearance of people around us.

_____ d. People who live in the country are more friendly than people who live in densely populated areas.

_____

*From Jeffrey Schrank, *Deception Detection* (Boston: Beacon Press, 1975), p. 43.

READING SELECTION 1: Technical Prose

When writing on technical subjects, authors sometimes include graphs and tables because such visual aids present information clearly and concisely. You will need information from the prose section and the charts to complete the following exercises.

Read "Crowded Earth—Billions More Coming" quickly to get a general understanding of the article; do not be concerned if you do not know the meanings of some vocabulary items. Then scan* to answer the Comprehension questions.

COMPREHENSION

Answer the following questions. Indicate if statements 1 through 18 are true (T) or false (F).

1. ___ In the year 2000, the world population may be 12 billion people.

2. ___ The population estimate of 6.4 billion for the year 2000 is based on the present growth rate of 2 per cent per year.

3. ___ The population is increasing fastest in the more highly-industrialized countries.

4. ___ Generally speaking, the nations with the highest rates of population increase are the same countries that even today find it difficult to feed all their people.

5. ___ By the year 2000, approximately four-fifths of the world's population will live in the "poorer" nations.

6. ___ By the year 2000, 37 per cent of the world population will be living in urban areas.

7. ___ It took millions of years for the world population to reach 1 billion.

8. ___ The world population doubled between 1830 and 1930.

9. ___ The world population doubled between 1930 and 1960.

10. ___ The world's birth rate is increasing while the death rate is decreasing.

11. ___ Chart I shows that the world population is increasing faster now than it ever has before.

12. ___ The percentage figures in Chart II indicate the expected percentage increase in population between 1972 and 2000.

13. ___ The population of Russia is increasing about twice as fast as the population of Europe.

14. ___ By the year 2000, it is estimated that Asia alone will have more people than are alive in the whole world today.

(*Continued on page 28.*)

---

*For an introduction to scanning, see Unit 1.

CROWDED EARTH— BILLIONS MORE COMING

MORE THAN 6 BILLION people in a world that already is having trouble supporting about 4 billion—

That is the prospect now being held out by population experts, and it frightens them.

A new projection by the United Nations shows that, if the present growth rate of 2 per cent per year continues, today's world population of 3.9 billion will hit 6.4 billion by the year 2000.

What's more, the great bulk of the growth—9 of every 10 people added to the earth's population—will be in the poorer, undeveloped countries. These are the nations where feeding billions of people already is proving a near-insurmountable challenge.

By the year 2000, today's "have not" nations will have a combined population of 5 billion people, comprising nearly four fifths of the world's population.

Food isn't the only problem that such a population explosion presents. The more people there are and the more crowded their living conditions, authorities warn, the greater grows the likelihood of violence and upheaval.

According to U. N. projections, half of all the earth's people will be living in urban areas by the year 2000, up from 37 per cent today.

From time of Christ—. To put this growth in perspective—

At the time of Christ, millions of years after man first appeared on the earth, demographers estimate there were 250 million people.

In 1830, world population reached 1 billion. It took only 100 more years to add another billion to world population; just 30 more to add a third billion. And it will have taken just 15 more years to reach the 4-billion mark in 1975.

Actually, the world's birth rate is on a decline. But so are death rates, as medical advances have increased life spans and reduced infant mortality.

Average world life expectancy, the U. N. says, has increased by 20 years over the past three decades.

It's mainly in advanced nations that population growth is being curbed.

The outlook beyond 2000 is even more threatening. Unless population growth is curtailed, a world population of 12 billion is foreseen in a century. One question raised by demographers:

Is the earth capable of providing a decent life for 12 billion people?

I.

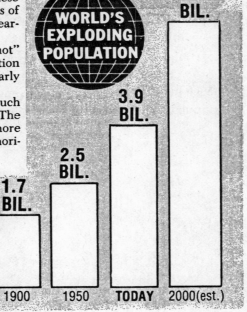

WORLD'S EXPLODING POPULATION

1750	791 MIL.
1800	978 MIL.
1850	1.3 BIL.
1900	1.7 BIL.
1950	2.5 BIL.
TODAY	3.9 BIL.
2000 (est.)	6.4 BIL.

II.

WHERE GROWTH IS LIKELY TO COME FASTEST

	Population 1972 (MILLIONS)	2000 (est.) (MILLIONS)	INCREASE
AFRICA	364	834	129%
LATIN AMERICA	300	625	108%
ASIA	2,154	3,757	74%
OCEANIA	20	33	65%
RUSSIA	248	321	29%
NORTH AMERICA	233	296	27%
EUROPE	469	540	15%

Source: United Nations

III.

THE 25 MOST POPULATED COUNTRIES

	Country	Population 1973	Years Until Population Will Double*
1.	China	792,677,000	41
2.	India	596,000,000	32
3.	U.S.S.R.	248,626,000	77
4.	United States	209,123,000	116
5.	Indonesia	128,121,000	26
6.	Japan	106,663,000	53
7.	Brazil	101,582,000	25
8.	Bangladesh	75,382,000	26
9.	Pakistan	64,461,000	24
10.	West Germany	61,806,000	†
11.	Nigeria	58,148,000	29
12.	United Kingdom	55,956,000	231
13.	Mexico	54,963,000	20
14.	Italy	54,642,000	116
15.	France	51,921,000	116
16.	Philippines	41,288,000	22
17.	Thailand	39,075,000	25
18.	Turkey	37,737,000	27
19.	Egypt	34,705,000	32
20.	Spain	34,675,000	63
21.	Korea	33,435,000	35
22.	Poland	33,202,000	77
23.	Iran	32,778,000	22
24.	Burma	29,213,000	30
25.	Ethiopia	26,947,000	27

*Years to double assumes continuation of 1972 rate of increase.

†No increase in 1972

Source: U.S. Census Bureau

Reprinted from *U.S. News and World Report*, October 21, 1974. Copyright © 1974 by U.S. News and World Report, Inc.

15. _____ Chart III lists the 25 countries with the highest rate of population increase.

16. _____ No figures are available on the rate of population increase in West Germany.

17. _____ The population of Poland is increasing faster than the population of Italy.

18. _____ According to Chart III, the United Kingdom has the lowest rate of population increase of any country in the world.

19. What two results of medical advances does the author say have caused the change in the world death rate?

20. The author mentions that it will be difficult to feed 6 billion people. What other danger of an overcrowded world is mentioned?

21. In chart III, the column titled "Years Until Population Will Double" is an estimation. What is it based on? What factors affect population growth?

READING SELECTION 2: Mystery

Mystery stories are written to involve readers in solving a problem. The problem is presented early in the passage and the tension grows gradually until it is solved.

In this story,* a man name Ausable will certainly die unless he can outsmart his enemy. Read the story carefully. You should be able to solve the problem before the end of the story.

The Midnight Visitor

1   Ausable did not fit the description of any secret agent Fowler had ever read about. Following him down the musty corridor of the gloomy French hotel where Ausable had a room, Fowler felt disappointed. It was a small room, on the sixth and top floor, and scarcely a setting for a romantic figure.

2   Ausable was, for one thing, fat. Very fat. And then there was his accent. Though he spoke French and German passably, he had never altogether lost the New England accent he had brought to Paris from Boston twenty years ago.

3   "You are disappointed," Ausable said wheezily over his shoulder. "You were told that I was a secret agent, a spy, dealing in espionage and danger. You wished to meet me because you are a writer, young and romantic. You envisioned mysterious figures in the night, the crack of pistols, drugs in the wine."

4   "Instead, you have spent a dull evening in a French music hall with a sloppy fat man who, instead of having messages slipped into his hand by dark-eyed beauties, gets only an ordinary telephone call making an appointment in his room. You have been bored!" The fat man chuckled to himself as he unlocked the door of his room and stood aside to let his frustrated guest enter.

5   "You are disillusioned," Ausable told him. "But take cheer, my young friend. Presently you will see a paper, a quite important paper for which several men and women have risked their lives, come to me in the next-to-last step of its journey into official hands. Some day soon that paper may well affect the course of history. In that thought is drama, is there not?" As he spoke, Ausable closed the door behind him. Then he switched on the light.

6   And as the light came on, Fowler had his first authentic thrill of the day. For halfway across the room, a small automatic pistol in his hand, stood a man.

Ausable blinked a few times.

"Max," he wheezed, "you gave me quite a start. I thought you were in Berlin. What are you doing in my room?"

7   Max was slender, not tall, and with a face that suggested the look of a fox. Except for the gun, he did not look very dangerous.

"The report," he murmured. "The report that is being brought to you tonight concerning some new missiles. I thought I would take it from you. It will be safer in my hands than in yours."

8   Ausable moved to an armchair and sat down heavily. "I'm going to raise the devil with the management this time; I am angry," he said grimly. "This is the second time in a month that somebody has gotten into my room off that confounded balcony!" Fowler's eyes went to the single window of the room. It was an ordinary window, against which now the night was pressing blackly.

9   "Balcony?" Max asked curiously. "No, I had a passkey. I did not know about the balcony. It might have saved me some trouble had I known about it."

---

*Adapted from "The Midnight Visitor" from *Mystery and More Mystery*, by Robert Arthur. Copyright © 1939, 1967 by Robert Arthur. Reprinted by permission of Random House, Inc.

10 "It's not my balcony," explained Ausable angrily. "It belongs to the next apartment." He glanced explanatorily at Fowler. "You see," he said, "this room used to be part of a large unit, and the next room—through that door there—used to be the living room. *It* had the balcony, which extends under *my* window now. You can get onto it from the empty room next door, and somebody did, last month. The management promised to block it off. But they haven't."

11 Max glanced at Fowler, who was standing stiffly a few feet from Ausable, and waved the gun with a commanding gesture. "Please sit down," he said. "We have a wait of a half an hour, I think."

 "Thirty-one minutes," Ausable said moodily. "The appointment was for twelve-thirty. I wish I knew how you learned about the report, Max."

12 The little spy smiled evilly. "And we wish we knew how your people got the report. But, no harm has been done. I will get it back tonight. What is that? Who is at the door?"

13 Fowler jumped at the sudden knocking at the door. Ausable just smiled, "That will be the police," he said. "I thought that such an important paper as the one we are waiting for should have a little extra protection. I told them to check on me to make sure everything was all right."

14 Max bit his lip nervously. The knocking was repeated.

 "What will you do now, Max?" Ausable asked. "If I do not answer the door, they will enter anyway. The door is unlocked. And they will not hesitate to shoot."

15 Max's face was black with anger as he backed swiftly toward the window; with his hand behind him, he opened the window and put his leg out into the night. "Send them away!" he warned. "I will wait on the balcony. Send them away or I'll shoot and take my chances!"

What will happen now? How will Ausable escape? Do you think he has a plan? In a few words, tell how you think the story will end. _____

_____

_____

Now continue reading.

---

16 The knocking at the door became louder and a voice was raised. "Mr. Ausable! Mr. Ausable!"

 Keeping his body twisted so that his gun still covered the fat man and his guest, the man at the window grasped the frame with his free hand to support himself as he rested his weight on one thigh. Then he swung his other leg up and over the window sill.

17 The doorknob turned. Swiftly Max pushed with his left hand to free himself and drop to the blacony. And then as he dropped, he screamed once, shrilly.

18 The door opened and a waiter stood there with a tray, a bottle and two glasses. "Here is the drink you ordered, sir." He set the tray on the table, deftly uncorked the bottle, and left the room.

19 White faced and shaking, Fowler stared after him. "But . . . but . . . what about . . . the police?" he stammered.

 "There never were any police." Ausable sighed. "Only Henry, whom I was expecting."

"But what about the man on the balcony . . . ?" Fowler began.

"No," said Ausable, "he won't return."

Why won't Max return? _____

COMPREHENSION CLUES

If you were not able to write an ending to the story, perhaps answering the following questions will help you. Mark each of the following statements true (T) or false (F).

1. _____ Max had never been to Ausable's room before.

2. _____ Max knew about the balcony because he had used it to enter the apartment.

3. _____ Ausable knew that someone would knock on the door.

4. _____ The apartment was on the sixth floor of the building.

5. _____ Max knew about the balcony because Ausable told him about it.

Now: Why won't Max return? _____

READING SELECTION 3: Conversation

This passage is taken from the book *Iberia* by James Michener. The author describes the book as a "nineteenth-century English-style travel book with much personal observation, much reflection, and much affection."* Michener expresses his philosophy in the following quotation:

If you reject the food, ignore the customs, fear the religion and avoid the people, you might better stay home: you are like a pebble thrown into water; you become wet on the surface, but you are never part of the water.†

"Toledo: A Problem of Menus"‡ provides a humorous account of Michener's attempt to put his philosophy to work in Spain.

Read the passage and do the exercises which follow. You may want to do the Vocabulary from Context exercise on page 36 before you begin.

Toledo: A Problem of Menus

1   The Spanish government, aware that the golden rewards of tourism could evaporate as quickly as they appeared, has taken sensible steps to protect the tourist. . . . Restaurants are required to offer, in addition to their à la carte menus, a special tourist menu from which one can get a good meal and a bottle of wine at a fixed price. By ordering from this menu one can eat really well in Spain and at about half the price he would expect to pay in either France or Italy.

2   But. I sat down, in a restaurant in Toledo, looked at the menu and said, "I'll take fish soup, Spanish omelette and flan."
"And what wine?"
"Whatever comes with the meal."
"Nothing comes with the meal."
"But it says right here . . ."
"You have to order that. Then it's extra."
"But the menu says. . ."
"You're pointing at the tourist menu."
"That's what I ordered."
"Oh, no! You didn't mention the tourist menu."
"I'm mentioning it now."
"You can't mention it now. You've got to mention it when you sit down."

3   "But you haven't even given the order to the kitchen."
"True. But I've written it in my book. And it's the writing that counts."
"You mean that if I'd said 'tourist menu' at the start, my meal would have cost me a dollar and sixty cents?"
"Clearly."
"But since I delayed three minutes the same meal is going to cost me two-sixty?"
"Plus sixty cents for the wine."

4   I tried to point out how ridiculous such a situation was, but the waiter was

---

*This quotation is from the jacket flap of Michener's book *Iberia*.
†*Reader's Digest*, August, 1975, p. 99.
‡Adapted from *Iberia: Spanish Travels and Reflections* by James Michener. Copyright © 1968 Random House, Inc., and Marjay Productions, Inc.

adamant, and soon the manager came up, looked at his waiter's book and shrugged his shoulders. "If you wanted the tourist menu you should have said so," he grumbled.

"I'm saying so now."

"Too late."

I rose and left the restaurant, with the waiter abusing me and the manager claiming loudly that I owed him for having soiled a napkin, which I admit I had unfolded.

5   I escaped but projected myself into an even worse mess, for I chose what seemed to be the best restaurant in Toledo, where I announced quickly and in a clear voice that I wanted the tourist menu.

"What a pity! With the tourist menu you can't have partridge."

"I don't believe I'd care for partridge." I had had it on a previous visit and was not too taken with it. "Just the tourist menu."

"But on the tourist menu you get only three dishes."

"That's exactly what I want."

"But on that menu you don't get special wine, and I know you Americans prefer a special wine."

"I'll drink whatever you Spaniards drink."

"We drink the special wine."

6   I insisted that I be served from the tourist menu, and grudgingly the waiter handed me a menu which offered an enticing choice of five soups, eleven egg or fish dishes, seven meat courses and six promising desserts, but of the twenty-nine dishes thus available, twenty-six carried a surcharge if ordered on the tourist menu. Technically, one could order a dinner that would cost the price advertised by the government, but if he did so he would have two soups, one cheap fish and no dessert. Madrid had laid down the law, but Toledo was interpreting it.

7   As a traveler I work on the principle which I commend to others: No man should ever protest two abuses in a row. Few men can be right twice running, and never three times straight, so I ordered three dishes, each of which carried a surcharge: soup, roasted chicken, flan. The soup was delicious and the ordinary wine was palatable and I sat back to enjoy the meal which had started off so badly.

8   Unfortunately, I had chosen a table that put me next to a good-looking, ruddy-faced Englishman whose tweed suit gave the impression that he must at home have been a hunting man. As he finished his soup he said to his wife, "First class, absolutely first class." He had, as I suspected he might, ordered the partridge, but when the waiter deposited the steaming casserole before him, the Englishman looked at it suspiciously, waited till the waiter had gone, then asked his wife quietly, "Do you smell something?"

"I think I do," she replied.

"And do you know what it is?"

9   Without speaking she pointed her fork at the partridge, whereupon her husband nodded silently and brought his nose closer to the casserole. "My goodness," he said in a whisper, "this is fairly raunchy." In gingerly manner he tasted the bird, folded his hands in his lap and said, "My goodness."

10   His wife got a piece of the bird onto her fork and tasted it, looked gravely at her husband and nodded.

"What to do?" he asked.

"You obviously can't eat it."

"I wonder should I call the waiter."

"I think you'd better."

11   I was now in a relaxed mood and had no desire to see the Englishman make a fool of himself, because obviously he wanted to avoid a scene. "With your permission, sir," I said, waiting for him to acknowledge me.

"Of course."

"I'm afraid there's nothing wrong with your partridge, sir. It's how they serve it in Spain. A delicacy. Well hung."

12   With admirable restraint the Englishman looked at me, then at the offending bird and said, "My good man, I've been accustomed to well-hung fowl all my life. Gamy. But this bird is rotten."

13   "May I, sir?" I tasted the partridge and it was exactly the way it should have been by Toledo standards. Gamy. Tasty. A little like a very strong cheese. Special taste produced by hanging the bird without refrigeration and much admired by Spanish hunters and countrymen. "It's as it should be," I concluded.

14   The Englishman, not one to make a scene, tasted the bird again but found it more objectionable than before. "I've shot a good many birds in my lifetime," he said, "but if I ever got one that smelled like this I'd shoot it again." He picked at the casserole for a moment and added, "This poor bird was hung so long it required no cooking. It had begun to fall apart of its own weight."

15   Once more I tried to console him: "I've had Toledo partridge twice before, and I promise you, it tasted just like yours."

"And you lived?" He pushed his plate away but refrained from complaining to the waiter. He did, however, look rather unpleasantly at me, as if to reprimand me for trying to convince him that he should eat such a bird.

16   At this point the waiter brought my chicken, and I am embarrassed to report that it smelled just like the partridge. It was one of the worst-cooked, poorly presented and evilest-smelling chickens I had ever been served and was obviously inedible. I tried cutting off a small piece, but blood ran out the end and the smell increased. I followed through and tasted it, but it was truly awful and I must have made a face, for the Englishman reached over, cut himself a helping, cut it into pieces and tried one while giving the other to his wife. Neither could eat the sample, whereupon the Englishman smiled indulgently and said very softly, "See what I mean?"

COMPREHENSION

Answer the following questions. Your teacher may want you to answer the questions orally, in writing, or by underlining appropriate parts of the text. True/False items are indicated by a T/F preceding a statement.

1. T / F   The Spanish government does not want Spanish merchants to take unfair advantage of tourists.

2. How does the tourist menu protect tourists? _____

   _____

3. T / F   In the first restaurant Michener wanted to order from the tourist menu.

4. T / F   Wine is included in the price of a tourist menu.

5. Why did the waiter refuse to give Michener the tourist menu in the first restaurant? _____

   _____

6. T / F   Michener left the first restaurant without paying anything.

7. T / F   Michener hoped to have better luck in the second restaurant because it looked better than the first.

8. T / F   Michener changed his manner of ordering in the second restaurant.

9. In the second restaurant, what were the objections the waiter offered concerning the tourist menu?

   a. _____

   b. _____

   c. _____

10. T / F   For the price of the tourist menu in the second restaurant, one could choose from twenty-nine dishes.

11. Write a definition, synonym, or description of *in a row* (paragraph 7). _____

   What two words in the same paragraph are synonyms of *in a row*? _____

12. T / F   Michener's meal cost more than the government's fixed price for the tourist menu.

13. What made Michener think that the Englishman was a hunter?

   _____

14. The Englishman describes his partridge casserole as "raunchy." What synonyms of *raunchy* appear in paragraph 12? _____

15. What was wrong with the Englishman's partridge? _____

   _____

(*Continued on page 36.*)

35

16. What is "well-hung" partridge? _____

17. T / F   The Englishman ate his casserole in spite of its foul odor.

18. Why did Michener speak up when the Englishman was thinking of returning his dinner?

_____

19. Write a definition, synonym, or description of *inedible* (paragraph 16). _____

_____

20. Do you think Michener returned his chicken? Why or why not? _____

_____

VOCABULARY FROM CONTEXT

Use the context provided to determine the meanings of the italicized words. Write a definition, synonym, or description of each of the italicized vocabulary items in the space provided.

1. _____ At the Regal Restaurant, there are two menus. On one menu, an entire meal is listed for a single price. On the other, an *à la carte* menu, each dish is priced individually and may be ordered separately. In many cases, ordering from the first kind of menu is the cheapest way to get a complete meal. On such menus, however,

2. _____ if you order something which is not included in the meal, there is a *surcharge* which makes the meal more expensive.

3. _____ I could not convince my friend to go on a picnic instead of to a restaurant. He was *adamant* in his desire to eat a formal meal.

4. _____ At a famous restaurant, I was once served food so old that it had gone bad. I could smell the *rotten* meat before the waiter put it on my table. Foolishly, I screamed insults at him. I should have realized that it wasn't the waiter's fault. I should have screamed

5. _____ those *abuses* at the cook.

6. _____ Usually if restaurant food is poorly prepared, I don't criticize the waiter. Instead, I *reprimand* the manager.

7. _____ When I am served bad food, I assume a very serious manner and say to the manager *gravely* that I will not

8. _____ pay for the *objectionable* meal.

9. _____ After eating at bad restaurants, the meals at the Elite Cafe look wonderfully *enticing*, as appealing as water to a man in a desert.

36

10. _____
11. _____
Restaurants sometimes keep food unrefrigerated until it is almost bad, until it smells *gamy* and looks *raunchy*.

12. _____
Although I enjoy a pleasant atmosphere when I dine at restaurants, what is most important to me is the quality of the food. Nothing can *console* me after the disappointment of a poor meal.

13. _____
Knowing that the slightest mistake meant losing his job, the waiter carried the expensive wine glasses *gingerly* from the kitchen.

NONPROSE READING: Newspaper Advertisements

Classified advertisements or want ads appear in most newspapers. The ads on page 39 come from a university newspaper.* If you were living in this university community, you might use the ads in this newspaper to find a job, to rent an apartment, or to advertise something you wanted to sell.

Read each question. Then scan the ads to find the answer.†

1. If you had lost your watch, under which section might you look? _Lost and Found_

2. If you wanted to earn money, under which section would you place an ad? _Help wanted_

3. If you were looking for an apartment, under which section would you place an ad? _Wanted to rent_

4. If you needed somebody to share your apartment, under which section would you place an ad? _Roommates_

5. If you were looking for a house to rent, which telephone number(s) would you call? _800-9846_

6. What is the earliest date on which you could sublet an apartment? _____

7. If you wanted to live in an apartment by yourself without spending more than $200, which ads would you be sure to answer? Circle them.

8. If you had trouble getting to work on time every morning, which business service could you call? _____

9. Whom would you call if you wanted to buy a radio?_____

10. If you were a man and wanted to share an apartment, which telephone number(s) would you be sure to call? _____

11. Whom would you call if you wanted to learn to play the guitar? _____

12. If you wanted a job taking care of children, which ad would you answer? _____

13. Which number(s) would you be sure to call if you were interested in apartments near the Medical Center? _____

14. If you wanted to place an ad, what number would you call? _____
    If you placed an ad at 4:00 P.M. on a Wednesday, when would it appear? _____

15. Would you answer the ad offering a job as a delivery person if you didn't have a car? _____

(*Continued on page 40.*)

_____
*Courtesy of the *Michigan Daily*.
† For an explanation of nonprose reading and an introduction to scanning, see Unit 1.

classified ads

FOR DIRECT CLASSIFIED SERVICE CALL 800-0557—10 A.M.-4 P.M. Monday-Friday

FOR RENT

BEST ON CAMPUS

Excellent room for girls begins Jan., 2, 4 or 8 month lease. Singles, $105-$125. Double, $140. Call for appointment. 800-1932.

LUXURY A/C STUDIO, modern kitchen, wall to wall carpet. Available immediately. On-campus location. $160/mo. 800-5808 persistently.

AVAILABLE IMMEDIATELY: MODERN, FURNISHED EFFICIENCY & 1-BEDRM. APTS.
DAHLMANN APARTMENTS
800-7600

ONE BDRM. modern furn. apt., $210 mo., air cond., balcony, avail. Jan. 1 or immediate occupancy. Close to campus. Call Rick. 800-0119 after 10 p.m.

FAMILY HOME, 3 bdrm., full partition basement, 2 car garage, large yard, children and well trained pets welcome. $275. See 11-21-76. Call Renter's Aid. 800-4300.

APT. 2-bedroom, air conditioned, furnished, convenient to Med. Center, for Jan. 1. 800-9846.

EFFICIENCY $165. Nice kitchen, basement storage space. Renter's Aid, 800-4300. Fee.

2 BEDROOM furnished apartment. Parking, laundry facilities. Dec.-Aug., $210/month. 800-9715.

APT. 2-bedroom, air conditioned, furnished, convenient to Med. Center, for Jan. 1. 800-9846.

SUBLET

SUBLETS: as of Jan. 1. 2-bedroom furnished apartments. $210; also, roommates wanted. Call Modern Apartments, 418 East Washington, 800-6906.

ASSUME LEASE 3-bdrm. 1½ bath apt. Hospital-campus area, carpeted, stove and refrig. $333/month plus elec. Avail. 1 Dec. Free bus to downtown and campus 10 times daily weekdays. Coin Laundry and free storage in basement. Underground parking avail. 800-7487.

TO SUBLET: Apt., 2½ rooms and bath, near campus, completely furnished, $145/mo. All utilities included. Available after Xmas. Call Larry persistently, 800-7213.

3-BEDROOM
apartment available for sublet in January. Furnished. 2 blocks from campus. Price negotiable. Call 800-2134.

SUBLET

DOUBLE ROOM in furnished house near campus. Parking. 800-5854.

WANTED TO RENT

2-BDRM. PLACE wanted. Hopefully under $180/mon. Thanks. 800-6839.

GARAGE OR PARKING SPACE wanted near campus. Call Rob, 800-4992 before 10:00 a.m. or after 6:00 p.m.

WANTED: ONE-BEDROOM APARTMENT for Jan. 1 through August. Preferably near campus, but not necessary. Call 800-7129.

ROOMMATES

FEMALE Grad Student wanted: to share a 2-bdrm., furnished apt., own rm. ½ block from Frieze Bldg. $112.50/mo. Starting Jan. 800-1090 after 5:30. Call persistently.

NEED PERSON to assume lease for own bedroom in apt. near campus, $92/mo. starting Jan. 1. Call 800-6157 after 5:00.

FEMALE ROOMMATE WANTED
Own room near campus. Available December 1. Rent $80 per month unt'l March 1st. $120 thereafter. Call Jill for details, 800-7839.

FOURTH WOMAN NEEDED: bi-level, modern apartment, near campus. $67.50/mo. Beginning January. 800-7866.

BUSINESS SERVICES

TUTORING, EE, Statistics, Math, Computers. Call Walt, 800-3594.

EARLY HOUR WAKE-UP SERVICE For prompt, courteous wake-up service. 800-0760.

WEDDING INVITATIONS—Mod. or traditional. Call 800-0942 anytime.

PASSPORT and Application Photos. Call 800-0552 or 800-9668, ask for Steve.

MATURE STUDENT would take care of children during Christmas vacation. 800-0441 eves.

TYPING AND EDITING. Call Jean. 800-3594. 10 a.m.-10 p.m.

EXPERIENCED GUITAR TEACHER wants students. Folk/jazz. Bob. 800-7535.

LOST AND FOUND

FOUND: Cat, 6 months old, black and white markings Found near Linden and South U. Steve. 800-4661.

LOST: Gold wire rim glasses in brown case. Campus area. Reward. Call Gregg 800-2896.

FOUND: Set of keys on Tappan near Hill intersection. Identify key chain. Call 800-9662 around 6.

FEMALE CAT: Black, white, and brown. Found two weeks ago at E. Ann and Glenn. 800-9286.

FOUND Nov. 8—A black and white puppy in Packard-Jewett area. 800-5770.

FOR SALE

COME to our moving sale—Plants, pottery, books, clothes, etc. Sat., Dec. 14—9:00-5:00. 1612 Ferndale, Apt. 1, 800-4696.

SHEEPSKIN COAT, man's size 42, 1 year old. $85. After 6 p.m., 800-5224.

MOVING: Must sell. TV b/w 12", $50; AM/FM transistor radio A/C or battery, $15; cassette tape recorder, $10; misc. records. Call Jon or Pat, 800-0739 after 5 or weekends.

USED FUR COATS and JACKETS. Good condition. $50-$125. Call 800-0436 after 12 noon.

SNOW TIRES: 12", used one winter. 800-7473.

PERSONAL

OVERSEAS JOBS — Australia, Europe, S. America, Africa. Students all professions and occupations $700 to $3000 monthly. Expenses paid, overtime, sight-seeing. Free information.

UNSURE WHAT TO DO? Life-Planning Workshop, Dec. 13-15. Bob and Margaret Blood, 800-0046.

THE INTERNATIONAL CENTER plans to publish a booklet of student travel adventures. If you'd like to write about your foreign experience, unusual or just plain interesting, call us (800-9310) and ask for Mike or Janet.

WITCHCRAFT ANYONE? Wish to join or organize people into witchcraft or the occult. Call Don, 800-6762.

HELP WANTED

BABYSITTER—MY HOME
If you are available a few hours during the day, some evenings and occasional weekends to care for 2 school-age children, please call Gayle Moore days 800-1111, evenings and weekends 800-4964.

HELP WANTED for housework ½ day per week. When—to be discussed for mutual convenience. Good wages. Sylvan Street. Call 800-2817.

PERSONS WANTED for delivery work. Own transportation. Good pay. Apply 2311 E. Stadium. Office 101, after 9 a.m.

TELEPHONE RECEPTIONIST wanted. No experience necessary. Good pay. Apply 2311 E. Stadium. Office 101. After 9 a.m.

WAITRESS WANTED: 10 a.m.-2 p.m. or 10:30 a.m.-5 p.m. Apply in person, 207 S. Main. Curtis Restaurant.

PLANT LOVERS interested in working part-time at The Greenhouse apply in person. Liberty at Division.

16. Rewrite the following ad using complete grammatical sentences: For Rent: 1-bdrm. mod. furn. apt. $210/mo. A/C avail. after Xmas. _____

_____

_____

_____

17. Write an ad from the following statement using abbreviations and eliminating unnecessary words.

I am leaving the country before January 31, and I must sell everything. I have a black and white television, an air conditioner, miscellaneous clothing and a used refrigerator. I also want to sell an artificial Christmas tree and my electric typewriter. The typewriter will be available after January 20. Please call 800-7351 before 9:00 in the evening. Ask for Bob.

_____

_____

_____

_____

_____

WORD STUDY: Stems and Affixes

Below is a list of some commonly occurring stems and affixes.* Study their meanings, then do the exercises which follow. Your teacher may ask you to give examples of words you know which are derived from these stems and affixes.

Prefixes:

ante-	before
circum-	around
contra-, anti-	against
inter-	between
intro-, intra-	within
post-	after
sub-, suc-, suf-, sug-, sup-, sus-	under, *follow*
super-	above, over
trans-	across

Stems:

-ced-	go, move, yield
-duc-	lead
-flect-	bend
-mit-, -miss-	send
-port-	carry
-sequ-, -secut-	follow
-spir-	breathe
-tele-	far
-vene-, -vent-	come
-voc-, -vok-	call

(handwritten notes: conduction, reflect, mission, transmit, passport, consecutive, respir, telegraph, convention, revok, ductil., admission, anipat, audible)

Suffixes:

-able-, -ible-, -ble	capable of, fit for
-ous, -ious, -ose	full of, of the nature of

Exercise 1
In each item, select the best definition of the italicized word or phrase or answer the question.

1. The first thing Jim did when he got off the train was look for a *porter*.

    _____ a. man who sells tickets   _____ c. man who carries luggage
    _____ b. taxi cab   _____ d. door to the luggage room

---
*For a list of all stems and affixes taught in *Reader's Choice*, see Appendix.

2. No matter what Fred said, Noam *contradicted him*.

    ____ a. said the opposite   ____ c. laughed at him
    ____ b. yelled at him   ____ d. didn't listen to him

3. The doctor is a specialist in the human *respiratory* system. She knows most about _____

    ____ a. bones.   ____ c. nerves.
    ____ b. lungs.   ____ d. the stomach.

4. He *circumvented* the problem.

    ____ a. described   ____ c. went around, avoided
    __✓_ b. solved   ____ d. wrote down, copied

5. Which is a postscript?

    ____ a.
    ____ b.
    ____ c.
    ____ d.

6. Use what you know about stems and affixes to explain how the following words were derived:

    telephone _____

    telegram _____

    television _____

7. When would a photographer use a telephoto lens for his camera? _____

8. Use word analysis to explain what *support* means _____

9. What is the difference between interstate commerce and intrastate commerce? _____

10. Use word analysis to explain what *supersonic* speed is. _____

11. At one time, many European towns depended on the system of aqueducts built by the Romans for their water supply. What is an aqueduct? _____

12. If a person has a *receding* hairline, what does he look like? _____

Exercise 2
Following is a list of words containing some of the stems and affixes introduced in this unit and the previous one. Definitions of these words appear on the right. Put the letter of the appropriate definition next to each word.

1. _____ anteroom
2. _____ portage
3. _____ portable
4. _____ antecedent
5. _____ flexible

a. capable of being carried easily
b. the carrying of boats or goods overland from one body of water to another
c. able to bend without breaking; not stiff
d. something which happened or existed before another thing
e. a room forming an entrance to another one

6. _____ superscript
7. _____ transport
8. _____ transmit
9. _____ supervisor
10. _____ deflect

a. to bend or turn to one side something which was following a straight path
b. a letter or symbol written immediately above and to the side of another symbol
c. an administrative officer; a boss
d. to carry from one place to another, especially over a distance
e. to send from one person or place to another

11. _____ vociferous
12. _____ revoke
13. _____ vocation
14. _b_ convene
15. _____ telemeter

a. to call back; to cancel
b. to come together as a group
c. characterized by a noisy outcry or shouting
d. instrument for measuring the distance of an object far from an observer
e. the career one believes himself called to; one's occupation or profession

16. _____ circumscribe
17. _____ subsequent
18. _____ introspection
19. _b_ intervene
20. _____ consequence

a. the observation or examination of one's own thought processes
b. to come between points of time or events
c. to draw a line around
d. following in time, order, or place
e. a logical result or conclusion; the relation of effect to cause

WORD STUDY: Dictionary Usage

In Unit 1, you were introduced to the types of information that a dictionary can provide. In this exercise, you will again scan* for information from a dictionary page, but here you will concentrate only on the definitions of words. Read the questions, then scan the dictionary page† (opposite) to find the answers.

1. In the following sentences, first determine the part of speech of the italicized word, then use the dictionary page to find a synonym for the word.

   a. Because of her all-night study sessions, Sandy is *run-down*.

      1. noun, verb, adjective, adverb
      2. synonym: _____

   b. John's telephone call to Peter caused a *rupture* in their four-year friendship.

      1. noun, verb, adjective, adverb
      2. synonym: _____

2. Find a synonym for *running* as it is used in the following sentence.

   We have won the contest four years *running*. _____

3. Which of the following is not listed as a synonym for *rural*?

   _____ a. rustic
   _____ b. rubric
   _____ c. pastoral

4. Under which word would you find synonyms of *run-of-the-mill*?

   _____ a. mill
   _____ b. average
   _____ c. run

5. Which word must you look up to find a description of a running knot?

   _____ a. slipknot
   _____ b. running
   _____ c. knot

6. According to this dictionary, a running mate is not _____

   _____ a. a horse.
   _____ b. a person.
   _____ c. a machine.

---

*For an introduction to scanning, see Unit 1.

†Copyright © 1969, 1970, 1971, 1973, 1975, 1976, Houghton Mifflin Company. Reprinted by permission from *The American Heritage Dictionary of the English Language*.

runcinate
Runcinate leaf of dandelion

rune

f u th a r k
g w h n i j e
p z s t b e
m l ng o d

basic Germanic runic alphabet

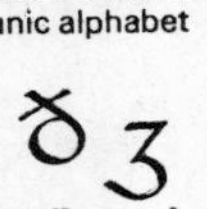

edh yogh

two later runes used in English

run·a·gate (rŭn′ə-gāt′) *n. Archaic.* **1.** A renegade or deserter. **2.** A vagabond. [Variant of RENEGADE (influenced by RUN).]
run·a·round (rŭn′ə-round′) *n.* Also **run·round** (rŭn′round′). **1.** Deception, usually in the form of evasive excuses. **2.** *Printing.* Type set in a column narrower than the body of the text, as on either side of a picture.
run·a·way (rŭn′ə-wā′) *n.* **1.** One that runs away. **2.** An act of running away. **3.** *Informal.* An easy victory. —*adj.* **1.** Escaping or having escaped from captivity or control. **2.** Of or done by running away. **3.** Easily won, as a race. **4.** Of or pertaining to a rapid price rise.
run·back (rŭn′băk′) *n.* **1.** The act of returning a kickoff, punt, or intercepted forward pass. **2.** The distance so covered.
run·ci·ble spoon (rŭn′sə-bəl). A three-pronged fork, as a pickle fork, curved like a spoon and having a cutting edge. [*Runcible,* a nonsense word coined by Edward Lear.]
run·ci·nate (rŭn′sə-nāt′, -nĭt) *adj. Botany.* Having saw-toothed divisions directed backward: *runcinate leaves.* [Latin *runcinātus,* past participle of *runcināre,* to plane, from *runcina,* carpenter's plane (formerly taken also to mean a saw), from Greek *rhukanē*†.]
run down. **1. a.** To slow down and stop, as a machine. **b.** To exhaust or wear out. **c.** To lessen in value. **2.** To pursue and capture. **3.** To hit with a moving vehicle. **4.** To disparage; decry. **5.** To give a brief or summary account of. **6.** *Baseball.* To put out a runner after trapping him between two bases.
run-down (rŭn′doun′) *n.* **1.** A summary or résumé. **2.** *Baseball.* A play in which a runner is put out when he is trapped between bases. —*adj.* **1.** In poor physical condition; weak or exhausted. **2.** Unwound and not running.
rune (ro͞on) *n.* **1.** One of the letters of an alphabet used by ancient Germanic peoples, especially by the Scandinavians and Anglo-Saxons. **2.** Any poem, riddle, or the like written in runic characters. **3.** Any occult characters. **4.** A Finnish poem or canto. [In sense 4, from Finnish *runo.* In other senses, Middle English *roun, rune,* secret writing, rune, from Old Norse *rūn* (unattested). See **rūno-** in Appendix.*] —**run′ic** *adj.*
rung¹ (rŭng) *n.* **1.** A rod or bar forming a step of a ladder. **2.** A crosspiece supporting the legs or back of a chair. **3.** The spoke in a wheel. **4.** *Nautical.* One of the spokes or handles on a ship's steering wheel. [Middle English *rung, rong,* Old English *hrung,* akin to Old High German *runga,* Gothic *hrugga*†.]
rung². Past tense and past participle of **ring.** See Usage note at **ring.**
run in. **1.** To insert or include something extra. **2.** *Printing.* To make a solid body of text without a paragraph or other break. **3.** *Slang.* To take into legal custody.
run-in (rŭn′ĭn′) *n.* **1.** A quarrel; an argument; a fight. **2.** *Printing.* Matter added to a text. —*adj.* Added or inserted in text.
run·let (rŭn′lĭt) *n.* A rivulet. [Diminutive of RUN (stream).]
run·nel (rŭn′əl) *n.* **1.** A rivulet; a brook. **2.** A narrow channel or course, as for water. [Middle English *rynel,* Old English *rynel,* from *rinnan,* to run, flow. See **er-¹** in Appendix.*]
run·ner (rŭn′ər) *n.* **1.** One who or that which runs, as: **a.** One that competes in a race. **b.** A fugitive. **c.** A messenger or errand boy. **2.** An agent or collector, as for a bank or brokerage house. **3.** One who solicits business, as for a hotel or store. **4.** A smuggler. **5.** A vessel engaged in smuggling. **6.** One who operates or manages something. **7.** A device in or on which a mechanism slides or moves, as: **a.** The blade of a skate. **b.** The supports on which a drawer slides. **8.** A long narrow carpet. **9.** A long narrow tablecloth. **10.** A roller towel. **11.** *Metallurgy.* A channel along which molten metal is poured into a mold; gate. **12.** *Botany.* **a.** A slender, creeping stem that puts forth roots from nodes spaced at intervals along its length. **b.** A plant, such as the strawberry, having such a stem. **c.** A twining vine, such as the **scarlet runner** *(see).* **13.** Any of several marine fishes of the family Carangidae, such as the blue runner, *Caranx crysos,* of temperate waters of the American Atlantic coast.
run·ner-up (rŭn′ər-ŭp′) *n.* One that takes second place.
run·ning (rŭn′ĭng) *n.* **1.** The act of one that runs. **2.** The power or ability to run. **3.** Competition: *in the running.* **4.** An operating: *the running of a machine.* **5. a.** That which runs or flows. **b.** The amount that runs. —*adj.* Continuous: *a running commentary.* —*adv.* Consecutively: *four years running.*
running board. A narrow footboard extending under and beside the doors of some automobiles and other conveyances.
running gear. **1.** The working parts of an automobile, locomotive, or other vehicle. **2. Running rigging** *(see).*
running hand. Writing done rapidly without lifting the pen from the paper.
running head. *Printing.* A title printed at the top of every page or every other page. Also called "running title."
running knot. A **slipknot** *(see).*
running light. **1.** One of several lights on a boat or ship kept lighted between dusk and dawn. **2.** One of several similar lights on an aircraft; a navigation light.
running mate. **1.** A horse used to set the pace in a race for another horse. **2.** The candidate or nominee for the lesser of two closely associated political offices.
running rigging. The part of a ship's rigging that comprises the ropes with which sails are raised, lowered, or trimmed, booms and gaffs are operated, etc. Also called "running gear."
running stitch. One of a series of small, even stitches.
run·ny (rŭn′ē) *adj.* **-nier, -niest.** Inclined to run or flow.
Run·ny·mede (rŭn′ĭ-mēd). A meadow on the Thames, 19 miles west of London, where King John is thought to have signed the Magna Carta in 1215. [Middle English *Runimede,* "meadow on the council island" : Old English *Rūnieg,* council island : *rūn,* secret, secret council (see **rūno-** in Appendix*) + *ieg, ig,* island (see **akwā-** in Appendix*) + *mede,* MEAD (meadow).]
run off. **1.** To print, duplicate, or copy. **2.** To run away; elope. **3.** To spill over; to overflow. **4.** To decide a contest or competition by a run-off.
run-off (rŭn′ôf′, -ŏf′) *n.* **1. a.** The overflow of a fluid from a container. **b.** Rainfall that is not absorbed by the soil. **2.** Eliminated waste products from manufacturing processes. **3.** An extra competition held to break a tie.
run-of-the-mill (rŭn′əv-*thə*-mĭl′) *adj.* Ordinary; not special; average. See Synonyms at **average.** [From *run of (the) mill,* products of a mill that are not graded for quality.]
run on. **1.** To continue on and on. **2.** *Printing.* To continue a text without a formal break.
run-on (rŭn′ŏn′, -ôn′) *n. Printing.* Matter that is appended or added without a formal break. —*adj.* Being run on.
run·round. Variant of **run-around.**
runt (rŭnt) *n.* **1.** An undersized animal; especially, the smallest animal of a litter. **2.** A person of small stature. Often used disparagingly. [Possibly from Dutch *rund,* small ox. See **ker-¹** in Appendix.*] —**runt′i·ness** *n.* —**runt·y** *adj.*
run through. **1.** To pierce. **2.** To use up (money, for example) quickly. **3.** To examine or rehearse quickly.
run-through (rŭn′thro͞o′) *n.* A complete but rapid review or rehearsal of something, such as a theatrical work.
run·way (rŭn′wā′) *n.* **1.** A path, channel, or track over which something runs. **2.** The bed of a water course. **3.** A chute down which logs are skidded. **4.** *Bowling.* A narrow track on which balls are returned after they are bowled. **5.** A smooth ramp for wheeled vehicles. **6.** A narrow walkway extending from a stage into an auditorium. **7.** A strip of level ground, usually paved, on which aircraft take off and land.
Run·yon (rŭn′yən), **(Alfred) Damon.** 1884–1946. American journalist and author of short stories.
ru·pee (ro͞o-pē′, ro͞o′pē) *n. Abbr.* **Re., r., R.** **1. a.** The basic monetary unit of Ceylon and Mauritius, equal to 100 cents. **b.** The basic monetary unit of India, equal to 100 paise. **c.** The basic monetary unit of Nepal, equal to 100 pice. **d.** The basic monetary unit of Pakistan, equal to 100 paisas. See table of exchange rates at **currency.** **2.** A coin worth one rupee. [Hindi *rupaīyā,* from Sanskrit *rūpya,* wrought silver, from *rūpa*†, shape, image.]
Ru·pert (ro͞o′pərt). A river of Quebec, Canada, flowing 380 miles westward from Mistassini Lake to James Bay.
Ru·pert (ro͞o′pərt), **Prince.** 1619–1682. German-born English military, naval, and political leader; supporter of Charles I; inventor.
Ru·pert's Land (ro͞o′pərts). The Canadian territory granted the Hudson's Bay Company in 1670, most of which was incorporated in The Northwest Territories after its purchase by Canada in 1870.
ru·pi·ah (ro͞o-pē′ä) *n., pl.* **rupiah** or **-ahs.** **1.** The basic monetary unit of Indonesia, equal to 100 sen. See table of exchange rates at **currency.** **2.** A note worth one rupiah. [Hindi *rupaīyā,* RUPEE.]
rup·ture (rŭp′chər) *n.* **1. a.** The act of breaking open or bursting. **b.** The state of being broken open or burst. **2.** A break in friendly relations between individuals or nations. **3.** *Pathology.* **a.** A **hernia** *(see),* especially of the groin or intestines. **b.** A tear in bodily tissue. —*v.* **ruptured, -turing, -tures.** —*tr.* To break open; burst. —*intr.* To undergo or suffer a rupture. —See Synonyms at **break.** [Middle English *ruptur,* from Old French *rupture,* from Latin *ruptūra,* from *rumpere* (past participle *ruptus*), to break. See **reup-** in Appendix.*] —**rup′tur·a·ble** *adj.*
ru·ral (ro͝or′əl) *adj.* **1.** Of or pertaining to the country as opposed to the city; rustic. **2.** Of or pertaining to people who live in the country. **3.** Of or relating to farming; agricultural. Compare **urban.** [Middle English, from Old French, from Latin *rūrālis,* from *rūs* (stem *rūr-*), country. See **rewe-** in Appendix.*] —**ru′ral·ism′** *n.* —**ru′ral·ist** *n.* —**ru′ral·ly** *adv.*

Synonyms: rural, arcadian, bucolic, rustic, pastoral, sylvan. These adjectives are all descriptive of existence or environment which is close to nature; those with a literary flavor are often used facetiously. *Rural* applies to sparsely settled or agricultural country, as distinct from settled communities. *Arcadian* implies ideal or simple country living. *Bucolic* is often used derisively of country people or manners. *Rustic,* sometimes uncomplimentary, applies to country people who seem unsophisticated, but may also apply favorably to living conditions or to natural environments which are pleasingly primitive. *Pastoral* implies the supposed peace of rural living and the shepherd's life, with a suggestion of artificiality. *Sylvan* refers to wooded as opposed to cultivated country, and carries the sense of unspoiled beauty.

rural free delivery. *Abbr.* **R.F.D., RFD** Free government delivery of mail in rural areas.
ru·ral·i·ty (ro͞o-răl′ə-tē) *n., pl.* **-ties.** **1.** The state or quality of being rural. **2.** A rural trait or characteristic.
ru·ral·ize (ro͝or′əl-īz′) *v.* **-ized, -izing, -izes.** —*tr.* To make rural. —*intr.* To live or visit in the country. —**ru′ral·i·za′tion** *n.*
rural route. *Abbr.* **R.R.** A rural mail route.
Ru·rik (ro͞o′rĭk). Died A.D. 879. Scandinavian warrior; founder of the dynasty that ruled Russia until 1598.
Rus. Russia; Russian.
Ru·se (ro͞o′sä). *Turkish* **Rus·chuk** (ro͞os′cho͝ok). A Danubian port in northeastern Bulgaria. Population, 118,000.
ruse (ro͞oz) *n.* An action or device meant to confuse or mislead. See Synonyms at **artifice.** [Middle English, detour of a hunted animal, from Old French, from *ruser,* to repulse, detour. See **rush** (to dash off).]

ă pat/ā pay/âr care/ä father/b bib/ch church/d deed/ĕ pet/ē be/f fife/g gag/h hat/hw which/ĭ pit/ī pie/îr pier/j judge/k kick/l lid, needle/m mum/n no, sudden/ng thing/ŏ pot/ō toe/ô paw, for/oi noise/ou out/o͝o took/o͞o boot/p pop/r roar/s sauce/sh ship, dish/

7. Which word must you look up to find the definition of *rung* as used in the following sentence:

I would have rung you earlier but I didn't have time.

_____ a. ring
_____ b. rang
_____ c. rung

8. From the dictionary definitions give the number of the appropriate definition for each of the italicized words in the following sentences:

a. We put a *runner* in the hall from the front door to the kitchen. _____

b. The singer walked onto the *runway* in order to get closer to the audience. _____

c. There were 24 *runes* in the Germanic alphabet. _____

9. Which of the following runes is a modern *m*?

_____ a.   ⋈
_____ b.   ᛘ
_____ c.   ᛗ

10. What is the meaning of the italicized word in the following sentence:

John complained that *Ruse* was dangerous.

_____ a. a misleading action
_____ b. a city
_____ c. an artifice

11. Complete the following sentence with the appropriate form of the word *rural*.

Because of his anti-urban feelings Kenworthy Piker is known as the leading

_____ of his time.

12. Choose the word that correctly completes the following sentences:

a. Let me give you a brief _____ of what we talked about before you arrived.

1. run-down
2. run down

b. We must have a _____ in order to decide which person will be the new president.

1. run-off
2. run off

SENTENCE STUDY: Introduction

The exercises in this book provide you with practice in using a number of reading skills and strategies to understand an author's message. Context Clues, Stems and Affixes, and Dictionary Usage exercises teach you strategies for discovering the meanings of unfamiliar vocabulary items. Scanning exercises provide you with practice in quickly finding specific pieces of information in a passage. Skimming, to be introduced in Unit 4, focuses on reading a passage quickly for a general idea of its meaning.

When you have difficulty understanding a passage, just reading further will often make the passage clearer. Sometimes, however, comprehension of an entire passage depends on your being able to understand a single sentence. Sentences which are very long, sentences which have more than one meaning, or sentences which contain difficult grammatical patterns often cause comprehension problems for readers. The sentence study exercise which follows as well as similar ones in later units give you the opportunity to develop strategies for attacking complicated sentences.

Although there is no easy formula that will help you to arrive at an understanding of a difficult sentence, you should keep the following points in mind.

1. Try to determine what makes the sentence difficult:

   a. If the sentence contains a lot of difficult vocabulary it may be that the sentence can be understood without knowing the meaning of every word. Try crossing out unfamiliar items:

      The West had sent armies to ~~capture and~~ hold Jerusalem; instead they themselves fell ~~victim~~ to ~~a host of~~ new ideas and ~~subtle~~ influences which left their mark on the development of European literature, ~~chivalry~~, warfare, ~~sanitation~~, commerce, political institutions, medicine, ~~and the papacy itself~~.

   b. If the sentence is very long, try to break it up into smaller parts:

      The West had sent armies to capture and hold Jerusalem. The West fell victim to a host of new ideas and subtle influences. These ideas and influences left their mark on the development of European literature, chivalry, warfare, sanitation, commerce, political institutions, medicine, and the papacy.

   c. Also, if the sentence is very long, try to determine which parts of the sentence express specific details supporting the main idea. Often clauses which are set off by commas, or introduced by words like *which*, *who*, and *that* are used to introduce extra information or to provide supporting details. Try crossing out the supporting details in order to determine the main idea:

      These ideas, ~~which left their mark on the development of European literature, chivalry, warfare, sanitation, commerce, political institutions, medicine, and the papacy~~, greatly changed Western culture.

Be careful! A good reader reads quickly but accurately.

2. Learn to recognize the important grammatical and punctuation clues which can change the meaning of a sentence.

a. Look for single words and affixes which can change the entire meaning of a sentence:

Summery weather is *not un*common.
The *average* daytime *high* temperature is *approximately* 56 .

b. Look for punctuation clues:

Wally ⊙sings⊙ at all of his friends' parties.
Barry said, "George has been elected president⊙"

Note that all of the italicized words or affixes and the circled punctuation above are essential to the meaning of the sentences; if any of these are omitted, the meaning of the sentence changes significantly.

c. Look for key words that tell you of relationships within a sentence:

The school has grown *from* a small building holding 200 students *to* a large institute which educates 4,000 students a year.

From . . . to indicates the beginning and end points of a period of change.

Many critics have proclaimed Doris Lessing as *not only* the best writer of the postwar generation, *but also* a penetrating analyst of human affairs.

Not only . . . but also indicates that both parts of the sentence are of equal importance.

In order to graduate on time, you will need to take five courses each semester.

In order to, is like *if*; it indicates that some event must occur before another event can take place.

The West had sent armies to capture and hold Jerusalem; *instead* they themselves fell victim to new ideas and subtle influences.

Instead indicates that something happened contrary to expectations.

As a result of three books, a television documentary, and a special exposition at the Library of Congress, the mystery has aroused considerable public interest.

As a result of indicates a cause and effect relationship. The clause that follows *as a result of* is the cause of some event. The three books, television program, and exposition are the *cause*; the arousal of public interest is the *effect*.

Because of the impact of these ideas, *which* had been introduced originally to Europe by soldiers returning from the East, the West was greatly changed.

Because of indicates a cause and effect relationship. The West was changed as a result of these ideas. The information between the word *which* and the final comma (,) refers to *these ideas*.

SENTENCE STUDY: Comprehension

Read the following sentences carefully. The questions which follow are designed to test your comprehension of complex grammatical structures. Select the *best* answer.

Example:
The student revolt is not only a thorn in the side of the president's newly established government, but it has international implications as well.

Who or what does this revolt affect?
_____ a. the students
_____ b. the side of the president's body
_____ c. only the national government
_____ d. national and international affairs

Explanation:
_____ a. According to the sentence, the students are the cause of certain events, not among those affected.
_____ b. Although you may not have been familiar with the idiom *a thorn in someone's side*, context clues should have told you that this phrase means *a problem* and does not actually refer to the side of the president's body.
_____ c. National government is an incomplete answer. The construction *not only . . . but . . . as well* should tell you that more than one element is involved. The president's newly established government (the national government) is not the only area affected by the revolt.
✓ d. The revolt affects both national and international affairs.

1. I disagreed then as now with many of John Smith's judgments, but always respected him, and this book is a welcome reminder of his big, honest, friendly, stubborn personality.
   How does the author of this sentence feel about John Smith?
   _____ a. He dislikes him but agrees with his ideas.
   _____ b. He considers him to be a disagreeable person.
   _____ c. He disagrees with his ideas but respects him.
   _____ d. He disagreed with him then but agrees with him now.

2. Concepts like *passivity*, *dependence*, and *aggression* may need further research if they are to continue to be useful ways of thinking about human personalities.
   What might require more research?
   _____ a. human thought processes
   _____ b. certain concepts
   _____ c. human personalities
   _____ d. useful ways of thinking

3. In order for you to follow the schedule set by the publisher, your paper must be looked over over the weekend, revised, and handed in in its final form on Monday.
   What must you do on Saturday and Sunday?
   _____ a. meet the publisher
   _____ b. examine your paper
   _____ c. hand in a paper
   _____ d. look over the weekend

4. The real reason why prices were, and still are, too high is complicated, and no short discussion can satisfactorily explain this problem.

        What word or phrase best describes prices?

        _____ a. complicated

        _____ b. adequately explained

        _____ c. too high in the past, but low now

        _____ d. too high in the past and in the present

5. This is not just a sad-but-true story; the boy's experience is horrible and damaging, yet a sense of love shines through every word.

        How does the author of this sentence feel about the story?

        _____ a. It transmits a sense of love.

        _____ b. It is just sad.

        _____ c. It is not true.

        _____ d. It is horrible and damaging.

6. In the past five years the movement has grown from unorganized groups of poorly armed individuals to a comparatively well-armed, well-trained army of anywhere from 10,000 to 16,000 members.

        What is the present condition of this movement?

        _____ a. The members are poorly armed.

        _____ b. There are only a few poor individuals.

        _____ c. There are over 16,000 members.

        _____ d. The members are organized and well armed.

7. The financial situation isn't bad yet, but we believe that we have some vital information and, if it is correct, unemployment will soon become a serious problem.

        What do we know about the financial situation?

        _____ a. It won't change.

        _____ b. It will become a serious problem.

        _____ c. It is not bad now.

        _____ d. It will improve.

8. The general then added, "The only reasonable solution to the sort of problems caused by the current unstable political situation is one of diplomacy and economic measures and not the use of military force."

        What type of solution does the general support?

        _____ a. economic and diplomatic action

        _____ b. diplomatic and economic action if military force fails

        _____ c. only diplomatic action

        _____ d. military actions in response to political problems

9. Because the supply of natural gas was plentiful in comparison to other choices like coal and fuel oil, and because it burns cleaner, many people changed their heating systems to natural gas, thereby creating shortages.

        Why did people prefer gas?

        _____ a. It was natural.

        _____ b. There were no other choices.

        _____ c. The other fuels were dirtier and less plentiful.

        _____ d. There is, even today, a plentiful supply of it.

PARAGRAPH READING: Main Idea

This exercise is similar to the one you did in Unit 1. Read the following paragraphs quickly. Concentrate on discovering the author's main idea. Remember, don't worry about details in the paragraphs. You only want to determine the author's general message. After each of the paragraphs, select the statement which best expresses the writer's main idea. Do not look back at the paragraphs.

Paragraph 1

John Cabot was the first Englishman to land in North America. However, this man who legitimized England's claim to everything from Labrador to Florida, left no sea journal, no diary or log, not even a portrait or a signature. Until 1956 most learned encyclopedias and histories indicated that Cabot's first landfall in America was Cape Breton, Nova Scotia. Then a letter was discovered in the Spanish archives, making it almost certain that he had touched first at the northernmost tip of Newfoundland, within five miles of the site of Leif Ericson's ill-fated settlement at L'Anse aux Meadows. Researchers studying the voyages of Columbus, Cartier, Frobisher, and other early explorers had a wealth of firsthand material with which to work. Those who seek to recreate the life and routes used by Cabot must make do with thirdhand accounts, the disloyal and untruthful boasts of his son, Sebastian, and a few hard dates in the maritime records of Bristol, England.*

Select the statement which best expresses the main idea of the paragraph.

_____ a. John Cabot claimed all the land from Labrador to Florida for England.

_____ b. Much of what is known about Cabot is based on the words of his son, Sebastian, and on records in Bristol, England.

_____ c. The lack of firsthand accounts of Cabot's voyage has left historians confused about his voyages to North America.

_____ d. Historians interested in the life and routes used by Cabot recently discovered an error they made in describing his discovery of North America.

---

*From Allan Keller, "The Silent Explorer: John Cabot in North America," *American History Illustrated* 8, no. 9 (January 1974): 5.

Paragraph 2

The Bible, while mainly a theological document written with the purpose of explaining the nature and moral imperatives of the Christian and Jewish God, is secondarily a book of history and geography. Selected historical materials were included in the text for the purpose of illustrating and underlining the religious teaching of the Bible. Historians and archaeologists have learned to rely upon the amazing accuracy of historical memory in the Bible. The smallest references to persons and places and events contained in the accounts of the Exodus, for instance, or the biographies of such Biblical heroes as Abraham and Moses and David, can lead, if properly considered and pursued, to extremely important historical discoveries. The archaeologists' efforts are not directed at "proving" the correctness of the Bible, which is neither necessary nor possible, any more than belief in God can be scientifically demonstrated. It is quite the opposite, in fact. The historical clues in the Bible can lead the archaeologist to a knowledge of the civilizations of the ancient world in which the Bible developed and with whose religious concepts and practices the Bible so radically differed. It can be considered as an almost unfailing indicator, revealing to the experts the locations and characteristics of lost cities and civilizations.*

Select the statement which best expresses the main idea of the paragraph.

——— a. The holy writings of the world's religions can provide valuable geographical information.

——— b. The Bible is primarily a religious document.

——— c. The Bible was intended by its authors to be a record of the history of the ancient world.

——— d. The Bible, though primarily a religious text, is a valuable tool for people interested in history.

Paragraph 3

At one time it was the most important city in the region—a bustling commercial center known for its massive monuments, its crowded streets and commercial districts, and its cultural and religious institutions. Then, suddenly, it was abandoned. Within a generation most of its population departed and the once magnificent city became all but a ghost town. This is the history of a pre-Columbian city called Teotihuacán (the Aztec Indians' word for "the place the gods call home"), once a metropolis of as many as 200,000 inhabitants 33 miles northeast of present-day Mexico City and the focus of a far-flung empire that stretched from the arid plains of central Mexico to the mountains of Guatemala. Why did this city die? Researchers have found no signs of epidemic disease or destructive invasions. But they have found signs that suggest the Teotihuacanos themselves burned their temples and some of their other buildings. Excavations revealed that piles of wood had been placed around these structures and set afire. Some speculate that Teotihuacán's inhabitants may have abandoned the city because it had become "a clumsy giant . . . too unwieldy to change with the times." But other archaeologists think that the ancient urbanites may have destroyed their temples and abandoned their city in rage against their gods for permitting a long famine.†

---

*From Nelson Glueck, "The Bible as Divining Rod," *Horizon* 2, no. 2 (November 1959): 6.
†From "Twilight of the Gods," *Time*, November 24, 1975, p. 107.

Select the statement which best expresses the main idea of the paragraph.

_____ a. Teotihuacán, once the home of 200,000 people, was the center of a large empire.

_____ b. Many archaeologists are fascinated by the ruins of a pre-Columbian city called Teotihuacán.

_____ c. Teotihuacán, once a major metropolitan area, was destroyed by an invasion.

_____ d. A still unsolved mystery is why the people of Teotihuacán suddenly abandoned their city.

Paragraph 4

In any archaeological study that includes a dig, the procedures are basically the same: 1) selecting a site 2) hiring local workmen 3) surveying the site and dividing it into sections 4) digging trenches to locate levels and places to excavate 5) mapping architectural features 6) developing a coding system that shows the exact spot where an object is found 7) and recording, tagging, cleaning and storing excavated materials. Neilson C. Debevoise, writing on an expedition to Iraq in the early 1930's, described the typical "route" of excavated pottery. Workers reported an object to staff members before removing it from the ground. The date, level, location and other important information were written on a piece of paper and placed with the object. At noon the objects were brought in from the field to the registry room where they were given a preliminary cleaning. Registry numbers were written with waterproof India ink on a portion of the object previously painted with shellac. The shellac prevented the ink from soaking into the object, furnished a good writing surface, and made it possible to remove the number in a moment. From the registry room objects were sent to the drafting department. If a clay pot, for example, was of a new type, a scale drawing was made on graph paper. Measurement of the top, greatest diameter, base, height, color of the glaze, if any, the quality and texture of the body and the quality of the workmanship were recorded on paper with the drawing. When the drafting department had completed its work the materials were placed on the storage shelves, grouped according to type for division with the Iraq government and eventually shipped to museums. Today, the steps of a dig remain basically the same, although specific techniques vary.*

Select the statement which best expresses the main idea of the paragraph.

_____ a. For a number of years, archaeologists have used basically the same procedure when conducting a dig.

_____ b. Neilson C. Debevoise developed the commonly accepted procedure for organizing a dig.

_____ c. Archaeologists take great care to assure that all excavated objects are properly identified.

_____ d. A great deal of important historical and archaeological information can be provided by a dig.

---

*From "Unearthing the Past," *Research News* 23, no. 5 (November 1972): 6.

Paragraph 5

   The unprecedented expansion of Modern architecture throughout the world must be considered one of the great events in the history of art. Within the space of the last generation, the contemporary movement has become the dominant style of serious building not only in the United States and Europe, where pioneers had been at work since the late nineteenth century, but also in nations such as Brazil and India, where almost no Modern architecture existed until much later. Only the Gothic perhaps, among all the styles of the past, gained popular acceptance with anything like the speed of the Modern. And like the Gothic—which required a full seventy-five years of experimentation before it produced the cathedral of Chartres—the Modern has continually improved its structural techniques, gained in scale, and revised its aesthetics as it has attempted to meet the full range of man's civilized needs.*

Select the statement which best expresses the main idea of the paragraph.

_____ a. Gothic architecture gained popular acceptance faster than Modern architecture did.

_____ b. Modern architecture has not changed fast enough to meet the needs of mankind.

_____ c. The rapid growth and development of Modern architecture (as an art form) is nearly unequaled in the history of art.

_____ d. If architectural styles are to endure, they must develop and improve in an attempt to meet society's needs.

---

*From Allan Temko, "The Dawn of the 'High Modern'," *Horizon* 2, no. 1 (September 1959): 5.

READING SELECTION 1: Newspaper Article

When reading the newspaper one often *skims* articles before deciding whether or not to read more carefully. To skim is to read quickly in order to get the general idea of a passage. Unlike scanning* which involves searching for details or isolated facts (see Unit 1), skimming requires you to note only information and clues which provide an idea of the central theme or topic of a piece of prose.

When you skim, it is necessary to read only selected sentences in order to get the main idea. You should also use textual clues such as italicized or underlined words, headlines or subtitles, spacing, paragraphing, etc. Do not read every word or sentence.

Once you have a general idea about an article you may decide to read the entire selection carefully, or only to scan for specific pieces of information in order to answer questions which have occurred to you.

The article† which begins on this page is presented to give you practice in scanning and skimming. Do NOT read the article carefully. Skim the passage to answer the following questions, then do the Scanning exercise on page 57. You will need to do the Vocabulary from Context exercise on page 57 before you begin reading.

SKIMMING

Skim the article for the answers to the following questions.

How have attitudes toward smokers changed recently? What kinds of actions are nations taking to curb smoking?

Christian Science Monitor, July 3, 1975

World's Nonsmokers Take Up Fight for Cleaner Air

By CLAYTON JONES
Christian Science Monitor Service

A useful expression is slipping into the list of key translations used by nonsmoking world travelers:

Don't puff on me.
Allez fumer ailleurs. (French)
No me eche humo. (Spanish)
Bolma inte rok pa mig. (Swedish)
Blasen Sie mir nicht den Rauch ins Gesicht. (German)

In country after country, talk of nonsmokers' rights is in the air.

This fresh voice is heard from Australia to Sweden. Its force is freeing clean air for nonsmokers—and tightening the situation for smokers.

In West Germany, for instance, taxi drivers—known for their independence—post signs saying "Nicht Raucher" (nonsmoker) and may refuse passengers who insist on smoking . . . . Sweden plans a generation of nonsmokers by the year 2000 . . . . Bans in Poland prevent smoking in factories, offices, snack bars, and other public places . . . . And Venezuelans can be fined $230 to $1000 for smoking in supermarkets, buses, and numerous other places.

Many countries also are moving in step to limit tobacco promotion (despite a 7 percent jump in world tobacco production last year) and to eliminate the "false claims of the glorification of smoking as a habit . . ." says Jean de Moerloose of the United Nations World Health Organization.

While a majority of countries have taken little or no action yet, some 30 nations have introduced legislative steps to control smoking abuse. Many laws have been introduced in other countries to help clear the air for nonsmokers, or to cut cigarette consumption.

In many developing nations, however, cigarette smoking is seen as a sign of economic progress—and is even encouraged.

"While it appears that in developed countries the consumption of cigarettes has become stabilized, there are some indications that it is still rising at a steady pace in Latin America," says Dr. Daniel J. Joly, an adviser to the Pan American Health Organization.

Despite progress in segregating nonsmokers and smokers, most countries see little change in the number of smokers. In fact, there is a jump in the number of girls and young women starting to smoke.

As more tobacco companies go international, new markets are sought to gain new smokers in developing countries. For example, great efforts are made by the American tobacco industry to sell cigarettes in the Middle East and North Africa—where U.S. tobacco exports increased by more than 27 percent last year, according to the U.S. Foreign Agriculture Service.

So far, any cooperation between tobacco interests and governments' campaigns against smoking has been in the area of tobacco advertising.

Restrictions on cigarette ads, plus health warnings on pack-

---

*For an introduction to scanning, see Unit 1.
†Adapted version of Zee Page article by Clayton Jones, "*Non Smokers Lib*. Shout heard 'round the world 'Don't puff on me' " (original title) July 3, 1975. Reprinted by permission from the *Christian Science Monitor*. Copyright © 1975 by The Christian Science Publishing Society. All rights reserved.

ages and bans on public smoking in certain places, are the most popular tools used by nations in support of nonsmokers or in curbing smoking.

But world attention also is focusing on other steps which will:

—Make the smoker increasingly self-conscious and uncomfortable about his habit by publicizing public awareness of the decline of social acceptability of smoking. (This method is receiving strong support in the U.S. and other countries.)

—Prevent pro-smoking scenes on television and films.

—Remove cigarette vending machines.

—Provide support for those who want to kick the habit of smoking.

—Make it illegal to sell or hand over tobacco products to minors—and prohibit smoking in meeting places for young people.

—Boost cigarette prices with higher tobacco taxes—and use the money for antismoking campaigns.

At a June UN conference on smoking, a goal set by Sir George E. Godber, chairman of the expert committee on smoking and health for the World Health Organization, stated: "We may not have eliminated cigarette smoking completely by the end of this century, but we ought to have reached a position where relatively few addicts still use cigarettes, but only in private at most in the company of consenting adults."

NATIONS ATTEMPT SOLUTIONS

Here are brief sketches of major or unique attempts around the world to insure nonsmokers' right to smoke-free air and to help smokers quit:

SWEDEN

An ambitious, concerted plan to raise a nation of nonsmokers is being implemented by the Swedish National Board of Health and Welfare.

Swedish children born after 1975 will grow up in environments that will be nonsmoking and antismoking as much as possible. General cigarette consumption will be cut from 1,700 cigarettes a year per person to a 1920 level of under 300 cigarettes a year, according to the 25-year plan.

A campaign to restrict tobacco advertising, raise cigarette prices to over $2 a pack, remove cigarette vending machines by 1979, ban pro-smoking content in films and television programs, restrict public smoking, and give intensive antismoking education in schools and the military, will promote the goal of a society which "should be so unfavorable toward smoking that smoking could not arise once again as a major factor harmful to public health."

By Swedish law, life-insurance premiums are lowered for nonsmokers.

WEST GERMANY

An image-reversing advertising campaign began a few years ago in West Germany whereby it is the nonsmoker who is shown to be living the swinging life previously claimed by the cigarette addict.

A government-sponsored program to warn the public about the dangers of smoking includes an attempt to encourage consideration of the nonsmoker at work and in public places. Tobacco television ads were stopped in 1973.

But there are no firm plans at the federal level to ban smoking in public places, although it is being considered as a legislative proposal. Health experts say that the legally required warning on cigarette packages in the United States has not helped. Hence there are strong doubts about strict laws in the whole area of smoking. The governing idea here is to encourage consideration of others. But this angle of attack (moral persuasion) does not rule out legislation. In two of Germany's 11 states there are laws to protect public employees who do not smoke from their smoking fellow workers. "Smoke breaks" are used to separate the smokers and nonsmokers.

"The nonsmoker today is just as much or more respected than the smoker," says one health official, "and this is a success in itself."

GREAT BRITAIN

A television advertising ban in 1965, a health warning on tobacco packages begun in 1971, a 20 percent price rise on cigarettes in 1974, and a constant campaign to isolate public smoking in airlines, trains, and other public places have fueled a forceful antismoking and nonsmokers' program in Britain.

In Ireland, an advertising code bans ads emphasizing the pleasure of smoking, featuring conventional heroes of the young as smokers, or implying that it is less harmful to smoke one brand than another.

VENEZUELA

Nonsmoking Venezuelans have begun a major campaign using newspapers, radio, and television to slow and reverse the country's spiraling consumption of cigarettes.

Numerous columns in **El Nacional**, a Caracas newspaper, detail many bad aspects of smoking, noting the worldwide movement to cut back on cigarettes.

A law passed last November forbids smoking in airlines, trains, buses, theaters, museums, supermarkets, hospitals, and other public places. Fines range from $230 to $1000. So far, however, the campaign has only had limited success because of weak enforcement.

ARGENTINA

A smoking ban in public transportation in Buenos Aires seems to be holding up, and bus drivers as well as subway and train conductors frequently remind passengers that smoking is prohibited.

In part, this may be due to the rather sophisticated attitude of Argentines who are increasingly concerned about the health effects of smoking.

Although a one-year ban on cigarette advertising on radio, television, and film has run out, some stations and theaters continue the ban—as do some newspapers.

CANADA

Tobacco companies in 1972 banned their own television and radio advertising in Canada.

Many nonsmokers' rights groups are successfully campaigning for nonsmoking areas in restaurants, public meetings, trains and planes, and food stores.

NORWAY

On July 1, 1975, it became a crime in Norway to offer a cigarette to a child under 16. The new law, which many countries are watching, also places a total ban on all tobacco advertising, including tobacco shop window displays. Field workers throughout the country are conducting educational and antismoking activities.

UNITED STATES

U.S. airlines are subject to $1,000 fines for failing to provide a smoke-free seat for any passanger who wants one. The Interstate Commerce Commission has made "no smoking" the rule, rather than the exception, on all interstate passenger trains and buses. The military segregates smokers and no longer distributes cigarettes in C-rations.

A growing number of restaurants now offer separate areas for nonsmokers. A ban on television and radio cigarette ads, health warnings, and restrictions on public smoking in many states and cities make the United States a participant in world nonsmoking and antismoking efforts. The number of U.S. nonsmokers is rising as well.

POLAND

Polish broadcasters restrict smoking on television except when it is necessary as part of the dramatic action, and are required to increase the number of television and radio programs devoted to antismoking activities.

Far-reaching restrictions on smoking in public areas went into effect last year to protect the health and comfort of nonsmokers.

AUSTRALIA

Cigarette commercials on Australian television are followed by a somber voice saying that "medical authorities warn that smoking is a health hazard." A similar message is on cigarette packs. In September, 1976, cigarette television ads will be phased out. Presently, the ads are not permitted before 9:30 p.m.

SCANNING

Scan the article for the answers to the following questions.

1. How many countries have introduced legislation to restrict smoking?

2. At a time when countries are moving to limit smoking:
   a. Did world tobacco production increase or decrease in 1974?
   b. Did the number of smokers in Latin America increase or decrease in 1974?
   c. Is the number of females starting to smoke increasing or decreasing?

3. How have tobacco companies reacted to government campaigns against smoking?

4. Has Great Britain developed a strong antismoking campaign?

5. What evidence is there that the U.S. antismoking campaign has been successful?

6. What is the antismoking goal of Swedish society?

7. What is the attitude of Argentines toward smoking?

8. Has the antismoking campaign in Venezuela been successful?

VOCABULARY FROM CONTEXT

Both the ideas and the vocabulary in the following passage are taken from the article on smoking. Use the context provided to determine the meanings of the italicized words. Write a definition, synonym, or description of each of the italicized vocabulary items in the space provided.

1. _____

2. _____
3. _____

4. _____
5. _____

6. _____
7. _____

Some people believe that cigarette smoking is dangerous and should therefore be considered a health *hazard*. They want their governments to create antismoking programs. People differ as to how strong these antismoking *campaigns* should be. Some of the strongest campaigns would try to completely *eliminate* cigarette smoking. Supporters of these programs would try to *ban* cigarette smoking completely in public places. Others would try only to *restrict* the number of places where people could smoke. Such restrictions would not try to eliminate public smoking completely, but only to *curb* smoking by reducing cigarette *consumption*.

VOCABULARY REVIEW

Two of the words in each line below are similar in meaning. Circle the word which does not belong.

1. ban   eliminate   campaign
2. curb   consume   restrict
3. danger   health   hazard

57

READING SELECTION 2: Newspaper Questionnaire

Efficient reading requires an understanding of the attitudes and experiences of the writer. Unless one has knowledge about or is able to infer an author's beliefs, it is possible to understand all of the sentences in a passage and yet not comprehend a writer's ideas.

Reading a newspaper in another language is an excellent way of drawing inferences about another culture. The following selection is a quiz which appeared in a newspaper in the United States.* It was designed to provide people with the opportunity to measure their ability to handle problems. By taking the quiz, you should be able to gain an understanding of the kinds of problems experienced in the United States and the ways in which people attempt to deal with them.

Answer each of the questions. If you have trouble deciding what you would do in a given situation, indicate how you predict people in the United States would answer the quesiton.

How Do You Handle Everyday Stress?

Psychologists are now convinced that day-to-day problems, which frequently seem unimportant, are what "take a lot out of you." Moreover, they can even affect the length of your life. Everybody faces day-to-day problems, but some can handle them better than others.

Would you like to know how well you can cope? In this quiz, circle the answer closest to the way you actually react in the situation described. If the situation is unfamiliar, circle the answer closest to the way you think you would handle it.

Answers at the end will tell you how well you are coping with everyday stress and may help you to improve your methods of dealing with problems.

1. Birthdays, weddings, anniversaries . . . it seems impossible to avoid spending money.
   a. You tell everyone to take you off their gift list so that you don't have to buy a gift.
   b. In spite of the expense you continue to enjoy selecting small, special gifts for any occasion.
   c. You give only to those who are most important to you.

2. You had an automobile accident with another car and you have to appear in court.
   a. The anxiety and inconvenience of appearing in court causes you to lose sleep.
   b. It's an unimportant event, one of those things that happen in life.You will reward yourself with a little gift after court.
   c. You forget about it. You will cope with it when the day comes.

3. Some furniture and carpeting in your house was damaged by a leak in the water pipes and you discover that your insurance doesn't cover the loss.
   a. You become depressed and complain bitterly about the insurance company.
   b. You recover the furniture yourself.
   c. You think about cancelling your insurance and writing a letter of complaint to the Better Business Bureau.

---

*Adapted from "How Do You Handle Everyday Stress?" by Dr. Syvil Marquit and Marilyn Lane. Features and News Service.

4. You've had a fight with your neighbor and nothing was resolved.
   a. You go home, fix a strong drink, try to relax and forget about it.
   b. You call your lawyer to discuss a possible lawsuit.
   c. You work off your anger by taking a walk.

5. The pressures of modern day living have made you and your wife/husband irritable.
   a. You decide to take it easy and not be forced into any arguments.
   b. You try to discuss irritating matters with a third person so that you can make your feelings known without an argument.
   c. You insist on discussing the problems with your wife/husband to see how you can take off some of the pressure.

6. A close friend is about to get married. In your opinion, it will be a disaster.
   a. You convince yourself that your early fears are incorrect, and hope for the best.
   b. You decide not to worry because there's still time for a change of plans.
   c. You decide to present your point of view; you explain your reasoning seriously to your friend.

7. You are worried about rising food prices.
   a. Despite rising prices, you refuse to change your eating habits.
   b. Your anger level rises every time you see an increase in price from the week before, but you buy anyway.
   c. You try to spend less and plan good menus anyway.

8. Finally your abilities have been recognized; you've been offered an important job.
   a. You think of turning down the chance because the job is too demanding.
   b. You begin to doubt if you can handle the added responsibilities successfully.
   c. You analyze what the job requires and prepare yourself to do the job.

9. You suspect that your rent or some other monthly expense will increase.
   a. You pick up the mail anxiously each day and give a sigh of relief when the letter isn't there.
   b. You decide not to be caught by surprise and you plan how to handle the situation.
   c. You feel everyone is in the same situation and that somehow you'll cope with the increase.

10. Someone close to you has been seriously injured in an accident, and you hear the news by phone.
    a. You hold back your feelings for the moment because other friends and relatives have to be told the news.
    b. You hang up and burst into tears.
    c. You call your doctor and ask for tranquilizers to help you through the next few hours.

11. You've won a big luxury car in a competition. You could use a car but it seems this is going to change your life considerably.
    a. You worry about the added problems your good luck will bring.
    b. You sell it and buy a smaller car, banking the money left over.
    c. You decide to enjoy the car and to worry about the added expense later.

12. Every holiday there is a serious argument in the family about whether to visit your parents or those of your husband/wife.
    a. You make a rigid 5-year plan, which will require you to spend each holiday with different members of the family.
    b. You decide that you'll spend important holidays with the members of the family you like best, and ask others to join you for the lesser holidays.
    c. You decide the fairest thing is not to celebrate with the family at all—and it's less trouble.

13. You're not feeling well.
    a. You diagnose your own illness, then read about it.
    b. You gather up your courage, talk about it at home and go to see your doctor.
    c. You delay going to the doctor thinking that you will eventually feel better.

14. Your youngest child is leaving home and going into the world.
    a. You discuss the development with friends to see how they're handling it.
    b. You give all the help you can and plan new interests for yourself.
    c. You try to talk the young person into staying home a bit longer.

To find out how you cope with stress, score your answers according to the following chart:

Questions 1-3:   A=3, B=1, C=2
Questions 4-8:   A=3, B=2, C=1
Questions 9-14: A=2, B=1, C=3

The lower your total score, the better able you are to cope with your problems. If you scored 23 or less, the advice that follows may be normal behavior for you. (Perhaps you can teach others how to be calm.)

If you scored over 23, here are some ways to handle stress conditions effectively. Don't put difficult situations to one side thinking they will go away. Eventually you will have to deal with them anyway. Don't make decisions that will cause you stress later. It's better to face reality at the beginning. For example, don't accept an invitation if you know you won't be able to attend when the time comes.

In order to avoid problems later, think things through in advance. In facing a problem, don't guess about the future or let your imagination run away with you; find out what the true situation is, then handle it.

Most of the time what you may be fearing will never happen. When you get upset about an unavoidable stress-filled event, do something physical to work it off. When tragedy strikes, as it does to all of us, don't be afraid to show your emotions.

DISCUSSION

1. What can you infer from this quiz about the kinds of problems faced by people in the United States?

2. The choices below each question in the quiz describe some of the ways people in the United States cope with problems. Which of these are similar to the ways people in your country deal with problems? Which do you find strange?

VOCABULARY

Circle the word or phrase which is not similar in meaning.

deal with   attempt   handle   cope with

READING SELECTION 3: Magazine Article

Read the following article quickly to determine the author's main ideas.* You may want to do the Vocabulary from Context exercise on page 66 before you begin reading.

Before Christopher Columbus discovered the New World, Europeans commonly believed that the world was flat. They believed that if you sailed too far from land you would fall off the edge of the earth to be eaten by fire-breathing monsters. Ridiculous, you say? Don't be too sure. Before making a final judgment, read about the:

Graveyard of the Atlantic

1   At 2 P.M. on Dec. 5, 1945, five Navy bombers took off in perfect flying weather from the Naval Air Station at Fort Lauderdale, Fla., on a routine training mission over the Atlantic Ocean. Less than two hours later, the flight commander radioed that he was "completely lost." Then there was silence. A rescue plane was sent to search for the missing aircraft and it, too, disappeared. In all, six planes and 27 men vanished that day without a trace. Despite one of history's most extensive search efforts, involving more than 300 planes and dozens of ships, the Navy was unable to discover even floating wreckage or a telltale oil slick.

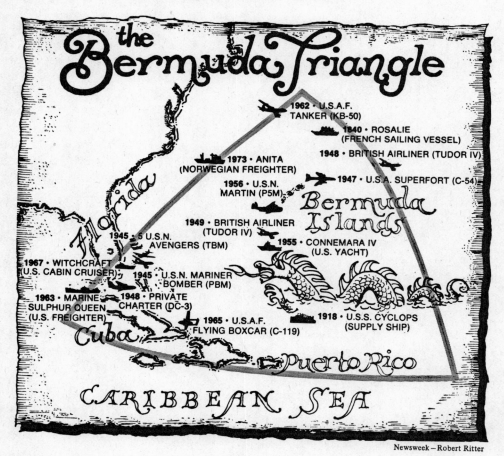

Newsweek—Robert Ritter

Limbo of the lost: Some of the triangle's victims and where they vanished

---

*Adapted from "Graveyard of the Atlantic." Copyright © 1974 by Newsweek, Inc. All rights reserved. Reprinted by permission.

2   This is just one of the many chilling stories told of "The Bermuda Triangle," a mysterious area of the Atlantic Ocean roughly stretching south from Bermuda to the Florida coast and Puerto Rico. During the past 30 years, the triangle has claimed the lives of some 1,000 seamen and pilots. Among sailors, it is known variously as "The Triangle of Death," "The Hoodoo Sea" and "The Graveyard of the Atlantic" because of the mysterious calms, waterspouts, and sudden storms that have bothered seafarers in its water. When he entered this stretch of the Atlantic, Christopher Columbus noted curious glowing streaks of "white water." The mysterious patches of light and foam are still visible today and so bright that they have been seen by U.S. astronauts from outer space.

3   In recent months, the triangle has aroused considerable public interest through three hot-selling books, a television documentary (narrated by horror master Vincent Price) and a special exposition at the Library of Congress. None of these investigations has produced convincing answers to the mystery of the triangle, but there is no shortage of interesting theories. Some scientists and popular authors go so far as to suggest that the triangle is the hunting ground of extraterrestrial beings in search of human specimens for their "cosmic zoos."

4   Whatever the truth may be, planes and ships disappear in the triangle with eerie regularity. On July 3, 1947, a U.S. Army C-54 Superfort disappeared 100 miles off Bermuda without broadcasting any word of difficulty. An immediate search over 100,000 square miles of sea failed to turn up a single piece of wreckage. On Jan. 30, 1948, a Tudor IV British airliner, the Star Tiger, vanished over the triangle with 31 passengers and crew aboard. A year later, the Star Tiger's sister plane, the Star Ariel, disappeared en route to Jamaica. Seventy-two search planes, plus dozens of ships, failed to turn up any sign of the missing aircraft.

5   One of the largest ships claimed by the mysterious triangle was the U.S.S. Cyclops, a 500-foot coaling ship that disappeared on March 4, 1918. Investigations revealed no evidence of foul weather, no messages for help, no wreckage and no sign of the 309 men aboard. Stranger yet are the numerous "ghost" ships that have been found floating crewless within the triangle. On one weird occasion in 1881, the cargo ship Ellen Austin discovered a schooner, sails flapping in the wind, a full cargo of mahogany intact, but no sign of human life. The captain of the Ellen Austin installed a new crew to sail it, but two days later, during a rough storm, the two ships temporarily lost sight of each other. When the captain again boarded the schooner, he found his crew had disappeared. After a second crew was assigned, the ship was again lost in a fog bank. This time, no trace of the schooner—or the crew—was ever found.

6   Officially, the U.S. Navy does not recognize the triangle as a danger zone and the U.S. Coast Guard is convinced that "the majority of disappearances [in the triangle] can be attributed to the area's unique environmental features." These include the swift Gulf Stream current, the unexplored underwater canyons of the Atlantic and the often violent weather patterns within the mystery zone. Then too, the triangle is one of only two places on earth where a compass needle points to true rather than magnetic north. (The other is "The Devil's Sea," an equally treacherous zone in the Pacific, southeast of Japan.) Thus, a navigator who does not remember this may find himself well off course. "There are mysterious and strange things going on out there," admits Richard Winer, author of The Devil's Triangle . . . a paperback that has sold 500,000 copies since its publication three months ago. "But I believe that all the answers lie in human error, mechanical malfunctions, freak weather or magnetic abnormalities."

7   Officials of the National Oceanic and Atmospheric Administration are not so

certain. "Despite efforts by the U.S. Air Force, Navy and Coast Guard," NOAA reports, "no reasonable explanation to date has been made for the vanishings." Because of these uncertainties, private investigators have sought more fanciful explanations. John Wallace Spencer, author of *Limbo of the Lost*, a paperback that has sold 1.5 million copies in the past fifteen months, argues that beings from outer space have established a highly advanced civilization in the unexplored depths of the Atlantic inside the triangle. There, he believes, most of the missing vessels—and their crews—may still be on display for study by these higher intelligences. "It sounds weird," Spencer admits, "until you realize that it's the only explanation that covers all the facts."

8   These and other theories are all examined in Charles Berlitz's current volume, *The Bermuda Triangle* . . . which has climbed onto the best-seller list less than three months after publication. A Yale graduate with a fascination for Atlantis, the legendary lost continent, Berlitz expands upon the theory that a giant solar crystal, which once supplied power for Atlantis, lies on the ocean floor. Periodically, he theorizes, passing ships and planes trigger the crystal, which confuses their instruments and sucks them into the impassable deep.

9   To test such theories, a parapsychological institute call the Isis Center for Research and Study of the Esoteric Arts, based in Silver Springs, Md., is planning to take 300 psychics and scientists on a cruise into the triangle next June. The researchers hope to make contact with whatever "higher intelligences" may lie under the sea. A similar expedition into the Devil's Sea was made by a group of Japanese scientists in 1955. Nothing has been heard of them since.

COMPREHENSION

Exercise 1

Indicate if each statement is true (T) or false (F) according to your understanding of the passage. Do not refer to the passage as you mark your answers.

1. _____ The Bermuda Triangle is an area of the Atlantic Ocean where a number of ships and planes have disappeared.

2. _____ The triangle has been a source of mystery for only thirty years.

3. _____ In spite of great public interest in the triangle, no theory has yet been suggested to explain the disappearances.

4. _____ According to the article, important information regarding the disappearances has come from people who lived through the experiences themselves.

5. _____ The U.S. Navy does not recognize the triangle as a danger zone.

6. _____ Although a great deal of publicity has been given to the mystery of the triangle, officials of the U.S. government all agree that natural causes account for the disappearances.

7. _____ If the team from the Isis Center for Research and Study of the Esoteric Arts is as successful as the team of Japanese scientists was in 1955, the mystery will soon be solved.

Exercise 2

This section tests your comprehension of details. You may refer to the passage to answer the following questions.

1. How many people have disappeared in the triangle in the last thirty years?

2. What curiosity of the triangle was reported by both Columbus and U.S. astronauts?

3. From the information you have here, what is the date of the most recent disappearance in the triangle?

4. What is meant by the term *ghost ship*?

5. What are the environmental features of the triangle which make it unique?

6. In the triangle, a compass needle points to true north rather than to magnetic north. How might this fact help explain the disappearances?

7. Richard Winer, John Wallace Spencer, and Charles Berlitz all offer theories concerning the triangle. What is your opinion of each of these theories?

8. Has the group from the Isis Center completed its voyage? How would you find this information?

VOCABULARY FROM CONTEXT

Use the context provided and your knowledge of stems and affixes to determine the meanings of the italicized words. Write a definition, synonym, or description of each of the italicized vocabulary items in the space provided.

The Bermuda Triangle is an area of the Atlantic Ocean which has puzzled people for several centuries.

1. _____ There are a number of environmental features that can be found only in the Bermuda Triangle. Because of these *unique* characteristics, the triangle is one of the most dangerous areas in the Atlantic Ocean.

2. _____ The weather in the triangle is *treacherous*; its sudden changes often endanger the lives of sailors.

3. _____ The triangle is well known for unexpected storms, hurricanes that are out of season, and other unnatural events. Many people feel that this *freak* weather can explain most of the strange events which have occurred there.

4. _____ Because of the many violent storms, the triangle is often *impassable*.

5. _____ Many ships leave land and disappear completely; the U.S.S. Cyclops, for example, *vanished* in 1918.

6. _____ Some missing ships carried *cargo* such as coal, oil, mahogany, and military supplies, while other ships carried only passengers.

7. _____ Engine *malfunction* might explain the disappearance of of old ships, but investigators must look for other explanations when a new ship disappears.

8. _____ When a ship is reported missing, searchers rush to the area to look for *evidence* which might explain the disappearance.

9. _____ One author tries to explain the disappearances of the ships by *attributing* them to natural events or human error.

10. _____ Another author believes that intelligences from another world are responsible for the disappearances. He says that these *extraterrestrial* beings have a zoo where they keep all the missing seamen.

11. _____   Many people agree that natural causes cannot explain the strange events in the triangle. "It just isn't natural for a ship to completely disappear like this. It's *weird*, no matter how you try to explain it," declared the seamen.

12. _____   "These *eerie* events make me afraid to sail out of sight of land."

READING SELECTION 4: Narrative

The following selection is taken from Gerald Durrell's book, *My Family and Other Animals.** The book is an account of the year the Durrell family spent on the Greek island of Corfu. As the title indicates, the book is not an ordinary autobiography. "Bootle-Bumtrinket" is a good example of the unusual incidents experienced by the Durrells during their stay on the island.

Read the passage quickly to appreciate the humor of the author. Do not worry about unfamiliar vocabulary.

Bootle-Bumtrinket

1   Our trips to the enchanted archipelago became less and less frequent in spite of all arguments on my part, and I was tortured by the thought of all the wonderful animal life waiting in the pools to be caught; but I was unable to do anything about it, simply because I had no boat. I suggested that I might be allowed to take the *Sea Cow* out myself, say once a week, but the family were, for a variety of reasons, against this. But then, just when I had almost given up hope, I was struck with a brilliant idea: my birthday was due fairly soon, and if I dealt with the family skillfully I felt sure I could not only get a boat, but a lot of other equipment as well. I therefore suggested to the family that, instead of letting them choose my birthday presents, I might tell them the things which I wanted most. In this way they could be sure of not disappointing me. The family, rather surprised, agreed, and then, somewhat suspiciously, asked me what I wanted. Innocently, I said that I hadn't thought about it much, but that I would work out a list for each person, and they could then choose one or more items on it.

2   My list took a lot of time and thought to work out, and a considerable amount of applied psychology. Mother, for instance, I knew would buy me everything on her list, so I put down some of the most necessary and expensive equipment for my insect collection. Margo's list was a little more difficult, for the items had to be chosen so that they would encourage her to go to her favourite shops. It was, I realized resignedly, quite useless to ask Larry for any equipment for my insect collection, but if my list showed some sort of literary leaning I stood a good chance. Accordingly I made out a formidable sheet covered with the titles, authors' names, publishers, and price of all the natural history books I felt in need of, and put an asterisk against those that would be most gratefully received. Since I had only one request left, I decided to tackle Leslie verbally instead of handing him a list, but I knew I should have to choose my moment with care. I had to wait some days for what I considered to be the right moment.

3   I had just helped him to the successful conclusion of some shooting experiments he was making, which involved tying an ancient gun to a tree and firing it by means of a long string attached to the trigger. At the fourth attempt we achieved what apparently Leslie considered to be success: the barrel burst and bits of metal whined in all directions. Leslie was delighted and made copious notes on the back of the envelope. Together we set about picking up the remains of the gun. While we were doing this I casually asked him what he would like to give me for my birthday.

4   "Hadn't thought about it," he replied absently. "I don't mind . . . anything you like . . . you choose."

5   I said I wanted a boat. Leslie, realizing how he had been trapped, said indignantly that a boat was far too large a present for a birthday, and anyway he couldn't afford

*Adapted from *My Family and Other Animals* by Gerald Durrell. Copyright © 1956 by Gerald Durrell. Reprinted by permission of The Viking Press and Granada Publishing Ltd.

it. I said, equally indignantly, that he had *told* me to choose what I liked. Leslie said yes, he had, but he hadn't meant a boat, as they were terribly expensive. I said that when one said *anything* one meant anything, which included boats, and anyway I didn't expect him to buy me one. I had thought, since he knew so much about boats, he would be able to build me one. However, if he thought that would be too difficult . . .

6   "Of course it's not difficult," said Leslie, unguardedly, and then added hastily, "Well . . . not terribly difficult. But it's the *time*. It would take ages and ages to do. Look, wouldn't it be better if I took you out in the *Sea Cow* twice a week?"

7   But I was adamant; I wanted a boat and I was quite prepared to wait for it.

"Oh, all right, all right," said Leslie exasperatedly, "I'll build you a boat. But I'm not having you hanging around while I do it, understand? You're to keep well away. You're not to see it until it's finished."

8   Delightedly I agreed to these conditions, and so for the next two weeks Spiro kept turning up with car-loads of wood, and the sounds of sawing, hammering, and blasphemy floated round from the back veranda. The house was littered with wood shavings, and everywhere he walked Leslie left a trail of sawdust.

9   The morning of my birthday was full of incident. My presents having been inspected and the family thanked, I then went round to the back veranda with Leslie, and there lay a mysterious shape hidden under a cover. Leslie drew this aside with the air of a magician, and there lay my boat. I gazed at it rapturously; it was surely the most perfect boat that anyone had ever had. Gleaming in her coat of new paint she lay there, my transportation to the enchanted archipelago.

10   The boat was some seven feet long, and almost circular in shape. Leslie explained hurriedly—in case I thought the shape was due to poor craftsmanship—that the reason for this was that the boards had been too short for the frame, an explanation I found perfectly satisfactory. After all, it was the sort of irritating thing that could have happened to anyone. I said stoutly that I thought it was a lovely shape for a boat, and indeed I thought it was. She was not sleek, slim, and rather predatory looking, like most boats, but round, peaceful, and somehow comforting in her circular solidarity. She reminded me of an earnest dung-beetle, an insect for which I had great affection. Leslie, pleased at my evident delight, said that he had been forced to make her flat-bottomed, since, for a variety of technical reasons, this was the safest. I said that I liked flat-bottomed boats the best, because it was possible to put jars of specimens on the floor without so much risk of them upsetting. Leslie asked me if I liked the colour scheme, as he had not been too sure about it. Now, in my opinion, the colour scheme was the best thing about it, the final touch that completed the unique craft. Inside she was painted green and white, while her bulging sides were tastefully covered in white, black, and brilliant orange stripes, a combination of colours that seemed to me both artistic and friendly. Leslie then showed me the long, smooth cypress pole he had cut for a mast, but explained that it could not be fitted into position until the boat was in water. Enthusiastically I suggested launching her at once. Leslie, who was very careful about procedure, said you couldn't launch a ship without naming her, and had I thought of a name yet? This was a difficult problem, and the whole family were called out to help me solve it. After much debate, I decided on the name of *Bootle-Bumtrinket*, which was not only an unusual name, but was an aristocratically hyphenated one as well.

11   The matter of the name being settled, we set about the job of launching her. It was not an easy task, but finally the *Bootle-Bumtrinket* bobbed steadily and confidently in the water.

12   "Now!" said Leslie, organizing things. "Let's get the mast in . . . Margo, you hold

her nose . . . that's it . . . Now, Peter, if you'll get into the stern, Larry and I will hand you the mast . . . all you have to do is stick it in that socket."

13   So, while Margo lay on her tummy holding the nose of the boat, Peter leapt nimbly into the stern and settled himself, with legs apart, to receive the mast which Larry and Leslie were holding.

14   "This mast looks a bit long to me, Les," said Larry, eyeing it critically.

"Nonsense! It'll be fine when it's in," retorted Leslie. "Now . . . are you ready, Peter?"

15   Peter nodded, braced himself, held the mast firmly in both hands, and plunged it into the hole. Then he stood back, dusted his hands, and the *Bootle-Bumtrinket*, with a speed remarkable for a craft of her size, turned turtle. Peter, clad in his one decent suit which he had put on in honour of my birthday, disappeared with scarcely a splash. All that remained on the surface of the water was his hat, the mast, and the *Bootle-Bumtrinket's* bright orange bottom.

16   "He'll drown! He'll drown!" screamed Margo, who always tended to look on the dark side of a crisis.

"Nonsense! It's not deep enough," said Leslie.

"I told you that mast was too long," said Larry.

"It *isn't* too long," Leslie snapped irritably; "that fool didn't set it right."

"Don't you dare call him a fool," said Margo.

"You can't fit a twenty-foot mast on to a thing like a washtub and expect it to keep upright," said Larry.

17   "If you're so damn clever why didn't *you* make the boat?"

"I wasn't asked to . . . Besides, you're supposed to be the expert, though I doubt if they'd employ you on Clydeside."

"Very funny. It's easy enough to criticize . . . just because that fool . . . "

"Don't call him a fool . . . How dare you?"

"Now, now, don't argue about it, dears," said Mother peaceably.

"Well, Larry's so damn patronizing . . . "

"Thank God! He's come up," said Margo in fervent tones as the bedraggled and sputtering Peter rose to the surface.

18   We hauled him out, and Margo hurried him up to the house to try to get his suit dry before the party. The rest of us followed, still arguing. Leslie, incensed at Larry's criticism, changed into trunks and, armed with a large manual on boat construction and a tape measure, went down to salvage the boat. For the rest of the morning he kept sawing bits off the mast until she eventually floated upright, but by then the mast was only about three feet high. Leslie was very puzzled, but he promised to fit a new mast as soon as he'd worked out the correct measurements. So the *Bootle-Bumtrinket*, tied to the end of the dock, floated there in all her glory, looking like a very vivid, overweight Manx cat.

COMPREHENSION

Answer the following questions. Your teacher may want you to answer the questions orally, in writing, or by underlining appropriate parts of the text. True/False items are indicated by a T/F preceding a statement. In many cases you will have to use your own judgment, because the answer is not specifically given.

1. Why did the author want a boat? _____
   _____

2. What is the *Sea Cow*? _____

3. Based on the gift lists the author prepared, what do you know about Mother, Margo, and
   Larry? _____
   _____
   _____

4. T / F   Leslie is older than the author.

5. T / F   Leslie tried to convince the author that building a boat was too difficult.

6. T / F   The author tricked Leslie into building a boat.

7. Write a synonym, definition, or description of *adamant* (paragraph 7). _____
   _____

8. T / F   Leslie said he would build the boat only if the author promised to help.

9. T / F   Leslie had no problems building the boat.

10. T / F   Leslie intended from the beginning to make the boat circular.

11. What did the author like best about the boat? _____
    _____

12. Write a synonym, definition, or description of *launch* (bottom, paragraph 10). _____
    _____

13. T / F   Leslie said that a boat could not be launched until it was given a name.

14. T / F   Peter was a close friend of Leslie.

15. What happened after Peter plunged the mast into the hole? What is the meaning of *to turn
    turtle*? _____
    _____

(Continued on page 72.)

16. T / F   Only Margo acted to save Peter.

17. T / F   Peter did not drown because he was a good swimmer.

18. T / F   *Bootle-Bumtrinket* turned turtle because Peter did not fix the mast properly.

19. Judging from Larry's remarks to Leslie (paragraph 17), what do you think Clydeside is?
_____

20. Write a synonym, definition, or description of *incensed* (paragraph 18). _____
_____

21. A Manx cat has a very short tail. Why does the author refer to *Bootle-Bumtrinket* as a "vivid, overweight Manx cat" (paragraph 18)? _____
_____

VOCABULARY FROM CONTEXT

This exercise should be done after you have finished reading "Bootle-Bumtrinket." The exercise is designed to give you additional clues to determine the meanings of unfamiliar vocabulary items in context. In the paragraph indicated by the number in parentheses, find the word or phrase that best fits the meaning given. Your teacher may want to read these aloud as you quickly scan the paragraph to find the answer.

1. (1)   Which word in sentence 1 means *felt great pain; suffered*?

2. (1)   Which word in sentence 1 means *a group of (small) islands*?

3. (2)   Which word in the next-to-the-last sentence means *to approach; to begin to do something difficult*?

4. (8)   Which word means *cursing; swearing; use of bad or unacceptable language in anger or frustration*?

5. (18) Which word means *to save; to recover*?

NONPROSE READING: Questionnaire

This questionnaire* requires following the same kind of directions you will encounter when applying for insurance or a visa, or in dealing with some government agencies. The directions on such forms are often complicated and difficult to understand. This exercise is designed to give you practice in following directions and providing information required by a questionnaire.†

The Odds for Long Life

This questionnaire came from Robert Collins, coordinator for health education in the Bellevue, Washington, Public Schools, who has used it to encourage class discussion of life expectancy. We thought we'd use it to stimulate personal thinking. on that subject among our readers. We hope you'll get a pencil and fill in the blanks.

But beware. The figures are unscientific and extremely imprecise—merely indicators of *some* characteristics and practices that may contribute to long life. Furthermore, the predictions here are based on the "average" person. They will predict for any one of us only in terms of very rough odds. As a result, if you are past middle age you may find that the "prediction" for you is death several years ago.

1) **Year of Birth**
   Find the period which includes your year of birth, then write your basic life expectancy in the space provided.

Period	Men	Women
1880-1900	35-40	37-42
1901-1904	46 & 2 mos.	48 & 8 mos.
1905-1908	48 & 8	51 & 5
1909-1912	50 & 7	54 & 4
1913-1916	51 & 8	55 & 5
1917-1920	52 & 6	56 & 5
1921-1924	58 & 2	61 & 2
1925-1928	58 & 5	61 & 10
1929-1932	58 & 10	63 & 2
1933-1936	60 & 6	65 & 5
1937-1940	62	66
1941-1944	64 & 6	68
1945-1948	65	70 & 4
1949-1952	65 & 11	71 & 6
1953-1956	67	74
1957-1961	67 & 6	74 & 2
1962-	67 & 8	74 & 4

Write down your basic life expectancy. . . . . years . . . . months

(*Continued on page 74.*)

---

*Adapted from "The Odds for Long Life" by Robert Collins. Copyright © 1973 by *Harper's* Magazine. Reprinted from the May 1973 issue by special permission.
†For an explanation of nonprose reading, see Unit 1.

2) **Present Age**

Age		Add		Age	Add		Age	Add	
1-4	yrs.	1	yr.	31-35	3	yrs.	61-65	8	yrs.
5-10		2	yrs.	36-40	3½		66-70	9½	
11-15		2		41-45	4		71-75	11½	
16-20		2		46-50	4½		76-80	12	
21-25		2½		51-55	5½		81-85	6½	
26-30		3		56-60	6½		85 plus	4½	

New total .... years .... months

3) **Family History**

Add 1 year for each 5-year period your father has lived past 70. Do the same for your mother.

New total .... years .... months

4) **Marital Status**

If you are married, add 5 years.
If you are over 25 and not married, deduct 1 year for every unwedded decade.

New total .... years.... months

5) **Where you live**

Small town—add 3-5 years.
City—subtract 2 years.

New total .... years .... months

6) **Economic Status**

If wealthy or poor for greater part of life, deduct 3 years.

New total .... years .... months

7) **Your Shape**

If you are over 40, deduct 1 year for every 5 lbs. you are overweight. For each inch your stomach measurement exceeds your chest measurement, deduct 2 years.

New total .... years.... months

8) **Exercise**

Regular and moderate add 3 years; regular and vigorous, add 5 years.

New total .... years .... months

9) **Disposition**

Good-natured and placid add 1-5 years. Tense and nervous subtract 1-5 years.

New total .... years .... months

10) **Alcohol**

Heavy drinker—subtract 5 years. Very heavy drinker—subtract 10 years.

New total .... years .... months

11) **Smoking**

1/2 to 1 pack per day	subtract 3 years
1 to 1 1/2 packs per day	subtract 5 years
1 1/2 to 2 packs per day	subtract 10 years
Pipe or cigar	subtract 2 years

New total .... years .... months

12) **Family Environment**

Regular medical checkups and regular dental care add 3 years.
Frequently ill subtract 2 years.

Final total .... years .... months

DISCUSSION

1. Why would marital status be a factor in life expectancy?

2. The questionnaire implies that living in a small town is healthier than living in a city. Do you agree? Why or why not?

3. Three years must be deducted from your life expectancy if you have been either wealthy or poor for a long period of time. How do you explain this?

4. The questionnaire implies that your personality affects your life expectancy. How do you explain this?

5. The basic life expectancy chart gives different life expectancies for men and women. Why is this? In your society is there a difference in life expectancy for the two sexes?

6. What are the credentials and qualifications of Mr. Collins, the author of the questionnaire? On what does he base his facts and figures?

WORD STUDY: Context Clues

In the following exercise, do NOT try to learn the italicized words. Concentrate on developing your ability to guess the meaning of unfamiliar words using context clues. Read each sentence carefully, and write a definition, synonym, or description of the italicized word on the line provided.

1. _____   The major points of your plan are clear to me, but the details are still *hazy*.

2. _____   By *anticipating* the thief's next move, the police were able to arrive at the bank before the robbery occurred.

3. _____   All of the palace's laundry, when gathered for washing, formed a *massive* bundle which required the combined efforts of all the servants to carry.

4. _____   "Give me specific suggestions when you criticize my work," said the employee. "*Vague* comments do not help me improve."

5. _____   The apple *appeased* my hunger temporarily, but I could still eat a big dinner.

6. _____   After the attacks on civilians by army troops, a committee met to try to discover what could have *provoked* such action.

7. _____   The king *manifested* his pleasure with a hearty laugh.

8. _____   The nation's highway death *toll* has increased every year since the invention of the automobile.

9. _____   The workers' lives were *wretched*; they worked from morning to night in all kinds of weather, earning only enough money to buy their simple food and cheap clothes.

10. _____   In a series of bold moves, government attorneys attacked the *mammoth* auto industry, saying that the size of the business endangered the financial freedom of the individual buyer.

WORD STUDY: Stems and Affixes

Below is a list of some commonly occurring stems and affixes.* Study their meanings then do the exercises which follow. Your teacher may ask you to give examples of words which are derived from these stems and affixes.

Prefixes:

bicycle	a-, an-	no, without, lacking
	bene-	well
	bi-	two *bigamy*
mistake	mis-	wrong, unfavorable
monopoly	mono-	one, alone *monogamy*
Polygamy	poly-	many
Synonim	syn-, sym-, syl-	with, together

Stems:

anthropology · *pathos* · *filling*

-anthro-, -anthropo-	man
-arch-	first, chief
-fact-, -fect-	make, do
-gam-	marriage
-hetero-	different, other
-homo-	same
-man-, -manu-	hand
-morph-	form
-onym-, -nomen-	name
-pathy-	feeling, suffering
-theo-, -the-	god

Suffixes:

	-ic, -al	relating to, having the nature of
catholisism	-ism, -ist	action or practice, state or condition
	-oid	like, resembling

misanthropist → Somebody who hate people.
Bible → (baibol)

---

*For a list of all stems and affixes taught in *Reader's Choice*, see Appendix.

Exercise 1
In each item, select the best definition of the italicized word or phrase.

1. The small country was ruled by a *monarch* for 500 years.

monarchy

____X____ a. king or queen _____ c. group of the oldest citizens
_____ b. single family _____ d. group of the richest citizens

2. He was interested in *anthropology*.

_____ a. the study of apes _____ c. the study of royalty
_____ b. the study of insects ___X___ d. the study of man

3. Some citizens say the election of William Blazer will lead to *anarchy*.

_____ a. a strong central government ___X___ c. the absence of a controlling government

_____ b. a government controlled by one man _____ d. an old-fashioned, out-dated government

4. If a man is a *bigamist*, he

___X___ a. is married to two women. _____ c. has two children.
_____ b. is divorced. _____ d. will never marry.

5. Which of the following pairs of words are *homonyms*?

same name

_____ a. good   bad _____ c. lie   die
_____ b. Paul   Peter ___X___ d. two   too

6. Which of the following pairs of words are *antonyms*?

_____ a. sea   see _____ c. read   read
_____ b. wet   dry _____ d. Jim   Susan

7. The reviewer criticized the poet's *amorphous* style.

without form

_____ a. unimaginative _____ c. stiff, too ordered
_____ b. unusual _____ d. lacking in organization and form

8. Dan says he is an *atheist*.

without form

_____ a. one who believes in one god _____ c. one who believes in many gods
___X___ b. one who believes there is no god _____ d. one who is not sure if there is a god

9. There was a great *antipathy* between the brothers.

_____ a. love _____ c. dislike
_____ b. difference _____ d. resemblance

10. How are the meanings of *manufacture* and *manuscript* different from the meanings of the stems from which they are derived? Use your dictionary if necessary.

_____

_____

Exercise 2
Following is a list of words containing some of the stems and affixes introduced in this unit and previous ones. Definitions of these words appear on the right. Put the letter of the appropriate definitions next to each word.

1. _____ manual
2. _____ manicure
3. _____ polygamy
4. _____ benediction
5. _____ benefactor
6. _____ monogamy

a. the practice or condition of having many or several marriage partners
b. professional care of the hands and fingernails
c. one who performs good deeds
d. the act of saying a blessing
e. the practice or condition of having one marriage partner
f. of or pertaining to the hands; done by the hand or hands

7. _____ anthropomorphous
8. _____ heteromorphic
9. _____ anthropometry
10. _____ misnomer
11. _____ heterochromatic
12. _____ synchronous

a. having or resembling the human form
b. occurring at the same time
c. of, having, or pertaining to more than one color
d. the measurement of the size and proportions of the human body
e. dissimilar in shape, structure, or magnitude
f. a wrongly applied name or designation; an error in naming a person or thing

13. _____ monochromatic
14. _____ polychrome
15. _____ monotheism
16. _____ polytheism
17. _____ anonymous
18. _____ theology

a. the belief that there is only one god
b. pertaining to one color or one wave length only
c. the belief in more than one god
d. the science or study of divine things or religious truths
e. being of many or various colors
f. giving no name; of unknown authorship

19. _____ archenemy
20. _____ archetype
21. _____ sympathy
22. _____ pathetic
23. _____ anthropoid
24. _____ synonym

a. agreement in feeling between persons
b. a chief opponent
c. the original model or form after which a thing is made
d. resembling man
e. causing pity; affecting the feelings
f. a word having the same, or nearly the same, meaning as another in the language

SENTENCE STUDY: Comprehension

Read the following sentences carefully.* The questions which follow are designed to test your comprehension of complex grammatical structures. Select the *best* answer.

1. My discovery of Tillie Olsen was a gift from a friend; years ago she gave me her copy of *Tell Me A Riddle*, because she liked the stories and wanted to share the experience.

    What do we know about Tillie Olsen?

    _____ a. She is a friend.

    _____ b. She likes stories.

    _____ c. She gives gifts.

    _____ d. She is an author.

2. A few government officials even estimate that the war has created more than half a million refugees who need immediate food, clothing, and shelter.

    Exactly how many refugees are there?

    _____ a. half a million

    _____ b. over half a million

    _____ c. We don't know exactly.

    _____ d. Only a few government officials know the exact figure.

3. The Green Tiger Press believes that the relatively unknown works of great children's illustrators are sources of vast beauty and power, and is attempting to make these treasures more easily available.

    What is the goal of this printing company?

    _____ a. to publish more children's books

    _____ b. to develop powerful stories

    _____ c. to make children's illustrations more easily available

    _____ d. to encourage artists to become children's illustrators

4. Although he calls the $1,000 donation "a very generous amount, especially in these times," the president expresses hope that the project will attract additional funds from companies and other sources so that it can continue beyond this first year.

    What does the president know about the project?

    _____ a. It will cost only $1,000.

    _____ b. It is very special.

    _____ c. Special sources will support it.

    _____ d. It cannot continue without additional funding.

5. Any thought that this new custom will remain unchanged—or in Europe will remain uniquely English—is ridiculous.

    What does the author believe about the new custom?

    _____ a. It will remain limited.

    _____ b. The custom will change.

    _____ c. Acceptance of the custom is ridiculous.

    _____ d. The custom will remain in Europe.

---

*For an introduction to sentence study, see Unit 1.

6. These robust and persistent sailors gathered from all the nations of western Europe, and set out on the voyages that laid foundations for four great empires with no other power than sail and oar.

 Why were these voyages important?

 _____ a. Sailors came from many countries in Europe.

 _____ b. The voyages laid the foundations for western Europe.

 _____ c. The foundations for empires were established.

 _____ d. Western Europe lost its power.

7. Young people need to develop the values, attitudes, and problem-solving skills essential to their participation in a political system which was designed, and is still based, on the assumption that all citizens would be so prepared.

 What is a basic assumption of this political system?

 _____ a. All people will be capable of participation.

 _____ b. All people participate in the system.

 _____ c. All people should have the same values and attitudes.

 _____ d. Most people cannot develop the skills to participate in the system.

8. While we may be interested in the possibilities of social harmony and individual fulfillment to be achieved through nontraditional education, one cannot help being cautious about accepting any sort of one-sided educational program as a cure for the world's ills.

 How does the author feel about nontraditional education?

 _____ a. He believes that it has no possibility of success.

 _____ b. He doubts that it can cure the world's ills.

 _____ c. He feels that it is a cure for the world's ills.

 _____ d. He believes it will bring social harmony.

9. The complexity of the human situation and the injustice of the social order demand far more fundamental changes in the basic structure of society itself than some politicians are willing to admit in their speeches.

 What is necessary to correct the problems of society?

 _____ a. basic changes in its structure

 _____ b. fewer political speeches

 _____ c. honest politicians

 _____ d. basic changes in political methods.

PARAGRAPH READING: Restatement and Inference

Each paragraph below is followed by five statements. The statements are of four types:
1. Some of the statements are *restatements* of ideas in the original paragraph. They give the same information in a different way.
2. Some of the statements are *inferences* (conclusions) which can be drawn from the information given in the paragraph.
3. Some of the statements are not true based on the information given.
4. Some of the statements cannot be judged true or false based on the information given in the original paragraph.

Put a check (✓) next to all restatements and inferences (types 1 and 2). Note: do not check a statement which is true of itself but cannot be inferred from the paragraph.

Example:

Often people who hold higher positions in a given group overestimate their performance, while people in the lowest levels of the group underestimate theirs. While this may not always be true, it does indicate that often the actual position in the group has much to do with the feeling of personal confidence a person may have. Thus, if a member holds a high position in a group or if he feels that he has an important part to play in the group, he will probably have more confidence in his own performance.

_____ a. If a person has confidence in his own performance, he will achieve a high position in a group.

_____ b. If we let someone know he is an important part of a group, he will probably become more self-confident.

_____ c. People who hold low positions in a group often overestimate their performance.

_____ d. People in positions of power in a group may feel they do better work than they really do.

_____ e. People with higher positions in a group do better work than other group members.

Explanation:

_____ a. This cannot be inferred from the paragraph. We know that people who hold high positions have more self-confidence than those who don't. However, we don't know that people with more confidence will achieve higher status. Confidence may come only *after* one achieves a higher position.

✓ b. This is an inference which can be drawn from the last sentence in the paragraph. We know that if someone feels he has an important part to play in a group, he will probably have more self-confidence. We can infer that if we let someone know (and therefore make him feel) that he has an important part to play, he will probably become more self-confident.

_____ c. This is false. The first sentence states that the people in the lowest levels of a group underestimate, not overestimate, their performance.

✓ d. This is a restatement of the first sentence. People who hold higher positions tend to overestimate their performance: they may feel they do better work than they really do.

_____ e. We do not know this from the paragraph. We know that people who hold higher positions often *think* they do better work than others in a group. (They "overestimate their performance.") We do not know that they actually do better work.

Paragraph 1

Like any theory of importance, that of social or cultural anthropology was the work of many minds and took on many forms. Some, the best known of its proponents, worked on broad areas and attempted to describe and account for the development of human civilization in its totality. Others restricted their efforts to specific aspects of the culture, taking up the evolution of art, or the state, or religion.

_____ a. Social anthropology concerns itself with broad areas while cultural anthropology concerns itself with specific aspects of culture.

_____ b. Cultural anthropologists, also known as social anthropologists, may work in either broad or restricted areas.

_____ c. Cultural anthropology is a new field of study.

_____ d. Any important area of study requires the work of many minds and is therefore likely to have different approaches.

_____ e. The best known people in cultural anthropology attempted to describe the development of human civilization.

Paragraph 2

I saw by the clock of the city jail that it was past eleven, so I decided to go to the newspaper immediately. Outside the editor's door I stopped to make sure my pages were in the right order; I smoothed them out carefully, stuck them back in my pocket, and knocked. I could hear my heart thumping as I walked in.

_____ a. The teller of this story has just left the city jail.

_____ b. He has been carrying his papers in his pocket.

_____ c. We know that the storyteller is a newspaper writer by profession.

_____ d. We might infer that the storyteller is going to show his papers to the editor.

_____ e. The meeting is important for the storyteller.

Paragraph 3

In recent years there have been many reports of a growing impatience with psychiatry, with its seeming foreverness, its high cost, its debatable results, and its vague, esoteric terms. To many people it is like a blind man in a dark room looking for a black cat that isn't there. The magazines and mental health associations say psychiatric treatment is a good thing, but what it is or what it accomplishes has not been made clear.

_____ a. Even mental health associations haven't been able to demonstrate the value of psychiatry.

_____ b. The author believes that psychiatry is of no value.

_____ c. People are beginning to doubt the value of psychiatry.

_____ d. In recent years psychiatry has begun to serve the needs of blind people.

_____ e. Only magazines and mental health associations believe that psychiatry is a good thing.

Paragraph 4

The Incas had never acquired the art of writing, but they had developed a complicated system of knotted cords called *quipus*. These were made of the wool of the alpaca or llama, dyed in various colors, the significance of which was known to the officials. The cords were knotted in such a way as to represent the decimal system. Thus an important message relating to the progress of crops, the amount of taxes collected, or the advance of an enemy could be speedily sent by trained runners along the post roads.

_____ a. Because they could not write, the Incas are considered a simplistic, poorly developed society.

_____ b. Through a system of knotted cords, the Incas sent important messages from one community to another.

_____ c. Because runners were sent with the cords, we can safely assume that the Incas did not have domesticated animals.

_____ d. Both the color of the cords and the way they were knotted formed part of the message of the *quipus*.

_____ e. The *quipus* were used for important messages.

Paragraph 5

There was a time when scholars held that early man lived in a kind of beneficent anarchy, in which each person was granted his rights by his fellows and there was no governing or being governed. Various early writers looked back to this Golden Age but the point of view that man was originally a *child of nature* is best known to us in the writings of Rousseau, Locke, and Hobbes. These men described the concept of *social contract*, which they said had put an end to the *state of nature* in which earliest man is supposed to have lived.

_____ a. For Rousseau, Locke, and Hobbes, the concept of *social contract* put an end to the time of beneficent anarchy in which early man lived.

_____ b. According to the author scholars today do not hold that early man lived in a state of anarchy.

_____ c. Only Rousseau, Locke, and Hobbes wrote about early man as a *child of nature*.

_____ d. The early writers referred to in this passage lived through the Golden Age of early man.

_____ e. We can infer that the author of this passage feels that concepts of government have always been present in human history.

READING SELECTION 1: Magazine Article

A high school teacher in Oregon has developed an unusual course for helping young people make intelligent decisions about marriage. Read the following article to see how you feel about Mr. Allen's "Conjugal Prep." Then answer the Comprehension questions. You may want to do the Vocabulary from Context exercise on page 88 before you begin reading.

Conjugal Prep

1) The bridegroom, dressed in a blue blazer and brown suede Adidas sneakers, nervously cleared his throat when his bride, in traditional white, walked down the classroom aisle. As the mock minister led the students—and ten other couples in the room—through the familiar marriage ceremony, the giggles almost drowned him out. But it was no laughing matter. In the next semester, each "couple" would buy a house, have a baby—and get a divorce.

2) In a most unusual course at Parkrose (Ore.) Senior High School, social-science teacher Cliff Allen leads his students through the trials and tribulations [trouble] of married life. Instead of the traditional course, which dwells on the psychological and sexual adjustments young marrieds must face, Allen exposes his students to the nitty-gritty problems of housing, insurance and child care. "No one tells kids about financial problems," says Allen, 36. "It's like sex—you don't talk about it in front of them."

3) Students act out in nine weeks what normally takes couples ten years to accomplish. In the first week, one member of each couple is required to get an after-school job—a real one. During the semester, the salary, computed on a full-time basis with yearly increases factored in, serves as the guideline for their lifestyle. The third week, the couples must locate an apartment they can afford and study the terms of the lease. [contract for rent]

4) **Disaster:** In the fifth week, the couples "have a baby" and then compute the cost by totaling hospital and doctor bills, prenatal and postnatal care, baby clothes and furniture. In week eight, disaster strikes: the marriages are strained to the breaking point by such calamities as a mother-in-law's moving in, death, or imprisonment. It's all over by week nine (the tenth year of marriage). After lectures by marriage counselors and divorce lawyers and computations of alimony [payment] and child support, the students get divorced.

5) Allen's course, which has "married" 1,200 students since its inception five years ago, is widely endorsed by parents and students. Some of the participants have found the experience chastening to their real-life marital plans. "Bride" Valerie Payne, 16, and her "groom," David Cooper, 19, still plan to marry in July, but, said Cooper, the course pointed out "the troubles you can have." The course was more unsettling to Marianne Baldrica, 17, who tried "marriage" last term with her boyfriend Eric Zook, 18. "Eric and I used to get along pretty well before we took the course together," Marianne said. "But I wanted to live in the city, he wanted the country. He wanted lots of kids, I wanted no kids. It's been four weeks since the course ended and Eric and I are just starting to talk to each other again."

—LINDA BIRD FRANCKE with MARY ALICE KELLOGG in Parkrose, Ore.

James D. Wilson—Newsweek

Classroom couple: Nine weeks to divorce

June 2, 1975

COMPREHENSION

Answer the following questions. Your teacher may want you to answer the questions orally, in writing, or by underlining appropriate parts of the text. True/False items are indicated by a T/F preceding the statement.

1. T / F   The course taught by Cliff Allen requires students to marry, buy a house, and get a divorce.

2. T / F   Allen believes that traditional courses do not adequately prepare young people for married life.

3. What are the nitty-gritty problems which Allen's students must face during the course?
   Housing, unusug and child care.
   _____

4. T / F   One member of a "newlywed couple" must get a job.

5. How long does the course last? _9 weeks_ How long are the couples "married"? _10 years._
   _____

6. What are some of the events of married life that the students "experience"? _They_
   have a baby _____

7. What are examples of the disasters which strike couples in the 8th week of the course? _____
   death, imprisonment _____
   _____

8. How has the course affected the marriage plans of some of the students? _____
   _____

9. Do you think young people in your country should be required to take such a course? _____

10. How do the customs and values of the United States (as revealed in this article) compare with customs and values in your country with respect to the following areas:

    a. age at which people marry
    b. role of the school in preparing young people for marriage
    c. amount of individual freedom in choosing marriage partners
    d. "crises" likely to be faced by married couples

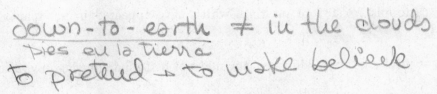

down-to-earth ≠ in the clouds
pies eu la tierra
to pretend → to make believe

VOCABULARY FROM CONTEXT

Both the ideas and the vocabulary from the passage below are taken from "Conjugal Prep." Use the context provided to determine the meanings of the italicized words. Write a definition, synonym, or description of each of the italicized vocabulary items in the space provided.

1. _____

2. _____

3. _____

4. _____

5. _____

6. _____

7. _____

8. _____

9. _____

10. _____

11. _____

In Mr. Allen's high school class, all the students have to "get married." However, the wedding ceremonies are not real ones but imitations. These *mock* ceremonies sometimes become so noisy that the loud laughter *drowns out* the voice of the "minister." Even the two students getting married often begin to *giggle*.

The teacher, Mr. Allen, believes that marriage is a difficult and serious business. He wants young people to understand that there are many changes that must take place after marriage. He believes that the need for these psychological and financial *adjustments* should be understood before people marry.

Mr. Allen doesn't only introduce his students to major problems faced in marriage such as illness or unemployment. He also *exposes* them to the *nitty-gritty* problems they will face every day. He wants to introduce young people to all the *trials and tribulations* that can *strain* a marriage to the breaking point. He even familiarizes his students with the problems of divorce and the fact that divorced men must pay child support money for their children and sometimes pay monthly *alimony* to their wives.

It has been *unsettling* for some of the students to see the problems that a married couple often faces. Until they took the course, they had not worried much about the problems of marriage. However, both students and parents feel that Mr. Allen's course is valuable and have *endorsed* the course publicly. Their statements and letters supporting the class have convinced the school to offer the course again.

CARTOONISTS LOOK AT MARRIAGE

On page 89 are some cartoonists' views of marriage which have appeared in newspapers in the United States.

Which cartoons do you find amusing? Which ones would not be found amusing in your culture?

Do any of these cartoons illustrate problems for which Allen's course attempts to prepare young people?

Are there situations presented here which reveal universal problems presented by marriage?

1. LAFF - A - DAY

"I can't help with your divorce expenses until I finish paying for your wedding!"

2. THE LOCKHORNS

"OF COURSE YOU'RE ALL I THINK ABOUT. THAT'S WHY I'M ALWAYS SO MISERABLE."

3. THE LOCKHORNS

"YOU FORGOT TO SET OUT STEAK KNIVES FOR THE MASHED POTATOS."

4. TRUDY

"Set the alarm clock a half an hour earlier — I want to finish our argument before you go to work."

5. THE LOCKHORNS

"I RAN INTO YOUR OLD BOYFRIEND CHARLIE WERNER TODAY. HE COULDN'T THANK ME ENOUGH FOR STEALING YOU AWAY FROM HIM."

6. TRUDY

"That's right, save your strength, Ted, you've got the long walk upstairs to bed in about an hour!"

READING SELECTION 2: Narrative

Would you consider a family unusual if:
- all the shopping was done by the children in committees?
- phonographs played constantly in the bathrooms so that everyone could learn foreign languages as they brushed their teeth?
- the mother was a psychologist who became as famous as her engineer husband in the field of scientific management?

All of these statements—and many more just as unusual—apply to the family of John and Lillian Gilbreth. These two remarkable people raised a family in the first quarter of the twentieth century, at a time when the United States was rapidly industrializing, and when large families were becoming less common. Through their research into scientific management, the Gilbreths showed many large companies how to increase profits by saving time and labor. They believed that the principles of good industrial management could also apply to the management of families, and they set out to prove it with their twelve children.

The following selection is taken from *Cheaper by the Dozen*, a book written by two of the Gilbreth children.* Read the passage quickly to appreciate the humor, then do the exercises which follow. You may want to do Vocabulary from Context exercise 1 on page 97 and the Dictionary Study exercise on page 99 before you begin reading.

Adaptation from
Cheaper by the Dozen

1   It was an off year that didn't bring a new Gilbreth baby. Both Dad and Mother wanted a large family. And if it was Dad who set the actual goal of an even dozen, Mother as readily agreed.

Dad mentioned the dozen figure for the first time on their wedding day.

"We're going to have a wonderful life, Lillie. A wonderful life and a wonderful family. A great big family."

"We'll have children all over the house," Mother smiled. "From the basement to the attic."

"From the floorboards to the chandelier."

"How many would you say we should have, just an estimate?" Mother asked.

"Just as an estimate, many."

"Lots and lots."

2   "We'll settle for an even dozen," said Dad. "No less. What do you say to that?"

"I say," said Mother, "a dozen would be just right. No less."

"That's the minimum."

"Boys or girls?"

"Well, boys would be fine," Dad whispered. "A dozen boys would be just right. But . . . well, girls would be all right too. Sure. I guess."

3   "I'd like to have half boys and half girls. Do you think it would be all right to have half girls?"

"If that's what you want," Dad said, "we'll plan it that way. Excuse me a minute while I make a note of it." He took out his memorandum book and solemnly wrote: "Don't forget to have six boys and six girls."

They had a dozen children, six boys and six girls, in seventeen years. Somewhat to Dad's disappointment, there were no twins or other multiple births. There was no

---

*Adapted from *Cheaper by the Dozen* by Frank B. Gilbreth, Jr., and Ernestine Gilbreth Carey, copyright © 1963, 1948. Reprinted by permission of Thomas Y. Crowell Company, Inc., publisher.

doubt in his mind that the most efficient way to raise a large family would be to have one huge litter and get the whole business over with at one time.

4   One reason Dad had so many children was that he was convinced anything he and Mother teamed up on was sure to be a success.

Dad always practiced what he preached, and it was just about impossible to tell where his scientific management company ended and his family life began.

Our house at Montclair, New Jersey, was a sort of school for scientific management and the elimination of wasted motions—or "motion study," as Dad and Mother named it.

5   Dad took moving pictures of us children washing dishes, so that he could determine how we could reduce our motions and thus hurry through the task. Irregular jobs, such as painting the back porch or removing a tree stump from the front lawn, were awarded on a low-bid basis. Each child who wanted extra pocket money submitted an offer saying what he would do the job for. The lowest bidder got the contract.

6   Dad put process and work charts in the bathrooms. Every child old enough to write—and Dad expected his offspring to start writing at a tender age—was required to initial the charts in the morning after he had brushed his teeth, taken a bath, combed his hair, and made his bed. At night, each child had to weigh himself, plot the figure on a graph, and initial the process charts again after he had done his homework, washed his hands and face, and brushed his teeth. Mother wanted to have a place on the charts for saying prayers, but Dad said as far as he was concerned prayers were voluntary.

7   It was regimentation, all right. But bear in mind the trouble most parents have in getting just one child off to school, and multiply it by twelve. Some regimentation was necessary to prevent bedlam.

8   Yes, at home or on the job, Dad was always the efficiency expert. He buttoned his vest from the bottom up, instead of from the top down, because the bottom-to-top process took him only three seconds, while the top-to-bottom took seven. He even used two shaving brushes to lather his face, because he found that by so doing he could cut seventeen seconds off his shaving time. For a while he tried shaving with two razors, but he finally gave that up.

9   "I can save forty-four seconds," he grumbled, "but I wasted two minutes this morning putting this bandage on my throat."

It wasn't the slashed throat that really bothered him. It was the two minutes.

10   Mother the psychologist and Dad the motion study man and general contractor decided to look into the new field of the psychology of management, and the old field of psychologically managing a houseful of children. They believed that what would work in the home would work in the factory, and what would work in the factory would work in the home.

Dad put the theory to a test shortly after we moved to Montclair. The house was too big for Tom Grieves, the handyman, and Mrs. Cunningham, the cook, to keep in order. Dad decided we were going to have to help them, and he wanted us to offer the help willingly. He had found that the best way to get cooperation out of employees in a factory was to set up a joint employer-employee board, which would make work assignments on a basis of personal choice and aptitude. He and Mother set up a Family Council, patterned after an employer-employee board. The Council met every Sunday afternoon, immediately after dinner.

11   Like most of Dad's and Mother's ideas, the Family Council was basically a good one and, although it verged sometimes on the hysterical, brought results. Family purchasing committees, duly elected, bought the food, clothes, furniture, and ath-

letic equipment. A utilities committee levied one-cent fines on wasters of water and electricity. A projects committee saw that work was completed as scheduled. The amount of money the children were to receive for allowances was decided by the Council, which also determined appropriate rewards and punishments.

12   One purchasing committee found a large department store which gave us wholesale rates on everything from underwear to baseball gloves. Another bought canned goods directly from a manufacturer, in truckload lots.

13   One Sunday, when Dad convened the meeting of the Council, we sat self-consciously around the table, waiting for the right moment. The chairman knew something was in the air, and it tickled him. He had trouble keeping a straight face when he called for new business.

Martha, who had been carefully instructed in private, arose.

"It has come to the attention of the membership," she began, "that the assistant chairman intends to buy a new rug for the dining room. Since the entire membership will be required to look upon, and sit in chairs resting upon, the rug, I move* that the Council be consulted before any rug is purchased."

"Second the motion," said Anne.

Dad didn't know what to make of this one. "Any discussion?" he asked, in a move designed to kill time while he planned his counter attack.

14   "Mr. Chairman," said Lillian. "We have to sweep it. We should be able to choose it."

"We want one with flowers on it," Martha put in. "When you have flowers, the crumbs don't show so easily, and you save motions by not having to sweep so often."

"We want to know what sort of a rug the assistant chairman intends to buy," said Ernestine.

"We want to make sure the budget can afford it," Fred announced.

"I recognize the assistant chairman," said Dad. "This whole Council business was your idea anyway, Lillie. What do we do now?"

15   "Well," Mother said doubtfully, "I had planned to get a plain violet-colored rug, and I had planned to spend a hundred dollars. But if the children think that's too much, and if they want flowers, I'm willing to let the majority rule."

"I move," said Frank, "that not more than ninety-five dollars be spent."

Dad shrugged his shoulders. If Mother didn't care, he certainly didn't.

"So many as favor the motion to spend only ninety-five dollars, signify by saying aye."

The motion carried unanimously.

"Any more new business?"

16   "I move," said Bill, "that we spend the five dollars we have saved to buy a collie puppy."

"Hey, wait a minute," said Dad. The rug had been somewhat of a joke, but the dog question was serious. We had wanted a dog for years. Dad thought that any pet which didn't lay eggs was an extravagance that a man with twelve children could ill afford. He felt that if he surrendered on the dog question, there was no telling what the Council might vote next. He had a sickening mental picture of a barn full of ponies, a car for Anne, motorcycles, a swimming pool, and, ultimately, the poor house or a debtors' prison, if they still had such things.

17   "Second the motion," said Lillian, yanking Dad out of his dreams.

"A dog," said Jack, "would be a pet. Everyone in the family could pat him, and I would be his master."

---

*"I move," "Second the motion," and "I recognize" are phrases taken from parliamentary procedure. They are generally used only in formal meetings in which each person's participation is rigidly controlled.

"A dog," said Dan, "would be a friend. He could eat scraps of food. He would save us waste and would save motions for the garbage man."

"A dog," said Fred, "would keep burglars away. He would sleep on the foot of my bed, and I would wash him whenever he was dirty."

"A dog," Dad mimicked, "would be an accursed nuisance. He would be our master. He would eat me out of house and home. He would spread fleas from the attic to the garage. He would be positive to sleep on the foot of *my* bed. Nobody would wash his filthy, dirty, flea-bitten carcass."

18   He looked pleadingly at Mother.

"Lillie, Lillie, open your eyes," he begged. "Don't you see where this is leading us? Ponies, cars, trips to Hawaii, silk stockings, rouge, and bobbed hair."

"I think, dear," said Mother, "that we must rely on the good sense of the children. A five-dollar dog is not a trip to Hawaii."

We voted; there was only one negative ballot—Dad's. Mother abstained. In after years, as the collie grew older, shed hair on the furniture, bit the mailman, and did in fact try to appropriate the foot of Dad's bed, the chairman was heard to remark on occasion to the assistant chairman:

19   "I give nightly praise to my Maker that I never cast a ballot to bring that lazy, ill-tempered beast into what was once my home. I'm glad I had the courage to go on record as opposing that illegitimate, shameless fleabag that now shares my bed and board. You abstainer, you!"

20   Mother took an active part in church and community work. She didn't teach a class, but she served on a number of committees. Once she called on a woman who had just moved to town, to ask her to serve on a fund-raising committee.

"I'd be glad to if I had the time," the woman said. "But I have three young sons and they keep me on the run. I'm sure if you have a boy of your own, you'll understand how much trouble three can be."

"Of course," said Mother. "That's quite all right. And I do understand."

"Have you any children, Mrs. Gilbreth?"

"Oh, yes."

"Any boys?"

"Yes, indeed."

"May I ask how many?"

"Certainly. I have six boys."

"Six boys!" gulped the woman. "Imagine a family of six!"

"Oh, there're more in the family than that. I have six girls, too."

"I surrender," whispered the newcomer. "When is the next meeting of the committee? I'll be there, Mrs. Gilbreth. I'll be there."

21   One teacher in the Sunday school, a Mrs. Bruce, had the next-to-largest family in Montclair. She had eight children, most of whom were older than we. Her husband was very successful in business, and they lived in a large house about two miles from us. Mother and Mrs. Bruce became great friends.

About a year later, a New York woman connected with some sort of national birth control organization came to Montclair to form a local chapter. Her name was Mrs. Alice Mebane, or something like that. She inquired among her acquaintances as to who in Montclair might by sympathetic to the birth control movement. As a joke, someone referred her to Mrs. Bruce.

"I'd be delighted to cooperate," Mother's friend told Mrs. Mebane, "but you see I have several children myself."

22   "Oh, I had no idea," said Mrs. Mebane. "How many?"

"Several," Mrs. Bruce replied vaguely. "So I don't think I would be the one to head up any birth control movement in Montclair."

"I must say, I'm forced to agree. We should know where we're going, and practice what we preach."

"But I do know just the person for you," Mrs. Bruce continued. "And she has a big house that would be simply ideal for holding meetings."

"Just what we want," purred Mrs. Mebane. "What is her name?"

"Mrs. Frank Gilbreth. She's community-minded, and she's a career woman."

23   "Exactly what we want. Civic minded, career woman, and—most important of all—a large house. One other thing—I suppose it's too much to hope for—but is she by any chance an organizer? You know, one who can take things over and militantly drive ahead?"

"The description," gloated Mrs. Bruce, "fits her like a glove."

"It's almost too good to be true," said Mrs. Mebane, wringing her hands in ecstasy. "May I use your name and tell Mrs. Gilbreth you sent me?"

"By all means," said Mother's friend. "Please do. I shall be disappointed, if you don't."

"And don't think that I disapprove of your having children," laughed Mrs. Mebane. "After all, many people do, you know."

24   "Careless of them," remarked Mrs. Bruce.

The afternoon that Mrs. Mebane arrived at our house, all of us children were, as usual, either upstairs in our rooms or playing in the back yard. Mrs. Mebane introduced herself to Mother.

"It's about birth control," she told Mother.

"What about it?" Mother asked, blushing.

"I was told you'd be interested."

"Me?"

"I've just talked to your friend, Mrs. Bruce, and she was certainly interested."

"Isn't it a little late for her to be interested?" Mother asked.

"I see what you mean, Mrs. Gilbreth. But better late than never, don't you think?"

"But she has eight children," said Mother.

Mrs. Mebane blanched, and clutched her head.

"My God," she said. Not really."

Mother nodded.

25   "How perfectly frightful. She impressed me as quite normal. Not at all like an eight-child woman."

"She's kept her youth well," Mother agreed.

"Ah, there's work to be done, all right," Mrs. Mebane said. "Think of it, living right here within eighteen miles of our national birth control headquarters in New York City, and her having eight children. Yes, there's work to be done, Mrs. Gilbreth, and that's why I'm here."

"What sort of work?"

"We'd like you to be the moving spirit behind a Montclair birth control chapter."

26   Mother decided at this point that the situation was too ludicrous for Dad to miss, and that he'd never forgive her if she didn't deal him in.

"I'll have to ask my husband," she said. "Excuse me while I call him."

Mother stepped out and found Dad. She gave him a brief explanation and then led him into the parlor and introduced him.

27   "It's a pleasure to meet a woman in such a noble cause," said Dad.

"Thank you. And it's a pleasure to find a man who thinks of it as noble. In general, I find the husbands much less sympathetic with our aims than the wives. You'd be surprised at some of the terrible things men have said to me."

"I love surprises," Dad leered. "What do you say back to them?"

"If you had seen, as I have," said Mrs. Mebane, "relatively young women grown old before their time by the arrival of unwanted young ones. And population figures show . . . Why Mr. Gilbreth, what are you doing?"

28   What Dad was doing was whistling assembly. On the first note, feet could be heard pounding on the floors above. Doors slammed, there was a landslide on the stairs, and we started skidding into the parlor.

"Nine seconds," said Dad pocketing his stopwatch. "Three short of the all-time record."

"God's teeth," said Mrs. Mebane. "What is it? Tell me quickly. Is it a school? No. Or is it . . . ? For Lord's sakes. It is!"

"It is what?" asked Dad.

"It's your family. Don't try to deny it. They're the spit and image of you, and your wife, too!"

"I was about to introduce you," said Dad. "Mrs. Mebane, let me introduce you to the family—or most of it. Seems to me like there should be some more of them around here somplace."

29   "God help us all."

"How many head of children do we have now, Lillie, would you say off hand?"

"Last time I counted, seems to me there was an even dozen of them," said Mother. "I might have missed one or two of them, but not many."

"I'd say twelve would be a pretty fair guess," Dad said.

"Shame on you! And within eighteen miles of national headquarters."

30   "Let's have tea," said Mother.

But Mrs. Mebane was putting on her coat. "You poor dear," she clucked to Mother. "You poor child." Then turning to Dad. "It seems to me that the people of this town have pulled my leg on two different occasions today."

"How revolting," said Dad. "And within eighteen miles of national headquarters, too."

COMPREHENSION

Indicate if each statement is true (T) or false (F) according to your understanding of the passage. Use information in the passage and inferences which can be drawn from the passage to make your decisions.

1. _____ Mr. Gilbreth had difficulty convincing his wife to have twelve children.

2. _____ Mr. Gilbreth would have liked to have a family of twelve boys.

3. _____ Mr. Gilbreth made every effort to separate his professional life from his family life.

4. _____ The Gilbreth Company showed other businesses how to save time.

5. _____ At the Gilbreth home, jobs which were performed regularly were studied so that they could be performed without wasted motion.

6. _____ Irregular jobs were assigned to the child who had the necessary amount of knowledge and free time.

7. _____ Each Gilbreth child was expected to perform certain duties before leaving for school.

8. _____ Mr. Gilbreth set up the Family Council to make sure that the household chores would be distributed among the family members.

9. _____ Apparently, the Gilbreth family had been run for a number of years without the Family Council.

10. _____ A cow is the type of pet Mr. Gilbreth would have liked.

11. _____ The Council voted 12 to 2 in favor of getting a dog.

12. _____ Although the Council was set up as a democracy, Mr. Gilbreth had complete control, and would defeat decisions he did not like.

13. _____ The children hoped that they would soon be able to buy ponies and cars.

14. _____ Mr. Gilbreth finally began to like the dog.

15. _____ Because of her large family, Mrs. Gilbreth was not able to participate in community affairs.

16. _____ Birth control organizations are in favor of small families.

17. _____ Mrs. Bruce and Mrs. Gilbreth were recommended to Mrs. Mebane because both women were very active in the community.

18. _____ Mrs. Bruce was correct when she recommended Mrs. Gilbreth as a good organizer.

19. _____ Mr. Gilbreth whistled to assemble the family.

(Continued on page 97.)

20. _____ Mrs. Mebane apparently felt that the closer one got to the national birth control head-quarters, the smaller families should be.

VOCABULARY FROM CONTEXT

Exercise 1
Use the context provided to determine the meanings of the italicized words. Write a definition, synonym, or description of each word in the space provided.

1. _____ Although dogs and cats often have large families, rabbits are famous for the size of their *litters*, which sometimes number more than twelve bunnies at one time.

2. _____ By putting his fingers in his mouth and blowing hard through his teeth and fingers, Mr. Gilbreth produced a loud *whistle*.

3. _____ Richard organized his staff with a rigid schedule of jobs and responsibilities which often occupied them twelve hours a day, seven days a week. Many people, unable to tolerate this *regimentation*, quit their jobs after the first week.

4. _____ In order to discover who had a natural ability to learn languages, the students were given tests to determine their language *aptitude*.

5. _____ His behavior became more and more unusual until, just as his family was on the *verge* of sending him to a mental hospital, he recovered.

6. _____ Mark became *hysterical* when his basketball team won, and he did not calm down for several days.

7. _____ Pets are a *nuisance*; if you have one, you can't go any-where or do anything without making arrangements for them to stay behind or accompany you.

8. _____ That horse won't work without some reward, but it is remarkable how much he can accomplish with a carrot as an *incentive*.

9. _____ Some of the jobs around the house were required, while others were done on a *voluntary* basis.

10. _____ With mud from head to toe, flowers still clutched in his hand, John looked so *ludicrous* that we couldn't help laughing.

97

Exercise 2

This exercise should be done after you have finished reading the selection from *Cheaper by the Dozen*. The exercise is designed to determine how well you have been able to use context clues to guess the meaning of unfamiliar vocabulary in the story. Give a definition, synonym, or description of each of the words below. The number in parentheses indicates the paragraph in which the word can be found. Your teacher may want you to do these orally or in writing.

1. (6) offspring _____

2. (6) tender _____

3. (9) slashed _____

4. (14) sweep _____

5. (17) mimicked _____

6. (18) abstained _____

FIGURATIVE LANGUAGE AND IDIOMS

In the paragraph indicated by the number in parentheses, find the phrase that best fits the meaning given. Your teacher may want to read these aloud as you quickly scan the paragraph to find the answer.

1. (4) What phrase in the second sentence means *do what he says others should do*?

2. (16) What phrase means *impossible to predict*?

3. (17) What phrase means *cost a great deal to support; cost too much to support*?

4. (23) What phrase means *fits exactly; is exactly correct or appropriate*?

5. (26) What phrase in the first sentence means *include him*?

6. (30) What phrase means *played a joke on*?

DICTIONARY STUDY

Many words have more than one meaning. When you use the dictionary to discover the meaning of an unfamiliar word, you need to use the context to determine which definition is appropriate. Use the portions of the dictionary provided on page 100 to select the best definition for each of the italicized words below.

1. "It was an *off* year that didn't bring a new Gilbreth baby."

   _____

2. "Some regimentation was necessary to prevent *bedlam*."

   _____

3. The Family Council determined the amount of the children's *allowances*.

   _____

4. Mr. Gilbreth knew that the children had planned a surprise and it *tickled* him.

   _____

5. He had trouble keeping a *straight face* when he asked for suggestions.

   _____

6. They're all your children. Don't try to deny it. "They're the *spit and image* of you, and your wife, too!"_____

7. "How many head of children do we have now, Lillie, would you say *off hand*?"

   _____

al·low·ance (ə-lou′əns), *n.* 1. an allowing. 2. something allowed. 3. an amount of money, food, etc. given regularly to a child, dependent, soldier, etc. 4. a reduction in the price of something in consideration of a large order or of turning in a used article, etc. 5. the amount by which something is allowed to be more or less than stated, as to compensate for the weight of the container, inaccuracy of machining, etc. *v.t.* [ALLOWANCED (-ənst), ALLOWANCING], 1. to put on an allowance or a ration. 2. to apportion economically.
make allowance (or **allowances**), to take circumstances, limitations, etc. into consideration.
make allowance (or **allowances**) **for,** 1. to forgive or excuse because of mitigating factors. 2. to leave room, time, etc. for; allow for.

bed·lam (bed′ləm), *n.* [ME. *Bedlem, Bethlem* < the London hospital of St. Mary of *Bethlehem*], 1. [B-], a famous old London hospital for the mentally ill. 2. any similar hospital. 3. any noisy, confused place or situation. 4. noise and confusion; uproar. *adj.* full of noise and confusion.

off (ôf), *adv.* [a Late ME. variant spelling of *of*, later generalized for all occurrences of *of* in stressed positions; *off* is thus merely *of* stressed], 1. so as to be away, at a distance, to a side, etc.: as, he moved *off* toward the door. 2. so as to be no longer on, attached, united, in contact, etc.: as, he took *off* his coat, he tore a sheet *off*. 3. (a specified distance) away: *a*) in space: as, the road is 200 yards *off*. *b*) in time: as, my vacation is only two weeks *off*. 4. *a*) so as to be no longer in operation, function, continuance, etc.: as, he turned the motor *off*. *b*) to the point of completion or exhaustion: as, drink it *off*. 5. so as to be less, smaller, fewer, etc.: as, the number of customers dropped *off*. 6. away from one's work or usual activity: as, let's take the week *off*. *prep.* 1. (so as to be) no longer (or not) on, attached, united, etc.: as, it rolled *off* the table, the car is *off* the road. 2. from the substance of; on: as, he lived *off* the fat of the land. 3. coming or branching out from: as, an alley *off* Main Street. 4. free or relieved from: as, *off* duty. 5. not up to the usual level, standard, etc. of: as, badly *off* one's game. 6. [Colloq.], no longer using, engaging in, supporting, etc.; abstaining from: as, he's *off* liquor for life. 7. in *nautical usage*, away from (shore): as, a mile *off* shore. *adj.* 1. not on, attached, united, etc.: as, his hat is *off*. 2. not in operation, function, continuance, etc.: as, the motor is *off*. 3. gone away; on the way: as, the children are *off* to school. 4. less, smaller, fewer, etc.: as, profits are *off* this year. 5. away from work, etc.; absent: as, the office force is *off* today. 6. not up to the usual level, standard, etc.: as, an *off* season. 7. more remote; further: as, on the *off* chance, *off* side. 8. on the right: said of a horse in double harness, etc. 9. in (specified) circumstances: as, they are well *off*. 10. wrong; in error: as, you are *off* in your calculations. 11. in *cricket*, designating the side of the field facing the batsman. 12. in *nautical usage*, toward the sea; seaward. *n.* 1. the fact or condition of being off: as, I've had my *off*s and ons. 2. in *cricket*, the off side. *interj.* go away! stay away! *Off* is also used in various idiomatic expressions, many of which are entered in this dictionary under the key words. Abbreviated **o.**
be (or **take**) **off,** to go away; depart.
off and on, now and then; intermittently.
off with, put off! take off! remove!
off with you! go away! depart!
off., 1. office. 2. officer. 3. official. 4. officinal.
off·cast, off-cast (ôf′kast′, ôf′käst′), *adj.* & *n.* castoff.
off-chance (ôf′chans′, ôf′chäns′), *n.* a slight chance.
off-col·or (ôf′kul′ēr), *adj.* 1. varying from the usual, standard, or required color. 2. not quite proper; in rather poor taste; risqué: as, an *off-color* joke.
off·hand (ôf′hand′), *adv.* without prior preparation or study; at once; extemporaneously. *adj.* 1. said or done offhand; extemporary; unpremeditated; hence, 2. casual, curt, informal, brusque, etc.
off·hand·ed (ôf′han′did), *adj.* offhand.

spit (spit), *n.* [ME. *spite*; AS. *spitu*; akin to OHG. *spizzi*, a point; IE. base *spei-, a point (cf. SPIRE)], 1. a thin, pointed rod or bar on which meat is impaled and held to be broiled or roasted over a fire. 2. a narrow point of land extending into a body of water. 3. a long, narrow reef, shoal, or sandbank extending from the shore. *v.t.* [SPITTED (-id), SPITTING], to thrust a pointed rod through; fix or impale on or as on a spit.

spit (spit), *v.t.* [SPAT (spat) or SPIT, SPITTING], [ME. *spitten*; AS. *spittan*; akin to Dan. *spytte*; IE. echoic base *sp(h)jēu-*, etc., as also in L. *sputum*, Eng. *spew*], 1. to eject from within the mouth. 2. to eject, throw out, emit, or utter explosively: as, the man *spat* an oath. 3. to light (a fuse). *v.i.* 1. to eject saliva from the mouth; expectorate. 2. to rain or snow lightly or briefly. 3. to make an explosive hissing noise, as an angry cat. *n.* 1. the act of spitting. 2. saliva. 3. something like saliva, as the frothy secretion of certain insects. 4. a light, brief shower of rain or fall of snow. 5. [Colloq.], the likeness or counterpart, as of a person.
spit and image, [Colloq.], perfect likeness; exact image.
spit on (or **at**), to express contempt for, hatred of, etc. by or as if by ejecting saliva on or at.

straight (strāt), *adj.* [ME. *streght* (pp. of *strecchen*, to stretch, used as *adj.*); AS. *streht*, pp. of *streccan*, to stretch; cf. STRETCH], 1. having the same direction throughout its length; having no curvature or angularity: as, a *straight* line. 2. not crooked, bent, bowed, wavy, curly, etc.; upright; erect: as, a *straight* back, *straight* hair. 3. with all cylinders in a direct line: said of some internal-combustion engines. 4. direct; undeviating; continuous; uninterrupted, etc.: as, a *straight* course. 5. following strictly the principles, slate of candidates, etc. of a political party: as, he votes a *straight* ticket. 6. following a direct or systematic course of reasoning, etc.; methodical; accurate. 7. in order; properly arranged, etc.: as, put your room *straight*. 8. *a*) honest; sincere; upright. *b*) [Colloq.], reliable, as information. 9. outspoken; frank. 10. unmixed; undiluted: as, *straight* whisky. 11. unqualified; unmodified: as, a *straight* answer. 12. at a fixed price per unit regardless of the quantity bought or sold: as, the apples are ten cents *straight*. 13. in *card games*, consisting of cards in sequence: as, a *straight* flush. *adv.* 1. in a straight line; unswervingly. 2. upright; erectly. 3. without deviation, detour, circumlocution, etc.; directly. *n.* 1. the quality or condition of being straight. 2. something straight; specifically, *a*) the straight part of a racecourse between the last turn and the winning post. *b*) in *poker*, a series of five cards in sequence.
straight away (or **off**), at once; without delay.
straight angle, an angle of 180 degrees.
straight-arm (strāt′ärm′), *v.t.* in *football*, to push away (a tackler) with the arm outstretched. *n.* the act of straight-arming.
straight·a·way (strāt′ə-wā′), *adj.* extending in a straight line. *n.* a track, or part of a track, that extends in a straight line.
straight·edge (strāt′ej′), *n.* a piece or strip of wood, etc. having a perfectly straight edge used in drawing straight lines, testing plane surfaces, etc.
straight·en (strāt′'n), *v.t.* & *v.i.* to make or become straight.
straight-faced (strāt′fāst′), *adj.* showing no amusement or other emotion.
straight·for·ward (strāt′fôr′wērd), *adj.* 1. moving or leading straight ahead; direct. 2. honest; frank; open. *adv.* in a straightforward manner; directly.
straight·for·wards (strāt′fôr′wērdz), *adv.* straightforward.
straight-line (strāt′lin′), *adj.* 1. composed of straight lines. 2. having the parts arranged in a straight line or lines. 3. designating a linkage or similar device (*straight-line motion*) used to produce or copy motion in straight lines.
straight man, in the *theater*, an actor who serves as a foil for a comedian.
straight-out (strāt′out′), *adj.* [Colloq.], 1. straightforward; direct. 2. unrestrained; outright. 3. thoroughgoing; unqualified.
straight·way (strāt′wā′), *adv.* at once; without delay.

tick·le (tik′'l), *v.t.* [TICKLED (-'ld), TICKLING], [ME. *tikelen*; akin to G. dial. *zickeln*; for the base see TICK (insect)], 1. to please; gratify: as, this dessert will *tickle* the palate. 2. to amuse; delight: as, the story *tickled* him. 3. to excite the surface nerves of by touching or stroking lightly with the finger, a feather, etc. so as to cause involuntary twitching, laughter, etc. 4. to rouse, stir, move, get, etc. by or as by touching lightly. *v.i.* 1. to have an itching or tingling sensation: as, my palm *tickles*. 2. to be affected by excitation of the surface nerves; be ticklish. *n.* 1. a tickling or being tickled. 2. a tickling sensation.
tickle one pink, [Slang], to please one greatly.
tick·ler (tik′lēr), *n.* 1. a person or thing that tickles. 2. a memorandum pad, file, or other device for aiding the memory. 3. an irritating problem; puzzle. 4. an account book showing notes due and the dates of these.
tick·lish (tik′lish), *adj.* 1. sensitive to tickling. 2. easily upset; unstable; unsteady; touchy; fickle. 3. needing careful handling; precarious; delicate.

READING SELECTION 3: Magazine Article

"Sonar for the Blind" is a magazine article which describes a new type of equipment designed to help blind people.* Read the passage quickly to determine the author's main ideas. Then use the questions which follow to guide you in a careful reading of the article. You will need to do the Vocabulary from Context exercise on page 104 before you begin reading.

Sonar for the Blind

1   A blind baby is doubly handicapped. Not only is it unable to see, but because it cannot receive the visual stimulus from its environment that a sighted child does, it is likely to be slow in intellectual development. Now the ten-month-old son of Dr. and Mrs. Dennis Daughters of San Ramon, Calif., is the subject of an unusual psychological experiment designed to prevent a lag in the learning process. With the aid of a sonar-type electronic device that he wears on his head, infant Dennis is learning to identify the people and objects in the world around him by means of echoes.

2   Dennis and a twin brother, Daniel, were born last September almost three months too early. Daniel died after five days, and Dennis developed retrolental fibroplasia, an eye disorder usually caused by overexposure to oxygen in an incubator.† He went blind, but through a pediatrician at the premature unit where he was treated, the Daughterses were contacted by Dr. Tom Bower, a psychologist from the University of Edinburgh then serving a fellowship at the Stanford University

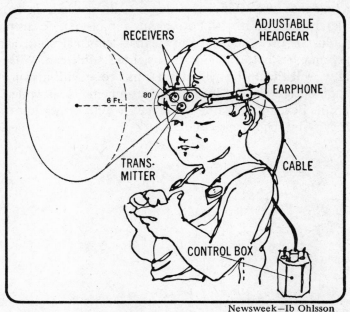

Newsweek—Ib Ohlsson

Center for Advanced Study in the Behavioral Sciences. Bower wanted to see how a blind infant might respond if given an echo-sounding device to help him cope with his surroundings—and the Daughterses agreed to help.

3   By the time the child was six weeks old, his parents noticed that he continuously uttered sharp clicking sounds with his tongue. Bower explained that blind people often use echoes to orient themselves, and that the clicking sounds were the boy's way of creating echoes. This, Bower believed, made the child an ideal subject for testing with an electronic echo-sounding device.

4   Signals: The device used in the study is a refinement of the "Sonicguide," an instrument produced by Telesensory Systems, Inc., of Palo Alto, Calif., and used by blind adults in addition to a cane or guide dog. As adapted for Dennis, it consists of a battery-powered system about the size of a half dollar that is worn on a headgear. A transmitter emits an ultrasonic pulse that creates an 80-degree cone of sound at 6

---

† incubator: a machine for the protection of small weak babies in which temperature and oxygen are controlled

feet. Echoes from objects within the cone are changed by two receivers into audible signals fed into each ear. The signals are perceived as sounds that vary in pitch and volume with the size and distance of the object.

5   The closer an object is, the lower the pitch, and the larger the object, the louder the signal. Hard surfaces produce a sharp ping, while soft ones send back signals with a slightly fuzzy quality. An object slightly to the right of Denny's head sends back a louder sound to his right ear than to the left. Thus, by simply moving his head right and left and up and down, he can not only locate an object but also get some notion of its shape and size, thanks to the varying qualities of sounds reaching his ears as the cone of ultrasound passes its edges. Dennis likes to use the device to play a kind of peek-a-boo with his mother. Standing on her knee and facing her directly, he receives a strong signal in both ears. By turning his head away, he makes her seem to disappear. "From the first time he wore it," says Mrs. Daughters, "it was like a light going on in his head."

6   The boy also learned to identify many objects, including his favorite toy, a rubber caterpillar with six antenna-like projections coming out of its body. And at six-and-a-half months, when a teething biscuit was held in front of Dennis, the child immediately grabbed it with both hands and put it into his mouth.

7   So far, the study has shown that a normal blind baby can employ echoes as well as, or even better than, an unsighted adult can. What remains to be determined is how well the device will help Dennis cope with his surroundings as he begins to walk and venture further into his environment. Meanwhile, Telesensory, Inc., is working on the development of a sonar device with somewhat the same sensitivity as Dennis's for use by school-age children.

COMPREHENSION

Exercise 1

Answer the following questions. Your teacher may want you to answer the questions orally, in writing, or by underlining appropriate parts of the text. True/False items are indicated by a T/F preceding a statement.

1. Why does the writer say that a blind baby is doubly handicapped in comparison to a sighted child? _____

   _____

2. T / F   Dennis was blind at birth.

3. Why did Bower believe Dennis would be an ideal subject for this experiment? _____

   _____

4. T / F   Dennis is the first blind person to use a sonar-type electronic device to help in identifying objects.

5. T / F   Dennis doesn't hear the sounds made by the transmitter.

6. T / F   With the headgear on, Dennis can identify objects behind him.

7. T / F   Dennis cannot identify anything closer than six feet from him.

8. T / F   Dennis has a wider range of "vision" 6 feet from his eyes than 2 feet from them.

9. There are two receivers on the headgear. How does this help Dennis locate objects? _____

   _____

10. If someone holds a book 6 feet directly in front of Dennis and then moves it to only 1 foot directly in front of him, what change in sound does Dennis hear?

    ___ a.   a lower-pitched sound   ___ c.   a sharper sound
    ___ b.   a higher-pitched sound   ___ d.   a softer sound

11. How could Dennis distinguish between a small ball and a large ball from a distance of 3 feet? The small ball would produce _____

    ___ a.   a sharper sound.   ___ c.   a softer sound.
    ___ b.   a higher-pitched sound.   ___ d.   a louder sound.

12. How could Dennis distinguish between a book and a pillow of the same size and at an equal distance in front of him?
    A book would produce _____

    ___ a.   a higher-pitched sound.   ___ c.   a sharper sound.
    ___ b.   a louder sound.   ___ d.   a fuzzier sound.

(Continued on page 104.)

13. How do you think the child's game of peek-a-boo is usually played? _____

_____

14. T / F It seems that blind babies are at least as good as blind adults at using echoes to "see."

Exercise 2

Indicate which of the following statements are inferences or conclusions which can be drawn from this article. Check (✓) all the correct inferences. Be prepared to defend your answers with portions of the text.

1. _____ Visual stimuli are helpful to intellectual development.

2. _____ When Dennis grows up he will not need to use a guide dog or a cane like other blind people.

3. _____ Dennis has learned the relationship between the echoes he hears and the shape and distance of an object in front of him.

4. _____ It is hoped that school-aged children will be able to use a device similar to Dennis's.

VOCABULARY FROM CONTEXT

Use the context provided to determine the meanings of the italicized words. Write a definition, synonym, or description of each italicized vocabulary item in the space provided.

1. _____ Sue has been blind from birth, but she did not let her *handicap* stop her from going to college.

2. _____ Rick spent all of his time playing sports instead of studying; as a result his reading ability has been handicapped. His mental development *lags* behind his physical development.

3. _____ Alice shouted into the cave calling for her brother, but the only sound she heard was the *echo* of her own voice bouncing off the stone walls.

4. _____ When the child moved to the city she frequently got lost if she went out alone. She could never remember which direction she had come from; she was unable to *orient* herself in her new surroundings.

5. _____ The singer's performance was not very good; the notes he sang were often the wrong *pitch*—sometimes they were too low and sometimes too high.

6. _____ Blind people face countless difficulties in their lives but, happily, they succeed in *coping* with many of them so they can live near-normal lives.

NONPROSE READING: Poetry

Because the goal of reading is to discover the author's message, we can say that reading involves solving a puzzle for which the clues are the words we read.* Reading poetry can be the most exciting kind of reading because more of the meaning seems hidden. The author provides the fewest but the richest clues. All of your reading skills will be needed if you are to "solve" the poems in this section.

Each of the following poems describes something.† Read each poem carefully to discover what is being described; do not be concerned if you do not know the meaning of some vocabulary items. If you are having trouble arriving at an answer, read the poem again. If the poem is still not clear, answering the questions on page 108 will give you more clues.

Living Tenderly

My body a rounded stone
with a pattern of smooth seams.
My head a short snake,
retractive, projective.
My legs come out of their sleeves
or shrink within,
and so does my chin.
My eyelids are quick clamps.
My back is my roof.
I am always at home.
I travel where my house walks.
It is a smooth stone.
It floats within the lake,
or rests in the dust.
My flesh lives tenderly
inside its bone.

What is it? _____

---

*For an explanation of nonprose reading, see Unit 1.

†Poems by May Swenson are used by permission of the author from *Poems to Solve*, copyright © 1966 by May Swenson.

Southbound on the Freeway

A tourist came in from Orbitville,
parked in the air, and said:

The creatures of this star
are made of metal and glass.

Through the transparent parts
you can see their guts.

Their feet are round and roll
on diagrams—or long

measuring tapes—dark
with white lines.

They have four eyes.
The two in the back are red.

Sometimes you can see a 5-eyed
one, with a red eye turning

on the top of his head.
He must be special—

The others respect him,
and go slow,

when he passes, winding
among them from behind.

They all hiss as they glide,
like inches, down the marked

tapes. Those soft shapes,
shadowy inside

the hard bodies—are they
their guts or their brains?

What is it? _____

By Morning

Some for everyone
    plenty

    and more coming

Fresh   dainty   airily arriving
    everywhere at once

Transparent at first
    each faint slice
    slow   soundlessly tumbling
    then quickly thickly a gracious fleece
    will spread like youth   like wheat
    over the city

Each building will be   a hill
    all sharps made round

    dark worn noisy arrows made still
    wide   flat   clean   spaces

Streets will be fields
    cars be   fumbling sheep

A deep bright harvest will be seeded
    in a night

By morning we'll be   children
    feeding on manna

    a new loaf on every doorsill

What is it? _____

COMPREHENSION CLUES

"Living Tenderly": What is it?

   1. What is the shape of its body?

   2. What does its head look like?

   3. T / F Its legs don't move.

   4. T / F It carries its home wherever it goes.

   5. T / F It lives only in dry places.

"Southbound on the Freeway": What does the tourist see?

   1. From where is the tourist observing the creatures?

   2. What are the creatures made of?
     (a) Describe their feet.
     (b) Describe their eyes.

   3. What is it that is described as "dark with white lines"?

   4. What is different about the special ones:
     (a) in appearance?
     (b) in the way they affect the behavior of the other creatures?

   5. What is a freeway?

"By Morning": What is it?

   1. Which adjectives describe how it arrives?

   2. How does it look at first?

   3. What could make buildings suddenly look like hills?

   4. What happens to the cars?

   5. What could happen in the night to change a city like this?

WORD STUDY: Context Clues

In the following exercise do NOT try to learn the italicized words. Concentrate on developing your ability to guess the meaning of unfamiliar words using context clues. Read each sentence carefully, and write a definition, synonym, or description of the italicized word on the line provided.

1. _____qualities_____ It is difficult to list all of my father's *attributes* because he has so many different talents and abilities

2. _____give_____ Mary, the president of the family council, *conferred* upon Robert the title of vice-president, because she thought he would do a good job.

3. _____fat_____ Mother was tall, fat, and middle aged. The principal of the school was an older woman, almost as *plump* as Mother, and much shorter.

4. _____ When Mark was in one of his *pedantic* moods, he assumed the manner of a distinguished professor and lectured for hours, on minute, boring topics.

5. _____ Many members of the old wealthy families in society held themselves *aloof* from Gatsby, refusing even to acknowledge his existence.

6. _Try to don't say nothing_ I became angrier and angrier as Don talked, but I *refrained* from saying anything.

7. _____ineffectious_____ Mr. Doodle is always busy in an *ineffectual* way; he spends hours running around accomplishing nothing.

8. _____ Ian was proud of the neat rows of *marigolds* in his flower beds which he tended with great care.

9. _____dark - sad_____ Most dentists' offices are *drab* places, but Emilio's new office is a bright, cheerful place.

10. _____ The inner and outer events of a plant are interdependent; but this isn't saying that the *skin, cortex, membrane,* or whatever you want to call the boundary of the individual is meaningless.

WORD STUDY: Stems and Affixes

Below is a list of some commonly occurring stems and affixes.* Study their meanings, then do the exercises which follow. Your teacher may ask you to give examples of words you know which are derived from these stems and affixes.

Prefixes:	
multi-	many
peri-	around
semi-	half
tri-	three
ultra-	beyond, excessive, extreme
uni-	one

Stems:	
-aster-, -astro-, -stellar-	star
-auto-	self
-bio-	life
-cycle-	circle
-mega-	great
-mort-	death
-phil-	love
-polis-	city
-psych-	mind
-soph-	wise

Suffixes:	
-ist	one who

Exercise 1

In each item, select the best definition of the italicized word or phrase or answer the question.

1. To apply to some universities, you must fill out the application form and include a short *autobiography*.

_____ a. sample of your writing

✓ b. account of your life written by you

_____ c. list of courses you have taken

_____ d. list of schools you have attended

_____

*For a list of all stems and affixes taught in *Reader's Choice*, see Appendix.

2. The policeman used a *megaphone*.

_____ a. a portable radio   ✓ c. an instrument to make his voice louder

_____ b. a long stick   _____ d. a telephone in his car

3. Dr. Swanson has written articles about *interstellar* travel.

_____ a. underwater   _____ c. high-speed
_____ b. long-distance   ✓ d. outer space

4. Janet is interested in *autographs* of famous people.

_____ a. pictures   _____ c. families
_____ b. personalities   ✓ d. signatures

5. An *asterisk* is a written symbol which looks like _____.

_____ a. /.   _____ c. %.
✓ b. *.   _____ d. @.

6. The government is financing a study of the effects on man of living in a *megalopolis*.

_____ a. an apartment in a large building   _____ c. a dangerous part of a city
✓ b. an extremely large city   _____ d. a city with a large police force

7. Children learning to ride bicycles probably already know how to ride a _____

_____ a. unicycle.   ✓ c. tricycle.
_____ b. megacycle.   _____ d. motorcycle.

8. What is the *perimeter* of this rectangle?

✓ a. 14   _____ c. 2
_____ b. 4   _____ d. 5

9. *Nautical* means *pertaining to seamen, ships, or navigation*. Explain how the word *astronaut* is formed.

_____

_____

10. Why are the clothes that nurses, policemen, and soldiers wear called *uniforms*?

___ it's used by all group = same clothes _____

_____

11. People who study population often speak of the world mortality rate. What is the opposite of *mortality rate*?

___ the birthrate rate _____

Exercise 2

Following is a list of words containing some of the stems and affixes introduced in this unit and the previous ones. Definitions of these words appear on the right. Put the letter of the appropriate definition next to each word.

1. _f_ psychologist
2. _e_ philanthropist
3. _a_ sophisticated
4. _d_ biochemist
5. _b_ biography
6. _c_ biology

a. worldly-wise; knowing; finely experienced
b. a written history of a person's life
c. the science of life or living matter in all its forms and phenomena
d. one who studies the chemical compounds and processes occurring in organisms
e. one who shows love for mankind by doing good works for society
f. one who studies mental processes and behavior

7. _e_ antibiotic
8. _c_ asteroid
9. _d_ megascopic
10. _a_ periscope
11. _b_ ultramicroscope
12. _f_ astronomer

a. an optical instrument which allows a submarine to observe the surface from below the water
b. an instrument used to detect an object too small to be seen with an ordinary microscope
c. resembling a star
d. visible to the unaided eye; enlarged, magnified
e. a substance capable of killing microorganisms
f. a scientific observer of the planets, stars, and outer space

13. _f_ cycle
14. _b_ semicircle
15. _c_ trichromatic
16. _a_ trilogy
17. _d_ astrology
18. _e_ triplet

a. a series or group of three related dramas, operas, novels, etc.
b. a half circle
c. pertaining to the use or combination of three different colors
d. the study of the influence of the stars on human affairs
e. one of three children born at one birth
f. a recurring period of time in which certain events repeat themselves in the same order and at the same intervals

19. _c_ unilateral
20. _d_ bilateral
21. _e_ ultraviolet
22. _a_ multimillionaire
23. _f_ ultranationalism
24. _b_ multicolored

a. a person who has many millions of dollars
b. having many colors
c. pertaining to, involving, or affecting only one side
d. affecting two sides or parties
e. invisible rays of the spectrum lying beyond the violet end of the visible spectrum
f. excessive devotion to national interests as opposed to international considerations

SENTENCE STUDY: Restatement and Inference

Each sentence below is followed by five statements.* The statements are of four types:
  1. Some of the statements are restatements of the original sentence. They give the same information in a different way.
  2. Some of the statements are inferences (conclusions) which can be drawn from the information given in the original sentence.
  3. Some of the statements are false based on the information given.
  4. Some of the statements cannot be judged true or false based on the information given in the original sentence.
Put a check (✓) next to all restatements and inferences (types 1 and 2). Note: do not check a statement which is true of itself but cannot be inferred from the sentence given.

Example:
Heavy smokers and drinkers run a fifteen-times greater risk of developing cancer of the mouth and throat than nonsmokers and nondrinkers.

_____ a. Cancer of the mouth and throat is more likely to occur in heavy smokers and drinkers than in nonsmokers and nondrinkers.

_____ b. People who never drink and smoke will not get mouth or throat cancer.

_____ c. Heavy drinkers who run have a greater risk of developing cancer than nondrinkers.

_____ d. People who don't smoke and drink have less chance of getting cancer of the mouth and throat than those who smoke and drink heavily.

_____ e. People would probably be healthier if they did not drink and smoke too much.

Explanation:
✓ a. This is a restatement of the original sentence. If heavy smokers and drinkers run a greater risk of developing cancer than those who do not drink or smoke, then cancer is more likely to occur in heavy smokers and drinkers.

_____ b. It is not true that people who never smoke and drink will never get mouth or throat cancer. We only know that they are _less likely_ to get this kind of cancer.

_____ c. The word _run_ in the original sentence is part of the phrase _to run a risk_ which means _to be in danger_. The sentence does not tell us anything about heavy drinkers who enjoy the sport of running.

✓ d. This is a restatement of the original sentence. If people who drink and smoke heavily have a greater chance of getting mouth and throat cancer than those who don't, then it must be true that those who don't smoke and drink heavily have less chance of developing this kind of cancer.

✓ e. This is an inference which can be drawn from the information given. If people who smoke and drink heavily run a high risk of developing cancer, then we can infer that people probably would be healthier if they didn't smoke and drink too much (heavily).

---

*For an introduction to sentence study, see Unit 1.

1. Nine out of ten doctors responding to a survey said they recommend our product to their patients if they recommend anything.

_____ a. Nine out of ten doctors recommend the product.

_____ b. Of the doctors who responded to a survey, nine out of ten doctors recommend the product.

__✓__ c. If they recommend anything, nine out of ten doctors responding to a survey recommend the product.

__✓__ d. Most doctors recommend the product.

_____ e. We don't know how many doctors recommend the product.

2. This organization may succeed marvelously at what it wants to do, but what it wants to do may not be all that important.

_____ a. The organization is marvelous.

_____ b. The organization may succeed.

__✓__ c. Although the organization may reach its goals, the goals might not be important.

_____ d. What the organization wants is marvelous.

__✓__ e. The author questions the goals of the organization.

3. This book contains a totally new outlook which combines the wisdom of the past with scientific knowledge to solve the problems of the present.

_____ a. Problems of the past and present are solved in this book.

__✓__ b. In this book, current knowledge and past wisdom are combined to solve current problems.

_____ c. Only by using knowledge of the past and present can we solve problems.

_____ d. None of today's problems can be solved without scientific knowledge.

__✓__ e. This book is different because it combines the wisdom of the past with scientific knowledge.

4. Like other timeless symbols, flags have accompanied mankind for thousands of years, gaining ever wider meaning, yet losing none of their inherent and original force.

_____ a. In spite of losing some of their original force, flags are a timeless symbol which have accompanied mankind for thousands of years.

__✓__ b. Flags have existed for thousands of years.

_____ ✓ c. Timeless symbols typically gain wider meaning while not losing their inherent force.

_____ d. Thousands of years ago flags accompanied mankind but through time they have lost their force.

_____ ✓ e. Because flags are considered a timeless symbol, they have gained continually wider meaning without losing their inherent original force.

5. When there is an absence of reliable information about drugs, the risks involved in using them are greatly increased.

_____ ✓ a. There is no reliable information about drugs.

_____ b. Using drugs is more dangerous when we don't know what effects and dangers are involved.

_____ ✓ c. The risks involved in using drugs have increased.

_____ d. People should try to find out about drugs before using them.

_____ ✓ e. There are no risks involved in using drugs if we have reliable information about them.

6. The project of which this book is the result was first suggested in the summer of 1962, in the course of some leisurely conversations at the foot of and (occasionally) on top of the Alps of western Austria.

_____ a. This book was written in 1962.

_____ b. This book was written in Austria.

_____ ✓ c. This book is a collection of conversations held in 1962.

_____ ✓ d. This book is the end result of a project.

_____ e. This book is about western Austria.

7. Los Angeles' safety record with school buses is generally a good one, but of course this record is only as good as the school bus drivers themselves.

_____ a. In spite of a generally good safety record for their school buses, Los Angeles school bus drivers are not very good.

_____ ✓ b. If school bus drivers are not very good, the town's school bus safety record will not be very good either.

_____ ✓ c. If cities wish to maintain good safety records with school buses, they should hire good school bus drivers.

_____ ✓ d. With better school buses, drivers will be able to maintain better safety records.

_____ ✓ e. Los Angeles' safety record with school buses has improved because better bus drivers have been hired.

115

8. Taxes being so high, the descendents of the wealthy class of the nineteenth century are being forced to rent out their estates to paying guests.

_____ a. In the nineteenth century, the wealthy class rented out its estates.

__✓__ b. Because of high taxes, families which were rich one hundred years ago now rent out their estates.

_____ c. Guests pay high taxes when they rent old estates.

__✓__ d. Some families which were once wealthy are having trouble paying their taxes.

__✓__ e. High taxes have changed the lives of some of the old wealthy families.

9. According to the definition of Chinese traditional medicine, acupuncture is the treatment of disease—not just the alleviation of pain—by inserting very fine needles into the body at specific points called loci.

_____ a. The author believes some people do not know that acupunture can be used to treat illness.

__✓__ b. Finely pointed needles called loci are used in acupuncture.

__✓__ c. In Chinese traditional medicine, acupuncture is known to treat disease and alleviate pain.

__✓__ d. Those using acupuncture treat disease by placing needles into the body at specific points.

_____ e. Only those who practice traditional Chinese medicine use acupuncture.

10. It would be difficult to overpraise this book.

_____ a. This is a difficult book.

__✓__ b. This book deserves much praise.

_____ c. It is difficult not to overpraise this book.

__✓__ d. It is difficult to praise this book.

_____ e. The author of this sentence thinks this is an excellent book.

PARAGRAPH ANALYSIS: Reading for Full Understanding

The paragraph exercises in Units 1 and 3 require you to determine the main idea of a passage. This exercise and the one in Unit 11 require much more careful reading. Each selection is followed by a number of questions. The questions are designed to give you practice in:

1. determining the main idea
2. understanding supporting details
3. drawing inferences
4. guessing vocabulary items from context
5. using syntactic and stylistic clues to understand selected portions of the paragraphs

Read each paragraph carefully. Try to determine the author's main idea while attempting to remember important details. For each of the questions below, select the *best* answer. You may refer to the passage to answer the questions.

Example:

1   It is not often realized that women held a high place in southern European
2   societies in the 10th and 11th centuries. As a wife, the woman was protected by the
3   setting up of a dowry or *decimum*. Admittedly, the purpose of this was to protect
4   her against the risk of desertion, but in reality its function in the social and family
5   life of the time was much more important. The *decimum* was the wife's right to
6   receive a tenth of all her husband's property. The wife had the right to withhold
7   consent, in *all* transactions the husband would make. And more than just a right:
8   the documents show that she enjoyed a real power of decision, equal to that of her
9   husband. In no case do the documents indicate any degree of difference in the legal
10   status of husband and wife.
11   The wife shared in the management of her husband's personal property, but the
12   opposite was not always true. Women seemed perfectly prepared to defend their own
13   inheritance against husbands who tried to exceed their rights, and on occasion they
14   showed a fine fighting spirit. A case in point is that of María Vivas, a Catalan woman
15   of Barcelona. Having agreed with her husband Miró to sell a field she had inherited,
16   for the needs of the household, she insisted on compensation. None being offered,
17   she succeeded in dragging her husband to the scribe to have a contract duly drawn
18   up assigning her a piece of land from Miró's personal inheritance. The unfortunate
19   husband was obliged to agree, as the contract says, "for the sake of peace." Either
20   through the dowry or through being hot-tempered, the Catalan wife knew how to
21   win herself, within the context of the family, a powerful economic position.*

---

*From Sylvia L. Thrupp, ed., *Early Medieval Society* (New York: Appleton-Century-Crofts, 1967), p. 120.

1. A *decimum* was _____

    ____ a. the wife's inheritance from her father.
    ____ b. a gift of money to the new husband.
    ____ c. a written contract.
    ✓ d. the wife's right to receive one-tenth of her husband's property.

2. In the society described in the passage, the legal standing of the wife in marriage was _____

    ____ a. higher than that of her husband.
    ____ b. lower than that of her husband.
    ✓ c. the same as that of her husband.
    ____ d. higher than that of a single woman.

3. What compensation did María Vivas get for the field?

    ✓ a. some of the land Miró had inherited
    ____ b. a tenth of Miró's land
    ____ c. money for household expenses
    ____ d. money from Miró's inheritance

4. Could a husband sell his wife's inheritance?

    ____ a. no, under no circumstances
    ____ b. yes, whenever he wished to
    ✓ c. yes, if she agreed
    ____ d. yes, if his father-in-law agreed

5. Which of the following is NOT mentioned as an effect of the dowry system?

    ____ a. The husband had to share the power of decision in marriage.
    ____ b. The wife was protected from desertion.
    ✗ c. The wife gained a powerful economic position.
    ✓ d. The husband was given control over his wife's property.

Explanation:

1. (d) This is a restatement of a part of the passage. If you did not remember the definition of the word *decimum*, you could have scanned for it quickly and found the answer in lines 5 and 6.

2. (c) This is the main idea of the paragraph. The high place of women in the society is introduced in the first sentence. In lines 9 and 10 the author states that a woman enjoyed a legal power of decision equal to that of her husband. The last sentence tells us that, within the context of the home, women held a powerful economic position.

3. (a) This tests your understanding of details. In lines 17 and 18 the author states that María Vivas forced her husband to agree to a contract giving her a piece of land from his inheritance.

4. (c) This is an inference. In lines 6 and 7 the author states that the wife could refuse to agree to any business agreements the husband might want to make. Thus, we can infer that a husband could only sell his wife's inheritance if she agreed. Furthermore, in lines 15 and 16, the fact that María Vivas allowed her husband to sell a field she had inherited, indicates that her agreement was necessary.

5. (d) Items a, b, and c serve as a summary of the ideas of the passage.

    (a) Lines 8 and 9 tell us that wives enjoyed a real power of decision; line 11 states that a wife shared in the management of her husband's estate.

    (b) Lines 3 and 4 state that the purpose of the dowry was to protect wives from desertion.

    (c) The final sentence states that, within the context of the family, the wife was able to win a powerful economic position.

    (d) Nowhere does it state that a husband was given control over a wife's property, and in several instances the opposite is stated (see questions 3 and 4).

Paragraph 1

1   Today is the anniversary of that afternoon in April a year ago that I first saw
2   the strange and appealing doll in the window of Abe Sheftel's stationery and toy
3   shop on Third Avenue near Fifteenth Street, just around the corner from my office,
4   where the plate on the door reads: Dr. Samuel Amory. I remember just how it was
5   that day: the first hint of spring floated across the East River, mixing with the
6   soft-coal smoke from the factories and the street smells of the poor neighborhood.
7   As I turned the corner on my way to work and came to Sheftel's, I was made once
8   more aware of the poor collection of toys in the dusty window, and I remembered
9   the approaching birthday of a small niece of mine in Cleveland, to whom I was in
10   the habit of sending modest gifts. Therefore, I stopped and examined the window
11   to see if there might be anything appropriate, and looked at the confusing collection
12   of unappealing objects—a red toy fire engine, some lead soldiers, cheap baseballs,
13   bottles of ink, pens, yellowed stationary, and garish cardboard advertisements for
14   soft-drinks. And thus it was that my eyes eventually came to rest upon the doll
15   tucked away in one corner, a doll with the strangest, most charming expression
16   on her face. I could not wholly make her out, due to the shadows and the film
17   through which I was looking, but I was aware that a tremendous impression had
18   been made upon me as though I had run into a person, as one does sometimes with
19   a stranger, with whose personality one is deeply impressed.*

1.   What made an impression on the author?

      ✓ ____ a. the doll's unusual face
      ____ b. the collection of toys
      ____ c. a stranger he met at the store
      ____ d. the resemblance of the doll to his niece

2.   Why does the author mention his niece?

      ____ a. She likes dolls.
      ____ b. The doll looks like her.
      ____ c. She lives near Sheftel's.
      ✓ ____ d. He was looking for a gift for her.

---

*From Paul Gallico, "The Enchanted Doll," in *Story and Structure*, ed. Laurence Perrine (New York: Harcourt, Brace and World, Inc., 1970), pp 327-28.

3.   Why did the author go past Sheftel's?

   ___ a. He was on his way to work.
   ___ b. He was looking for a present for his niece.
   ___ c. He wanted to buy some stationery.
   ___ d. He liked to look in the window.

4.   The story takes place in the ___

   ___ a. early summer.
   ___ b. midsummer.
   ___ c. early spring.
   ___ d. late spring.

5.   When was the story written?

   ___ a. one year after the incident
   ___ b. right after the incident
   ___ c. in the author's old age
   ___ d. on the author's birthday

6.   Most of the things in the store window were ___

   ___ a. expensive.
   ___ b. appealing.
   ___ c. neatly arranged.
   ___ d. unattractive.

Paragraph 2

1   The great advance in rocket theory 40 years ago showed that liquid-fuel rockets
2   were far superior in every respect to the skyrocket with its weak solid fuel, the
3   only kind of rocket then known. However, during the last decade, large solid-fuel
4   rockets with solid fuels about as powerful as liquid fuels have made their appear-
5   ance, and it is a favorite layman's question to inquire which one is "better." The
6   question is meaningless; one might as well ask whether a gasoline or a diesel engine
7   is "better." It all depends on the purpose. A liquid-fuel rocket is complicated, but
8   has the advantage that it can be controlled beautifully. The burning of the rocket
9   engine can be stopped completely; it can be reignited when desired. In addition,
10   the thrust can be made to vary by adjusting the speed of the fuel pumps. A solid-
11   fuel rocket, on the other hand, is rather simple in construction, though hard to
12   build when a really large size is desired. But once you have a solid-fuel rocket,
13   it is ready for action at very short notice. A liquid-fuel rocket has to be fueled
14   first and cannot be held in readiness for very long after it has been fueled. However,
15   once a solid-fuel rocket has been ignited, it will keep burning. It cannot be stopped
16   and reignited whenever desired (it could conceivably be stopped and reignited after
17   a pre-calculated time of burning has elapsed) and its thrust cannot be varied. Be-
18   cause a solid-fuel rocket can be kept ready for a long time, most military missiles
19   employ solid fuels, but manned spaceflight needs the fine adjustments that can
20   only be provided by liquid fuels. It may be added that a liquid-fuel rocket is an
21   expensive device; a large solid-fuel rocket is, by comparison, cheap. But the solid
22   fuel, pound per pound, costs about 10 times as much as the liquid fuel. So you have,
23   on the one hand, an expensive rocket with a cheap fuel and on the other hand a
24   comparatively cheap rocket with an expensive fuel.*

1. The author feels that a comparison of liquid- and solid-fuel rockets shows that ____

     ____ a. neither type is very economical.
     ____ b. the liquid-fuel rocket is best.
     ____ c. each type has certain advantages.
     ____ d. the solid-fuel rocket is best.

2. The most important consideration for manned space flight is that the rocket be ____

     ____ a. inexpensive to construct.
     ____ b. capable of lifting heavy spacecraft into orbit.
     ____ c. easily controlled.
     ____ d. inexpensive to operate.

3. Solid-fuel rockets are expensive to operate because of their ____

     ____ a. size.   ____ c. burning time.
     ____ b. fuel.   ____ d. complicated engines.

4. Which of the following statements is *not* characteristic of liquid-fuel rockets?

     ____ a. The fuel is cheap.   ____ c. They are cheap to build.
     ____ b. They can be stopped and reignited.   ____ d. They must be used soon after fueling.

---

*From Willy Ley, "Space Race," in *Information Please Almanac*, ed. D. Golenpaul (New York: Simon and Schuster).

Paragraph 3

1　　　It was not yet eleven o'clock when a boat crossed the river with a single passenger
2　who had obtained his transportation at that unusual hour by promising an extra
3　fare. While the youth stood on the landing-place searching in his pockets for money,
4　the ferryman lifted a lantern, by the aid of which, together with the newly risen
5　moon, he took a very accurate survey of the stranger's figure. He was a young man
6　of barely eighteen years, evidently country bred, and now, as it seemed, on his
7　first visit to town. He was wearing a rough gray coat, which was in good shape,
8　but which had seen many winters before this one. The garments under his coat were
9　well constructed of leather, and fitted tightly to a pair of muscular legs; his stockings
10　of blue yarn must have been the work of a mother or sister, and on his head was a
11　three-cornered hat, which in its better days had perhaps sheltered the grayer head
12　of the lad's father. In his left hand was a walking stick, and his equipment was
13　completed by a leather bag not so abundantly stocked as to inconvenience the
14　strong shoulders on which it hung. Brown, curly hair, well-shaped features, bright,
15　cheerful eyes were nature's gifts, and worth all that art could have done for his
16　adornment. The youth, whose name was Robin, paid the boatman, and then walked
17　forward into the town with a light step, as if he had not already traveled more than
18　thirty miles that day. As he walked, he surveyed his surroundings as eagerly as if
19　he were entering London or Madrid, instead of the little metropolis of a New England
20　colony.*

1.　What time of year was it in this story?

　　____ a. spring
　　____ b. summer
　　____ c. fall
　　____ d. winter

2.　At what time of day did Robin cross the river?

　　____ a. morning
　　____ b. midday
　　____ c. late afternoon
　　__✓_ d. night

3.　The boatman was willing to take Robin across the river because ____

　　____ a. he wanted to make extra money.
　　____ b. he saw that Robin was young and rich.
　　____ c. he was going to row across the river anyway.
　　____ d. he felt sorry for him because Robin looked poor.

---

*From Nathaniel Hawthorne, *Selected Tales and Sketches*, ed. H. Waggooner Hyatt (Chicago: Holt, Rinehart and Winston, 1962), pp. 13-14.

4. The stockings that Robin wore were obviously____

    ____ a. well worn.
    ____ b. very expensive.
    ____ c. handmade.
    ____ d. much too big.

5. From the way he looked, it was evident that Robin was ____

    ____ a. a wealthy merchant's son.
    ____ b. a country boy.
    ____ c. a soldier.
    ____ d. a foreigner.

6. Robin was apparently going to the town ____

    ____ a. to buy new clothes.
    ____ b. for the first time.
    ____ c. for the first time in several years.
    ____ d. on one of his regular trips there.

7. How did Robin appear as he walked into town?

    ____ a. He was cheerful and excited.
    ____ b. He was tired.
    ____ c. He seemed very sad.
    ____ d. He seemed frightened by his strange surroundings.

8. How far had Robin traveled?

    ____ a. over thirty miles
    ____ b. from Madrid
    ____ c. from a nearby town
    ____ d. from London

Paragraph 4

1   Fifty volunteers were alphabetically divided into two equal groups, Group A to
2   participate in a 7 week exercise program, and Group B to avoid deliberate exercise
3   of any sort during those 7 weeks. On the day before the exercise program began,
4   all 50 men participated in a step-test. This consisted of stepping up and down on
5   a 16-inch bench at 30 steps a minute for 5 minutes. One minute after completion
6   of the step-test, the pulse rate of each subject was taken and recorded. This served
7   as the pretest for the experiment. For the next 7 weeks, subjects in the experimental
8   group (Group A) rode an Exercycle (a motor-driven bicycle-type exercise machine)
9   for 15 minutes each day. The exercise schedule called for riders to ride relaxed
10   during the first day's ride, merely holding on to the handle bars and foot pedals as
11   the machine moved. Then, for the next 3 days, they rode relaxed for 50 seconds of
12   each minute, and pushed, pulled, and pedaled actively for 10 seconds of each
13   minute. The ratio of active riding was increased every few days, so that by the
14   third week it was half of each minute, and by the seventh week the riders were
15   performing 15 solid minutes of active riding.
16   At the end of the 7 weeks, the step-test was again given to both groups of sub-
17   jects, and their pulses taken. The post-exercise pulse rates of subjects in the experi-
18   mental group were found to have decreased an average of 30 heart beats per minute,
19   with the lowest decrease 28 and the highest decrease 46. The pulse rates of subjects
20   in the control group remained the same or changed no more than 4 beats, with an
21   average difference between the initial and final tests of zero.*

1.   How many people were in each group?

    ___ a. 100
    ___ b. 50
    ___ c. 25
    ___ d. 15

2.   The step-test was given ____

    ___ a. after each exercise period.
    ___ b. at the beginning and at the end of the seven week period.
    ___ c. only once, at the beginning of the seven week period.
    ___ d. twice to the men in Group A and once to the men in Group B.

---

*From James E. Haney, "Health and Motor Behavior: Measuring Energy Expenditures," *Research News* 22, no. 5 (November 1971): 7.

3.   When were pulse rates taken?

    ____ a. after every exercise period
    ____ b. every day
    ____ c. after the step-tests
    ____ d. every time the ratio of active riding was increased

4.   The exercise schedule was planned so that the amount of active riding ____

    ____ a. increased every few days.
    ____ b. varied from day to day.
    ____ c. increased until the third week and then was kept constant.
    ____ d. increased every exercise period.

5.   What did Group A do in their program?

    ____ a. They stepped up and down on a bench each day.
    ____ b. They pushed and pulled on exercise handles every day.
    ____ c. They rode on an Exercycle every day.
    ____ d. They refrained from any exercise.

6.   The post-exercise pulse rates of Group B were found on the average to have ____

    ____ a. not changed.
    ____ b. gone down 28 beats per minute.
    ____ c. gone down 30 beats per minute.
    ____ d. gone down 4 beats per minute.

7.   This paragraph implies that ____

    ____ a. most people do not get enough exercise.
    ____ b. a high pulse rate is desirable.
    ____ c. regular exercise can strengthen your heart.
    ____ d. everyone should exercise 15 minutes a day.

Paragraph 5

1   In the second half of each year, many powerful storms are born in the tropical
2 Atlantic and Caribbean seas. Of these, only about a half a dozen generate the strong,
3 circling winds of 75 miles per hour or more that give them hurricane status, and
4 several usually make their way to the coast. There they cause millions of dollars
5 of damage, and bring death to large numbers of people.
6   The great storms that hit the coast start as innocent circling disturbances hun-
7 dreds—even thousands—of miles out to sea. As they travel aimlessly over water
8 warmed by the summer sun, they are carried westward by the trade winds. When
9 conditions are just right, warm, moist air flows in at the bottom of such a distur-
10 bance, moves upward through it and comes out at the top. In the process, the
11 moisture in this warm air produces rain, and with it the heat that is converted to
12 energy in the form of strong winds. As the heat increases, the young hurricane
13 begins to swirl in a counter-clockwise motion.
14   The average life of a hurricane is only about nine days, but it contains almost
15 more power than we can imagine. The energy in the heat released by a hurricane's
16 rainfall in a single day would satisfy the entire electrical needs of the United States
17 for more than six months. Water, not wind, is the main source of death and destruc-
18 tion in a hurricane. A typical hurricane brings 6- to 12-inch downpours resulting
19 in sudden floods. Worst of all is the powerful movement of the sea—the mountains
20 of water moving toward the low-pressure hurricane center. The water level rises as
21 much as 15 feet above normal as it moves toward shore.*

1. When is an ordinary tropical storm called a hurricane?

    _____ a. when it begins in the Atlantic and Caribbean seas
    _____ b. when it hits the coastline
    _____ c. when it is more than 75 miles wide
    _____ d. when its winds reach 75 miles per hour

2. What is the worst thing about hurricanes?

    _____ a. the destructive effects of water
    _____ b. the heat they release
    _____ c. that they last about nine days on the average
    _____ d. their strong winds

3. The counter-clockwise swirling of the hurricane is brought about by _____

    _____ a. the low-pressure area in the center of the storm.
    _____ b. the force of waves of water.
    _____ c. the trade winds.
    _____ d. the increasing heat.

4. Apparently the word *downpour* means _____

    _____ a. heavy rainfall.
    _____ b. dangerous waves.
    _____ c. the progress of water to the hurricane center.
    _____ d. the energy produced by the hurricane.

---

*From E. Hughes, "Hurricane Warning," *Reader's Digest*, September 1969, p. 21.

READING SELECTION 1: Magazine Article

Some magazine articles attempt to summarize scientific research for the general public. The author of the article on page 129 draws from the work of a number of experts in presenting an explanation for why we laugh.*

    Read the article carefully and do the exercises which follow. You may want to do Vocabulary from Context exercise 1 on page 131 before you begin reading.

COMPREHENSION

Exercise 1
Indicate if each statement is true (T) or false (F) according to your understanding of the article.

1. _____ We laugh as a release for our normally repressed drives.

2. _____ Laughter strengthens social bonds.

3. _____ We laugh to express mastery over anxiety.

4. _____ We laugh to release energy after a crisis.

5. _____ We laugh at jokes of which we are the target.

6. _____ We never laugh when we are alone because we require company to laugh.

7. _____ We laugh immediately at birth.

8. _____ We sometimes laugh in times of sorrow.

9. _____ We sometimes laugh when nothing is funny.

10. _____ The ability to laugh takes a lifetime to perfect.

11. _____ We laugh to break tension.

12. _____ Laughter is an unpleasant physical sensation.

13. _____ A sense of humor is a result of the mastery of human relationships.

14. _____ We always laugh when we understand a joke.

---

*"Why We Laugh" by Janet Spencer from *Ladies' Home Journal*, November 1974.

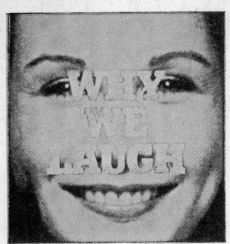

Are you a quiet giggler? Or can you let loose with hearty laughter? Your ability to laugh may mean more than you think. By Janet Spencer

Picture this cartoon: A man is watering his lawn just as an attractive blonde walks by. As he ogles her, he accidentally turns the hose on his dowdy wife, who is sitting on the porch.

2) Men usually think the cartoon is funny. Women do not. And there's a good reason for the difference in opinion.

3) We start finding things laughable—or not laughable—early in life. An infant first smiles at approximately eight days of age. Many psychologists feel this is his first sign of simple pleasure—food, warmth and comfort. At six months or less, the infant laughs to express complex pleasures—such as the sight of Mother's smiling face.

4) In his book *Beyond Laughter*, psychiatrist Martin Grotjahn says that the earlier an infant begins to smile and laugh, the more advanced is his development. Studies revealed that children who did not develop these responses (because they lacked an intimate, loving relationship) "developed a schizophrenic psychosis in later life, or simply gave up and died."

5) Between the ages of six months and one year, the baby learns to laugh for essentially the same reasons he will laugh throughout his life, says Dr. Jacob Levine, associate professor of psychology at Yale University. Dr. Levine says that people laugh to express mastery over an anxiety. Picture what happens when a father tosses his child into the air. The child will probably laugh—but not the first time. In spite of his enjoyment of "flying," he is too anxious to laugh. How does he know Daddy will catch him? Once the child realizes he will be caught, he is free to enjoy the game. But more importantly, says Dr. Levine, the child laughs because he has mastered an anxiety.

6) Adult laughter is more subtle, but we also laugh at what we used to fear. The feeling of achievement, or lack of it, remains a crucial factor. Giving a first dinner party is an anxious event for a new bride. Will the food be good? Will the guests get along? Will she be a good hostess? All goes well; the party is over. Now she laughs freely. Her pleasure from having proved her success is the foundation for her pleasure in recalling the evening's activities. She couldn't enjoy the second pleasure without the first, more important one—her mastery of anxiety.

7) Laughter is a social response triggered by cues. Scientists have not determined a brain center for laughter, and they are perplexed by patients with certain types of brain damage who go into laughing fits for no apparent reason. The rest of us require company, and a reason to laugh.

8) When we find ourselves alone in a humorous situation, our usual response is to smile. Isn't it true that our highest compliment to a humorous book is to say that "it made me laugh out loud"? Of course, we do occasionally laugh alone; but when we do, we are, in a sense, socializing with ourselves. We laugh at a memory, or at a part of ourselves.

9) Practically every philosopher since Plato has written on how humor and laughter are related, but Sigmund Freud was the first to evolve a conclusive theory. Freud recognized that we all repress certain basic but socially "unacceptable" drives, such as sex and aggression. Jokes, not accidentally, are often based on either sex or aggression, or both. We find these jokes funny because they provide a sudden release of our normally suppressed drives. We are free to enjoy the forbidden, and the energy we normally use to inhibit these drives is discharged in laughter.

10) Another reason laughter is pleasurable is because of the physical sensations involved. Laughter is a series of minor facial and respiratory convulsions that stimulates our respiratory and circulatory systems. It activates the secretion of adrenalin and increases the blood flow to the head and brain. The total effect is one of euphoria.

11) Of course, we don't always need a joke to make us laugh. People who survive frightening situations, such as a fire or an emergency plane landing, frequently intersperse their story of the crisis with laughter. Part of the laughter expresses relief that everything is now all right. During a crisis, everyone mobilizes energy to deal with the potential problem. If the danger is averted, we need to release that energy. Some people cry; others laugh.

12) Part of the integral pleasure of a joke *is* getting the point. But if the sexual or aggressive element of the joke is too thinly disguised, as in "sick" humor, the joke will leave us feeling guilty instead of amused. We may laugh—but in embarrassment. According to Dr. Grotjahn, "The disguise must go far enough to avoid guilt," but "not so far that the thrill of aggression is lost."

13) Which brings us to why women may not have found the joke about the man watering his wife very funny—because they get the point only too well. Many psychiatrists agree that the reason women aren't amused by this kind of joke is that most sex jokes (a hefty percentage of all jokes) employ women as their target. Women sometimes make poor joke tellers for the same reason; consciously or subconsciously, they express their resentment by "forgetting" the story.

14) When we are made the butt of a joke, either on a personal or impersonal level, we are emotionally involved in it. Consequently, we won't be able to laugh (except as a pretense). While we are feeling, we cannot laugh. The two do not mix. French essayist Henri Bergson called laughter a "momentary anesthesia of the heart." We call it comic relief.

15) Knowing that laughter blunts emotion, we can better understand why we sometimes laugh when nothing is funny. We laugh during moments of anxiety because we feel no mastery over the situation, claims Dr. Levine. He explains, "Very often compulsive laughter is a learned response. If we laugh, it expresses good feelings and the fact that we are able to cope. When we're in a situation in which we *can't* cope, we laugh to reassure ourselves that we *can!*"

16) How often have we laughed at a funeral or upon hearing bad news? We laugh to deny an unendurable reality until we are strong enough to accept it. Laughter also breaks our tension. However, we may also be laughing to express relief that the tragedy didn't happen to us. We laugh before giving a big party, before delivering a speech, or while getting a traffic ticket, to say, "This isn't bothering me. See? I'm laughing."

17) But if we sometimes laugh in sorrow, more often we laugh with joy. Laughter creates and strengthens our social bonds. And the ability to share a laugh has guided many marriages through hard periods of adjustment.

18) According to Dr. Levine, we can measure our adjustment to the world by our capacity to laugh. When we are secure about our abilities, we can poke fun at our foibles. If we can laugh through our anxieties, we will not be overpowered by them.

19) The ability to laugh starts early, but it takes a lifetime to perfect. Says Dr. Grotjahn, "When social relationships are mastered, when the individual has mastered . . . a peaceful relationship with himself, then he has . . . the sense of humor." And then he can throw back his head and laugh. **END**

Exercise 2

The sentences in exercise 1 are general statements about laughter. Often authors will give specific examples to make an argument stronger or clearer. Following is a list of situations which the author of this article uses to illustrate some of the true statements in exercise 1. Match each of the examples below with the number of the appropriate general statement from the previous exercise. Some items have more than one possible answer. Choose what you feel to be the best answer. Be prepared to defend your choice.

Example:

___3___ Infants laugh when their fathers throw them in the air.

1. _____ A new bride laughs after she gives her first successful dinner party.

2. _____ People who survive an emergency plane landing intersperse their story with laughter.

3. _____ We laugh before delivering a speech.

4. _____ We sometimes laugh at a funeral or when we hear bad news.

5. _____ We laugh at a sexual joke.

6. _____ Married couples laugh through hard periods of social adjustment.

CRITICAL READING

Exercise 1

In order to evaluate an author's arguments, it is important to notice whom she quotes to support her statements. A number of experts are cited in this article. Next to each name below write the person's profession.

Example:

Sigmund Freud ___psychiatrist___

1. Henri Bergson _____

2. Martin Grotjahn _____

3. Jacob Levine _____

4. Plato _____

Exercise 2

When an article combines information from many sources, it is sometimes difficult to determine the source of an individual piece of information. In this article it is especially difficult to determine if individual statements are those of the author or are based on the work of the experts cited.

Following is a list of statements made in the article. Indicate if each one has been made by the author or one of her sources.

Example:

_____Levine_____ We laugh to express mastery over anxiety.

1. _____ We laugh as a release for our normally repressed drives.

2. _____ Laughter strengthens social bonds.

3. _____ We laugh to release energy after a crisis.

4. _____ A sense of humor is a result of the mastery of human relationships.

5. _____ We sometimes laugh when nothing is funny.

6. _____ Laughter is a pleasurable physical sensation.

DISCUSSION

This article discusses situations which bring about laughter in the United States. Which situations given are similar to those in your country? Which are different? Which elements of laughter do you think are the same for all people?

VOCABULARY FROM CONTEXT

Exercise 1

Use the context provided to determine the meanings of the italicized words. Write a definition, synonym, or description of each of the italicized vocabulary items in the space provided.

1. _Concerned, nervousness_
2. _offende, don't want_
3. _knowledge_
4. _nervous_
5. _cover_
6. _hide_
7. _central_

Some people feel very nervous when they fly in airplanes. No matter how hard they try, they cannot lower their *anxiety*. Some of them enjoy talking about their fears while others *resent* being asked to discuss their personal feelings. Many are aware that they feel anxious but only a few are *conscious* of the way they express their *tension*. Some people try to hide their nervousness; they try to *disguise* their anxiety by telling jokes. Others become loud and *aggressive*, attacking people by making them the *butt* of cruel jokes.

8. _____ central

9. _____ principal

10. _____ way facts

11. _____ important

12. _____ control

13. _____ contain - keep in

14. _____ impulse way

15. get rid of _____ through out

16. _____ cause - not - function

17. _____ begin

18. problem _____

19. _____ no innocent

20. _____ complete

Sometimes making someone else the *target* of jokes is an attempt to control one's own fears—to *master* anxiety.

A number of *factors* can be mentioned as important in explaining why some people have a fear of flying: early childhood experiences, general sense of security, fear of heights, trust in others, percent of alcohol in blood, etc., but the *crucial* factor seems to be a feeling of no control.

Usually, we are able to *suppress* our feelings so that they do not affect our behavior.

By smiling foolishly and talking loudly, we are able to *repress* the rising feeling of fear so that it does not affect the way we behave.

Most of us learn very young in life to control basic *drives* such as sex, hunger, and aggression.

Sometimes the tension produced by our fears is so great that we cannot suppress it. At such times we need to *discharge* the tension by laughing or crying.

The memory of a bad experience can sometimes *trigger* the same fear caused by that experience. Thus, a child might be frightened by the sight of a dog even though he is safe, merely because he once had a bad experience with a dog. A bad experience can be the *cue* that triggers our fears.

Everyone experiences fear during major *crises*—such as fires, automobile accidents, etc.—but some people are even afraid of the dark.

At the time of the crime, the man felt no emotion but later he began to feel *guilty*, so he went to the police and told them the whole story.

Because it is necessary to recognize a problem before it can be solved, admitting that we are afraid is an *integral* part of the process of mastering our fears.

Exercise 2

The following groups of sentences have been adapted from the article "Why We Laugh." Use context clues to determine the meanings of the italicized words. Write a definition, synonym, or description of each of the italicized vocabulary items in the space provided.

1. People who survive frightening situations frequently *intersperse* their story of the crisis with laughter. Part of the laughter expressed is relief that everything is all right. During a crisis, everyone mobilizes energy to deal with the potential problem. If the danger is avoided we need to release that energy. For example, if a pilot *averts* a plane crash by making a safe emergency landing, he may laugh as he describes his experience.   intersperse: _____

   averts: _____

2. We find these jokes funny because they provide a sudden release of our normally suppressed drives. We are free to enjoy the forbidden, and the energy we normally use to *inhibit* these drives is discharged as laughter. _____

3. When we are secure about our abilities, we can joke about our *foibles*. If we can laugh at our small faults, we will not be overpowered by them. _____

4. A man is watering his lawn just as an attractive, well-dressed blond walks by. As he *ogles* her, he accidently turns the hose on his ugly, *dowdy* wife.   ogle: _____

   dowdy: _____

VOCABULARY REVIEW

Two of the words on each line in the following exercise are similar in meaning. Circle the word which does not belong.

1. cue	butt	target
2. inhibit	suppress	trigger
3. resent	release	discharge
4. crucial	conscious	integral
5. aggression	repression	suppression

READING SELECTION 2: Narrative

The following passage, like the one in Unit 4, is taken from Gerald Durrell's book, *My Family and Other Animals*.* In this selection the author's habit of collecting strange and wonderful animal life throws the house into complete confusion.

Read the selection to get a general understanding of the story, then do the exercises which follow. You may want to do Vocabulary from Context exercise 1 on page 137 before you begin reading.

An Attack on the Family

1   I grew very fond of the scorpions in the garden wall. I found them to be pleasant, unassuming creatures with, on the whole, the most charming habits. Provided you did nothing silly or clumsy (like putting your hand on one) the scorpions treated you with respect, their one desire being to get away and hide as quickly as possible. They must have found me rather a trial, for I was always ripping sections of the plaster away so that I could watch them, or capturing them and making them walk about in jam-jars so that I could see the way their feet moved. By means of my sudden and unexpected assaults on the wall I discovered quite a bit about the scorpions.

2   By crouching under the wall at night with a torch, I managed to catch some brief glimpses of the scorpions' wonderful courtship dances. I saw them standing, claws joined, their bodies raised to the skies, their tails lovingly intertwined; I saw them waltzing slowly in circles, claw in claw. But my view of these performances was all too short, for almost as soon as I switched on the torch the partners would stop, pause for a moment, and then, seeing that I was not going to extinguish the light, they would turn round and walk firmly away, claw in claw, side by side. They were definitely beasts that believed in keeping themselves *to* themselves. If I could have kept a colony in captivity I would probably have been able to see the whole of the courtship, but the family had forbidden scorpions in the house, despite my arguments in favour of them.

3   Then one day I found a fat female scorpion in the wall, wearing what at first glance appeared to be a pale brown fur coat. Closer inspection proved that this strange garment was made up of a mass of tiny babies clinging to the mother's back. I was enraptured by this family, and I made up my mind to smuggle them into the house and up to my bedroom so that I might keep them and watch them grow up. With infinite care I manoeuvred the mother and family into a matchbox, and then hurried to the villa. It was rather unfortunate that just as I entered the door lunch should be served; however, I placed the match box carefully on the mantelpiece in the drawing-room, so that the scorpions could get plenty of air, and made my way to the dining-room and joined the family for the meal. Dawdling over my food, feeding Roger under the table and listening to the family arguing, I completely forgot about my exciting new captures. At last Larry, having finished, brought the cigarettes from the drawing-room, and lying back in his chair he put one in his mouth and picked up the matchbox he had brought. Unaware of my impending doom I watched him interestedly as, still talking glibly, he opened the matchbox.

4   Now, I maintain to this day that the female scorpion meant no harm. She was agitated and annoyed at being shut up in a matchbox for so long, and so she seized the first opportunity to escape. She hoisted herself out of the box with great rapidi-

---

*Adapted from *My Family and Other Animals* by Gerald Durrell. Copyright © 1956 by Gerald Durrell. Reprinted by permission of The Viking Press and Granada Publishing Ltd.

ty, her babies clinging on desperately, and scuttled on to the back of Larry's hand. There, not quite certain what to do next, she paused, her sting curved up at the ready. Larry, feeling the movement of her claws, glanced down to see what it was, and from that moment things got increasingly confused.

5   He uttered a roar of fright that made Lugaretzia drop a plate and brought Roger out from beneath the table, barking wildly. With a flick of his hand he sent the unfortunate scorpion flying down the table, and she landed midway between Margo and Leslie, scattering babies like confetti as she thumped on the cloth. Thoroughly enraged at this treatment, the creature sped towards Leslie, her sting quivering with anger. Leslie leapt to his feet, overturning his chair, and flicked out desperately with his napkin, sending the scorpion rolling across the cloth towards Margo, who promptly let out a scream that any railway engine would have been proud to produce. Mother, completely bewildered by this sudden and rapid change from peace to chaos, put on her glasses and peered down the table to see what was causing the pandemonium, and at that moment Margo, in a vain attempt to stop the scorpion's advance, hurled a glass of water at it. The shower missed the animal completely, but successfully drenched Mother, who, not being able to stand cold water, promptly lost her breath and sat gasping at the end of the table, unable even to protest. The scorpion had now gone to ground under Leslie's plate, while her babies swarmed wildly all over the table. Roger, mystified by the panic, but determined to do his share, ran round and round the room, barking hysterically.

6   "It's that bloody boy again . . ." bellowed Larry.
"Look out! Look out! They're coming!" screamed Margo.
"All we need is a book," roared Leslie; "don't panic, hit 'em with a book."
"What on earth's the *matter* with you all?" Mother kept asking, wiping her glasses.
"It's that bloody boy . . . he'll kill the lot of us . . . Look at the table . . . knee-deep in scorpions . . ."
"Quick . . . quick . . . do something . . . Look out, look out!"
"Stop screeching and get a book, for God's sake . . . You're worse than the dog . . . Shut *up*, Roger."
"By the Grace of God I wasn't bitten . . ."
"Look out . . . there's another one . . . Quick . . . quick . . ."
"Oh, shut up and get me a book or something . . ."
"But *how* did the scorpions get on the table, dear?"
"That bloody boy . . . Every matchbox in the house is a deathtrap . . ."
"Look out, it's coming towards me . . . Quick, quick, do something . . ."
"Hit it with your knife . . . *your knife* . . . Go on, hit it . . ."

7   Since no one had bothered to explain things to him, Roger was under the mistaken impression that the family were being attacked, and that it was his duty to defend them. As Lugaretzia was the only stranger in the room, he came to the logical conclusion that she must be the responsible party, so he bit her in the ankle. This did not help matters very much.

8   By the time a certain amount of order had been restored, all the baby scorpions had hidden themselves under various plates and bits of cutlery. Eventually, after impassioned pleas on my part, backed up by Mother, Leslie's suggestion that the whole lot be killed was defeated. While the family, still simmering with rage and fright, retired to the drawing-room, I spent half an hour collecting the babies, picking them up in a teaspoon, and returning them to their mother's back. Then I carried them outside on a saucer and, with the utmost reluctance, released them on the garden wall. Roger and I went and spent the afternoon on the hillside, for I felt it would be wise to allow the family to have a siesta before seeing them again.

COMPREHENSION

Exercise 1

Answer the following questions. Your teacher may want you to answer the questions orally, in writing, or by underlining appropriate parts of the text. True/False items are indicated by a T/F preceding a statement. In many cases you will have to use your own judgment because the answer is not specifically given in the passage.

1. T / F   Scorpions are not dangerous.

2. T / F   The author likes scorpions.

3. Why wasn't the author able to observe the whole courtship dance? _____
_____

4. T / F   The author knew that his family would not allow scorpions in the house.

5. How did the mother scorpion carry her babies? _____

6. T / F   The author caught the scorpion family in a jam-jar.

7. When was the scorpion family discovered? _____
_____

8. Why did Margo throw water on Mother? _____
_____

9. T / F   The author tried to kill the scorpions with a book.

10. T / F   The author felt that the scorpions were attacking his family.

11. T / F   Mother supported the writer in his attempt to save the scorpions.

12. How were the scorpions removed from the house? _____
_____

13. T / F   The author stayed outside for the rest of the day because he didn't want to see the family until everyone had rested.

Exercise 2

To answer the following questions you will have to make decisions about the story based on careful reading. Many questions do not have clear-cut answers; you will have to decide what *you* think the best answer is. Be prepared to defend your choices with portions of the text.

1. Who is Roger? _____

2. Who is Lugaretzia? _____

3. How many people are in the Durrell family? _____ Name them, and indicate if they are male or female. _____

    _____

4. Who keeps yelling for a book? _____

5. Who says that every matchbox in the house is a death-trap? _____

6. Who is "screeching"? _____

7. Who says, "But *how* did the scorpions get on the table, dear?" _____

8. Who is the youngest member of the family? _____

9. In your opinion, who seems the most confused? _____

VOCABULARY FROM CONTEXT

Exercise 1

Use the context provided to determine the meanings of the italicized words. Write a definition, synonym, or description of each of the italicized vocabulary items in the space provided.

1. _____   Because the light frightened the scorpions away, I wasn't able to observe them for very long. However, by appearing suddenly with my electric torch, I was able to get brief *glimpses* of their behavior.

2. _____   I was completely *enraptured* with the scorpion family. My happiness at finding them was so great that I decided I would keep them in my room for closer study.

(*Continued on page 138.*)

3. _____ The members of the family were so angry that I decided to stay away from the house until dinner. Their *rage* truly frightened me.

4. _____ Because she had not seen the scorpions, Mother was completely *bewildered* by the sudden confusion.

5. _____ I begged the family not to kill the scorpions, and they finally listened to my *pleas*.

6. _____ Mr. and Mrs. Firth had a long *courtship*. They dated for nine years before they got married.

7. _____ He *crouched* down to look under the table for his shoes.

8. _____ After the scorpion affair the whole family tried *in vain* to get me to stop collecting animals and insects. They should have known that I wouldn't stop collecting just because of one little scare.

Exercise 2

This exercise is designed to give you additional clues to determine the meanings of unfamiliar vocabulary items in context. In the paragraph indicated by the number in parentheses, find the word or phrase that best fits the meaning given. Your teacher may want to read these aloud as you quickly scan the paragraph to find the answer.

1. (1) Which word means *a bother; an annoyance; a problem*?

2. (3) Which word in the third sentence means *to bring in secretly*?

3. (3) Which word at the end of the paragraph means *fate; future problems*?

4. (5) Which two words in the middle of the paragraph mean *confusion*?

5. (8) Which word in the first sentence means *peace and quiet; organization*?

Exercise 3
This exercise should be done after you have finished reading "An Attack on the Family." The exercise is designed to determine how well you have been able to use context clues to guess the meaning of unfamiliar vocabulary in "An Attack on the Family." Give a definition, synonym, or description of each of the words or phrases below. This exercise can be done orally or in writing.

1. assaults (last sentence, paragraph 1) _____

2. clinging (second sentence, paragraph 3) _____

3. manoeuvred (middle, paragraph 3) _____

4. maintain (paragraph 4) _____

5. hoisted (paragraph 4) _____

6. scuttled (paragraph 4) _____

7. peered (middle, paragraph 5) _____

8. hurled (bottom, paragraph 5) _____

9. drenched (bottom, paragraph 5) _____

10. swarmed (bottom, paragraph 5) _____

11. screeching (middle, paragraph 6) _____

12. reluctance (bottom, paragraph 8) _____

READING SELECTION 3: Short Story

What is a lottery? Why do you think lotteries have become popular throughout the world?

When "The Lottery" first appeared in *The New Yorker* in 1948, letters flooded the magazine expressing admiration, anger, and confusion at the story.* For a long time, Shirley Jackson refused to discuss the story, apparently believing that people had to make their own evaluation of it and come to a personal understanding of its meaning. Whatever people may think of it, they all agree that it is unusual.

Read "The Lottery" carefully and make your own judgment. You may want to do Vocabulary from Context exercise 1 on page 148 before you begin reading.

The Lottery

1   The morning of June 27th was clear and sunny, with the fresh warmth of a full-summer day; the flowers were blossoming profusely, and the grass was richly green. The people of the village began to gather in the square, between the post office and the bank, around ten o'clock; in some towns there were so many people that the lottery took two days and had to be started on June 26th, but in this village, where there were only about three hundred people, the whole lottery took only about two hours, so it could begin at ten o'clock in the morning and still be through in time to allow the villagers to get home for noon dinner.

2   The children assembled first, of course. School was recently over for the summer, and the feeling of liberty sat uneasily on most of them; they tended to gather together quietly for a while before they broke into boisterous play, and their talk was still of the classroom and the teacher, of books and reprimands. Bobby Martin had already stuffed his pockets full of stones, and the other boys soon followed his example, selecting the smoothest and roundest stones; Bobby and Harry Jones and Dickie Delacroix—the villagers pronounced the name "Dellacroy"—eventually made a great pile of stones in one corner of the square and guarded it against the raids of the other boys. The girls stood aside, talking among themselves, looking over their shoulders at the boys, and the very small children rolled in the dust or clung to the hands of their older brothers or sisters.

3   Soon the men began to gather, surveying their own children, speaking of planting and rain, tractors and taxes. They stood together, away from the pile of stones in the corner, and their jokes were quiet, and they smiled rather than laughed. The women, wearing faded house dresses and sweaters, came shortly after their menfolk. They greeted one another and exchanged bits of gossip as they went to join their husbands. Soon the women, standing by their husbands, began to call to their children, and the children came reluctantly, having to be called four or five times. Bobby Martin ducked under his mother's grasping hand and ran, laughing, back to the pile of stones. His father spoke up sharply, and Bobby came quickly and took his place between his father and his oldest brother.

4   The lottery was conducted—as were the square dances, the teen-age club, the Halloween program—by Mr. Summers, who had time and energy to devote to civic activities. He was a round-faced, jovial man, and he ran the coal business; and people were sorry for him, because he had no children and his wife was a scold. When he

---

*Reprinted with the permission of Farrar, Straus and Giroux, Inc., from "The Lottery" by Shirley Jackson, copyright © 1948, 1949 by Shirley Jackson, copyright renewed 1976 by Laurence Hyman, Barry Hyman, Mrs. Sarah Webster, and Mrs. Joanne Schnurer. "The Lottery" originally appeared in *The New Yorker*.

arrived in the square, carrying the black wooden box, there was murmur of conversation among the villagers, and he waved and called, "Little late today, folks." The postmaster, Mr. Graves, followed him, carrying a three-legged stool; and the stool was put in the center of the square, and Mr. Summers set the black box down on it. The villagers kept their distance, leaving a space between themselves and the stool, and when Mr. Summers said, "Some of you fellows want to give me hand?" there was a hesitation before two men, Mr. Martin and his oldest son, Baxter, came forward to hold the box steady on the stool while Mr. Summers stirred up the papers inside it.

5   The original paraphernalia for the lottery had been lost long ago, and the black box now resting on the stool had been put into use even before Old Man Warner, the oldest man in town, was born. Mr. Summers spoke frequently to the villagers about making a new box, but no one liked to upset even as much tradition as was represented by the black box. There was a story that the present box had been made with some pieces of the box that had preceded it, the one that had been constructed when the first people settled down to make a village here. Every year, after the lottery, Mr. Summers began talking again about a new box, but every year the subject was allowed to fade off without anything's being done. The black box grew shabbier each year; by now it was no longer completely black but splintered badly along one side to show the original wood color, and in some places faded or stained.

6   Mr. Martin and his oldest son, Baxter, held the black box securely on the stool until Mr. Summers had stirred the papers thoroughly with his hand. Because so much of the ritual had been forgotten or discarded, Mr. Summers had been successful in having slips of paper substituted for the chips of wood that had been used for generations. Chips of wood, Mr. Summers had argued, had been all very well when the village was tiny, but now that the population was more than three hundred and likely to keep on growing, it was necessary to use something that would fit more easily into the black box. The night before the lottery, Mr. Summers and Mr. Graves made up the slips of paper and put them into the box, and it was then taken to the safe of Mr Summers' coal company and locked up until Mr. Summers was ready to take it to the square next morning. The rest of the year, the box was put away, sometimes one place, sometimes another; it had spent one year in Mr. Graves's barn and another year underfoot in the post office, and sometimes it was set on a shelf in the Martin grocery and left there.

7   There was a great deal of fussing to be done before Mr. Summers declared the lottery open. There were the lists to make up—of heads of families, heads of households in each family, members of each household in each family. There was the proper swearing-in of Mr. Summers by the postmaster, as the official of the lottery; at one time, some people remembered, there had been a recital of some sort, performed by the official of the lottery, a perfunctory, tuneless chant that had been rattled off duly each year; some people believed that the official of the lottery used to stand just so when he said or sang it; others believed that he was supposed to walk among the people; but years and years ago this part of the ritual had been allowed to lapse. There had been also a ritual salute, which the official of the lottery had had to use in addressing each person who came up to draw from the box, but this also had changed with time, until now it was felt necessary only for the official to speak to each person approaching. Mr. Summers was very good at all this; in his clean white shirt and blue jeans, with one hand resting carelessly on the black box, he seemed very proper and important as he talked interminably to Mr. Graves and the Martins.

8   Just as Mr. Summers finally left off talking and turned to the assembled villagers, Mrs. Hutchinson came hurriedly along the path to the square, her sweater thrown

over her shoulders, and slid into place in the back of the crowd. "Clean forgot what day it was," she said to Mrs. Delacroix, who stood next to her, and they both laughed softly. "Thought my old man was out back stacking wood," Mrs. Hutchinson went on, "and then I looked out the window and the kids was gone, and then I remembered it was the twenty-seventh and came a-running." She dried her hands on her apron, and Mrs. Delacroix said, "You're in time, though. They're still talking away up there."

9   Mrs. Hutchinson craned her neck to see through the crowd and found her husband and children standing near the front. She tapped Mrs. Delacroix on the arm as a farewell and began to make her way through the crowd. The people separated good-humoredly to let her through; two or three people said, in voices just loud enough to be heard across the crowd, "Here comes your Mrs., Hutchinson," and "Bill, she made it after all." Mrs. Hutchinson reached her husband, and Mr. Summers, who had been waiting, said cheerfully, "Thought we were going to have to get on without you, Tessie." Mrs. Hutchinson said, grinning, "Wouldn't have me leave m'dishes in the sink, now, would you Joe?" and soft laughter ran through the crowd as the people stirred back into position after Mrs. Hutchinson's arrival.

10   "Well, now," Mr. Summers said soberly, "guess we better get started, get this over with, so's we can go back to work. Anybody ain't here?"

"Dunbar," several people said. "Dunbar, Dunbar."

Mr. Summers consulted his list. "Clyde Dunbar," he said. "That's right. He's broke his leg, hasn't he? Who's drawing for him?"

11   "Me, I guess," a woman said, and Mr. Summers turned to look at her. "Wife draws for her husband," Mr. Summers said. "Don't you have a grown boy to do it for you, Janey?" Although Mr. Summers and everyone else in the village knew the answer perfectly well, it was the business of the official of the lottery to ask such questions formally. Mr. Summers waited with an expression of polite interest while Mrs. Dunbar answered.

"Horace's not but sixteen yet," Mrs. Dunbar said regretfully. "Guess I gotta fill in for the old man this year."

"Right," Mr. Summers said. He made a note on the list he was holding. Then he asked, "Watson boy drawing this year?"

12   A tall boy in the crowd raised his hand, "Here," he said. "I'm drawing for m'mother and me." He blinked his eyes nervously and ducked his head as several voices in the crowd said things like "Good fellow, Jack," and "Glad to see your mother's got a man to do it."

"Well," Mr. Summers said, "guess that's everyone. Old Man Warner make it?"

"Here," a voice said, and Mr. Summers nodded.

13   A sudden hush fell on the crowd as Mr. Summers cleared his throat and looked at the list. "All ready?" he called. "Now, I'll read the names—heads of families first—and the men come up and take a paper out of the box. Keep the paper folded in your hand without looking at it until everyone has had a turn. Everything clear?"

14   The people had done it so many times that they only half listened to the directions; most of them were quiet, wetting their lips, not looking around. Then Mr. Summers raised one hand high and said, "Adams." A man disengaged himself from the crowd and came forward. "Hi, Steve," Mr. Summers said, and Mr. Adams said, "Hi, Joe." They grinned at one another humorlessly and nervously. Then Mr. Adams reached into the black box and took out a folded paper. He held it firmly by one corner as he turned and went hastily back to his place in the crowd, where he stood a little apart from his family, not looking down at his hand.

"Allen," Mr. Summers said. "Anderson . . . Bentham."

15   "Seems like there's no time at all between lotteries any more," Mrs. Delacroix said to Mrs. Graves in the back row. "Seems like we got through with the last one only last week."

"Time sure goes fast," Mrs. Graves said.

"Clark . . . Delacroix."

"There goes my old man," Mrs. Delacroix said. She held her breath while her husband went forward.

"Dunbar," Mr. Summers said, and Mrs. Dunbar went steadily to the box while one of the women said, "Go on, Janey," and another said, "There she goes."

16   "We're next," Mrs. Graves said. She watched while Mr. Graves came around from the side of the box, greeted Mr. Summers gravely, and selected a slip of paper from the box. By now, all through the crowd there were men holding the small folded papers in their large hands, turning them over and over nervously. Mrs. Dunbar and her two sons stood together, Mrs. Dunbar holding the slip of paper.

"Harburt . . . Hutchinson."

"Get up there, Bill," Mrs. Hutchinson said, and the people near her laughed. "Jones."

17   "They do say," Mr. Adams said to Old Man Warner, who stood next to him, "that over in the north village they're talking of giving up the lottery."

Old Man Warner snorted. "Pack of crazy fools," he said. "Listening to the young folks, nothing's good enough for them. Next thing you know, they'll be wanting to go back to living in caves, nobody work any more, live *that* way for a while. Used to be a saying about 'Lottery in June, corn be heavy soon.' First thing you know, we'd all be eating stewed chickweed and acorns. There's always been a lottery," he added petulantly. "Bad enough to see young Joe Summers up there joking with everybody."

18   "Some places have already quit lotteries," Mrs. Adams said.

"Nothing but trouble in that." Old Man Warner said stoutly. "Pack of young fools."

"Martin." And Bobby Martin watched his father go forward. "Overdyke . . . Percy."

"I wish they'd hurry," Mrs. Dunbar said to her older son. "I wish they'd hurry."

"They're almost through," her son said.

"You get ready to run tell Dad," Mrs. Dunbar said.

19   Mr. Summers called his own name and then stepped forward precisely and selected a slip from the box. Then he called, "Warner."

"Seventy-seventh year I been in the lottery," Old Man Warner said as he went through the crowd. "Seventy-seventh time."

"Watson." The tall boy came awkwardly through the crowd. Someone said, "Don't be nervous, Jack," and Mr. Summers said, "Take your time, son."

"Zanini."

20   After that, there was a long pause, a breathless pause, until Mr. Summers, holding his slip of paper in the air, said, "All right, fellows." For a minute, no one moved, and then all the slips of paper were opened. Suddenly, all the women began to speak at once, saying, "Who is it?" "Who's got it?" "Is it the Dunbars?" "Is it the Watsons?" Then the voices began to say, "It's Hutchinson. It's Bill." "Bill Hutchinson's got it."

"Go tell your father," Mrs. Dunbar said to her older son.

21   People began to look around to see the Hutchinsons. Bill Hutchinson was standing

quiet, staring down at the paper in his hand. Suddenly, Tessie Hutchinson shouted to Mr. Summers, "You didn't give him time enough to take any paper he wanted. I saw you. It wasn't fair!"

"Be a good sport, Tessie," Mrs. Delacroix called, and Mrs. Graves said, "All of us took the same chance."

"Shut up, Tessie," Bill Hutchinson said.

22   "Well, everyone," Mr. Summers said, "that was done pretty fast, and now we've got to be hurrying a little more to get done in time." He consulted his next list. "Bill," he said, "you draw for the Hutchinson family. You got any other households in the Hutchinsons?"

"There's Don and Eva," Mrs. Hutchinson yelled. "Make *them* take their chance!"

"Daughters draw with their husbands' families, Tessie," Mr. Summers said gently. "You know that as well as anyone else."

"It wasn't *fair!*" Tessie said.

23   "I guess not, Joe," Bill Hutchinson said regretfully. "My daughter draws with her husband's family, that's only fair. And I've got no other family except the kids."

"Then, as far as drawing for families is concerned, it's you," Mr. Summers said in explanation, "and as far as drawing for households is concerned, that's you, too. Right?"

"Right," Bill Hutchinson said.

"How many kids, Bill?" Mr. Summers asked formally.

"Three," Bill Hutchinson said. "There's Bill, Jr., and Nancy, and little Dave. And Tessie and me."

"All right, then," Mr. Summers said. "Harry, you got their tickets back?"

24   Mr. Graves nodded and held up the slips of paper. "Put them in the box, then," Mr. Summers directed. "Take Bill's and put it in."

"I think we ought to start over," Mrs. Huchinson said, as quietly as she could. "I tell you it wasn't *fair*. You didn't give him time enough to choose. *Everybody* saw that."

Mr. Graves had selected the five slips and put them in the box, and he dropped all the papers but those onto the ground, where the breeze caught them and lifted them off.

"Listen, everybody," Mrs. Hutchinson was saying to the people around her.

"Ready, Bill?" Mr. Summers asked, and Bill Hutchinson, with one quick glance around at his wife and children, nodded.

25   "Remember," Mr. Summers said, "take the slips and keep them folded until each person has taken one. Harry, you help little Dave." Mr. Graves took the hand of the little boy, who came willingly with him up to the box. "Take a paper out of the box, Davy," Mr. Summers said. Davy put his hand into the box and laughed. "Take just one paper," Mr. Summers said. "Harry, you hold it for him." Mr. Graves took the child's hand and removed the folded paper from the right fist and held it while little Dave stood next to him and looked up at him wonderingly.

26   "Nancy next," Mr. Summers said. Nancy was twelve, and her school friends breathed heavily as she went forward, switching her skirt, and took a slip daintily from the box. "Bill, Jr.," Mr. Summers said, and Billy, his face red and his feet overlarge, nearly knocked the box over as he got a paper out. "Tessie," Mr. Summers said. She hesitated for a minute, looking around defiantly, and then set her lips and went up to the box. She snatched a paper out and held it behind her.

27   "Bill," Mr. Summers said, and Bill Hutchinson reached into the box and felt around, bringing his hand out at last with the slip of paper in it.

The crowd was quiet. A girl whispered, "I hope it's not Nancy," and the sound of the whisper reached the edges of the crowd.

"It's not the way it used to be," Old Man Warner said clearly. "People ain't the way they used to be."

"All right," Mr. Summers said. "Open the papers. Harry, you open little Dave's."

28   Mr. Graves opened the slip of paper, and there was a general sigh through the crowd as he held it up and everyone could see that it was blank. Nancy and Bill, Jr., opened theirs at the same time, and both beamed and laughed, turning around to the crowd and holding their slips above their heads.

"Tessie," Mr. Summers said. There was a pause, and then Mr. Summers looked at Bill Hutchinson, and Bill unfolded his paper and showed it. It was blank.

"It's Tessie," Mr. Summers said, and his voice was hushed. "Show us her paper, Bill."

29   Bill Hutchinson went over to his wife and forced the slip of paper out of her hand. It had a black spot on it, the black spot Mr. Summers had made the night before with the heavy pencil in the coal-company office. Bill Hutchinson held it up, and there was a stir in the crowd.

"All right, folks," Mr. Summers said, "Let's finish quickly."

30   Although the villagers had forgotten the ritual and lost the original black box, they still remembered to use stones. The pile of stones the boys had made earlier was ready; there were stones on the ground with the blowing scraps of paper that had come out of the box. Mrs. Delacroix selected a stone so large she had to pick it up with both hands and turned to Mrs. Dunbar. "Come on," she said. "Hurry up."

Mrs. Dunbar had small stones in both hands, and she said, gasping for breath, "I can't run at all. You'll have to go ahead and I'll catch up with you."

31   The children had stones already, and someone gave little Davy Hutchinson a few pebbles.

Tessie Hutchinson was in the center of a cleared space by now, and she held her hands out desperately as the villagers moved in on her. "It isn't fair," she said. A stone hit her on the side of the head.

Old Man Warner was saying, "Come on, come on, everyone." Steve Adams was in the front of the crowd of villagers, with Mrs. Graves beside him.

"It isn't fair, it isn't right," Mrs. Hutchinson screamed, and then they were upon her.

COMPREHENSION

Exercise 1
Without referring to the story, indicate if each statement below is true (T) or false (F).

1. _____ The lottery was always held in summer.

2. _____ The lottery had not changed for many generations.

3. _____ The villagers were angry at Mrs. Huchinson for being late.

4. _____ In the first drawing, only one person from each family drew a paper from the black box.

5. _____ The lottery was a custom only in this small village.

6. _____ Bill Hutchinson thought the first drawing was unfair.

7. _____ Tessie Hutchinson drew the paper with the black dot in the final drawing.

8. _____ The people wanted to finish in a hurry because they didn't like Tessie.

9. _____ The lottery was a form of human sacrifice.

Exercise 2
The following exercise requires a careful reading of "The Lottery." Indicate if each statement below is true (T) or false (F) according to your understanding of the story. Use information in the passage and inferences which can be drawn from the passage to make your decisions. You may refer to the story if necessary.

1. _____ Old Man Warner believed that the lottery assured the prosperity of the village.

2. _____ The date of the lottery was not rigidly fixed but occurred any time in summer when all of the villagers could be present.

3. _____ Mr. Summers never managed to make a new box for the lottery because people were unwilling to change the traditions that remained from the past.

4. _____ A family might contain several households.

5. _____ Mr. Warner felt that stopping the lottery would be equal to returning to prehistoric times.

6. _____ Only Mr. Warner remembered when the lottery was started.

7. _____ The villagers were hesitant to take part in the final step in the lottery.

DRAWING INFERENCES

1. When did you first realize that this was a strange lottery? That winning the lottery was not desirable?

2. What details did the author add to make the lottery seem like a "normal" lottery? What details indicated that the lottery was strange? What details had double meanings?

3. Why do you think everyone had to take part in the final step of the lottery?

4. What was Mr. Warner's attitude toward the lottery? In what way and why did his attitude differ from other members of the community? What group in every society does Mr. Warner represent?

5. Why did Tessie want to include Tom and Eva in the final drawing?

6. Which aspects of the lottery have changed? Which have not changed?

DISCUSSION

1. How do you think the lottery began? Why was it started? Why does it take place at that time of year?

2. Why do you think the community continues the lottery?

3. Was the lottery fair?

4. Would you take part in the lottery if you were a member of the community?

5. This story is about a physical sacrifice in which a person is killed. Sacrifice is characterized by the suffering of one member of a group for the benefit of the group as a whole, and by a sense of relief when one realizes that he or she has not been selected. This relief is so great that it leads to unconcern toward the fate of the person(s) to be sacrificed. Using this definition, can you think of specific institutions in modern societies in which sacrifices take place? Aside from physical sacrifice, what other types of sacrifice are possible?

VOCABULARY FROM CONTEXT

Exercise 1

Use the context provided to determine the meanings of the italicized words. Write a definition, synonym, or description of each of the italicized vocabulary items in the space provided.

1. _____

2. _____

3. _____
4. _____
5. _____
6. _____

7. _____
8. _____

I like any game of chance, but I most enjoy taking part in a lottery. The lottery is like an unchanging religious ceremony, and it is perhaps this *ritual* quality of the lottery that people enjoy. Unlike other games of chance, a lottery does not require a great deal of *paraphernalia*. The only equipment needed is a bowl filled with slips of paper. I enjoy the excitement of watching the official pick the winning number. The moment before the *drawing* is very serious. The judge *gravely* approaches the bowl and looks at the crowd *soberly*. The crowd is quiet except for the low *murmur* of excitement. Suddenly the winner is selected. After the lottery is over, everyone but the winner throws away his piece of paper, and the *discarded* slips are soon blown away by the wind. People begin to *disengage* themselves from the crowd and the lottery is over.

Exercise 2

This exercise is designed to give you additional clues to determine the meanings of unfamiliar vocabulary items in context. In the paragraph indicated by the number in parentheses, find the word that best fits the meaning given. Your teacher may want to read these aloud as you quickly scan the paragraph to find the answer.

1. (2) Which word means *noisy and excited*?

2. (2) Which word means *criticisms; severe or formal scoldings*?

3. (3) Which word means *information, usually about other people, not always factual*?

4. (7) Which word at the beginning of the paragraph means *taking care of details*?

5. (7) Which word at the bottom of the paragraph means *endlessly*?

Exercise 3
This exercise should be done after you have finished reading "The Lottery." The exercise is designed to determine how well you have been able to use context clues to guess the meaning of unfamiliar vocabulary in "The Lottery." Give a definition, synonym, or description of each of the words and phrases below. The number in parentheses indicates the paragraph in which the word can be found. This exercise can be done orally or in writing.

1. devote (first sentence, paragraph 4) _____

2. stirred up (last sentence, paragraph 4) _____

3. fade off (bottom, paragraph 5) _____

4. shabbier (last sentence, paragraph 5) _____

5. lapse (middle, paragraph 7) _____

6. craned (first sentence, paragraph 9) _____

7. tapped (second sentence, paragraph 9) _____

8. consulted (paragraph 10) _____

NONPROSE READING: Train Schedule

Below is a schedule of trains which travel between Chicago and Toronto. Train schedules are often difficult to read.* This exercise is designed to help you solve typical problems encountered by train travelers. Skim the schedule, then use the questions on page 151 to guide you in finding specific information.

These are abbreviations you may need to know:

p P.M.	CT Central Time	Ar arrive
a A.M.	ET Eastern Time	Dp depart

CHICAGO-DETROIT/PORT HURON LINE-(TORONTO)

Read Down   *(Local Time)*   Read Up

362	364	360		Train Number	365	361	363
The St.Clair	The Blue Water	The Wolverine		Train Name	The Blue Water	The Wolverine	The St.Clair
Daily	♠ Daily	Daily		Frequency of Operation	♠ Daily	Daily	Daily
🥤🛄	🥤	🥤	Miles	Type of Service	🥤	🥤🛄	🥤
4 15 p	3 15 p	7 45 a	0	Dp.CHICAGO, IL (Union Sta.) .(CT)Ar	12 10 p	1 45 p	10 30 p
7 10 p	6 10 p	10 40 a	89	............Niles, MI.......(ET).	11 15 a	12 50 p	9 35 p
8 10 p	7 10 p	11 40 a	136	...........KALAMAZOO..........	10 15 a	11 55 a	8 40 p
8 40 p	7 50 p	12 10 p	160	Ar........Battle Creek........ Dp	9 40 a	11 25 a	8 10 p
	7 55 p		160	Dp........Battle Creek........Ar	9 35 a		
	9 25 p		208	...........LANSING.............	8 00 a		
	f10 07 p		238	.........Durand⊕.........	f 7 18 a		
	10 49 p		255	..........Flint..........	6 38 a		
	f11 16 p		275	..........Lapeer⊕.........	f 6 10 a		
	12 25 a		319	Ar.........Port Huron.........Dp	5 15 a		
				(via Canadian Nat'l. Railways)			
	7 45 a		0	Dp........Sarnia, ON..........Ar	11 15 p		
	11 15 a		174	Ar..TORONTO, ON (Union Sta.).Dp	7 10 p		
8 40 p		12 10 p	160	Dp........Battle Creek..........Ar		11 25 a	8 10 p
9 35 p		1 05 p	205	...........Jackson..............		10 30 a	7 15 p
10 20 p		1 50 p	243	..........ANN ARBOR............		9 45 a	6 30 p
11 05 p		2 35 p	279	Ar..........DETROIT..........Dp		9 00 a	5 45 p
				(via Canadian Nat'l. Railways)			
6 50 a		6 05 p	0	Dp.......Windsor, ON...........Ar		1 10 a	4 20 p
8 40 a		7 55 p	108	Ar.........London..........Ar		10 10 p	2 25 p
10 50 a		10 10 p	223	Ar TORONTO,ON (Union Sta.)(ET)Dp		7 45 p	12 05 p

⊕ - Tickets not available at station for some or all trains. Tickets may be purchased from authorized Amtrak travel agent or train conductor (no penalty for cash fare on trains if no agent on duty at train time). Assistance with baggage will be provided by on-train attendants.

🛄 - Checked Baggage Service; consult Services listing or agent.

♠ - Service financed in part by a grant from Department of Transportation, State of Michigan.

🥤 - Light Meal and Beverage Service.

f - Flag Stop; stops only on signal to receive or discharge passengers.

Schedule courtesy of AMTRAK

---

*For an explanation of nonprose reading, see Unit 1.

Use the schedule on page 150 to answer the following questions. Your teacher may want you to do this exercise orally or in writing.

1. How many trains are available for trips from Chicago to Toronto? What are their names?
   _____
   How often do they run? _____

2. Traveling from Chicago to Toronto, where do you cross the time zone? _____
   _____ Given that Chicago is west of Toronto, what time is it in
   Chicago when it is 3:15 P.M. in Toronto? _____

3. Which train would you take if you wanted to get off at Flint? _____

4. Is there direct train service between Lansing and Ann Arbor? _____

5. How far is it from Sarnia to Toronto? From Windsor to Toronto? _____
   _____

6. How long is the trip from Chicago to Niles? (miles and hours) _____
   _____

7. Traveling from Chicago to Toronto, which train might you take if you had a lot of luggage?
   _____

8. Leaving from Lapeer, would you expect to buy your ticket before you board the train? _____
   Would it cost more to buy your ticket on the train? _____

9. Which train offers the fastest service from Chicago to Toronto? _____

10. If you were traveling from Chicago to Toronto and had to choose between the St. Clair and
    the Wolverine, which train would you take? Consider the following questions:
    a. Which train is faster? _____
    b. Do these trains take you directly to Toronto? _____
    c. How much time do you have between your arrival in Detroit and your departure from
       Windsor? _____
    d. Which schedule might require you to stay in a hotel in Detroit or Windsor? _____
    _____

    Which train would you take? _____

WORD STUDY: Stems and Affixes

Below is a list of some commonly occurring stems and affixes.* Study their meanings, then do the exercises which follow. Your teacher may ask you to give examples of words you know which are derived from these stems and affixes.

Prefixes:		
	by-	aside or apart from the common, secondary
	de-	down from, away
	dia-	through, across
	epi-	upon, over, outer
	hyper-	above, beyond
	hypo-	under, beneath, down

Stems:		
	-capit-	head
	-corp-	body
	-derm-	skin
	-geo-	earth
	-hydr-, -hydro-	water, liquid
	-lith-	stone
	-ortho-	straight, correct
	-pod-, -ped-	foot
	-therm-, -thermo-	heat
	-ver-	true

Suffixes:		
	-ate	to make
	-fy	to make
	-ize	to make

*For a list of all stems and affixes taught in *Reader's Choice*, see Appendix.

Exercise 1

Read each of the following sentences carefully, and write a definition, synonym, or description of the italicized word or words. Your teacher may want you to do this exercise orally or in writing.

1. Mr. Adams is employed at a *hydroelectric* plant. _____

2. Before Cindy gets dressed in the morning, she looks at the *thermometer* hanging outside her kitchen window. _____

3. Some doctors prescribe medication to slow down *hyperactive* children.

   _____

4. I'm not sure if that information is correct, but I'll look in our records to *verify* it.

   _____

5. Susan wants to replace the *pedals* on her bicycle with a special kind which racers use.

   _____

6. After spending so many days lost in the desert, he was suffering from severe *dehydration*.

   _____

7. June's father's hobby is photography, so she bought him a top-quality *tripod* for his birthday.

   _____

8. He will never learn how to improve his writing unless he stops being so *hypersensitive* to criticism. _____

9. Dr. Robinson said that just the sight of a *hypodermic* needle is enough to frighten many of his patients. _____

10. Although she finished her degree in dentistry in 1960, she wants to go back to school next year to specialize in *orthodontics*. _____

11. The immigration authorities *deported* Mr. Jensen because he did not have a legal passport.

    _____

12. The average *per capita* annual income in this country for people between the ages of sixteen and sixty-five has risen dramatically in the last ten years. _____

13. Mr. Thompson made an appointment with a *dermatologist* because he noticed small red spots on his hands. _____

14. Scientists have developed a sensitive instrument to measure *geothermal* variation.

    _____

15. Anthropologists say that bipedalism played an important role in the cultural evolution of the human species. Because early man was *bipedal*, his hands were free to make and use tools.

    _____

Exercise 2

Following is a list of words containing some of the stems and affixes introduced in this unit and the previous ones. Definitions of these words appear on the right. Put the letter of the appropriate definition next to each word.

1. _____ hypodermis
2. _____ diameter
3. _____ diachronic
4. _____ epicenter
5. _____ epidermis
6. _____ epigraph

a. the length of a straight line which passes through the center of an object
b. the outer layer of skin of some animals
c. the part of the earth's surface directly above the place of origin of an earthquake
d. the tissue immediately beneath the outer layer of tissue of plants
e. of or relating to phenomena as they occur over a period of time
f. a quotation printed at the beginning of a book or chapter to suggest its theme

7. _____ orthography
8. _____ hydrate
9. _____ decapitate
10. _____ orthodox
11. _____ hydrophobia
12. _____ corpulent

a. fear of water
b. conventional; agreeing with established or accepted doctrine
c. fat; large of body
d. to cut off the head of
e. correct spelling; writing words with the proper, accepted letters
f. to cause to combine with water or the element of water

13. _____ lithoid
14. _____ pedestrian
15. _____ megalith
16. _____ corporeal
17. _____ corpse
18. _____ podiatry

a. of or related to walking; a person who walks
b. stone-like
c. a stone of great size, especially one used in primitive monuments
d. a dead body
e. the care and treatment of the human foot in health and disease
f. bodily, of the nature of the physical body; not spiritual

19. _____ decentralize
20. _____ bypass
21. _____ diaphanous
22. _____ verisimilitude
23. _____ by-product
24. _____ geomorphic

a. a passage to one side; a route which goes around a town
b. to divide and distribute what has been concentrated or united
c. characterized by such fineness of texture as to permit seeing through
d. of or relating to the form of the earth or its surface features
e. the quality of appearing to be true
f. a secondary and sometimes unexpected result; something produced (as in manufacturing) in addition to the principal product

SENTENCE STUDY: Comprehension

Read these sentences carefully.* The questions which follow are designed to test your comprehension of complex grammatical structures. Select the *best* answer.

1. Like physical anthropology, orthodontics (dentistry dealing with the irregularities of teeth) tries to explain how and why men are different; unlike anthropology it also tries to correct those differences for functional or aesthetic reasons.
    How does orthodontics differ from physical anthropology?
    _____ a. Physical anthropology is concerned with aesthetics; orthodontics is not.
    _____ b. Physical anthropology deals with the irregularities of teeth.
    _____ c. Orthodontics tries to explain why men are different, anthropology does not.
    _____ d. Anthropology does not try to correct differences among men; orthodontics does.

2. What is most obvious in this book are all those details of daily living which make Mrs. Richards anything but common.
    According to this statement, what kind of person is Mrs. Richards?
    _____ a. She is very obvious.
    _____ b. She is an unusual person.
    _____ c. She is anything she wants to be.
    _____ d. She is quite ordinary.

3. A third island appeared gradually during a period of volcanic activity that lasted over four years. Later, the 1866 eruptions, which brought to Santorin those volcanologists who first began archeological work there, enlarged the new island through two new crater vents.
    What enlarged the third island?
    _____ a. the eruptions of 1866
    _____ b. a four-year period of volcanic activity
    _____ c. the activities of the men who came to study volanoes
    _____ d. archeological work, which created two new crater vents

4. Just before his tenth birthday John received a horse from his father; this was the first of a series of expensive gifts intended to create the impression of a loving parent.
    Why did John receive the horse?
    _____ a. because he was ten
    _____ b. because his father loved him
    _____ c. because his father wanted to seem loving
    _____ d. because his father wouldn't be able to give him expensive gifts in the future

5. Since industry and commerce are the largest users of electrical energy, using less electricity would mean a reduced industrial capacity and fewer jobs in the affected industries and therefore an unfavorable change in our economic structure.
    According to this sentence, decreasing the use of electricity _____
    _____ a. must begin immediately.
    _____ b. isn't important.
    _____ c. will cause difficulties.
    _____ d. won't affect industry.

---

*For an introduction to sentence study, see Unit 1.

6. The medical journal reported that heart attack victims who recover are approximately five times as likely to die within the next five years as those people without a history of heart disease.

What did this article say about people who have had a heart attack?
_____ a. They are more likely to die in the near future than others.
_____ b. They will die in five years.
_____ c. They are less likely to die than people without a history of heart disease.
_____ d. They are likely to recover.

7. Few phenomena in history are more puzzling than this one: that men and women with goals so vague, with knowledge so uncertain, with hopes so foggy, still would have risked dangers so certain and tasks so great.

What historical fact is puzzling?
_____ a. that people had such vague goals
_____ b. that people took such great risks
_____ c. that people had foggy hopes and uncertain knowledge
_____ d. that people completed such great tasks

8. Next he had to uncover the ancient secret—so jealously guarded by the ancients that no text of any kind, no descriptive wall painting, and no tomb inscriptions about making papyrus are known to exist.

What secret did this man want to discover?
_____ a. how to understand wall paintings
_____ b. how to read tomb inscriptions
_____ c. how to read the ancient texts
_____ d. how to produce papyrus

9. Alexis, ruler of a city where politics was a fine art, concealed his fears, received the noblemen with extravagant ceremonies, impressed them with his riches, praised them, entertained them, bribed them, made promises he had no intention of keeping—and thus succeeded in keeping their troops outside his city walls.

Why did Alexis give money and attention to the noblemen?
_____ a. because they praised him
_____ b. in order to prevent their armies from entering the city
_____ c. in order to impress them with his riches
_____ d. because they were his friends

PARAGRAPH READING: Restatement and Inference

This exercise is similar to the one found in Unit 5. Each paragraph below is followed by five statements. The statements are of four types:

1. Some of the statements are restatements of ideas in the original paragraph. They give the same information in a different way.
2. Some of the statements are inferences (conclusions) which can be drawn from the information given in the paragraph.
3. Some of the statements are false based on the information given.
4. Some of the statements cannot be judged true or false based on information given in the original paragraph.

Put a check (✓) next to all restatements and inferences (types 1 and 2). Note: do not check a statement which is true of itself but cannot be inferred from the paragraph.

Paragraph 1

It was the weekend before the exam. We were at the Walker's house and it was pouring rain. Jack came in late, drenched to the skin. He explained that a car had broken down on the road and he had stopped to help push it onto the shoulder and out of the traffic. I remember thinking then how typical that was of Jack. So helpful, so accommodating.

_____ a. Jack came in late because it was raining.

_____ b. Jack came in late because his car had broken down.

_____ c. The narrator thinks Jack is typical.

_____ d. The narrator bases his opinion of Jack on this one experience.

_____ e. Jack often helps other people.

Paragraph 2

The illustrations in books make it easier for us to believe in the people and events described. The more senses satisfied, the easier is belief. Visual observation tends to be the most convincing evidence. Children, being less capable of translating abstractions into actualities, need illustration more than adults. Most of us, when we read, tend to create only vague and ghostlike forms in response to the words. The illustrator, when he reads, must see. The great illustrator sees accurately.

_____ a. Illustrations help us to believe events described in words.

_____ b. When most people read, they do not picture events as accurately as can a great illustrator.

_____ c. Children are less able than adults to visualize events described in books.

_____ d. The author believes illustrators are especially able to imagine visual details described with words.

_____ e. The author believes all illustrators see accurately.

Paragraph 3

Surveys reveal that most adults consider themselves "well informed about the affairs of the nation and the world." Yet a regularly taken Roper poll that asks, "From where do you obtain most of your information about the world?" has found the percentage of people who reply, "Television" has been increasing steadily over the past decade. The latest questionnaire found that well over 60 percent of the respondents chose television over other media as their major source of information. These two facts are difficult to reconcile since even a casual study of television news reveals it is only a headline service and not a source of information enabling one to shape a world view.

_____ a. Most adults obtain most of their information about world affairs from the newspaper.

_____ b. The author of this passage does not believe that television provides enough information to make people well informed.

_____ c. The number of people answering the questionnaire has increased.

_____ d. Sixty percent of the people questioned get all their news from television.

_____ e. Most adults are well informed about the affairs of the nation and the world.

Paragraph 4

The dusty book room whose windows never opened, through whose panes the summer sun sent a dim light where gold specks danced and shimmered, opened magic windows for me through which I looked out on other worlds and times than those in which I lived. The narrow shelves rose halfway up the walls, their tops piled with untidy layers that almost touched the ceiling. The piles on the floor had to be climbed over, columns of books flanked the window, falling at a touch.

_____ a. The room is dusty and shadowy, filled with books from floor to ceiling.

_____ b. The sun never enters the room.

_____ c. The author spent time in this room as a child.

_____ d. The author did not like the room.

_____ e. Through the windows in the room, the author saw worlds other than those in which he lived.

Paragraph 5

By voting against mass transportation, voters have chosen to continue on a road to ruin. Our interstate highways, those much praised golden avenues built to whisk suburban travelers in and out of downtown have turned into the world's most expensive parking lots. That expense is not only economic—it is social. These highways have created great walls separating neighborhood from neighborhood, disrupting the complex social connections that help make a city livable.

_____ a. Interstate highways have created social problems.

_____ b. Highways create complex social connections.

_____ c. By separating neighborhoods, highways have made cities more livable.

_____ d. The author supports the idea of mass transportation.

_____ e. The author agrees with a recent vote by the citizens.

READING SELECTION 1: Satire

Satire is a style of writing which pretends to be serious in order to demonstrate the humor of a particular situation. Read the following article to determine what the author is satirizing.*

    You may want to do the Vocabulary from Context exercise on page 163 and the Dictionary Study exercise on page 164 before you begin reading.

Pockety Women Unite?

1   Pockets are what women need more of. The women's movement in the past decade has made giant strides in achieving greater social justice for females, but there's a great deal of work yet to be done. And it can't be done without pockets.

2   It has been commonly thought that men get the best jobs and make the most money and don't have to wash the dinner dishes simply because they're men, that cultural traditions and social conditioning have worked together to give them a special place in the world order.

3   While there is undoubtedly some truth to this, the fact remains that no one has investigated the role that pockets have played in preventing women from attaining the social status and rights that could and should be theirs.

4   Consider your average successful executive. How many pockets does he wear to work? Two in the sides of his trousers, two in the back, one on the front of his shirt, three on his suit coat, and one on the inside of the suit coat. Total: nine.

5   Consider your average woman dressed for office work. If she is wearing a dress or skirt and blouse, she is probably wearing zero pockets, or one or two at the most. The pantsuit, that supposedly liberating outfit, is usually equally pocketless. And it usually comes with a constricting elastic waist to remind women that they were meant to suffer. Paranoid, you say? Well, how many men's trousers come with elasticized waists?

6   Now, while it is always dangerous to generalize, it seems quite safe to say that, on the whole, the men of the world, at any given time, are carrying about a much greater number of pockets than are the women of the world. And it is also quite clear that, on the whole, the men enjoy more power, prestige, and wealth than women do.

7   Everything seems to point to a positive correlation between pockets, power, prestige, and wealth. Can this be?

8   An examination of the function of the pocket seems necessary. Pockets are for carrying money, credit cards, identification (including access to those prestigious clubs where people presumably sit around sharing powerful secrets about how to run the world), important messages, pens, keys, combs, and impressive-looking handkerchiefs.

9   All the equipment essential to running the world. And held close to the body. Easily available. Neatly classified. Pen in the inside coat pocket. Keys in the back left trouser pocket. Efficiency. Order. Confidence.

10   What does a woman have to match this organization? A purse.

    The most hurried examination will show that a purse, however large or important-looking, is no match for a suitful of pockets. If the woman carrying a purse is so lucky as to get an important phone number or market tip from the executive with

---

*Adapted from "Pockety Women Unite?" by Jane Myers, Staff Reporter, *Ann Arbor News*, September 22, 1975.

whom she is lunching, can she write it down? Can she find her pen? Perhaps she can, but it will probably be buried under three old grocery lists, two combs, a checkbook, and a wad of Kleenex. All of which she will have to pile on top of the lunch table before she can find the pen.

11   Will she ever get another tip from this person of power? Not likely. Now she has lost any psychological advantage she may have had. He may have been impressed with her intelligent discussion of the current economic scene before she opened her handbag, but four minutes later, when she is still digging, like a busy little prairie dog, for that pen, he is no longer impressed.

12   He knows he could have whipped his pen in and out of his pocket and written fourteen important messages on the table napkin in the time she is still searching.

What can a pocketless woman do?

Two solutions seem apparent. The women can form a pocket lobby (Pocket Power?) and march on the New York garment district.*

13   Or, in the event that effort fails (and well it might, since it would, by necessity, have to be run by a bunch of pocketless women) an alternate approach remains.

14   Every man in the country for his next birthday finds himself the lucky recipient of one of those very stylish men's handbags, and to go with it, one of those great new no-pocket body shirts.

---

*A major center of fashion design in the United States

COMPREHENSION

Exercise 1
Answer the following questions. Your teacher may want you to do this exercise orally, in writing, or by underlining appropriate parts of the text.

1. What are reasons commonly given to explain why men hold better positions in society than women? _____
   _____

2. How many pockets does the average successful male executive wear to work? _____

3. How many pockets does the average woman wear for office work? _____

4. According to the author, what is the correlation between power and pockets?
   _____

5. According to the author, why do people need pockets? _____
   _____

6. According to the author, what are the disadvantages of women's purses? _____
   _____

7. What two solutions does the author propose for women's pocket problems? _____
   _____

Exercise 2
In your opinion which of the following groups of people does the author find humorous (make fun of)? Be prepared to defend your choices with portions of the text.

1. _____ people who are well organized

2. _____ people who judge the efficiency of others on the basis of the way they dress

3. _____ people who feel that women can improve their situation in life by being more like men

4. _____ women

5. _____ businessmen

6. _____ people who make correlations between unrelated events

7. _____ people who describe human behavior by counting things

VOCABULARY FROM CONTEXT

Both the ideas and the vocabulary in this exercise are taken from "Pockety Women Unite?" Use the context provided to determine the meanings of the italicized words. Write a definition, synonym, or description of each of the italicized vocabulary items in the space provided.

1. _____ It is always dangerous to generalize; however, it seems obvious that, on the whole, men hold a higher position in society than women. Because of this *status*, men enjoy more power than women.

2. _____ A person's *prestige* often depends on his title or profession. For example, in many countries, doctors and lawyers are greatly admired.

3. _____ There seems to be a *correlation* between one's sex and one's status in society. On the whole, men enjoy higher status than women.

4. _____ Most women's clothing is made without pockets. As a result, women are forced to carry their belongings in a *purse*.

5. _____ Despite the fact that women often make valuable contributions, they have not been able to *attain* the same social and economic status as men.

DICTIONARY STUDY

Many words have more than one meaning. When you use the dictionary to discover the meaning of an unfamiliar word, you need to use the context to determine which definition is appropriate. Use the portions of the dictionary provided to select the best definition for each of the italicized words below.

1. As long as women insist on using purses, they will never be as organized as men. A purse, however large or important-looking, is no *match* for a suitful of pockets.

2. If a woman with a purse is lucky enough to get a business *tip* from the executive with whom she is lunching, she will not be able to find a pen with which to write it down.

3. Women should become *lobbyists* and try to influence the garment industry.

lob·by (lob'i), *n.* [*pl.* LOBBIES (-iz)], [ML. *lobium, lobia;* see LODGE], 1. a hall or large anteroom; waiting room or vestibule, as of an apartment house, hotel, theater, etc. 2. a large hall adjacent to the assembly hall of a legislature and open to the public. 3. a group of lobbyists representing the same special interest: as, a cotton *lobby*. *v.i.* [LOBBIED (-id), LOBBYING], to act as a lobbyist. *v.t.* to get or try to get legislators to vote for (a measure) by acting as a lobbyist (often with *through*).
lob·by·ism (lob'i-iz'm), *n.* the practice of lobbying.
lob·by·ist (lob'i-ist), *n.* [*lobby* + *-ist*], a person who tries to get legislators to introduce or vote for measures favorable to a special interest that he represents.

match (mach), *n.* [ME. *macche;* OFr. *mesche* (Fr. *mèche*), wick of a candle, match; prob. < L. *myxa*, wick of a candle; Gr. *myxa*, nozzle of a lamp], 1. originally, a wick or cord prepared to burn at a uniform rate, used for firing guns or explosives. 2. a slender piece of wood, cardboard, waxed cord, etc. tipped with a composition that catches fire by friction, sometimes only on a specially prepared surface. 3. [Obs.], a slip of paper, splinter of wood, etc. dipped in sulfur so that it can be ignited with a spark, for lighting candles, lamps, etc.
match (mach), *n.* [ME. *macche;* AS. *gemæcca*, one suited to another, mate < base of *macian*, to make, form (see MAKE, *v.* & *n.*); sense development: what is put to-gether—what is suitable (for putting together), etc.], 1. any person or thing equal or similar to another in some way; specifically, *a*) a person, group, or thing able to cope with or oppose another as an equal in power, size, etc.; peer. *b*) a counterpart or facsimile. *c*) either of two corresponding things or persons; one of a pair. 2. two or more persons or things that go together in appearance, size, or other quality; pair: as, her purse and shoes were a good *match*. 3. a contest or game involving two or more contestants. 4. *a*) an agreement to marry or mate. *b*) a marriage or mating: as, she made a good *match*. 5. a person regarded as a suitable or possible mate. *v.t.* 1. to join in marriage; get a (suitable) match for; mate. 2. *a*) formerly, to meet as an antagonist; hence, *b*) to compete with suc-cessfully. 3. to put in opposition (*with*); pit (*against*). 4. to be equal, similar, suitable, or corresponding to in some way: as, his looks *match* his character. 5. to make, show, produce, or get a competitor, counterpart, or equivalent to: as, I want to *match* this cloth. 6. to suit or fit (one thing) to another. 7. to fit (things) together; make similar or corresponding. 8. to com-pare. 9. *a*) to flip or reveal (coins) as a form of gam-bling or to decide something contested, the winner being determined by the combination of faces thus exposed. *b*) to match coins with (another person), usually betting that the same faces will be exposed. *v.i.* 1. to get married; mate. 2. to be equal, similar, suitable, or corresponding in some way.

tip (tip), *n.* [ME. *tippe;* prob. < MD. or MLG. *tip,* point, top; akin to G. *zipf-* in *zipfel,* an end, tip; prob. IE. base **dā(i)-,* to part, divide up (cf. TIDE, TIME)], 1. the pointed, tapering, or rounded end or top of something long and slim. 2. something attached to the end, as a cap, ferrule, etc. 3. a top or apex, as of a mountain. *v.t.* [TIPPED (tipt), TIPPING], 1. to make a tip on. 2. to cover the tip or tips of (*with* something). 3. to serve as the tip of.
tip (tip), *v.t.* [TIPPED (tipt), TIPPING], [prob. < ME. *tippe,* a tip, or its base], 1. to strike lightly and sharply; tap. 2. to give a small present of money to (a waiter, porter, etc.) for some service. 3. [Colloq.], to give secret information to in an attempt to be helpful: often with *off.* 4. in *baseball,* etc., to hit (the ball) a glancing blow. *v.i.* to give a tip or tips. *n.* 1. a light, sharp blow; tap. 2. a piece of information given secretly or confidentially in an attempt to be helpful: as, he gave me a *tip* on the race. 3. a sugges-tion, hint, warning, etc. 4. a small present of money given to a waiter, porter, etc. for services; gratuity.
tip (tip), *v.t.* [TIPPED (tipt), TIPPING], [ME. *tipen* (short vowel prob. < p.t. *tipte*); Northern word, prob. < ON.], 1. to overturn or upset: often with *over.* 2. to cause to tilt or slant. 3. to raise slightly or touch the brim of (one's hat) in salutation. *v.i.* 1. to tilt or slant. 2. to overturn or topple: often with *over.* *n.* a tipping or being tipped; tilt; slant.

READING SELECTION 2: Feature Article

Most newspapers print both news articles and feature articles. Unlike news articles which seek to inform the public about important events, feature articles are essays which describe persons and topics of general interest.

The following article was adapted from the *New York Times*.* Read quickly to discover the major ways in which the author contrasts the Japanese and United States style of decision-making. You will need to do Vocabulary from Context exercise 1 on page 168 before you begin reading.

THE NEW YORK TIMES, SUNDAY, MAY 12, 1974

POINT OF VIEW

Japanese Style in Decision-Making

By YOSHIO TERASAWA

1) To talk about problem-solving or decision-making within a national environment means examining many complex cultural forces. It means trying to measure the impact of these forces on contemporary life, and also coming to grips with changes now taking place.

2) It also means using dangerous comparisons—and the need to translate certain fundamental concepts which resist translation and comparisons.

3) For example, the concept of vocational or professional identity differs markedly between the United States and Japan.

4) In the West, the emphasis is on what a man, or woman does for a living. Here in the U.S., if you ask a boy what his father does, he will say "My daddy drives a truck" or "My daddy is a stock broker" or "My daddy is an engineer."

5) But in Japan, the boy will tell you "My daddy works for Mitsubishi" or "My daddy works for Nomura Securities" or for "Hitachi." But you will have no idea whether his father is president of Hitachi or a chauffeur at Hitachi.

6) In Japan, the most important thing is what organization you work for. This becomes very significant when you try to analyze the direction-taking or decision-making process. At the least, it explains the greater job stability in Japan, in contrast to the great job mobility in America.

7) While we differ in many ways, such differences are neither superior nor inferior to each other. A particular pattern of management behavior develops from a complexity of unique cultural factors — and will only work within a given culture.

8) Let me try to describe three or four characteristics of the Japanese environment that in some way affect decision-making or direction-taking and problem-solving. These characteristics are interrelated.

9) First, in any approach to a problem and in any negotiations in Japan, there is the "you to you" approach, as distinguished

In Japan, negotiations seek a basis of harmony rather than confrontation, as in West.

from the Western "I to you" approach.

10) The difference is this: in "I to you," each side presents his arguments forthrightly from his own point of view—he states what he wants and what he expects to get. Thus, a confrontation situation is set up, and Westerners are very adroit in dealing with this.

11) The "you to you" approach practiced in Japan is based on each side — automatically and often unconsciously — trying to understand the other man's point of view, and for the purpose of the discussion actually declaring this understanding. Thus, the direction of the meeting is a mutual attempt at minimizing confrontation and achieving harmony.

12) A second characteristic is based on "consensus opinion" and "bottom-up direction."

In Japan great consideration is given to and reliance placed on the thoughts and opinions of everyone at all levels. This is true of corporate enterprises and Government agencies.

13) To understand this, it is important to realize that Japan is a very densely populated homogeneous country. Moreover, the people are aware and are articulate. Literacy is almost 100 per cent. Problems are shared. In Japan there is a drive for the group—whether it is family, company, or Government—to act as a unit.

14) Tremendous weight is given to the achievement of solidarity and unanimity. Unilateral decision-making or direction-taking is generally avoided, or where it does occur for very practical urgent reasons, it usually happens along with a sounding out of all concerned.

15) This brings us to the second part of this characteristic. When I use the term "bottom-up," I am referring to a style of management — perhaps what you would call keeping your finger on the pulse of the public, or the labor force, or other audiences.

16) The difference is that in Japan we record the pulse and it has real meaning, and it influences the direction finally taken at the top regarding a specific important issue. In other words, Western style decision-making proceeds predominantly from top management and often does not consult middle management or the worker while in Japan, direction can be formulated at the lowest levels, travel upward through an organization and have an impact on the eventual decision. This is "bottom up."

17) There is also a characteristic style of communications in Japan that is different from the Western way.

18) The Japanese businessman works to achieve harmony, even if the deal falls through, and he will spend whatever time is necesary to determine his "you to you" approach and he will communicate his own views indirectly and with great sensitivity.

19) This places time in a different perspective. In Japan the Western deadline approach is secondary to a thorough job. Japanese are thorough in their meetings as well as in their production. Thus Americans are often exasperated by the seemingly endless sequences of meetings of many Japanese businessmen.

20) But where the American is pressing for a specific decision, the Japanese is trying to formu-

---

late a rather broad direction.

21) On the other hand, once agreement is established, it is the Japanese who sometimes wonder at the leisurely pace of execution of Westerners. The Japanese are eager for execution and Westerners, perhaps, like to take the time for in-depth planning.

22) Now, while Japan's industry and technology are highly developed, they have not replaced the fundamental force of human energy and motivation. By that I mean that the Japanese take great pride in doing a job well and getting it done no matter how much time is required.

23) There is a dedication and sense of responsibility which have not been replaced by the machine age. Perhaps we are not so sophisticated yet.

24) In my field—finance and securities—I am often asked by Westerners how Nomura Securities has managed to escape the paper logjam that American brokerage firms have faced. We, too have had that problem.

25) The Tokyo Stock Exchange often has a turnover of between 200 and 300 million shares a day. This volume is many times more than that of the New York Stock Exchange. How can we possibly handle this load?

26) First, we have very advanced computerization. Second, and most important, the personnel responsible for processing all these transactions stay and stay till all hours until the job is done. And their families understand that this is something that they must do, for the survival and progress of the company and for their own mutual security as well.

27) Perhaps in 20 years—or sooner—they will be more Westernized and insist on going home at five o'clock. But today, still, most insist on staying until the job is done. There is concern for workmanship.

28) This willingness to pitch in is an important aspect of Japanese problem-solving, and you find it at every level.

29) Some years ago, the Matsushita company was having a very bad time. Among the many measures taken, Mr. Matsushita, the founder and then chairman, became the manager of the sales department.

30) Also, when we at Nomura converted to computers about five years ago, the new system eliminated the jobs of 700 bookkeepers and accountants who were using abacuses. We got rid of the abacuses but we did not get rid of the people. We converted our bookkeepers and accountants to securities salesmen and some of these today are our leading sales people.

31) Where there is willingness and intelligence, there is a place within the company to try and to succeed. In Japan, a person's capabilities are not forced into an inflexible specialty. And we feel the company owes him something for his loyalty and commitment.

* * *

This article is adapted from a recent speech by Mr. Terasawa, president of Nomura Securities International, Inc., befor the Commonwealth Club of San Francisco.

COMPREHENSION

Exercise 1

Each of the statements below would be true of the business world in either the United States or Japan according to the information in the article or inferences which can be drawn from the article. Indicate whether each statement below is characteristic of Japan (J) or the United States (US). Be prepared to use parts of the article to support your decisions.

1. _____ In business meetings, confrontations are avoided by communicating one's personal views indirectly.

2. _____ An important decision is made by the president of a company and a memo is sent to all employees informing them of the decision.

3. _____ Several weeks of meetings pass before a policy decision is made.

4. _____ Several weeks pass after agreement is reached before action is taken.

5. _____ A new machine is installed to increase production and as a result 100 workers lose their jobs.

6. _____ When asked what his father does, a child answers, "My daddy is an engineer."

7. _____ A young employee moves from one company to another in order to improve his position.

8. _____ Employees often stay at work after hours, until a job is finished.

9. _____ Most companies employ workers of several different cultural and national backgrounds.

Exercise 2

The following questions will help you summarize "Japanese Style in Decision-Making."

1. According to the article, how does the concept of professional identity differ between the United States and Japan?

2. According to the article, what is the difference between the Western "I to you" approach and the Japanese "you to you" approach? What is the difference between Western-style unilateral decision-making and Japanese "consensus opinion" and "bottom-up direction"?

3. Compare the American and Japanese sense of time in business transactions.
   a. Why do Japanese seem to take longer to reach an agreement?
   b. Why do Americans seem to take longer to act after an agreement has been reached?

4. According to the author, how have the Japanese managed to "escape the paper logjam that American . . . firms have faced"?

5. Who is the author of this article? From what source has the article been adapted?

DISCUSSION

1. Do you think a similar article could be written contrasting the United States and your country? What sorts of things would you mention if you wrote such an article?

2. The author admits that "to talk about problem-solving or decision-making within a national environment . . . means using dangerous comparisons." Are there generalizations in the article which you find unconvincing either for lack of information or because of your personal experience?

VOCABULARY FROM CONTEXT

Exercise 1
Both the ideas and the vocabulary in the exercise below are taken from "Japanese Style in Decision-Making." Use the context provided to determine the meanings of the italicized words. Write a definition, synonym, or description of each of the italicized vocabulary items in the space provided.

1. _____

2. _____

When *formulating* business decision, Japanese businessmen do not depend only on the opinions of a few people at the top of the company; rather *reliance* is placed on the opinions of everyone, at all levels.

3. _____

4. _____

In the United States businessmen are skilled at handling strong disagreements in meetings. The Japanese, on the other hand, are *adroit* at avoiding such *confrontations*.

5. _____

6. _____

The Japanese businessman tries to create a situation in which all people present feel comfortable. Only in such an atmosphere of *harmony* are decisions made. *Consensus* decision-making, a process by which action is taken only after everyone is in agreement, is very important to the Japanese businessman.

7. _____

It is important that people from different cultures come to understand each other and develop *mutual* trust. Only when people trust each other is international cooperation possible.

8. _____

9. _____

The majority of people in Japan are *literate*: Because most people are able to read newspapers and magazines, they generally have opinions on most important matters. In addition, they are quite *articulate* and therefore able to state their ideas clearly to their superiors.

10. _____

11. _____

People are more likely to change jobs in the United States than they are in Japan. There are several possible explanations for the greater job *stability* in Japan in contrast to the great job *mobility* in the United States.

12. _____ The Japanese are often *exasperated* by the seriousness with which Americans approach time limits. Similarly, Americans are often impatient with the Japanese seeming lack of concern for *deadlines*.

13. _____

14. _____ Because the Japanese worker willingly stays after hours to finish work, he is well known for his *dedication* to his company.

15. _____ We thought we were in complete agreement and we expected a *unanimous* vote. However, one person voted against the plan.

16. _____ Unlike the United States where many different nationalities make up the population, Japan's population is quite *homogeneous*.

17. _____ A company's structure should not be so *inflexible* that it does not allow a person to change jobs as his abilities and the needs of the company change.

18. _____ Unlike decisions which are made on the basis of mutual concerns, *unilateral* decisions can be unpopular because they are made by only one of the parties concerned.

19. _____ Some *firms* offer their employees company-paid health insurance.

Exercise 2

This exercise should be done after you have finished reading "Japanese Style in Decision-Making." The exercise is designed to determine how well you have been able to use context clues to guess the meaning of unfamiliar vocabulary in the article. Give a definition, synonym, or description of each of the words below. The number in parentheses indicates the paragraph in which the word can be found. Your teacher may want you to do these orally or in writing.

1. (3) vocational (Find a synonym in the same paragraph.) _____

2. (10) forthrightly _____

3. (13) densely _____

4. (16) consult _____

5. (16) impact _____

6. (30) converted _____

FIGURATIVE LANGUAGE AND IDIOMS

In the paragraph indicated by the number in parentheses, find the phrase which best fits the definition given. Your teacher may want to read these aloud as you quickly scan the paragraph to find the answer.

1. (1)   What phrase means *understanding and taking appropriate action*?

2. (4)   What phrase means *as a profession; to support himself*?

3. (14) What phrase means *trying to find out someone's opinion*?

4. (15) What phrase means *knowing the feelings of a group of people*?

5. (18) What phrase means *fails; comes to nothing*?

6. (24) What phrase means *a situation in which progress is stopped because there is too much paper work*?

7. (28) What phrase means *begin to work energetically; help do a job*?

VOCABULARY REVIEW

Exercise 1
Place the appropriate word from this list in each of the blanks below. Do not use any word more than once.

formulate	exasperated
dedicated	transactions
articulate	adroit
deadlines	reliance

There are two reasons why Herman was made president of his company last week. First, Herman is very _____ at handling people. He is a(n) _____ man who is able to express his thoughts and desires very precisely. His ability helps him in business _____ . When other people become _____ because they cannot find the right words to express their thoughts, Herman can make everyone feel comfortable by helping them to find the right words.

Herman's second characteristic is his ability to get work done on time, to meet _____ . He has always been a(n) _____ employee whose _____ on hard work has earned him the respect of his superiors. In fact, Herman's success is due to his hard work and his ability to _____ plans which will get work done efficiently.

Exercise 2
The words in this list are opposite in meaning to the italicized words in the following passage. Change the story below by substituting an *antonym* for each of the italicized words or phrases. Each word should be used at least once.

    unilaterally   inflexible
    confrontation   unilateral
    mobility   heterogeneous

1. _____
2. _____
3. _____
4. _____
5. _____
6. _____

In my company all decisions are made *by consensus* in an atmosphere of *harmony*. The employees are educationally *homogeneous*. Like most workers in this country, employees here experience great job *stability*. However, the policy for changing jobs within the company is quite *flexible*. Requests to change jobs are approved on the basis of *mutual* concerns.

READING SELECTION 3: Short Story

Alan Austen is a troubled young man. Luckily, he finds a strange old man who can help him. There's just one problem. . .

Read the selection,* then do the exercises which follow. Your teacher may want you to do Vocabulary from Context exercise 1 on page 175 before you begin reading.

The Chaser

1   Alan Austen, as nervous as a kitten, went up certain dark and creaky stairs in the neighborhood of Pell Street, and peered about for a long time on the dim hallway before he found the name he wanted written obscurely on one of the doors.

2   He pushed open this door, as he had been told to do, and found himself in a tiny room, which contained no furniture but a plain kitchen table, a rocking-chair, and an ordinary chair. On one of the dirty buff-coloured walls were a couple of shelves, containing in all perhaps a dozen bottles and jars.

3   An old man sat in the rocking-chair, reading a newspaper. Alan, without a word, handed him the card he had been given. "Sit down, Mr. Austen," said the old man very politely. "I am glad to make your acquaintance."

4   "Is it true," asked Alan, "that you have a certain mixture that has-er-quite extra-ordinary effects?"

     "My dear sir," replied the old man, "my stock in trade is not very large—I don't deal in laxatives and teething mixtures—but such as it is, it is varied. I think nothing I sell has effects which could be precisely described as ordinary."

     "Well, the fact is . . ." began Alan.

5   "Here, for example," interrupted the old man, reaching for a bottle from the shelf. "Here is a liquid as colourless as water, almost tasteless, quite imperceptible in coffee, wine, or any other beverage. It is also quite imperceptible to any known method of autopsy."†

6   "Do you mean it is a poison?" cried Alan, very much horrified.

     "Call it a glove-cleaner if you like," said the old man indifferently. "Maybe it will clean gloves. I have never tried. One might call it a life-cleaner. Lives need cleaning sometimes."

7   "I want nothing of that sort," said Alan.

     "Probably it is just as well," said the old man. "Do you know the price of this? For one teaspoonful, which is sufficient, I ask five thousand dollars. Never less. Not a penny less."

     "I hope all your mixtures are not as expensive," said Alan apprehensively.

8   "Oh dear, no," said the old man. "It would be no good charging that sort of price for a love potion, for example. Young people who need a love potion very seldom have five thousand dollars. Otherwise they would not need a love potion."

     "I am glad to hear that," said Alan.

9   "I look at it like this," said the old man. "Please a customer with one article, and he will come back when he needs another. Even if it is more costly. He will save up for it, if necessary."

     "So," said Alan, "you really do sell love potions?"

10   "If I did not sell love potions," said the old man, reaching for another bottle, "I should not have mentioned the other matter to you. It is only when one is in a position to oblige that one can afford to be so confidential."

---

*"The Chaser" by John Collier. Copyright © 1941, 1968 by John Collier. Reprinted by permission of Harold Matson Company, Inc. Originally published in *The New Yorker*.
†autopsy: the examination of a dead body, to determine the cause of death

"And these potions," said Alan. "They are not just-just-er-"

11   "Oh, no," said the old man. "Their effects are permanent, and extend far beyond the mere casual impulse. But they include it. Oh, yes, they include it. Bountifully, insistently. Everlastingly."

"Dear me!" said Alan, attempting a look of scientific detachment. "How *very* interesting!"

12   "But consider the spiritual side," said the old man.

"I do, indeed," said Alan.

"For indifference," said the old man, "they substitute devotion. For scorn, adoration. Give one tiny measure of this to the young lady—its flavour is imperceptible in orange juice, soup, or cocktails—and however gay and giddy she is, she will change altogether. She will want nothing but solitude and you."

13   "I can hardly believe it," said Alan. "She is so fond of parties."

"She will not like them *any* more," said the old man. "She will be afraid of the pretty girls you may meet."

"She will actually be jealous?" cried Alan in a rapture. "Of me?"

"Yes, she will want to be everything to you."

"She is, already. Only she doesn't care about it."

14   "She will, when she has taken this. She will care intensely. You will be her sole interest in life."

"Wonderful!" cried Alan.

"She will want to know *all* you do," said the old man. "*All* that has happened to you during the day. *Every* word of it. She will want to know what you are thinking about, why you smile suddenly, why you are looking sad."

"That is love!" cried Alan.

15   "Yes," said the old man. "How carefully she will look after you! She will never allow you to be tired, to sit in a draught, to neglect your food. If you are an hour late, she will be terrified. She will think you are killed, or that some siren has caught you."

"I can hardly imagine Diana like that!" cried Alan, overwhelmed with joy.

16   "You will not have to use your imagination," said the old man. "And, by the way, since there are always sirens, if by any chance you *should*, later on, slip a little, you need not worry. She will forgive you, in the end. She will be terribly hurt, of course, but she will forgive you—in the end."

"That will not happen," said Alan fervently.

17   "Of course not," said the old man. "But, if it did, you need not worry. She would never divorce you. Oh, no! And, of course, she will never give you the least, the very least, grounds for—uneasiness."

"And how much," said Alan, "is this wonderful mixture?"

"It is not as dear," said the old man, "as the glove-cleaner, or life-cleaner, as I sometimes call it. No. That is five thousand dollars, never a penny less. One has to be older than you are, to indulge in that sort of thing. One has to save up for it."

18   "But the love potion?" said Alan.

"Oh, that," said the old man, opening the drawer in the kitchen table, and taking out a tiny, rather dirty-looking phial. "That is just a dollar."

"I can't tell you how grateful I am," said Alan, watching him fill it.

19   "I like to oblige," said the old man. "Then customers come back, later in life, when they are better off, and want more expensive things. Here you are. You will find it very effective."

"Thank you again," said Alan. "Good-bye."

"*Au revoir*,"* said the old man.

---

au revoir: (French) goodbye; until we meet again

COMPREHENSION

Answer the following questions. Your teacher may want you to do this exercise orally, in writing, or by underlining appropriate parts of the text. True/False items are indicated by a T/F preceding a statement.

1. T / F   Alan Austen accidentally discovered the old man's room.

2. T / F   The old man sold a large number of mixtures commonly found in pharmacies.

3. What did the old man call the $5,000.00 mixture? _____

4. What was the $5,000.00 mixture? _____

5. T / F   Alan Austen loved Diana more than she loved him.

6. How would you describe Diana? _____
_____

7. According to the old man, what effect would the love potion have on Diana? _____
_____

8. T / F   Alan felt that he could never love anyone but Diana.

9. A chaser is a drink taken to cover the unpleasant taste of a preceding drink. What is the first drink in this story? What is its unpleasant "taste"? What is the chaser? _____
_____

10. How could the old man make enough money to live if he sold his love potion for only one dollar? _____

DRAWING INFERENCES

In part, what makes "The Chaser" an interesting story is the fact that the author and the reader share a secret: they know something that Alan Austen doesn't know. Each reader will discover the meaning of the title, "The Chaser" at a different moment in the story. However, even if you finished the story before you realized the real meaning of the old man's words, you were probably able to go back and find double meanings in many of the passages in the story.

The following quotations are taken from "The Chaser." Read each one, then give two possible meanings: (1) the meaning Alan Austen understands, and (2) what you consider to be the real meaning. The number in parentheses indicates the paragraph where the quotation can be found. Your teacher may want you to do this exercise orally or in writing.

1. (14) "She will want to know *all* you do." said the old man. "*All* that has happened to you during the day. *Every* word of it. She will want to know what you are thinking about, why you smile suddenly, why you are looking sad."

2. (17) "... you need not worry. She would never divorce you."

3. (19) "I like to oblige," said the old man. "Then customers come back, later in life, when they are better off, and want more expensive things."

4. (19) "Thank you again," said Alan. "Goodbye."
"*Au revoir*," said the old man.

VOCABULARY FROM CONTEXT

Exercise 1
Use the context provided to determine the meanings of the italicized words. Write a definition, synonym, or description of each of the italicized vocabulary items in the space provided.

1. _____ The doctor said that if a person ate even one leaf of the hemlock plant, he would die, because the plant is a deadly *poison*.

2. _____ The murderer had developed a poison which could not be tasted or smelled when mixed with food. Because it was *imperceptible*, he was able to murder a number of people without being caught.

3. _____ "When making this mixture," the man said, "you don't need two teaspoons of salt, because one teaspoon is *sufficient*."

4. _____ "Since you are my best friend, and because I can trust you, I know I can be *confidential* with you. Listen carefully, because what I am going to tell you is a secret," said Henry.

5. _____ "I am able to *oblige* you sir; I can give you the item you wanted so badly."

6. _____ There are times when one wants to be surrounded by people, and there are times when one needs *solitude*.

7. _____ The man was so *jealous* of his wife that he would not allow her to talk to other men.

Exercise 2
This exercise is designed to give you additional clues to determine the meanings of unfamiliar vocabulary items in context. In the paragraph indicated by the number in parentheses, find the word that best fits the meaning given. Your teacher may want to read these aloud as you quickly scan the paragraph to find the answer.

1. (1)   Which word means *poorly lighted; dark?* _____

2. (4)   Which word means *objects for sale; items kept for sale?* _____

3. (7)   Which word means *worriedly; with alarm or concern?* _____

4. (10) Which word means *to perform a service; to please or help someone?* _____

5. (16) Which word means *women who attract, seduce, lure men?* _____

6. (17) Which word means *reason; basis; foundation?* _____

Exercise 3
This exercise should be done after you have finished reading "The Chaser." The exercise is designed to determine how well you have been able to use context clues to guess the meaning of unfamiliar vocabulary. Give a definition, synonym, or description of each of the words or phrases below. The number in parentheses indicates the paragraph in which the word can be found. Your teacher may want you to do these orally or in writing.

1. (1)   peered _____

2. (8)   potion _____

3. (16) slip a little _____

4. (17) dear _____

5. (19) better off _____

NONPROSE READING: Road Map

If you travel by car in an English-speaking country, you will need to read road maps in English. This exercise is designed to give you practice in many aspects of map reading.*

INTRODUCTION

Exercise 1
Examine the parts of the map you will need to use in order to answer the questions below.†

1. On page 180 is a section of a *map* of Tennessee (Tenn.) and Kentucky (Ky.), two states of the United States.

   Find the Kentucky-Tennessee border.

2. On page 181 is a section of the *Tennessee City and Town Index*. This lists the larger cities and towns in Tennessee with coordinates to help you find these cities and towns on the map.

   a. What are the coordinates of Clarksville, Tenn.? _____
   b. Locate Clarksville on the map on page 180.

3. Also on page 181 is an *inset* (a larger, more detailed reproduction) of Nashville, Tenn. You will need to use the inset of Nashville to find information about major roads and landmarks within Nashville.

   Riverside Hospital (on the north side of the city) is located near the intersection of which

   two streets? _____

4. On page 182 is a *legend*, that is, a list of symbols to help you interpret the map on page 180. On the legend is the *distance scale* which tells you the relationship of both miles and kilometers to inches on the map. Examine the legend carefully to see if you have any questions.

   a. Using the distance scale, estimate the distance in both miles and kilometers from

   Bowling Green, Ky. (coordinates: I-12), to the Ky.-Tenn. border. _____
   b. What is the difference between the two roads, route 31W and route 65, which connect

   Bowling Green and Nashville? _____

   _____

5. Finally, on page 182 you will find a *driving distance map*. This map will tell you the exact distance in miles between many of the large cities in Kentucky, Tennessee, and surrounding states. It also estimates the driving time from city to city.

   What is the distance between Bowling Green, Ky., and Nashville, Tenn.? _____

---

*For an explanation of nonprose reading, see Unit 1.
†Material adapted from Kentucky-Tennessee road map. Basic map reproduced by permission of the American Automobile Association, copyright owner.

Exercise 2
This exercise is designed to give you practice in deciding where to look for specific pieces of information. Below are questions you might ask if you needed to find information from a map. Read each question, then decide if you would look for the answer on the map itself, in the Tennessee City and Town Index, on the inset of Nashville, on the legend, or on the driving distance map. Put the appropriate letter in the blank provided.

     a. map
     b. city and town index
     c. inset
     d. legend
     e. driving distance map

Where should you look to find:

1. _____ the distance between Bowling Green, Ky., and Cincinnati, Ohio?
2. _____ the coordinates of McMinnville, Tenn.?
3. _____ the best route from Ashland City, Tenn., to Murfreesboro, Tenn.?
4. _____ the location in Nashville of the Country Music Hall of Fame?
5. _____ what the symbol **⅄** means?
6. _____ how to get to Vanderbilt University in Nashville from Interstate highway 65?

MAP READING

Use all the information provided on pages 180-82 to do the exercises which follow.

Exercise 1
Indicate if each statement below is true (T) or false (F). Work as quickly as you can.

1. _____ There is a direct route going northwest between Nashville and Clarksville, Tenn.

2. _____ Franklin, located north of Nashville, is in Tennessee.

3. _____ Cincinnati, Ohio, is about 300 miles driving distance from Nashville, Tenn.

4. _____ In southwest Nashville, route 70S will take you directly to the Tennessee Botanical Gardens and Fine Arts Center.

5. _____ There is a major commercial airport in Bowling Green, Ky.

6. _____ Going toward downtown Nashville from the southeast, you can get onto route 40 from route 24.

7. _____ Northwest of Nashville, a state highway connects Ashland City and Clarksville.

8. _____ Bellwood, Tenn., is west of Bellsburg, Tenn.

9. _____ Ashland City, Tenn., northwest of Nashville, is less than 15 miles/24 kilometers from Bellsburg.

10. _____ Nashville is the capital of Tennessee.

11. _____ Coming into downtown Nashville from the north on route 431 (Whites Creek Pike), you can exit directly onto route 65.

Exercise 2

If you were to take a trip by car through Kentucky and Tennessee, you would have to solve problems such as the ones posed by the questions in this exercise. Answer each question as completely as possible. Often there is more than one correct answer. Your teacher may ask you to do these orally or in writing.

1. Could you leave Chattanooga, Tenn., at 8:00 A.M. and get to Bowling Green, Ky., in time for a 12:00 lunch? _____ How fast would you have to drive? _____

2. Which route would you take going northeast from Bowling Green to Mammoth Cave National Park? _____
Can you spend the night at Mammoth Cave National Park? _____

3. Which route would you take from McMinnville, Tenn., to Nashville, Tenn., if you wanted to see the Great Falls Dam (northeast of McMinnville) and Cedars of Lebanon State Park (north of Murfreesboro)? _____

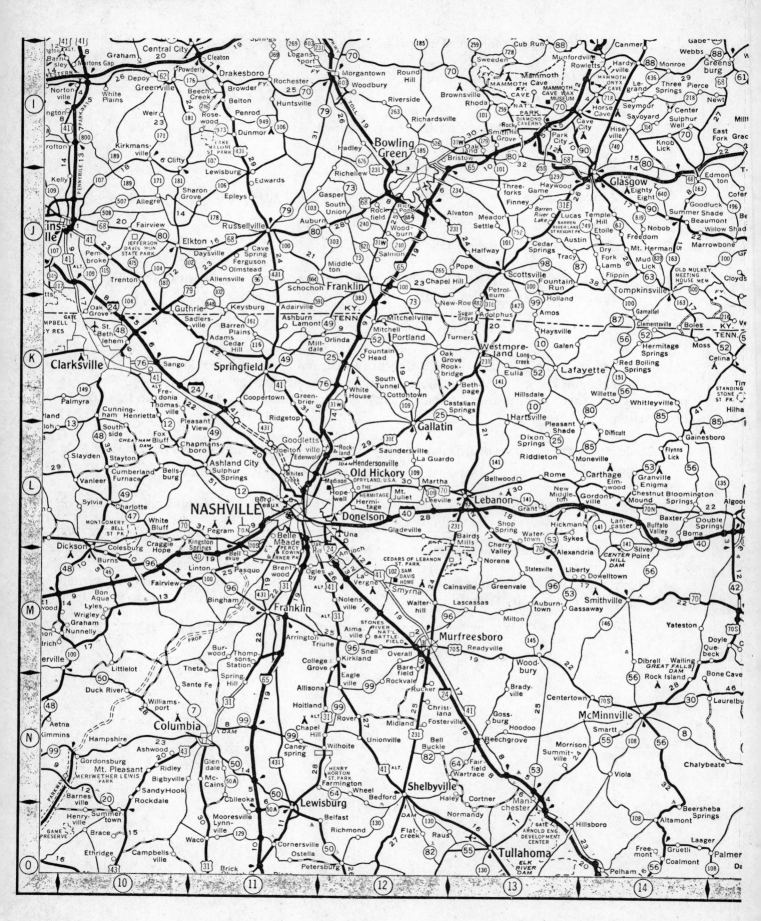

TENNESSEE CITY AND TOWN INDEX

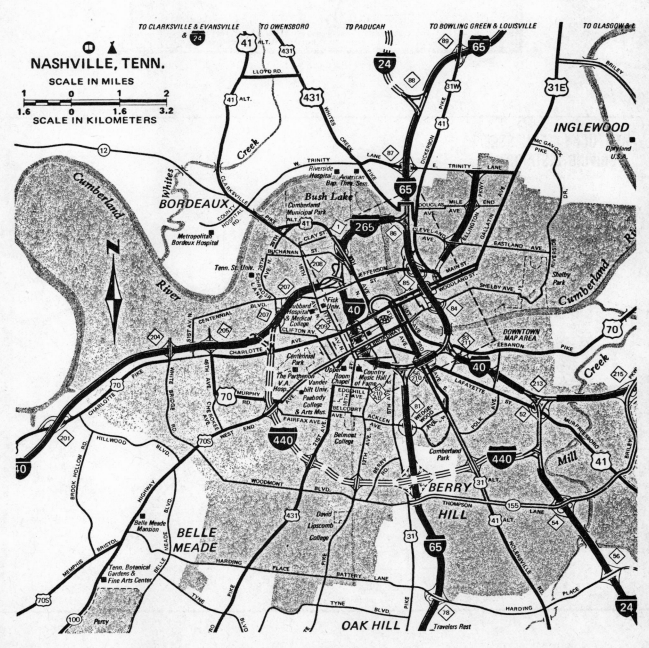

NASHVILLE, TENN.

SCALE IN MILES

SCALE IN KILOMETERS

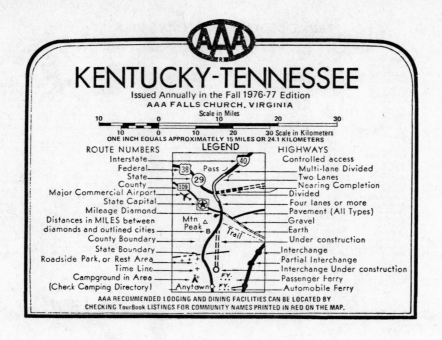

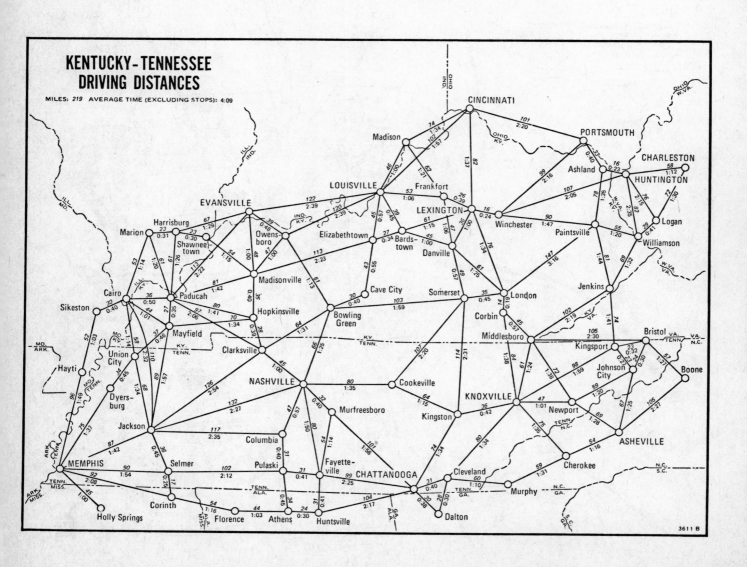

WORD STUDY: Context Clues

In the following exercise, do NOT try to learn the italicized words. Concentrate on developing your ability to guess the meaning of unfamiliar words using context clues. Read each sentence carefully, and write a definition, synonym, or description of the italicized word on the line provided.

1. _____ As he reached for the rock above him, his rope broke and he hung *precariously* by one hand as the rescuers ran toward him.

2. _____ The tired soldiers *trudged* through knee-deep mud for hours before they found a dry place to sleep.

3. _____ In the past, the world seemed to run in an orderly way. Now, however, everything seems to be in a state of *turmoil*.

4. _____ Monkeys are well known for their *grooming* habits; they spend hours carefully cleaning bits of dirt and straw from their coats.

5. _____ *Matrimony* doesn't seem to agree with Liz—she's been unhappy ever since she got married.

6. _____ Using a long, slender instrument called a *probe*, doctors are able to locate and remove pieces of metal from a patient's wounds.

7. _____ The following Monday, when the president *convened* the second meeting of the committee, we all sat down quietly and waited for him to begin.

8. _____ We think of plants in general as absorbing water and food; of animals as *ingesting* or "eating it."

9. _____ Robben is considered an *autocratic* administrator because he makes decisions without seeking the opinions of others.

10. _____ There is an element of word magic here: entomology and *limnology* sound more important than merely insect biology and fresh water biology.

SENTENCE STUDY: Restatement and Inference

This exercise is similar to the one found in Unit 7.* Each sentence below is followed by five statements. The statements are of four types:

1. Some of the statements are restatements of the original sentence. They give the same information in a different way.
2. Some of the statements are inferences (conclusions) which can be drawn from the information given in the original sentence.
3. Some of the statements are false based on the information given.
4. Some of the statements cannot be judged true or false based on the information given in the original sentence.

Put a check (✓) next to all restatements and inferences (types 1 and 2). Note: do not check a statement which is true of itself but cannot be inferred from the sentence given.

1. A favorite definition of joking has long been the ability to find similarity between dissimilar things—that is, hidden similarities.

   _____ a. Joking is the ability to find similarity in dissimilar things.

   _____ b. It takes a long time to develop the ability to tell good jokes.

   _____ c. This definition of joking is a new one in literary theory.

   _____ d. Many people define joking as the ability to find similarity in dissimilar things.

   _____ e. The author agrees with this definition.

2. Since the Romantic period, most modern theory has dealt with the peculiar act of the poet rather than his product or its effect on the audience.

   _____ a. Most modern theory does not deal with the poem itself or its effect on the audience.

   _____ b. Most modern theory of poetry deals with the act of the poet.

   _____ c. Since the Romantic period, literary theory has dealt with the effect of poetry on the reader.

   _____ d. The author believes that literary theory should only deal with the peculiar act of the poet.

   _____ e. Modern theory is considered to begin at the Romantic period.

3. Although housewives still make up the majority of volunteer groups, male participation is reported on the rise nationwide as traditional distinctions between men's work and women's work begin to fade.

   _____ a. As traditional societal roles change, more men are becoming members of volunteer groups.

   _____ b. Most members of volunteer groups are women.

---
*For an introduction to sentence study, see Unit 1.

_____ c. In the past, volunteer work was done mainly by women.

_____ d. Male participation in volunteer groups is increasing in all cities.

_____ e. The author believes there is a relationship between the changing societal roles and the increasing willingness of men to do work previously done by females.

4. The overall picture of this very early settled Peruvian population is that of a simple, peaceful people living in a small cultivable oasis by the sea, fishing, raising a few food crops, living in small, simple, nonmasonry houses and making the objects necessary for their economic and household life, with slight attention to art.

_____ a. This early Peruvian population had all the basic necessities of life available to it.

_____ b. We can assume that art only exists in very advanced societies.

_____ c. This society moved many times during the year.

_____ d. Because the people worked so hard they had no time for art.

_____ e. The author believes this society provides nothing of interest for historians.

5. Only a small number of scholars can be named who have entered at all deeply into the problems of jokes.

_____ a. Only a few scholars have studied jokes.

_____ b. The area of jokes is so complex that only a small number of people have been able to study it.

_____ c. Few scholars have studied the problem of jokes at all deeply.

_____ d. The author cannot remember the names of scholars who have studied jokes.

_____ e. It is not possible to name all those who have studied jokes at all deeply.

6. There is a question about the extent to which any one of us can be free of a prejudiced view in the area of religion.

_____ a. Probably everyone is prejudiced in his views on religion.

_____ b. Any one of us can be free of prejudice in the area of religion.

_____ c. To some extent we can never be free of prejudice in the area of religion.

_____ d. A prejudiced view in the area of religion is undesirable.

_____ e. Because we can't be free of prejudice in the area of religion, we should not practice a religion.

7. Although the November election may significantly change the face of the county Board of Commissioners, the group will still have to confront the same old problems.

_____ a. The November election may give the Board of Commissioners a new building.

_____ b. The Board of Commissioners consists of several members.

_____ c. The November election may change the membership of the Board of Commissioners.

_____ d. Although board members may change, the problems will remain the same.

_____ e. The author does not believe that this election will change the difficulties facing the commissioners.

8. If this book begins with a familiar theme—the Indian experience of the last 120 years—the author brings to it great power and deep understanding.

_____ a. This book was written 120 years ago.

_____ b. The Indian experience of the last 120 years is a familiar experience, and nothing new can be written about it.

_____ c. The book lacks understanding of the Indian experience.

_____ d. The book begins with a familiar theme.

_____ e. The author of this sentence likes the book.

9. In this part of the world, the political and social changes of the past 20 years have by no means eliminated the old upper class of royalty and friends and advisors of royalty, the holders of state monopolies, the great landlords and lords of commercial fiefs, tribal shiekhs, and village headmen.

_____ a. In this part of the world, political and social change have eliminated great landlords, lords of commercial fiefs, and village headmen.

_____ b. In this part of the world, the upper class and their friends and advisors have not been eliminated by political and social change.

_____ c. No means can eliminate the old upper class of royalty in this part of the world.

_____ d. The upper class of royalty has not changed in the past 20 years in this part of the world.

_____ e. In this part of the world, village headmen hold as much power as the advisors of royalty.

10. People should and do choose their elected representatives partly on the basis of how well they believe these representatives, once in office, can convince them to do or support whatever needs to be done.

_____ a. It is the author's belief that people should choose representatives whom they believe will convince them to take action.

_____ b. People choose representatives on the basis of whether or not they believe the representatives can be convinced to do what needs to be done.

_____ c. Although people should choose representatives whom they believe will convince them to take action, often they do not.

_____ d. People choose representatives whom they believe will convince them to take action.

_____ e. Representatives are elected only on the basis of their ability to take action.

PARAGRAPH ANALYSIS: Reading for Full Understanding

This exercise is similar to the one found in Unit 7. Read each paragraph carefully. Try to determine the author's main idea while attempting to remember important details. For each of the questions below, select the best answer. You may refer to the passage to answer the questions.

Paragraph 1

1 Summers with father were always enjoyable. Swimming, hiking, boating, fishing—
2 the days were not long enough to contain all of our activities. There never seemed to
3 be enough time to go to church, which disturbed some friends and relations. Ac-
4 cused of neglecting this part of our education, my father instituted a summer school
5 for my brother and me. However, his summer course included ancient history, which
6 Papa felt our schools neglected, and navigation, in which we first had a formal exam-
7 ination in the dining room, part of which consisted of tying several knots in a given
8 time limit. Then we were each separately sent on what was grandly referred to as a
9 cruise in my father's 18-foot knockabout, spending the night on board, and loaded
10 down, according to my mother, with enough food for a week. I remember that on
11 my cruise I was required to formally plot our course, using the tide table, even
12 though our goal was an island I could see quite clearly across the water in the
13 distance.*

1. What was the original reason for holding the summer school?

    ____ a. Friends and relatives thought the children should learn religion.
    ____ b. The father wanted the children to learn more about religion.
    ____ c. The children got poor grades in their regular school.
    ____ d. The regular school teachers neglected the children.

2. The purpose of the cruise mentioned in the passage was to _____

    ____ a. have fun.
    ____ b. test the author's sailing ability.
    ____ c. reward the author for completing summer school.
    ____ d. get to the island.

3. Why did the author have to plot the course of her cruise?

    ____ a. She had to demonstrate her ability to do so.   ____ c. The coast was dangerous.
    ____ b. She was afraid of getting lost.   ____ d. The tides were strong.

4. How long did the author's cruise last?

    ____ a. all summer   ____ c. overnight
    ____ b. a week   ____ d. one day, morning till night

5. Apparently a knockabout is _____

    ____ a. an island.   ____ c. a boat.
    ____ b. a cruise.   ____ d. a seaman's knot.

*From Sylvia Wright, Introduction to *Islandia*, by Austin Tappan Wright (New York: Rinehart and Co., 1959), pp. vii-viii.

Paragraph 2

1   The cicada exemplifies an insect species which uses a combinatorial communica-
2 tion system. In their life cycle, communication is very important, for only through
3 the exchange of sounds do cicadas know where to meet and when to mate. Three
4 different calls are employed for this purpose. Because of their limited sound pro-
5 ducing mechanisms, cicadas can make only ticks and buzzes. The only way they can
6 distinguish between congregation and courtship calls is by varying the rate with
7 which they make ticks and buzzes. The congregation call consists of 12 to 40 ticks,
8 delivered rapidly, followed by a two-second buzz. It is given by males but attracts
9 cicadas of both sexes. Once they are all together, the males use courtship calls. The
10 preliminary call, a prolonged, slow ticking, is given when the male notices a female
11 near him. The advanced call, a prolonged series of short buzzes at the same slow
12 rate, is given when a female is almost within grasp. The preliminary call almost in-
13 variably occurs before the advanced call, although the latter is given without the
14 preliminary call occurring first if a female is suddenly discovered very near by.
15 During typical courtship, though, the two calls together result in ticking followed by
16 a buzzing—the same pattern which comprises the congregation call but delivered at a
17 slower rate. In this way, cicadas show efficient use of their minimal sound producing
18 ability, organizing two sounds delivered at a high rate as one call and the same
19 sounds delivered at a slow rate as two more calls.*

1.   The cicada congregation call _____

_____ a. attracts only males.
_____ b. is given by both sexes.
_____ c. is given only by males.
_____ d. attracts only females.

2.   During typical courtship, when a male first notices a female near him, he gives _____

_____ a. the two courtship calls together.
_____ b. a series of slow ticks.
_____ c. 12 to 40 rapid ticks.
_____ d. a two-second buzz.

3.   How does the congregation call differ from the two courtship calls together?

_____ a. It is delivered at a slower rate.
_____ b. It is delivered at a faster rate.
_____ c. The ticks precede the buzzes.
_____ d. The buzzes precede the ticks.

4.   According to this passage, why is communication so important for cicadas?

_____ a. It helps them defend themselves against other insect species.
_____ b. It warns them of approaching danger.
_____ c. It separates the males from the females.
_____ d. It is necessary for the continuation of the species.

---

*From David McNeill, *The Acquisition of Language* (New York: Harper and Row, 1970), pp. 48-49.

Paragraph 3

1   Robert Spring, a 19th century forger, was so good at his profession that he was
2   able to make his living for 15 years by selling false signatures of famous Americans.
3   Spring was born in England in 1813 and arrived in Philadelphia in 1858 to open a
4   bookstore. At first he prospered by selling his small but genuine collection of early
5   U.S. autographs. Discovering his ability at copying handwriting, he began imitating
6   signatures of George Washington and Ben Franklin and writing them on the title
7   pages of old books. To lessen the chance of detection, he sent his forgeries to
8   England and Canada for sale and circulation.
9   Forgers have a hard time selling their products. A forger can't approach a respect-
10   able buyer but must deal with people who don't have much knowledge in the field.
11   Forgers have many ways to make their work look real. For example, they buy old
12   books to use the aged paper of the title page, and they can treat paper and ink with
13   chemicals.
14   In Spring's time, right after the Civil War, Britain was still fond of the Southern
15   states, so Spring invented a respectable maiden lady known as Miss Fanny Jackson,
16   the only daughter of General "Stonewall" Jackson. For several years Miss Fanny's
17   financial problems forced her to sell a great number of letters and manuscripts
18   belonging to her famous father. Spring had to work very hard to satisfy the demand.
19   All this activity did not prevent Spring from dying in poverty, leaving sharp-eyed
20   experts the difficult task of separating his forgeries from the originals.*

1.   Why did Spring sell his false autographs in England and Canada?

____ a. There was a greater demand there than in America.
____ b. There was less chance of being detected there.
____ c. Britain was Spring's birthplace.
____ d. The prices were higher in England and Canada.

2.   After the Civil War, there was a great demand in Britain for _____

____ a. Southern money.   ____ c. Southern manuscripts and letters.
____ b. signatures of George Washington   ____ d. Civil War battle plans.
            and Ben Franklin.

3.   Robert Spring spent 15 years _____

____ a. running a bookstore in Philadelphia.   ____ c. as a forger.
____ b. corresponding with Miss Fanny Jackson. ____ d. as a respectable dealer.

4.   According to the passage, forgeries are usually sold to _____

____ a. sharp-eyed experts.   ____ c. book dealers.
____ b. persons who aren't experts.   ____ d. owners of old books.

5.   Who was Miss Fanny Jackson?

____ a. the only daughter of General "Stonewall" Jackson
____ b. a little-known girl who sold her father's papers to Robert Spring
____ c. Robert Spring's daughter
____ d. an imaginary person created by Spring

---

*From the *Michigan Daily*, September 20, 1967.

Paragraph 4

1   In science the meaning of the word "explain" suffers with civilization's every
2 step in search of reality. Science cannot really explain electricity, magnetism, and
3 gravitation; their effects can be measured and predicted, but of their nature no more
4 is known to the modern scientist than to Thales who first speculated on the electri-
5 fication of amber. Most contemporary physicists reject the notion that man can ever
6 discover what these mysterious forces "really" are. Electricity, Bertrand Russell
7 says, "is not a thing, like St. Paul's Cathedral; it is a way in which things behave.
8 When we have told how things behave when they are electrified, and under what
9 circumstances they are electrified, we have told all there is to tell." Until recently
10 scientists would have disapproved of such an idea. Aristotle, for example, whose
11 natural science dominated Western thought for two thousand years, believed that
12 man could arrive at an understanding of reality by reasoning from self-evident
13 principles. He felt, for example, that it is a self-evident principle that everything in
14 the universe has its proper place, hence one can deduce that objects fall to the
15 ground because that's where they belong, and smoke goes up because that's where it
16 belongs. The goal of Aristotelian science was to explain *why* things happen. Modern
17 science was born when Galileo began trying to explain *how* things happen and thus
18 originated the method of controlled experiment which now forms the basis of
19 scientific investigation.

1.   The aim of controlled scientfic experiments is _____

____ a. to explain why things happen.
____ b. to explain how things happen.
____ c. to describe self-evident principles.
____ d. to support Aristotelian science.

2.   What principles most influenced scientific thought for two thousand years?

____ a. the speculations of Thales
____ b. the forces of electricity, magnetism, and gravity
____ c. Aristotle's natural science
____ d. Galileo's discoveries

3.   Bertrand Russell's notion about electricity is _____

____ a. disapproved of by most modern scientists.
____ b. in agreement with Aristotle's theory of self-evident principles.
____ c. in agreement with scientific investigation directed toward "how" things happen.
____ d. in agreement with scientific investigation directed toward "why" things happen.

4.   The passage says that until recently scientists disagreed with the idea _____

____ a. that there are mysterious forces in the universe.
____ b. that man cannot discover what forces "really" are.
____ c. that there are self-evident principles.
____ d. that we can discover why things behave as they do.

Paragraph 5

1   Dice, the plural of die, are small cubes used in games. They are usually made of
2 ivory, bone, wood, bakelite, or similar materials. The six sides are numbered by dots
3 from 1 to 6, so placed that the sum of the dots on a side and the opposite side
4 equals 7.
5   A simple form of play with dice is for each player to throw, or shoot, for the
6 highest sum. However, the most popular dice game in the United States is called
7 craps. It is played with 2 dice and the underlying principle of the game is the fact
8 that the most probable throw is a 7. On the first throw, if a player shoots a 7 or 11
9 (called a natural), he wins and begins again, but if he shoots 2, 3, or 12 (called craps)
10 on the first throw, he loses. If on the first throw he shoots 4, 5, 6, 8, 9, or 10, that
11 number becomes his point. He continues to throw until he shoots that number again
12 (makes his point), in which case he wins and begins again. However, if he shoots a 7
13 before he makes his point, he loses and relinquishes the dice to the next player.
14 Usually all others in the game bet against the thrower, and in gambling halls bets are
15 made against the house.*

1. In craps, a throw of 11 _____

    _____ a. always wins.
    _____ b. sometimes loses.
    _____ c. sometimes wins.
    _____ d. becomes the point.

2. If one side of a die has three dots on it, the opposite side has _____

    _____ a. 6.
    _____ b. 4.
    _____ c. 3.
    _____ d. 7.

3. To shoot the dice means to _____

    _____ a. throw them.
    _____ b. lose.
    _____ c. make a natural.
    _____ d. make one's point.

4. In a game of craps, if a player throws a 5 and then a 3, he _____

    _____ a. wins.
    _____ b. loses.
    _____ c. shoots again.
    _____ d. makes his point.

---

*From *Columbia Encyclopedia*, 2d ed. (New York: Columbia University Press, 1950).

5. In a game of craps, if a player throws a 6, 3, 4, 4, 6, 11, in that order, he has _____

    ____ a. won twice.
    ____ b. made his point twice.
    ____ c. made two naturals.
    ____ d. shot craps.

6. In a game of craps, if the player throws a 12 on his first throw _____

    ____ a. he has the highest sum, so he wins.
    ____ b. that number is his point.
    ____ c. he has shot craps.
    ____ d. he has made a natural.

7. What number is most probable on a throw of the dice?

    ____ a. 7 and 11 have equal probabilities
    ____ b. 7
    ____ c. 11
    ____ d. craps

READING SELECTION 1: Textbook

"The Sacred 'Rac' " is taken from an introductory social anthropology textbook written for students in the United States.* The article describes the customs of a tribe of people studied by the Indian anthropologist Chandra Thapar. Read the passage, and answer the questions which follow. You may want to do the Vocabulary from Context exercise on page 196 before you begin.

The Sacred "Rac"

1   An Indian anthropologist, Chandra Thapar, made a study of foreign cultures which had customs similar to those of his native land. One culture in particular fascinated him because it reveres one animal as sacred, much as the people in India revere the cow. The things he discovered might interest you since you will be studying India as part of this course.

2   The tribe Dr. Thapar studied is called the Asu and is found on the American continent north of the Tarahumara of Mexico. Though it seems to be a highly developed society of its type, it has an overwhelming preoccupation with the care and feeding of the rac—an animal much like a bull in size, strength and temperament. In the Asu tribe, it is almost a social obligation to own at least one if not more racs. Anyone not possessing at least one is held in low esteem by the community because he is too poor to maintain one of these beasts properly. Some members of the tribe, to display their wealth and social prestige, even own herds of racs.

3   Unfortunately the rac breed is not very healthy and usually does not live more than five to seven years. Each family invests large sums of money each year to keep its rac healthy and shod, for it has a tendency to throw its shoes often. There are rac specialists in each community, perhaps more than one if the community is particularly wealthy. These specialists, however, due to the long period of ritual training they must undergo and to the difficulty of obtaining the right selection of charms to treat the rac, demand costly offerings whenever a tribesman must treat his ailing rac.

4   At the age of sixteen in many Asu communities, many youths undergo a puberty rite in which the rac figures prominently. The youth must petition a high priest in a grand temple. He is then initiated into the ceremonies that surround the care of the rac and is permitted to keep a rac.

5   Although the rac may be used as a beast of burden, it has many habits which would be considered by other cultures as detrimental to the life of the society. In the first place the rac breed is increasing at a very rapid rate and the Asu tribesmen have given no thought to curbing the rac population. As a consequence the Asu must build more and more paths for the rac to travel on since its delicate health and its love of racing other racs at high speeds necessitates that special areas be set aside for its use. The cost of smoothing the earth is too costly for any one individual to undertake; so it has become a community project and each tribesman must pay an annual tax to build new paths and maintain the old. There are so many paths needed that some people move their homes because the rac paths must be as straight as possible to keep the animal from injuring itself. Dr. Thapar also noted that unlike the cow, which many people in his country hold sacred, the excrement of

*"The Sacred 'Rac' " by Patricia Hughes, *Focusing on Global Poverty and Development* by Jayne C. Millar (Washington, D.C.: Overseas Development Council, 1974), pp. 357-58.

the rac cannot be used as either fuel or fertilizer. On the contrary, its excrement is exceptionally foul and totally useless. Worst of all, the rac is prone to rampages in which it runs down anything in its path, much like stampeding cattle. Estimates are that the rac kills thousands of the Asu in a year.

6   Despite the high cost of its upkeep, the damage it does to the land, and its habit of destructive rampages, the Asu still regard it as being essential to the survival of their culture.

COMPREHENSION

Answer the following questions. Your teacher may want you to answer the questions orally, in writing, or by underlining appropriate parts of the text. True/False items are indicated by a T/F preceding a statement.

1. What society reveres the rac? _____

_____

2. Where is the tribe located? _____

3. T / F   People who don't own racs are not respected in the Asu community.

4. Why does it cost so much to have a rac specialist treat an ailing rac? _____

_____

5. T / F   An Asu must pass through a special ceremony before being permitted to keep a rac.

6. How is the rac helpful to the Asu? _____

_____

7. What effects does the size of the rac population have on the life of the Asu? _____

_____

8. T / F   Rac excrement can be used as fuel or as fertilizer.

9. According to the author, what is the worst characteristic of the rac? _____

10. T / F   The Asu feel that their culture cannot survive without the rac.

11. What is *rac* spelled backward? _____

DRAWING INFERENCES

What is the author's attitude toward the rac? Why does she choose to present her opinion using this story about the Asu society?

DISCUSSION

Is the rac essential to the survival of the Asu society? Of your society? What effects is the rac having on your society? Do people in your society revere the rac as much as the Asu do?

VOCABULARY FROM CONTEXT

Use the context provided and your knowledge of stems and affixes to determine the meanings of the italicized words. Write a definition, synonym, or description of the italicized vocabulary items in the space provided.

1. _____ Alex has had trouble studying for the final examination because he has been too *preoccupied* with happy thoughts of his summer vacation.

2. _____ Alice's dog is gentle and friendly; unfortunately, my dog doesn't have such a pleasant *temperament*.

3. _____ Peter wants to be a doctor because he feels it is a very *prestigious* occupation, and he has always wanted to hold a high position in society.

4. _____ Do you know a doctor who has experience *treating* children?

5. _____ Instead of complaining to me that you're *ailing*, you should see a doctor to find out what's wrong with you.

6. _____ Many people believe that only primitive societies have a special ceremony to celebrate the time when a child becomes an adult; however, anthropologists say that advanced cultures also have *puberty rites*.

7. _____ The criminal was to be killed at dawn; but he *petitioned* the king to save him and his request was granted.

8. _____ Doctors believe that smoking cigarettes is *detrimental*
9. _____ to your health. They also *regard* drinking as harmful.

READING SELECTION 2: Narrative

The following passage, like those by Gerald Durrell in Units 4 and 8, is taken from *My Family and Other Animals.** The author is ten years old in this story, a young boy with a vivid imagination and a sharp eye for detail.

   Read the story carefully to appreciate Durrell's colorful description of people and things. You may want to do Vocabulary from Context exercise 1 on page 203 before you begin reading.

The Talking Flowers

1   I had worked for some weeks with Kralefsky before I discovered that he did not live alone. At intervals during the morning he would pause suddenly in the middle of a lesson and cock his head on one side, as if listening.
   "Excuse me a moment," he would say. "I must go see Mother."

2   At first this rather puzzled me, for I was convinced that Kralefsky was far too old to have a mother still living. After considerable thought, I came to the conclusion that this was merely his polite way of saying that he wished to use the toilet, for I realized that not everyone shared my family's lack of embarrassment when discussing this topic. It never occurred to me that, if this was so, Kralefsky closeted himself more often than any other human being I had met. One morning I had to use the bathroom. Since Kralefsky was so finicky about the subject of lavatories I decided that I would have to phrase my request politely, so I thought it best to adopt his own curious term. I looked him firmly in the eye and said that I would like to pay a visit to his mother.

3   "My mother?" he repeated in astonishment. "Visit my mother? Now?" I could not see what the problem was, so I merely nodded.
   "Well," he said doubtfully, "I'm sure she'll be delighted to see you, of course, but I'd better just go and see if it's convenient."
   He left the room, still looking puzzled, and returned after a few minutes.
   "Mother would be delighted to see you," he announced, "but she says will you please excuse her being a little untidy?"

4   I thought it was carrying politeness to an extreme to talk about the lavatory as if it were a human being, but, since Kralefsky was obviously a bit eccentric on the subject, I felt I had better humour him. I said I did not mind a bit if his mother was in a mess, as ours frequently was as well.

5   "Ah . . . er . . . yes, yes, I expect so," he murmured, giving me rather a startled glance. He led me down the corridor, opened a door, and, to my complete surprise, ushered me into a large shadowy bedroom. The room was a forest of flowers; vases, bowls, and pots were everywhere, and each contained a mass of beautiful blooms that shone in the gloom, like walls of jewels in a green-shadowed cave. At one end of the room was an enormous bed, and in it, propped up on a heap of pillows, lay a tiny figure not much bigger than a child. She must have been very old, I decided as we drew nearer, for her fine, delicate features were covered with a network of wrinkles that crossed a skin as soft and velvety-looking as a baby mushroom's. But the astonishing thing about her was her hair. It fell over her shoulders in a thick cascade, and then spread half way down the bed. It was the richest and most beautiful auburn colour imaginable, shining as though on fire, making me think of autumn leaves and the brilliant winter coat of a fox.

---

*Adapted from *My Family and Other Animals* by Gerald Durrell. Copyright © 1956 by Gerald Durrell. Reprinted by permission of The Viking Press and Granada Publishing Ltd.

6   "Mother dear," Kralefsky called softly, bobbing across the room and seating himself on a chair by the bed, "Mother dear, here's Gerry come to see you."

The minute figure on the bed lifted thin, pale lids and looked at me with great
tawny eyes that were as bright and intelligent as a bird's.

"I am so very flattered that you asked to see me," she said in a soft, husky voice.
"So many people nowadays consider a person of my age a bore."

"Do sit down," she invited; "do sit down and talk for a minute."

7   Gingerly I picked up the mass of auburn hair and moved it to one side so that I
could sit on the bed. The hair was soft, silky, and heavy, like a flame-coloured wave
swishing through my fingers. Mrs. Kralefsky smiled at me, and lifted a strand of it in
her fingers, twisting it gently so that it sparkled.

"My one remaining vanity," she said; "all that is left of my beauty."

She gazed down at the flood of hair as though it were a pet, or some other creature that had nothing to do with her, and patted it affectionately.

8   "They say," she announced—"they *say* that when you get old, as I am, your body
slows down. I don't believe it. No, I think that is quite wrong. I have a theory that
you do *not* slow down at all, but that *life slows down for you*. You understand me?
Everything becomes languid, as it were, and you can notice so much more when
things are in slow motion. The things you see! The extraordinary things that happen
all around you, that you never even suspected before! It is really a delightful adven-
ture, quite delightful!"

She sighed with satisfaction, and glanced round the room.

9   "Take flowers," she said, pointing at the blooms that filled the room. "Have you
heard flowers *talking*?"

Greatly intrigued, I shook my head; the idea of flowers talking was quite new to
me.

"Well, I can assure you that they *do* talk," she said. "They hold long conversations with each other . . . at least I presume them to be conversations, for I don't
understand what they're saying, naturally. When you're as old as I am you'll probably be able to hear them as well; that is, if you retain an open mind about such
matters. *Most* people say that as one gets older one believes nothing and is surprised
at nothing, so that one becomes more receptive to ideas. Nonsense! All the old
people I know have had their minds locked up like grey, scaly oysters since they
were in their teens."

10   She glanced at me sharply.

"D'you think I'm queer? Touched, eh? Talking about flowers holding conversations?"

Hastily and truthfully I denied this. I said that I thought it was more than likely
that flowers conversed with each other. "Another thing that you don't notice when
you're young is that flowers have personality. They are different from each other,
just as people are. Look, I'll show you. D'you see that rose over there, in the bowl
by itself?"

11   On a small table in the corner, in a small silver bowl, was a magnificent velvety
rose, so deep a garnet red that it was almost black. It was a gorgeous flower, the
petals curled to perfection, the bloom on them as soft and unblemished as the down
on a newly-hatched butterfly's wing.

12   "Isn't he a beauty?" inquired Mrs. Kralefsky. "Isn't he wonderful? Now I've had
him two weeks. You'd hardly believe it, would you? And he was not a bud when he
came. No, no, he was fully open. But, do you know, he was so sick that I did not
think he would live? The person who plucked him was careless enough to put him in
with a bunch of Michaelmas daisies. Fatal, absolutely fatal! You have no idea how

cruel the daisy family is, on the whole. They are very rough-and-ready sort of flowers, very down to earth, and, of course, to put such an aristocrat as a rose amongst them is just *asking* for trouble. By the time he got here he had drooped and faded to such an extent that I did not even notice him among the daisies. But, luckily, I heard them at it. I was dozing here when they started, particularly, it seemed to me, the yellow ones, who always seem so belligerent. Well, of course, I didn't know what they were saying, but it sounded *horrible*. I couldn't think *who* they were talking to at first; I thought they were quarrelling among themselves. Then I got out of bed to have a look and I found that poor rose, crushed in the middle of them, being harried to death. I got him out and put him by himself and gave him half an aspirin. Aspirin is so good for roses. Well, removed from the company of the daisies and given that pick-me-up, he revived in no time, and he seems so grateful; he's obviously making an effort to remain beautiful for as long as possible in order to thank me."

13   She gazed at the rose affectionately, as it glowed in its silver bowl.

"Yes, there's a lot I have learnt about flowers. They're just like people. Put too many together and they get on each other's nerves and start to die. Mix some kinds and you get what appears to be a dreadful form of class distinction. And, of course, the water is so important. Do you know that some people think it's kind to change the water every day? Dreadful! You can *hear* the flowers dying if you do that. I change the water once a week, put a handful of earth in it, and they thrive."

14   It was time for me to go home.

"Well, Gerry, we have been having a most interesting conversation. At least, I found it interesting, anyway."

Getting to my feet, I said that I had found it most interesting as well.

"You must come and see me again, if it would not bore you," she said. "You will find my ideas a little eccentric, I think, but they are worth listening to."

15   She smiled up at me, lying on the bed under her great cloak of hair, and lifted a hand in a courteous gesture of dismissal. I followed Kralefsky across the room, and at the door I looked back and smiled. She was lying quite still, submissive under the weight of her hair. She lifted her hand again and waved. It seemed to me, in the gloom, that the flowers had moved closer to her, had crowded eagerly about her bed, as though waiting for her to tell them something. A ravaged old queen, lying in state, surrounded by her whispering court of flowers.

COMPREHENSION

The following exercise checks your understanding of the story. You may refer to the passage to help you determine if each statement below is true (T) or false (F).

1. _____ Kralefsky was too old to have a living mother.

2. _____ Kralefsky used the toilet more than any other human being the author had met.

3. _____ The Durrells were very careful not to discuss matters relating to the bathroom.

4. _____ The author's mother was often a mess.

5. _____ Mrs. Kralefsky's room was filled with flowers.

6. _____ Mrs. Kralefsky enjoyed life.

7. _____ Mrs. Kralefsky's hair was very long and very beautiful.

8. _____ The author was bored by Mrs. Kralefsky.

9. _____ Mrs. Kralefsky held long discussions with her flowers.

10. _____ Daisies, according to Mrs. Kralefsky, are a lower class than roses.

11. _____ The author didn't use the Kralefsky's bathroom on this occasion.

READING FOR DETAILS

The following exercises check your understanding of the descriptions in the passage.

Exercise 1
You cannot remember every descriptive phrase in a story like this, but you should have a mental image of the people, places, and things described by Durrell. Test your general impression of Mrs. Kralefsky by checking (✓) the words which you think describe her. Your impression may not agree with that of other readers. Be prepared to use parts of the passage to support your choices.

1. _____ old

2. _____ boring

3. _____ imaginative

4. _____ kind

5. _____ ugly

6. _____ happy

7. _____ intelligent

8. _____ bored

9. _____ sad

Exercise 2

This exercise requires you to focus on the specific phrases the author uses to describe people. Scan the passage to find the phrases which Durrell uses to describe Mrs. Kralefsky. Check (✓) each of the phrases below which is an accurate description of Mrs. Kralefsky.

1. _____ not much larger than a child

2. _____ as old as a mushroom

3. _____ rich red-brown hair

4. _____ bright eyes

5. _____ smart as a fox

6. _____ as beautiful as a bird

Exercise 3

By now you should be familiar with the descriptions in the story. Read each of the phrases below and write the name of the person, place, or thing described next to the appropriate phrase.

1. _____ the color of autumn leaves

2. _____ a green-shadowed cave

3. _____ soft and velvety-looking as the skin of a baby mush-room

4. _____ a forest of flowers

5. _____ a thick cascade

VOCABULARY FROM CONTEXT

Exercise 1
Use the context provided to determine the meanings of the italicized words. Write a definition, synonym, or description of each of the italicized vocabulary items in the space provided.

1. _____ Her son's foolish behavior at the party is such an *embarrassing* subject that she refuses to speak about it.

2. _____ Mr. Fleming was surprised to see me sitting behind his desk. He gave me a *startled* look, then smiled and said, "I didn't know you were in town."

3. _____ The length of her hair *astonished* me; I don't think I have ever seen hair so long.

4. _____ Not wanting to disturb the sleeping kitten, I *gingerly* lifted her from the box and put her on a blanket near the heater.

5. _____ Jane was *intrigued* by the behavior of animals; she could sit for hours observing a bird making a nest or an ant carrying a leaf.

6. _____ Kenneth has only one *vanity*; his hair. He spends hours every day washing, brushing, and styling it before he leaves his apartment.

7. _____ Roses seem to *thrive* under certain conditions; the more sunlight and water they receive the more beautiful they are.

8. _____ The boy was *flattered* that he had been asked to give his opinion; he was happy to find that others wanted to know how he felt about things.

Exercise 2

This exercise is designed to give you additional clues to determine the meaning of unfamiliar vocabulary items in context. In the paragraph indicated by the number in parentheses, find the word that best fits the meaning given. Your teacher may want to read these aloud as you quickly scan the paragraph to find the answer.

1. (2) Which word means *very careful; too careful or proper*?

2. (4) Which word means *strange; unusual; different from most people*?

3. (12) Which word in the last half of the paragraph means *war-like; unfriendly; quick to quarrel or fight*?

Exercise 3

This exercise should be done after you have finished reading "The Talking Flowers." The exercise is designed to determine how well you have been able to use context clues to guess the meaning of unfamiliar vocabulary. Give a definition, synonym, or description of each of the words or phrases below. The number in parentheses indicates the paragraph in which the item can be found. Your teacher may want you to do these orally or in writing.

1. (2) lavatories _____

2. (2) adopt _____

3. (5) ushered _____

4. (5) propped up _____

5. (5) auburn _____

6. (8) languid _____

7. (10) touched _____

8. (12) plucked _____

9. (12) pick-me-up _____

READING SELECTION 3: Essay

An essay is a literary composition on a single subject which usually presents the author's personal opinion. The following essay, written by John V. Lindsay when he was mayor of New York City, is taken from his book, *The City*.*

Read the passage, then do the exercises which follow. You may want to do Vocabulary from Context exercise 1 on page 209 before you begin reading.

The City

1   In one sense, we can trace all the problems of the American city back to a single starting point: we Americans don't like our cities very much.

2   That is, on the face of it, absurd. After all, more than three-fourths of us now live in cities, and more are flocking to them every year. We are told that the problems of our cities are receiving more attention in Washington, and scholarship has discovered a whole new field in urban studies.

3   Nonetheless, it is historically true: in the American psychology, the city has been a basically suspect institution, filled with the corruption of Europe, totally lacking that sense of spaciousness and innocence of the frontier and the rural landscape.

4   I don't pretend to be a scholar on the history of the city in American life. But my thirteen years in public office, first as an officer of the U.S. Department of Justice, then as Congressman, and now as Mayor of the biggest city in America, have taught me all too well the fact that a strong anti-urban attitude runs consistently through the mainstream of American thinking. Much of the drive behind the settlement of America was in reaction to the conditions in European industrial centers—and much of the theory supporting the basis of freedom in America was linked directly to the availability of land and the perfectibility of man outside the corrupt influences of the city.

5   What has this to do with the predicament of the modern city? I think it has much to do with it. For the fact is that the United States, particularly the federal government, which has historically established our national priorities, has simply never thought that the American city was "worthy" of improvement—at least not to the extent of expending any basic resources on it.

6   Antipathy to the city predates the American experience. When industrialization drove the European working man into the major cities of the continent, books and pamphlets appeared attacking the city as a source of crime, corruption, filth, disease, vice, licentiousness, subversion, and high prices. The theme of some of the earliest English novels—*Moll Flanders* for example—is that of the innocent country youth coming to the big city and being subjected to all forms of horror until justice—and a return to the pastoral life—follow.

7   The proper opinion of Europe seemed to support the Frenchman who wrote: "In the country, a man's mind is free and easy...; but in the city, the persons of friends and acquaintances, one's own and other people's business, foolish quarrels, ceremonies, visits, impertinent discourses, and a thousand other fopperies and diversions steal away the greatest part of our time and leave no leisure for better and necessary employment. Great towns are but a larger sort of prison to the soul, like cages to birds or pounds to beasts."

---

*Adapted from *The City* by John V. Lindsay. By permission of W.W. Norton and Company, Inc. Copyright © 1969, 1970 by W. W. Norton and Company, Inc.

8   This was not, of course, the only opinion on city life. Others maintained that the city was "the fireplace of civilization, whence light and heat radiated out into the cold dark world." And William Penn planned Philadelphia as the "holy city," carefully laid out so that each house would have the appearance of a country cottage to avoid the density and overcrowding that so characterized European cities.

9   Without question, however, the first major thinker to express a clear antipathy to the urban way of life was Thomas Jefferson. For Jefferson, the political despotism of Europe and the economic despotism of great concentrations of wealth, on the one hand, and poverty on the other, were symbolized by the cities of London and Paris, which he visited frequently during his years as a diplomatic representative of the new nation. In the new world, with its opportunities for widespread land-holding, there was the chance for a flowering of authentic freedom, with each citizen, freed from economic dependence, both able and eager to participate in charting the course of his own future. America, in a real sense, was an escape from all the injustice that had flourished in Europe—injustice that was characterized by the big city.

10   This Jeffersonian theme was to remain an integral part of the American tradition. Throughout the nineteenth century, as the explorations of America pushed farther outward, the new settlers sounded most like each other in their common celebration of freedom from city chains.

11   The point is that all this opinion goes beyond ill feelings; it suggests a strong national sense that encouragement and development of the city was to be in no sense a national priority—that our manifest destiny* lay in the untouched lands to the west, in constant movement westward, and in maximum dispersion of land to as many people as possible.

12   Thus, the Northwest Ordinance of 1787—perhaps the first important declaration of national policy—explicitly encouraged migration into the Northwest Territory and provided grants of land and free public lands for schools. New York City, by contrast, did not begin a public-education system until 1842—and received, of course, no federal help at all. Similarly, the Homestead Act of 1862† was based on an assumption—supported by generations of American theory—that in the West could be found genuine opportunity and that the eastern-seaboard cities of the United States were simply hopeless collections of vice and deprivation.

13   This belief accelerated after the Civil War, for a variety of reasons. For one thing, the first waves of immigration were being felt around the country as immigrants arrived in urban areas. The poverty of the immigrants, largely from Ireland and Northern Europe, caused many people in rural America to equate poverty with personal inferiority—a point of view that has not yet disappeared from our national thinking. Attacks on the un-American and criminal tendencies of the Irish, the Slavs, and every other ethnic group that arrived on America's shore were a steady part of national thinking, as were persistent efforts to bar any further migration of "undesirables" to our country.

14   With the coming of rapid industrialization, all the results of investigations into city poverty and despair that we think of as recent findings were being reported—and each report served to confirm the beliefs of the Founding Fathers that the city was no place for a respectable American.

---

*The nineteenth century doctrine that the United States had the right and duty to expand throughout the North American continent

†A law which gave a 160-acre piece of land to anyone who lived on it for five years

15   Is all this relevant only to past attitudes and past legislative history? I don't think so. The fact is that until today, this same basic belief—that our cities ought to be left to fend for themselves—is still a powerful element in our national tradition.

16   Consider more modern history. The most important housing act in the last twenty-five years was not the law that provided for public housing; it was the law that permitted the FHA* to grant subsidized low-interest mortgages to Americans who want to purchase homes. More than anything else, this has made the suburban dream a reality. It has brought the vision of grass and trees and a place for the kids to play within the reach of millions of working Americans, and the consequences be damned. The impact of such legislation on the cities was not even considered— nor was the concept of making subsidized money available for neighborhood renovation in the city so that it might compete with the suburbs. Instead, in little more than a decade 800,000 middle income New Yorkers fled the city for the suburbs and were replaced by largely unskilled workers who in many instances represented a further cost rather than an economic asset.

17   And it was not a hundred years ago but two years ago that a suggested law giving a small amount of federal money for rat control was literally laughed off the floor of the House of Representatives amid much joking about discrimination against country rats in favor of city rats.

18   What happened, I think, was not the direct result of a "the city is evil and therefore we will not help it" concept. It was more indirect, more subtle, the result of the kind of thinking that enabled us to spend billions of dollars in subsidies to preserve the family farm while doing nothing about an effective program for jobs in the city; to create government agencies concerned with the interests of agriculture, veterans, small business, labor, commerce, and the American Indian but to create no Department of Urban Development until 1965; to so restrict money that meaningful federal aid is still not possible.

19   In other words, the world of urban America as a dark and desolate place undeserving of support or help has become fixed in the American consciousness. And we are paying for that attitude in our cities today.

---

*Federal Housing Administration

COMPREHENSION

Exercise 1
Check (✓) those statements which the author believes accurately reflect Americans' attitudes toward their cities.

1. _____ Americans don't like their cities very much.

2. _____ Americans have not thought their cities worthy of receiving financial support from the federal government.

3. _____ Americans were suspicious of cities because cities reminded them of the corruption of Europe.

4. _____ Most Americans believe that cities are centers of civilization.

5. _____ Americans believed that the federal government should provide support for establishing public school systems in urban areas.

6. _____ The United States government thought it was more important to develop the American West than to develop the cities.

7. _____ Rural Americans have been sympathetic to the problems of newly arrived immigrants in the city.

8. _____ No one considered the effect on cities of laws to help people build homes in the suburbs.

9. _____ The American attitude toward cities is changing.

10. _____ The American attitude toward cities has been harmful to the United States.

Exercise 2
As you read you should be able to differentiate between facts and opinions. Facts are statements of information which can be shown to be true. Opinions are beliefs, conclusions, or judgments not confirmed by positive knowledge or proof.

In this essay some of the opinions presented are those of the author; some are those of other people. Read the following sentences carefully. Indicate if each statement is a fact (F), (it could be demonstrated to be true) or an opinion (O), (not everyone would agree with the statement; it probably could not be convincingly proved to be true or false). If the statement is an opinion, indicate whose opinion it is. The number in parentheses indicates the paragraph in which each idea may be found.

Examples:

__F__ _____ New York City is the largest city in the United States. (4)

__O__ __Founding Fathers__ Good Americans should not live in cities. (14)

1. _____ _____   More than three-fourths of the American people now live in cities. (2)

2. _____ _____   There is a strong anti-urban attitude in America. (4)

3. _____ _____   When industrialization began, many Europeans went to work in cities. (6)

4. _____ _____   Cities are like prisons. (7)

5. _____ _____   Cities are centers of civilization. (8)

6. _____ _____   Although Thomas Jefferson often visited London and Paris, he did not like these cities. (9)

7. _____ _____   Because of the widespread opportunity to own land, America represented an escape from the injustices of Europe. (9)

8. _____ _____   The Northwest Ordinance gave free land to people. (12)

9. _____ _____   When New York City began its public school system, the federal government did not help. (12)

10. _____ _____   The cities on the east coast of the United States were corrupt. (12)

11. _____ _____   Many of the immigrants who came to America after the Civil War were poor. (13)

12. _____ _____   Poor immigrants are inferior to hard-working Americans. (13)

VOCABULARY FROM CONTEXT

Exercise 1

Use the context provided to determine the meanings of the italicized words. Write a definition, synonym, or description of each of the italicized vocabulary items in the space provided.

1. _____   The American people have never trusted the city; it has always appeared in literature and history as a *suspect* institution.

2. _____   A high *priority* should be given to providing public transportation; money for highways is less important.

3. _____   It is *absurd* to spend more money on highways. The wise solution for overcrowded roads is public transportation.

(*Continued on page 210.*)

4. _____ The government gave money to people to help buy homes outside of the cities. This system of *subsidized* housing caused many people to leave urban areas.

5. _____ Lack of public transportation in the suburbs has caused a terrible *predicament* for poor people who live there; they must either buy a car or depend on friends for transportation.

6. _____ Hotels and restaurants are an *integral* part of the city; without them, the city's tourist industry could not exist.

7. _____ When Governor Holmes was first elected, he was probably an honest man. However, since then, he has become as *corrupt* as all of the dishonest people around him. Now he is as bad as the rest of the state officials.

8. _____ Although Richard Weeks has accomplished many good things during his terms as mayor, the fact that he totally controls the city makes him a *despot*, and he should be forced to give up some of his power.

Exercise 2

This exercise is designed to give you additional clues to determine the meaning of unfamiliar vocabulary items from context. In the paragraph indicated by the number in parentheses, find the word that best fits the meaning given. Your teacher may want to read these aloud as you quickly scan the paragraph to find the answer.

1. (11) Which word means *distribution*?

2. (15) Which word means *provide for; take care of*?

3. (16) Which word means *improvement by repairing*?

Exercise 3
This exercise should be done after you have finished reading "The City." The exercise is designed to determine how well you have been able to use context clues to guess the meaning of unfamiliar vocabulary in the essay. Give a definition, synonym, or description of each of the words below. The number in parentheses indicates the paragraph in which the word can be found. Your teacher may want you to do these orally or in writing.

1. (1)   trace _____

2. (2)   flocking _____

3. (6)   antipathy _____

4. (6)   pastoral _____

5. (9)   charting _____

6. (13) waves _____

7. (13) ethnic _____

8. (13) bar _____

9. (16) fled _____

10. (18) subtle _____

LONGER READING: Suspense

Is it possible to rob a bank and not commit a crime?

Why would someone want to rob a bank? Money of course. But is that the only reason?

Read "The Dusty Drawer" carefully.* It is a special kind of mystery story which raises some interesting questions about human nature and about the difference between breaking the law and doing something which is wrong.

You may want to do the Vocabulary from Context exercise on page 225 and the Dictionary Study on page 227 before you begin reading. In addition, after you have read the first eleven paragraphs, you may want to do the first four items of the Figurative Language and Idioms exercise on page 226.

The Dusty Drawer

1   Norman Logan paid for his apple pie and coffee, then carried his tray toward the front of the cafeteria. From a distance, he recognized the back of William Tritt's large head. The tables near Tritt were empty, and Logan had no desire to eat with him, but they had some unfinished business that Logan wanted to clear up. He stopped at Tritt's table and asked, "Do you mind if I join you?"

2   Tritt looked up as he always looked up from inside his teller's cage in the bank across the street. He acted like a servant—like a fat, precise butler that Logan used to see in movies—but behind the film of obsequiousness was an attitude of vast superiority that always set Logan on edge.

3   "Why, yes, Mr. Logan. Do sit down. Only please, I must ask you not to mention that two hundred dollars again."

"Well, we'll see about that," said Logan, pulling out a chair and seating himself. "Rather late for lunch, isn't it?"

"Oh, I've had lunch," Tritt said. "This is just a snack." He cut a large piece of roast beef from the slab in front of him and thrust it into his mouth. "I don't believe I've seen you all summer," he added, chewing the meat.

4   "I took a job upstate," Logan said. "We were trying to stop some kind of blight in the apple orchards."

"Is that so?" Tritt looked like a concerned bloodhound.

"I wanted to do some research out West," Logan went on, "but I couldn't get any money from the university."

"You'll be back for the new term, won't you?"

5   "Oh, yes," Logan said with a sigh, "we begin again tomorrow." He thought for a moment of the freshman faces that would be looking up at him in the lecture room. A bunch of high-strung, mechanical New York City kids, pushed by their parents into his botany class. They were brick-bound people who had no interest in growing things, and Logan sometimes felt sad that in five years of teaching he had communicated to only a few of them his own delight with his subject.

6   "My, one certainly gets a long vacation in the teaching profession," Tritt said. June through September."

*"The Dusty Drawer" by Harry Miles Muheim. Copyright © 1969 by Harry Miles Muheim. Published in *Alfred Hitchcock Presents a Month of Mystery* (New York: Random House, 1969). Reprinted by permission of the author.

"I suppose," Logan said. "Only trouble is that you don't make enough to do anything in all the spare time."

Tritt laughed a little, controlled laugh and continued chewing. Logan began to eat the pie. It had the drab, neutral flavor of all cafeteria pies.

"Mr. Tritt," he said after a long silence.

"Yes?"

"When are you going to give me back my two hundred dollars?"

7   "Oh, come now, Mr. Logan. We had this all out ten months ago. We went over it with Mr. Pinkson and the bank examiners and everyone. I did *not* steal two hundred dollars from you."

"You did, and you know it."

"Frankly, I'd rather not hear any more about it."

"Mr. Tritt, I had three hundred and twenty-four dollars in my hand that day. I'd just cashed some bonds. I know how much I had."

"The matter has been all cleared up," Tritt said coldly.

8   "Not for me, it hasn't. When you entered the amount in my checking account, it was for one hundred and twenty-four, not three hundred twenty-four."

9   Tritt put down his fork and carefully folded his hands. "I've heard you tell that story a thousand times, sir. My cash balanced when you came back and complained."

"Sure it balanced," Logan exploded. "You saw your mistake when Pinkson asked you to check the cash. So you took my two hundred out of the drawer. No wonder it balanced!"

Tritt laid a restraining hand on Logan's arm. "Mr. Logan, I'm going a long, long way in the bank. I simply can't afford to make mistakes."

10   "You also can't afford to admit it when you do make one!"

"Oh, come now," said Tritt, as though he were speaking to a child. "Do you think I'd jeopardize my entire career for two hundred dollars?"

"You didn't jeopardize your career," Logan snapped. "You knew you could get away with it. And you took my money to cover your error."

11   Tritt sat calmly and smiled a fat smile at Logan. "Well, that's your version, Mr. Logan. But I do wish you'd quit annoying me with your fairy tale." Leaving half his meat untouched, Tritt stood up and put on his hat. Then he came around the table and stood looming over Logan. "I will say, however, from a purely hypothetical point of view, that if I *had* stolen your money and then staked my reputation on the lie that I hadn't, the worst thing I could possibly do would be to return the money to you. I think you'd agree with that."

"I'll get you, Tritt," said Logan, sitting back in the chair. "I can't stand to be had."

"I know, I know. You've been saying that for ten months, too. Good-by, now."

12   Tritt walked out of the cafeteria. Norman Logan sat there motionless watching the big teller cross the street and enter the bank. He felt no rage—only an increased sense of futility. Slowly, he finished his coffee.

A few minutes later, Logan entered the bank. Down in the safe-deposit vaults, he raised the lid of his long metal box and took out three twenty-five-dollar bonds. With a sigh, he began to fill them out for cashing. They would cover his government insurance premium for the year. In July, too, he'd taken three bonds from the box, when his father had overspent his pension money. And earlier in the summer, Logan had cashed some more of them, after slamming into a truck and damaging his Plymouth. Almost every month there was some reason to cash bonds, and Logan reflected that he hadn't bought one since his Navy days. There just wasn't enough money in botany.

13   With the bonds in his hand, he climbed the narrow flight of stairs to the street floor, then walked past the long row of tellers' cages to the rear of the bank. Here he opened an iron gate in a low marble fence and entered the green-carpeted area of the manager and assistant manager. The manager's desk was right inside the gate, and Mr. Pinkson looked up as Logan came in. He smiled, looking over the top of the glasses pinched on his nose.

14   "Good afternoon, Mr. Logan." Pinkson's quick eyes went to the bonds, and then, with the professional neutrality of a branch manager, right back up to Logan's thin face. "If you'll just sit down, I'll buzz Mr. Tritt."

"Mr. Tritt?" said Logan, surprised.

"Yes. He's been moved up to the first cage now."

Pinkson indicated a large, heavy table set far over against the side wall in back of his desk, and Logan sat in a chair next to it.

"Have a good summer?" The little man had revolved in his squeaky executive's chair to face Logan.

"Not bad, thanks."

"Did you get out of the city?"

"Yes, I had a job upstate. I always work during my vacations."

15   Mr. Pinkson let out a controlled chuckle, a suitable reply when he wasn't sure whether or not the customer was trying to be funny. Then he revolved again; his chubby cue-ball head bobbed down, and he was back at his figures.

Logan put the bonds on the clean desk blotter and looked over at Tritt's cage. It was at the end of the row of cages, with a door opening directly into the manager's area. Tritt was talking on the telephone inside, and for a long, unpleasant minute Logan watched the fat, self-assured face through the greenish glass. I'll get him yet, Logan thought. But he didn't see how. Tritt had been standing firmly shielded behind his lie for nearly a year now, and Norman Logan didn't seem to know enough about vengeance to get him.

16   Restive, Logan sat back and tipped the chair onto its hind legs. He picked ineffectually at a gravy stain on his coat; then his eye was attracted to a drawer, hidden under the overhang of the tabletop. It was a difficult thing to see, for it had no handle, and its face was outlined by only a thin black crack in the darkstained wood. Logan could see faintly the two putty-filled holes that marked the place where the handle had once been. Curious, he rocked forward a little and slipped his fingernails into the crack along the bottom of the drawer. He pulled gently, and the drawer slid smoothly and silently from the table.

17   The inside was a dirty, cluttered mess. Little mounds of grayish mold had formed on the furniture glue along the joints. A film of dust on the bottom covered the bits of faded yellow paper and rusted paper clips that were scattered about. Logan rocked the chair back farther, and the drawer came far out to reveal a delicate spider web. The spider was dead and flaky, resting on an old page from a desk calendar. The single calendar sheet read October 2, 1936. Logan pushed the drawer softly back into the table, wondering if it had actually remained closed since Alf Landon was running against Roosevelt.

18   The door of Tritt's cage clicked open, and he came out, carrying a large yellow form. William Tritt moved smoothly across the carpet, holding his fat young body erect and making a clear effort to keep his stomach in.

"Why, hello, Mr. Logan," he said. "I'm sorry for the delay. The main office called me. I can't hang up on them, you know."

"I know," Logan said.

The teller smiled as he lowered himself into the chair opposite Logan. Logan slid the bonds across the table.

19   "It's nice to see you again," Tritt said pleasantly as he opened his fountain pen. "Preparing for the new semester, I suppose?" There was no indication of their meeting across the street. Logan said nothing in reply, so Tritt went to work, referring rapidly to the form for the amount to be paid on each bond. "Well, that comes to sixty-seven dollars and twenty-five cents," he said, finishing the addition quickly.

Logan filled out a deposit slip. "Will you put it in my checking account, please?" He handed his passbook across the table. "And will you please enter the right amount?"

20   "Certainly, Mr. Logan," Tritt said, smiling indulgently. Logan watched carefully as Tritt made the entry. Then the teller walked rapidly back to his cage, while Logan, feeling somehow compelled to do so, took another glance into the dusty drawer. He kept thinking about the drawer as he got on a bus and rode up to the university. It had surprised him to stumble upon a dirty, forgotten place like that in a bank that was always so tidy.

21   Back in the biology department, Logan sat down at his desk, planning to prepare some roll sheets for his new classes. He stayed there for a long time without moving. The September sun went low behind the New Jersey Palisades, but he did not prepare the sheets, for the unused drawer stayed unaccountably in his mind.

Suddenly he sat forward in his chair. In a surprising flash of creative thought, he had seen how he could make use of the drawer. He wasn't conscious of having tried to develop a plan. The entire plan simply burst upon him all at once, and with such clarity and precision that he hardly felt any responsibility for it. He would rob the bank and pin the robbery on Tritt. That would take care of Tritt . . .

22   In the weeks that followed, Norman Logan remained surprisingly calm about his plan. Each time he went step by step over the mechanics of the robbery, it seemed more gemlike and more workable. He made his first move the day he got his November pay check.

Down on Fifty-first Street, Logan went into a novelty-and-trick store and bought a cigarette case. It was made of a dark, steel-blue plastic, and it looked like a trim thirty-eight automatic. When the trigger was pressed, a section of the top of the gun flipped upon a hinge, revealing the cigarettes inside the handle.

23   With this in his pocket, Logan took a bus way down to the lower part of Second Avenue and entered a grimy little shop displaying pistols and rifles in the window. The small shopkeeper shuffled forward, and Logan asked to see a thirty-eight.

"Can't sell you a thing until I see your permit," the man said. "The Sullivan Law."

"Oh, I don't want to buy a weapon," Logan explained. He took out his plastic gun. "I just want to see if the real thing looks like mine here."

24   The little man laughed a cackle laugh and brought up a thirty-eight from beneath the counter, placing it next to Logan's. "So you'll just be fooling around, eh?"

"That's right," said Logan, looking at the guns. They were almost identical.

"Oh, they look enough alike," said the man. "But lemme give you a tip. Put some Scotch tape over that lid to keep it down. Friend of mine was using one of those things, mister. He'd just polished off a stick-up when he pulled the trigger and the lid flopped open. Well, he tried to offer the victim a cigarette, but the victim hauled off and beat the hell out of him."

"Thanks," Logan said with a smile. "I'll remember that."

"Here, you can put some Scotch tape on right now."

25   Logan walked over to the Lexington Avenue line and rode uptown on the subway. It was five minutes to three when he got to the bank. The old, gray-uniformed guard touched his cap as Logan came through the door. The stand-up desks were crowded, so it was natural enough for Logan to go through the little iron gate and

215

cross to the table with the drawer. Mr. Pinkson and the new assistant manager had already left; their desks were clear. As Logan sat down, Tritt stuck his head out the door of his cage.

"More bonds, Mr. Logan?" he asked.

"No," said Logan. "Just a deposit."

26   Tritt closed the door and bent over his work. Logan took out his wallet, removed the pay check, then looked carefully the length of the bank. No one was looking in his direction. As he put the wallet back into his inside coat pocket, he withdrew the slim plastic gun and eased open the drawer. He dropped the gun in, shut the drawer, deposited the check, and went home to his apartment. In spite of the Sullivan Law, he was on his way.

27   Twice during November he used the table with the drawer. Each time he checked on the gun. It had not been moved. By the time he deposited his December check, Logan was completely certain that nobody ever looked in there. On the nineteenth of the month, he decided to take the big step.

28   Next morning, after his ten-o'clock class, Logan walked six blocks through the snow down the hill to the bank. He took four bonds out of his safe-deposit box and filled them out for cashing. The soothing sound of recorded Christmas carols floated down from the main floor.

29   Upstairs, he seated himself at the heavy table to wait for Tritt. Pinkson had nodded and returned to his figuring; the nervous assistant manager was not around. The carols were quite loud here, and Logan smiled at this unexpected advantage. He placed the bonds squarely on the blotter. Then he slipped open the drawer, took out the gun with his left hand, and held it below the table.

30   Tritt was coming toward him, carrying his bond chart. They said hello, and Tritt sat down and went to work. He totaled the sum twice and said carefully, still looking at the figures, "Well, Mr. Logan, that comes to eighty-three fifty."

"I'll want something in addition to the eighty-three fifty," said Logan, leaning forward and speaking in an even voice.

"What's that?" asked Tritt.

"Ten thousand dollars in twenty-dollar bills."

Tritt's pink face smiled. He started to look up into Logan's face, but his eyes froze on the muzzle of the gun poking over the edge of the table. He did not notice the Scotch tape.

"Now just go to your cage and get the money." Logan said.

31   It was William Tritt's first experience with anything like this. "Mr. Logan. Come now, Mr. Logan . . . " He swallowed and tried to start again, but his self-assurance had deserted him. He turned toward Pinkson's back.

"Look at me," snapped Logan.

Tritt turned back. "Mr. Logan, you don't know what you're doing."

"Keep still."

"Couldn't we give you a loan or perhaps a—"

32   "Listen to me, Tritt." Logan's voice was just strong enough to carry above "The First Noel." He was amazed at how authoritative he sounded. "Bring the money in a bag. Place it on the table here."

Tritt started to object, but Logan raised the gun slightly, and the last resistance drained from Tritt's fat body.

"All right, all right. I'll get it." As Tritt moved erratically toward his cage, Logan dropped the gun back into the drawer and closed it. Tritt shut the door of the cage, and his head disappeared below the frosted part of the glass. Immediately, Mr. Pinkson's telephone buzzed, and he picked it up. Logan watched his back, and after a few seconds, Pinkson's body stiffened. Logan sighed, knowing then that he would not get the money on this try.

33   Nothing happened for several seconds; then suddenly the little old guard came rushing around the corner of the cages, his big pistol drawn and wobbling as he tried to hold it on Logan.

"Okay, Okay. Stay there! Put your hands up, now!"

Logan raised his hands, and the guard turned to Pinkson with a half-surprised face. "Okay, Mr. Pinkson. Okay, I've got him covered now."

34   Pinkson got up as Tritt came out of the cage. Behind the one gun, the three men came slowly toward Logan.

"Careful, Louie, he's armed," Tritt warned the guard.

"May I ask what this is all about?" Logan said, his hands held high.

"Mr. Logan," said Pinkson, "I'm sorry about this, but Mr. Tritt here tells me that—that—"

"That you tried to rob me of ten thousand dollars," said Tritt, his voice choppy.

"I—I *what*?"

"You just attempted an armed robbery of this bank," Tritt said slowly. "Don't try to deny it."

35   Logan's face became the face of a man so completely incredulous that he cannot speak. He remembered not to overplay it, though. First he simply laughed at Tritt. Then he lowered his hands, regardless of the guard's gun, and stood up, the calm, indignant faculty member.

"All I can say, Mr. Tritt, is that I do deny it."

"Goodness," said Pinkson.

"Better take his gun, Louie," Tritt ordered the guard.

The guard stepped gingerly forward to Logan and frisked him, movie style. "Hasn't got a gun, Mr. Tritt," he said.

36   "Of course he's got a gun," snapped Tritt. He pushed the guard aside. "It's right in his coat." Tritt jammed his thick hand into Logan's left coat pocket and flailed it about. "It's not in that pocket," he said after a moment.

"It's not in any pocket," Logan said. "I don't have one."

37   "You do. You *do* have a gun. I saw it," Tritt answered, beginning to sound like a child in an argument. He spun Logan around and pulled the coat off him with a jerk. The sleeves turned inside out. Eagerly, the teller pulled the side pockets out, checked the inside pocket and the breast pocket, then ran his hands over the entire garment, crumpling it. "The—the gun's not in his coat," he said finally.

"It's not in his pants," the guard added.

38   Tritt stepped over to the table quickly. "It's around here somewhere," he said. "We were sitting right here." He stood directly in front of the closed drawer, and his hands began to move meaninglessly over the tabletop. He picked up the neat stack of deposit slips, put them down again, then looked under the desk blotter, as though it could have concealed a gun.

39   Logan knew he had to stop this. "Is there any place I can remove the rest of my clothes?" he asked loudly, slipping the suspenders from his shoulders. Several depositors had gathered on the other side of the marble fence to watch, and Mr. Pinkson had had enough.

40   "Oh, no, no," he said, almost shouting. "That won't be necessary, Mr. Logan. Louie said you were unarmed. Now, Louie, put *your* gun away, and for goodness' sake, request the customers to please move on."

"But Mr. Pinkson, you must believe me," Tritt said, coming over to the manager. "This man held a gun on me and—"

"It's hard to know what to believe," said Pinkson. "But no money was stolen, and I don't see how we can embarrass Mr. Logan further with this matter. Please, Mr. Logan, do pull up your suspenders."

41   It was a shattering moment for the teller—the first time his word had ever been doubted at the bank.

"But sir, I insist that this man—"

"I must ask you to return to your cage now, Mr. Tritt," Pinkson said, badly agitated. Tritt obeyed.

The manager helped Logan put on his coat, then steered him over to his desk. "This is all a terrible mistake, Mr. Logan. Please do sit down now, please." The friendly little man was breathing heavily. "Now, I just want you to know that if you should press this complaint, it—it would go awfully bad for us down in the main office downtown, and I—"

42   "Please don't get excited, Mr. Pinkson," Logan said with a smile. "I'm not going to make any complaint." Logan passed the whole thing off casually. Mr. Tritt imagined he saw a gun, that's all. It was simply one of those aberrations that perfectly normal people get occasionally. Now, could Mr. Pinkson finish cashing his bonds? The manager paid him the eighty-three fifty, continuing to apologize.

Logan left the bank and walked through the soft snowfall, whistling a Christmas carol. He'd handled himself perfectly.

43   In the weeks that followed, Logan continued to do business with Tritt, just as though nothing had happened. The teller tried to remain aloof and calm, but added sums incorrectly, and his hands shook. One day late in January, Tritt stood up halfway through a transaction, his great body trembling, "Excuse me, Mr. Logan," he murmured, and rushed off into the corridor behind the cages. Pinkson followed him, and Logan took advantage of the moment to check on the gun. It lay untouched in the drawer. Then Pinkson came back alone. "I'm awfully sorry to delay you again, sir," he said. "Mr. Tritt doesn't feel too well."

44   "Did he imagine he saw another gun?" Logan asked quietly.

"No. He just upsets easily now. Ever since that incident with you last month, he's been like a cat on a hot stove."

"I've noticed he's changed."

"He's lost that old, calm banking touch, Mr. Logan. And of course, he's in constant fear of a new hallucination."

"I'm sorry to hear that," Logan said, looking genuinely concerned. "It's very sad when a person loses his grip."

45   "It's particularly disappointing to me," the manager said sadly. "I brought Tritt into the bank myself, you see. Had him earmarked for a big spot downtown someday. Fine man. Intelligent, steady, accurate—why he's been right down the line on everything. But now—now he's—well, I *do* hope he gets over this."

46   "I can understand how you feel," Logan said sympathetically. He smiled inside at the precision of his planning. Fat William Tritt had been undermined just enough—not only in Pinkson's mind, but in his own.

47   On the tenth of March, Norman Logan acted again. When Tritt was seated across from him, Logan said, "Well, here we go again, Mr. Tritt." Tritt's head came up, and once more he was looking into the barrel of the toy automatic. He did not try to speak. "Now go get the ten thousand," ordered Logan. "And this time, do it."

48   Without objecting, the teller moved quickly to his cage. Logan slipped the gun back into the drawer; then he picked up his brief case and stood it near the edge of the table. Pinkson's telephone didn't buzz, and the guard remained out of sight. After a few minutes, Tritt came out of the cage, carrying a small cloth bag.

49   "All right, continue with the bonds," Logan said. "The bag goes on the table between us." Logan shifted forward and opened the bag, keeping the money out of sight behind the brief case. The clean new bills were wrapped in thousand-dollar units, each package bound with a bright yellow strip of paper. Logan counted through one package, and, with Tritt looking right at him, he placed the package of money carefully in the brief case.

50   "There," he said. "Now finish with the bonds." Tritt finished filling out the form and got Logan's signature. He was not as flustered as Logan had thought he'd be. "Now listen, Tritt," Logan went on, "My getaway is all set, of course, but if you give any signal before I'm out of the bank, I'll put a bullet into you—right here." Logan pointed to the bridge of his own nose. "Please don't think I'd hesitate to do it. Now get back to your cage."

51   Tritt returned to the cage. While his back was turned, Logan slipped the bag of money from his brief case and dropped it into the drawer, next to the gun. He eased the drawer into the table, took the brief case, and walked out of the bank.

    Outside, he stood directly in front of the entrance, as though he were waiting for a bus. After just a few seconds, the burglar alarm went off with a tremendous electrical shriek, and the old guard came running out of the door after him.

    He was followed immediately by Pinkson, the assistant manager, and Tritt.

52   "Well, gentlemen," said Logan, his hands raised again in front of the guard's gun, "here we are again, eh?"

    A crowd was gathering, and Pinkson sent the assistant to turn off the alarm. "Come, let's all go inside," he said. "I don't want any fuss out here."

    It was the same kind of scene they'd played before, only now Logan—the twice-wronged citizen—was irate, and now ten thousand dollars was missing from William Tritt's cage. Tritt was calm, though.

53   "I was ready for him this time," he said proudly to Pinkson. "I marked ten thousand worth of twenties. My initial is on the band. The money's in his brief case."

    "Oh, for Heaven's sake, Tritt," Logan shouted suddenly, "who ever heard of making a getaway by waiting for a bus. I don't know what your game is, but—"

    "Never mind my game," said Tritt. "Let's just take a look in your brief case."

54   He wrenched it from Logan's hand, clicked the lock, and turned the brief case upside down. A group of corrected examination books fell out. That was all.

    "See?" said Logan. "Not a cent."

    The guard put away his gun as Pinkson began to pick up the scattered books.

55   Tritt wheeled, threw the brief case against the wall, and grabbed Logan by the lapels. "But I gave you the money. I did. I did!" His face was pasty gray, and his voice was high. "You put it in the brief case. I saw you. I *saw* you do it! He began to shake Logan in a kind of final attempt to shake the ten thousand dollars out of him.

    Pinkson straightened up with the exam books and said, "For goodness' sake, Mr. Tritt. Stop it. Stop it."

    Tritt stopped shaking Logan, then turned wildly to Pinkson. "You don't believe me!" he shouted. "You don't believe me!"

    "It's not a question of—"

56   "I'll find that money. I'll show you who's lying." He rushed over to the big table and swept it completely clear with one wave of his heavy arm. The slips fluttered to the floor, and the inkwell broke, splattering black ink over the carpet. Tritt pulled the table in a wild, crashing arc across the green carpet, smashing it into Pinkson's desk. Logan saw the dusty drawer come open about a half-inch.

57   The big man dropped clumsily to his knees and began to pound on the carpet with his flattened hands as he kept muttering, "It's around here someplace—a cloth

bag." He grabbed a corner of the carpet and flipped it back with a grunt. It made a puff of dust and revealed only a large triangle of empty, dirty floor. A dozen people had gathered outside the marble fence by now, and all the tellers were peering through the glass panes of the cages at Tritt.

58   "I'll find it! I'll find it!" he shouted. A film of sweat was on his forehead as he stood up, turned, and advanced again toward the table. The slightly opened drawer was in plain sight in front of him, but everyone's eyes were fixed on Tritt, and Tritt did not see the drawer under the overhang of the table.

   Logan turned quickly to Pinkson and whispered, "He may be dangerous, Mr. Pinkson. You've got to calm him." He grabbed Pinkson by the arm and pushed him backward several feet, so that the manager came to rest on the edge of the table, directly over the drawer. The exam books were still in his hand.

59   "Mr. Tritt, you *must* stop this!" Mr. Pinkson said.

   "Get out of my way, Pinkson," said Tritt, coming right at him, breathing like a bull. "You believe him, but I'll show you. I'll find it!" He placed his hands on Pinkson's shoulders. "Now get away, you fool."

   "I won't take that from anyone," snapped Pinkson. He slapped Tritt's face with a loud, stinging blow. The teller stopped, stunned, and suddenly began to cry.

   "Mr. Pinkson. Mr. Pinkson, you've *got* to trust me."

   Pinkson was immediately ashamed of what he had done. "I'm sorry my boy. I shouldn't have done that."

60   "I tell you he held a gun on me again. A real gun—it's not my imagination."

   "But why didn't you call Louie?" Pinkson said. "That's the rule, you know."

   "I wanted to catch him myself. He—he made such a fool of me last time."

   "But that business last time was hallucination," said Pinkson, looking over at Logan. Logan nodded.

   "It's no hallucination when ten thousand dollars is missing," Tritt shouted.

   "That's precisely where the confusion arises in my mind," Mr. Pinkson said slowly. "We'll get it straight, but in the meantime, I must order your arrest, Mr. Tritt."

61   Logan came and stood next to Pinkson, and they both looked sympathetically at the teller as he walked slowly, still sobbing, back to the cage.

   "I'm just sick about it," Pinkson said.

   "I think you'll find he's not legally competent," said Logan, putting a comforting thought into Pinkson's head.

   "Perhaps not."

62   Logan showed his concern by helping to clean up the mess that Tritt had made. He and the assistant manager placed the table back into its position against the far wall, Logan shoving the dusty drawer firmly closed with his fingertips as they lifted it.

   Norman Logan returned to the bank late the next day. He sat at the table to make a deposit, and he felt a pleasantly victorious sensation surge through him as he slipped the gun and the ten thousand dollars out of the drawer and into his overcoat pocket. As he walked out the front door past the guard, he met Mr. Pinkson, who was rushing in.

63   "Terrible. Terrible," the little man said without even pausing to say hello.

   "What's that?" Logan asked calmly.

   "I've just been talking to the doctors at Bellevue about Tritt," Pinkson said. "He seems all right, and they've released him. Unfortunately, he can answer every question except 'Where's the money?'" Logan held firmly to the money in his pocket and continued to extend his sympathies.

Back at his apartment, Logan borrowed a portable typewriter from the man upstairs. Then he sat down and wrote a note:

> *Dear Mr. Pinkson:*
> *I'm returning the money. I'm so sorry. I guess I didn't know what I was doing. I guess I haven't known for some time.*

After looking up Tritt's initials on an old deposit slip, he forged a small tidy *W.T.* to the note.

64 Logan wiped his fingerprints from the bills and wrapped them, along with the note, in a neat package. For one delicious moment he considered how nice it would be to hang on to the money. He could resign from the university, go out West, and continue his research on his own. But that wasn't part of the plan, and the plan was working too well to tamper with it now. Logan drove to the post office nearest Tritt's apartment and mailed the money to Pinkson at the bank.

65 In the morning, Mr. Pinkson telephoned Logan at the university. "Well, it's all cleared up," he said, relieved but sad. "Tritt returned the money, so the bank is not going to press the charges. Needless to say, we're dropping Tritt. He not only denies having taken the money, he also denies having returned it."

"I guess he just doesn't know what he's doing," Logan said.

66 "Yes. That's what he said in the note. Anyway, Mr. Logan, I—I just wanted to call and apologize for the trouble we've caused you."

"Oh, it was no trouble for me," Logan replied, smiling.

"And you've been very helpful, too," Pinkson added.

"I was glad to be of help," Logan said quietly. "Delighted, in fact."

They said good-by then, and Logan walked across the hall to begin his ten o'clock botany lecture.

COMPREHENSION

1. Before you can appreciate a suspense story, you must understand the characters involved. Below is a list of physical and personality characteristics. Put a *T* next to those which describe Tritt and an *L* next to those which describe Logan. Some adjectives may describe both men. Be prepared to defend your choices with portions of the text.

     _____ a. fat   _____ f. careful

     _____ b. stubborn   _____ g. greedy

     _____ c. dishonest   _____ h. careless

     _____ d. ambitious   _____ i. self-assured

     _____ e. thin   _____ j. clever

2. The most important factor in enjoying a suspense story is a complete understanding of the plot. The following sentences will tell the story of "The Dusty Drawer" when they are arranged in the correct sequence. Read all of the sentences quickly, then number the sentences according to the order in which the events occur.

     _____ a. Logan writes a note to the bank and forges Tritt's initials, then returns the money by mail.

     _____ b. Tritt steals $200.00 from Logan to cover a mistake he had made while depositing money in Logan's account.

     _____ c. Logan learns that Tritt has been fired from his position at the bank.

     _____ d. Logan buys a toy gun and hides it in the dusty drawer.

     _____ e. Logan gets $10,000.00 from Tritt and hides it in the drawer.

     _____ f. Logan's first attempt to rob the bank causes Tritt to lose his banker's touch.

3. What was Tritt's position in the bank? _____

4. What was Logan's profession? _____

5. T / F   Tritt was considered a valuable employee who would make great progress in the bank if he made no mistakes.

6. Logan believed that Tritt stole the $200.00 because _____

     _____ a. he needed the money.

     _____ b. he had made an error and didn't want to admit it.

     _____ c. he hated Logan and wanted a safe way to hurt him.

     _____ d. he knew he would not be caught.

7. Logan suspected that $200.00 had been stolen when _____

    _____ a. he noticed that the wrong amount of money had been deposited in his account by Tritt.
    _____ b. he didn't receive the right amount of cash when his bonds were cashed by Tritt.
    _____ c. he checked his wallet after talking to Tritt.
    _____ d. he returned from his summer vacation and the money wasn't in his account.

8. T / F   As they were talking in the cafeteria, Tritt admitted to Logan that he had taken the money.

9. Although Tritt denied taking the $200.00, he did say that _____

    _____ a. Mr. Pinkson might have made a mistake when he counted the money.
    _____ b. he would have told Logan if he had stolen it.
    _____ c. he thought he knew who did.
    _____ d. he certainly wouldn't return the money if he had stolen it.

10. Logan wanted to get even with Tritt because _____

    _____ a. he had difficulty living without that $200.00.
    _____ b. he hated Tritt.
    _____ c. he did not like to be cheated.
    _____ d. he wanted to prevent Tritt from cheating other people.

11. T / F   Logan made regular trips to the bank.

12. Logan's plan to pin the robbery on Tritt _____

    _____ a. had been carefully developed over a period of ten months.
    _____ b. developed because he learned that Tritt had been promoted to the first cage.
    _____ c. was suggested to him by something that a shop owner told him.
    _____ d. came to him suddenly after he found an unused drawer in the bank.

13. T / F   Tritt had received a promotion while Logan was away on summer vacation.

14. T / F   The Sullivan Law prevents the sale of guns unless the customer has a permit.

15. T / F   In order to convince Tritt that the robbery was genuine, Logan bought a .38 caliber pistol.

16. T / F   The shopkeeper of the gun store assumed that Logan was going to attempt a robbery.

17. Logan became convinced the old drawer was never used because _____

    _____ a. the handles had been removed before the desk was painted.
    _____ b. the rest of the bank was so clean and efficient.
    _____ c. the gun was not moved during the time that he watched it.
    _____ d. neither Mr. Pinkson nor Mr. Tritt ever mentioned it.

18. The first time Logan tried to rob the bank _____

   _____ a. Tritt placed the money in a cloth bag after initialing the packets of bills.
   _____ b. Tritt said he would not bring the money from his cage.
   _____ c. Tritt signaled Mr. Pinkson from his cage.
   _____ d. Tritt thought it was all a joke.

19. T / F Logan offered to remove all his clothes because he was afraid that Tritt might accidentally find the drawer.

20. In the months following the first robbery attempt, Tritt _____

   _____ a. questioned Logan carefully about the robbery whenever he entered the bank.
   _____ b. tried to prove that Logan had had a gun.
   _____ c. became nervous and easily upset.
   _____ d. lost his position in the first cage because of his frequent errors.

21. T / F The second time Logan attempted the robbery, Tritt brought the money.

22. T / F When no one was looking, Logan moved the money from the brief case to the drawer.

23. Logan didn't keep the $10,000.00 because _____

   _____ a. the plan was working so well that he didn't want to change it.
   _____ b. he was too honest.
   _____ c. he was afraid that someone would find the drawer.
   _____ d. he knew that crime never benefits anyone.

DISCUSSION - COMPOSITION

1. Do you believe that Tritt stole $200.00 from Logan? On what do you base your opinion? (How did you learn that the money was missing?)

2. What is the nature of the crimes committed in "The Dusty Drawer"? What is the difference between the consequences of Tritt's actions as compared to Logan's? Is there any moral difference between the two men? Is one better than the other?

3. Was Logan justified in doing what he did? How would you defend him? Has he committed a crime? Are there other considerations that should be used to judge his actions besides the question of whether or not he has broken the law?

4. Has justice been served in "The Dusty Drawer"?

VOCABULARY FROM CONTEXT

Both the ideas and the vocabulary in the following sentences are taken from "The Dusty Drawer." Use the context provided to determine the meanings of each italicized word. Your teacher may want you to do this exercise orally or in writing.

1. _____   The man's *obsequious* behavior made everyone nervous. Like a servant, he was always rushing to open doors and perform other small tasks, apologizing unnecessarily for any inconvenience that he might have caused.

2. _____   Although he really did not want to open the mysterious drawer again, his curiosity *compelled* him to take one last look.

3. _____   The shop was dusty and dirty. Everything seemed to be covered with grease. He was very happy to escape that *grimy* place.

4. _____   Logan wanted to hit Tritt in the nose, but he *restrained* himself because he knew that violence would not help him get his money back.

5. _____   Tritt never allowed himself to become angry with customers. Like a parent with spoiled children, he always listened *indulgently* to their complaints.

6. _____   Both men had convincing stories to tell concerning the missing money, but Mr. Logan's *version* of what happened was by far more believable.

7. _____   Logan felt that the situation was hopeless, and the *futility* of his efforts bothered him a great deal.

8. _____   Logan finally decided that, although he might not recover the money that had been stolen from him, he would have the pleasure of seeing the thief punished. Soon, Logan could think of little else but *vengeance*.

9. _____   The floor of the grimy little store was covered with paper, boxes, pieces of metal and wood, empty paint cans and used brushes. The floor was so *cluttered* that Carl had difficulty walking to the door.

10. _____   Tritt was sure that he had seen a pistol, but everyone else felt that the robbery was just a product of Tritt's imagination—the *hallucination* of an overworked man.

(*Continued on page 226.*)

11. _____ The banker was *incredulous* when the money did not fall out of the thief's brief case; he couldn't believe that it wasn't there because he had seen him put the bills inside just before leaving the bank.

12. _____ Logan certainly had reason to be *indignant*; twice he had been unjustly accused of trying to rob the bank.

13. _____ After the first time someone tried to rob him, the banker became *flustered* easily, and in his confusion he would make many careless errors.

14. _____ Although he often had the opportunity, Mr. Tritt never stole money from a customer. This would have endangered his position at the bank, and he did not want to *jeopardize* his future.

FIGURATIVE LANGUAGE AND IDIOMS

In the second half of the section indicated by the number in parentheses, find the word or phrase that best fits the meaning given. Your teacher may want to read these aloud as you quickly scan the paragraph to find the answer.

1. (9) What phrase means *advancing greatly in one's career*?

2. (10) What phrase means *escape without punishment*?

3. (11) What phrase is used to promise vengeance?

4. (11) What phrase means *not able to tolerate being cheated*?

5. (21) What phrase means *put the blame on someone for something*?

6. (24) What phrase means *completed*?

7. (24) Which word means *a robbery*?

DICTIONARY STUDY

Many words have more than one meaning. When you use the dictionary to discover the meaning of an unfamiliar word or phrase, you need to use the context to determine which definition is appropriate. Use the portions of the dictionary provided to select the best definition for each of the italicized words below.

1. Logan *reflected* that all had gone well for him in the bank so far.

2. As he sat waiting for the cashier, Logan *stumbled* across the old drawer.

3. After the first robbery attempt, the cashier began to lose his *grip* on reality.

4. Tritt knew that if he were caught stealing money from the bank, he would lose his position and go to prison, but he *staked* his future on the hope that the manager would believe his version of the robbery.

grip (grip), *n.* [ME.; AS. *gripe;* a clutch, *gripa,* handful < var. of the base of AS. *gripan* (see GRIPE) with a reduced vowel; akin to G. *griff;* some senses < the *v.*], 1. the act of taking firmly and holding fast with the hand, teeth, an instrument, etc.; secure grasp; firm hold. 2. the manner in which this is done. 3. any special manner of clasping hands by which members of a secret or fraternal society identify each other as such. 4. the power of grasping firmly: as, his hand has lost its *grip.* 5. the power of understanding; mental grasp. 6. firm control; mastery: as, in the *grip* of disease, get a *grip* on yourself. 7. a mechanical contrivance for clutching or grasping. 8. the part by which a tool weapon, etc. is grasped in the hand; handle. 9. [prob. < or after D.], a small bag for holding clothes, etc. in traveling; valise. 10. a sudden, intense pain. 11. [Slang], in a motion-picture studio, a stagehand. 12. in *sports,* the manner of holding a bat, club, racket, etc. *v.t.* [GRIPPED or GRIPT (gript), GRIPPING], 1. to take firmly and hold fast with the hand, teeth, an instrument, etc. 2. to give a grip (sense 3) to. 3. to fasten or join firmly (*to*). 4. to get and hold the attention of. 5. to take hold upon; control (the attention, emotions, etc.). *v.i.* to get a grip.
  come to grips, 1. to engage in hand-to-hand fighting. 2. to struggle; try to cope (*with*).

re·flect (ri-flekt′), *v.t.* [ME. *reflecten;* OFr. *reflecter;* L. *reflectere; re-,* back + *flectere,* to bend], 1. to bend or throw back, as light, heat, or sound. 2. to give back an image of; mirror or reproduce. 3. to cast or bring back as a consequence (with *on*): as, his deeds *reflect* honor on the nation. 4. [Rare], to fold or turn back. *v.i.* 1. to be bent or thrown back: as, the light *reflected* from the water into his eyes. 2. to bend or throw back light, heat, sound, etc. 3. *a*) to give back an image or likeness. *b*) to be mirrored. 4. to think seriously; contemplate; ponder (with *on* or *upon*). 5. to cast blame or discredit (with *on* or *upon*). —*SYN.* see **consider, think.**

stake (stāk), *n.* [ME.; AS. *staca;* akin to D. *staak;* base as in *stick*], 1. a length of wood or metal pointed at one end for driving into the ground. 2. the post to which a person is tied for execution by burning. 3. execution by burning. 4. a pole or post fitted upright into a socket, as at the edge of a railway flatcar, truck bed, etc., to help hold a load. 5. a truck having a stake body. 6. *often pl.* something, especially money, risked or hazarded, as in a wager, game, or contest: as, the gamblers were playing for high *stakes.* 7. *often pl.* a reward given a winner, as in a race; prize. 8. a race in which a prize is offered. 9. a share or interest, especially a financial one, in property, a person, a business venture, or the like. 10. [Colloq.], a grubstake. *v.t.* [STAKED (stākt), STAKING], 1. to mark the location or boundaries of with or as with stakes, specifically so as to establish a claim (with *out,* etc.). 2. to fasten or support with a stake or stakes. 3. to hitch or tether to a stake. 4. to close (*up* or *in*), shut (*out*), etc. by stakes in the form of a fence or barrier. 5. [influenced by MD. *staken,* to fix, place], to risk or hazard; gamble; bet: as, he *staked* his winnings on the next hand. 6. [Colloq.], to furnish with money or resources, as for a business venture. 7. [Colloq.], to grubstake.
  at stake, being risked or hazarded, or dependent upon the outcome (of something specified or implied).
  pull up stakes, [Colloq.], to change one's place of residence, business, etc.
stake body, a flat truck body having sockets into which stakes may be fitted, as to support railings.
stake·hold·er (stāk′hōl′dĕr), *n.* one who holds money, etc. bet by others and pays it to the winner.

stum·ble (stum′b'l), *v.i.* [STUMBLED (-b'ld), STUMBLING], [ME. *stomblen, stomelen;* prob. < ON. **stumla* (cf. Norw. *stumla,* to stumble in the dark, etc.) < the base seen in *stammer*], 1. to trip or miss one's step in walking, running, etc. 2. to walk or go in an unsteady or awkward manner, as from age, weakness, etc. 3. to speak, act, or proceed in a confused, blundering manner: as, he *stumbled* through his recitation. 4. to fall into sin or error; do wrong. 5. to come by chance; happen: as, I *stumbled* across a clue. *v.t.* to cause to stumble. *n.* 1. the act of stumbling. 2. a blunder, error, or sin.
stumbling block, something that causes stumbling; obstacle, hindrance, or difficulty.

VOCABULARY REVIEW

Exercise 1
Place the appropriate word or phrase from the following list in each of the blanks below. Do not use any word more than once.

indulgent	go a long way	incredulous
get away with it	hallucinations	flustered
futile	vengeance	version
obsequiousness	jeopardize	clutter
reflect	grime	restraint
indignantly	compelled	grip

1. Although it is true that a good employee should be respectful and helpful, Harry's extreme _____ makes everyone uncomfortable.

2. John is intelligent, hardworking, and honest. He should _____ in his profession.

3. Douglas is well-known for his self-_____; it is said that, no matter how angry he becomes, he never allows himself to show it.

4. John becomes _____ easily these days. Merely by asking him a simple question you can confuse him.

5. My aunt Vera suffers from frequent _____; just last night she thought she saw a pink elephant in a tree.

6. If you don't clean your kitchen regularly, the _____ on the wall above the stove will become too thick to remove with soap and water alone.

7. Dick knew that the bank officials regularly examined his records. He should have known that he couldn't steal any money and _____.

8. After he was robbed, Robert ran around madly shouting "I'll get him, I'll get him!" It was obvious that he could think of nothing but _____.

9. Arthur's behavior became stranger every day until he seemed to completely lose his _____ on reality.

10. The judge told us not to be impatient; after the other man told his story, we could tell our _____ of what had happened.

11. I have tried for a number of years to get my grandfather to buy a new car, but my attempts have been _____; he just won't part with his old Ford.

12. Although I didn't particularly want to accompany the children to the zoo, my sense of responsibility _____ me to go with them.

13. No matter how often we reminded the children, they never cleaned their room; the _____ in the room became so bad that we couldn't even open the door.

14. Before I make an important decision, I need some time to just sit and _____.

15. As Uncle Andy described the size of the fish he had caught, I became more and more _____. (You just never know when he is telling the truth.)

16. Grandparents are always more _____ of children than parents. For that reason, we always enjoyed our vacations on our grandparents' farm.

17. Angry and insulted because he had been accused of stealing the money, Dean calmly but _____ demanded to see his lawyer.

18. Corey had been working so hard that he decided to take a vacation, even though he knew he might _____ his chances of doing well on the upcoming examination.

Exercise 2
Complete the sentences below with the correct form of the word provided on the left.

1. obsequiousness

   Quite apart from any question of the man's honesty, I would not hire him because I dislike his _____ manner.

2. incredulity

   The policeman watched _____ as the family proceeded to do their laundry in the public swimming pool.

3. futility

   "If wishes were horses, beggars would ride," is an old saying which emphasizes the _____ of dreaming about unrealistic good fortune.

4. vengeful

   The man promised the judge that he would not seek _____ against the person who had robbed him.

5. indulgence

   Some people believe that modern parents are far too _____ of their children.

6. grimy

   No matter how hard we try, we will not be able to remove the _____ from public monuments.

7. jeopardy

   Most of us would not _____ our lives without a good reason, but firemen are in almost constant danger.

LONGER READING: Anthropology

The author of this selection, Jane van Lawick-Goodall, spent six years observing chimpanzees at the Gombe Stream Chimpanzee Reserve on the shores of Lake Tanganyika in Tanzania before she wrote *In the Shadow of Man.** In this selection, a chapter from that book, she compares chimpanzees and people in five areas: brain development, tool-using and making, communicatory gestures, speech, and awareness of self. As you read, look for the similarities and differences.

You may want to do the Vocabulary from Context exercise on page 236 before you begin reading.

In the Shadow of Man

1   The amazing success of man as a species is the result of the evolutionary development of his brain which has led, among other things, to tool-using, toolmaking, the ability to solve problems by logical reasoning, thoughtful cooperation, and language. One of the most striking ways in which the chimpanzee biologically resembles man lies in the structure of his brain. The chimpanzee, with his capacity for primitive reasoning, exhibits a type of intelligence more like that of man than does any other mammal living today. The brain of the modern chimpanzee is probably not too dissimilar to the brain that so many millions of years ago directed the behavior of the first ape man.

2   For a long time, the fact that prehistoric man made tools was considered to be one of the major criteria distinguishing him from other creatures. As I pointed out earlier, I have watched chimpanzees modify grass stems in order to use them to probe for termites. It is true that the chimpanzee does not fashion his tools to "a regular and set pattern"—but then, prehistoric man, before his development of stone tools, undoubtedly poked around with sticks and straws, at which stage it seems unlikely that he made tools to a set pattern, either.

3   It is because of the close association in most people's minds of tools with man that special attention has always been focused upon any animal able to use an object as a tool; but it is important to realize that this ability, on its own, does not necessarily indicate any special intelligence in the creature concerned. The fact that the Galàpagos woodpecker finch uses a cactus spine or twig to probe insects from crevices in the bark is indeed a fascinating phenomenon, but it does not make the bird more intelligent than a genuine woodpecker that uses its long beak and tongue for the same purpose.

4   The point at which tool-using and toolmaking, as such, acquire evolutionary significance is surely when an animal can adapt its ability to manipulate objects to a wide variety of purposes, and when it can use an object spontaneously to solve a brand-new problem that without the use of a tool would prove insoluble.

5   At the Gombe Stream alone we have seen chimpanzees use objects for many different purposes. They use stems and sticks to capture and eat insects, and, if the material picked is not suitable, then it is modified. They use leaves to sop up water they cannot reach with their lips—and first they chew on the leaves and thus increase their absorbency. We have seen them use handfuls of leaves to wipe dirt from their bodies or to dab at wounds.

6   In captivity chimpanzees often use objects as tools quite spontaneously. One group that was studied intensively by Wolfgang Köhler used sticks to try to pry open

---

*Adapted from *In the Shadow of Man* by Jane van Lawick-Goodall, Copyright © 1971 by Hugo and Jane van Lawick-Goodall. Reprinted by permission of Houghton Mifflin Company.

box lids and dig in the ground for roots. They wiped themselves with leaves or straw, scratched themselves with stones and poked straws into columns of ants in order to eat the insects much like the Gombe Stream chimpanzees probe for termites. They often used sticks and stones as weapons during aggressive encounters. Extensive tests have been carried out in laboratory settings in order to find out more about the tool-*making* ability of the chimpanzee. Results show that he can pile up to five boxes one on top of the other in order to climb to hanging food, that he can fit up to three tubes together to reach food placed outside the bars of his cage, and that he can unwind part of a length of wire for the same purpose. So far, however, no chimpanzee has succeeded in using one tool to make another. Even with teaching, one chimpanzee, the subject of exhaustive tests, was not able to use a stone hand ax to break a piece of wood into splinters suitable for obtaining food from a narrow pipe. She could do this when the material was suitable for her to break off pieces with her teeth but, although she was shown how to use the hand ax on tougher wood many times, she never even attempted to make use of it when trying to solve the problem. However, many other chimpanzees must be tested before we say that the chimpanzee as a species is unable to perform this act. Some humans are mathematicians—others are not.

7   When the performance of the chimpanzee in the field is compared with his actual abilities in test situations, it would seem that, in time, he might develop a more sophisticated tool-culture. After all, primitive man continued to use his early stone tools for thousands of years, virtually without change. Then we find a more sophisticated type of stone tool-culture suddenly appearing widespread across the continents. Possibly a stone-age genius invented the new culture and his fellows, who undoubtedly learned from and imitated each other, copied the new technique.

8   If the chimpanzee is allowed to continue living he, too, might suddenly produce a race of chimp superbrains and evolve an entirely new tool-culture. For it seems almost certain that, although the ability to manipulate objects is innate in a chimpanzee, the actual tool-using patterns practiced by the Gombe Stream chimpanzees are learned by the infants from their elders. We saw one very good example of this. It happened when a female had diarrhea: she picked a large handful of leaves and wiped her messy bottom. Her two-year-old infant watched her closely and then twice picked leaves and wiped his own clean bottom.

9   To Hugo and me, and assuredly to many scientists interested in human behavior and evolution, one significant aspect of chimpanzee behavior lies in the close similarity of many of their communicatory gestures and postures to those of man himself. Not only are the actual positions and movements similar to our own but also the contexts in which they often occur.

10   When a chimpanzee is suddenly frightened he frequently reaches to touch or embrace a chimpanzee nearby, much like a child watching a horror film may seize his companion's hand. Both chimpanzees and humans seem reassured in stressful situations by physical contact with another individual. Once David Graybeard caught sight of his reflection in a mirror. Terrified, he seized Fifi, then only three years old. Even such contact with a very small chimp appeared to reassure him; gradually he relaxed and the grin of fear left his face. Humans may sometimes feel reassured by holding or stroking a dog or some other pet in moments of emotional crisis.

11   This comfort, which chimpanzees and humans alike appear to derive from physical contact with each other, probably originates during the years of infancy, when for so long the touch of the mother, or the contact with her body, serves to calm the frights and soothe the anxieties of both ape and human infants. So, when the child grows older and his mother is not always close at hand, he seeks the next best

thing—close physical contact with another individual. If his mother is around, however, he may deliberately pick her out as his comforter. Once when Figan was about eight years old he was threatened by Mike. He screamed loudly and hurried past six or seven other chimps nearby until he reached Flo; then he held his hand toward her and she held it with hers. Calmed, Figan stopped screaming almost at once. Young human beings, too, continue to unburden their hearts to their mothers long after the days of childhood have passed—provided, of course, that an affectionate relationship exists between them.

12   When chimpanzees are overjoyed by the sight of a large pile of bananas they pat and kiss and embrace one another as two friends might embrace when they hear good news, or as a child may leap to hug his mother when told of a special treat. We all know those feelings of intense excitement or happiness which cause people to shout and leap around, or to burst into tears. It is not surprising that chimpanzees, if they feel anything like this, should seek to calm themselves by embracing their companions.

13   A chimpanzee, after being threatened or attacked by a superior, may follow the aggressor, screaming and crouching to the ground or holding out his hand. He is, in fact, begging a reassuring touch from the other. Sometimes he will not relax until he has been touched or patted, kissed or embraced. Figan several times flew into a tantrum when such contact was withheld, hurling himself about on the ground, his screams cramping in his throat until the aggressor finally calmed him with a touch. I have seen a human child behaving in the same sort of way, following his mother around the house after she has told him off, crying, holding on to her skirt, until finally she picked him up and kissed and cuddled him in forgiveness. A kiss or embrace or some other gesture of endearment is an almost inevitable outcome once a matrimonial disagreement has been resolved, and in many cultures the clasping of hands occurs to demonstrate renewal of friendship and forgiveness after a quarrel.

14   When one human begs forgiveness from or gives forgiveness to another there are, however, moral issues involved; it is when we consider these that we get into difficulties in trying to draw parallels between chimpanzees and human behavior. In chimpanzee society the principle involved when a subordinate seeks reassurance from a superior, or when a high-ranking individual calms another, is in no way concerned with the right or wrong of an aggressive act. A female who is attacked for no reason other than that she happens to be standing too close to a charging male is quite as likely to approach the male and beg a reassuring touch as is the female who is bowled over by a male while she attempts to take a fruit from his pile of bananas.

15   Again, while we may make a direct comparison between the effect on an anxious chimpanzee or human of a touch or embrace of reassurance, the issue becomes complicated if we probe into the motivation that directs the gesture of the ape or the human who is doing the reassuring. Human beings are capable of acting from purely unselfish motives; we can be genuinely sorry for someone and try to share in his troubles in an effort to offer comfort. It is unlikely that a chimpanzee acts from feelings quite like these; I doubt whether even members of one family, united as they are by strong mutual affections, are ever motivated by pure altruism in their dealings with one another.

16   On the other hand, there may be parallels in some instances. Most of us have experienced sensations of extreme discomfort and unease in the presence of an abject, weeping person. We may feel compelled to try to calm him, not because we are sorry for him in the altruistic sense, but because his behavior disturbs our own feeling of well-being. Perhaps the sight— and especially the sound—of a crouching, screaming subordinate similarly makes a chimpanzee uneasy; the most efficient way of changing the situation is for him to calm the other with a touch.

17   Another area of similarity between chimpanzees and humans is greeting behavior. When two chimpanzees greet each other after a separation, their behavior often looks amazingly like that shown by two humans in the same context. Chimpanzees may bow or crouch to the ground, hold hands, kiss, embrace, touch, or pat each other on almost any part of the body, especially the head and face. A male may chuck a female or an infant under the chin. Humans in many cultures, show one or more of these gestures.

18   In human societies much greeting behavior has become ritualized. A man who smiles when greeting a friend, or who inclines his head when passing an acquaintance in the street, is not necessarily acknowledging that the other has a superior social status. Yet the nod undoubtedly derives from submissive bowing or prostration and the smile from a nervous grin. Often, though, human greetings still do serve to clarify the relative social status of the individuals concerned, particularly on formal occasions.

19   A greeting between two chimpanzees nearly always serves such a purpose—it reestablishes the dominance status of the one relative to the other. When nervous Olly greets Mike she may hold out her hand toward him, or bow to the ground, crouching submissively with downbent head. She is, in effect, acknowledging Mike's superior rank. Mike may touch or pat or hold her hand, or touch her head, in response to her submission. A greeting between two chimps is usually more demonstrative when the individuals concerned are close friends, particularly when they have been separated for days rather than hours. Goliath often used to fling his arms around David, and the two would press their lips to each other's faces or necks when they met; whereas a greeting between Goliath and Mr. Worzle seldom involved more than a casual touch even when the two had not seen each other for some time.

20   If we survey the whole range of the communication signals of chimpanzees on the one hand and humans on the other, we find striking similarities in many instances. It would appear, then, that man and chimp either have evolved gestures and postures along a most remarkable parallel or that we share with the chimpanzees an ancestor in the dim and very distant past; an ancestor, moreover, who communicated with his kind by means of kissing and embracing, touching and patting and holding hands.

21   One of the major differences between man and his closest living relative is, of course, that the chimpanzee has not developed the power of speech. Even the most intensive efforts to teach young chimps to talk have met with almost no success. Verbal language represents a truly gigantic step forward in man's evolution.

22   Chimpanzees do have a wide range of calls, and these certainly serve to convey some types of information. When a chimp finds good food he utters loud barks; other chimps in the vicinity instantly become aware of the food source and hurry to join in. An attacked chimpanzee screams and this may alert his mother or a friend, either of whom may hurry to his aid. A chimpanzee confronted with an alarming and potentially dangerous situation utters his spine-chilling *wraaaa*—again, other chimps may hurry to the spot to see what is happening. A male chimpanzee, about to enter a valley or charge toward a food source, utters his pant-hoots—and other individuals realize that another member of the group is arriving and can identify which one. To our human ears each chimpanzee is characterized more by his pant-hoots than by any other type of call. This is significant since the pant-hoot in particular is the call that serves to maintain contact between the separated groups of the community. Yet the chimps themselves can certainly recognize individuals by other calls; for instance, a mother knows the scream of her offspring. Probably a chimpanzee can recognize the calls of most of his acquaintances.

23   While chimpanzee calls do serve to convey basic information about some situa-

tions and individuals, they cannot for the most part be compared to a spoken language. Man by means of words can communicate abstract ideas; he can benefit from the experiences of others without having to be present at the time; he can make intelligent cooperative plans.

24 Recently it has been proved that the chimpanzee is capable of communicating with people in quite a sophisticated manner. There are two scientists in America, R. Allen and Beatrice Gardner, who have trained a young chimpanzee in the use of the approved sign language of the deaf. The Gardners felt that, since gesture and posture formed such a significant aspect of *chimpanzee* communication patterns, such a sign language might be more appropriate than trying to teach vocal words.

25 Washoe was brought up from infancy constantly surrounded by human companions. These people from the start communicated in sign language with Washoe and also with each other when in the chimp's presence. The only sounds they made were those approximating chimpanzee calls such as laughter, exclamations, and imitations of Washoe's own sounds.

26 Their experiment has been amazingly successful. At five years of age Washoe can understand some three hundred and fifty different symbols, many of which signify clusters of words rather than just a single word, and she can also use about one hundred and fifty of them correctly.

27 I have not seen Washoe; but I have seen some film demonstrating her level of performance and, strangely enough, I was most impressed by an error she made. She was required to name, one after the other, a series of objects as they were drawn from a sack. She signed off the correct names very fast—but even so, it could be argued that an intelligent dog would ultimately learn to associate the sight of a bowl with a correct response. And then a brush was shown to Washoe, and she made the sign for a comb. That to me was very significant. It is the sort of mistake a small child might make, calling a shoe a slipper or a plate a saucer—but never calling a shoe a plate.

28 Perhaps one of the Gardners' most fascinating observations concerns the occasion when for the first time Washoe was asked (in sign language) "Who is that?" as she was looking into a mirror. Washoe, who was very familiar with mirrors by that time, signaled back, "Me, Washoe."

29 This is, in a way, a scientific proof of a fact we have long known—that, in some way, the chimpanzee has a primitive awareness of Self. Undoubtedly there are people who would prefer not to believe this, since even more firmly rooted than the old idea that man alone is the only toolmaking being is the concept that man alone in the animal kingdom is Self-conscious. Yet, this should not be disturbing. It has come to me, quite recently, that it is only through a real understanding of the ways in which chimpanzees and men show similarities in behavior that we can reflect with meaning on the ways in which men and chimpanzees *differ*. And only then can we really begin to appreciate, in a biological and spiritual manner, the full extent of man's uniqueness.

30 Yes, man definitely overshadows the chimpanzee. The chimpanzee is, nevertheless, a creature of immense significance to the understanding of man. Just as he is overshadowed by us, so the chimpanzee overshadows all other animals. He has the ability to solve quite complex problems, he can use and make tools for a variety of purposes, his social structure and methods of communication with his fellows are elaborate, and he shows the beginnings of Self-awareness. Who knows what the chimpanzee will be like forty million years hence? It should be of concern to us all that we permit him to live, that we at least give him the chance to evolve.

COMPREHENSION

Exercise 1

Indicate if each statement below is true (T) or false (F) according to your understanding of the passage. Use information in the passage and inferences which can be drawn from the passage to make your decisions.

1. _____ The brain structure of the chimpanzee probably resembles that of early man.

2. _____ Toolmaking distinguishes man from all other animals.

3. _____ Using a familiar tool to solve an unfamiliar problem is common among animals.

4. _____ No chimp can learn to use one tool to make another tool.

5. _____ In the future there might be chimpanzee geniuses.

6. _____ Baby chimpanzees learn how to use tools by watching older chimpanzees.

7. _____ Hugo, mentioned in paragraph 9, is apparently one of the Gombe Stream chimpanzees.

8. _____ Chimpanzee gestures are very different from human gestures.

9. _____ A touch or embrace is reassuring to both anxious chimpanzees and anxious humans.

10. _____ Both apes and humans comfort an upset individual for unselfish reasons.

11. _____ The greeting behavior of chimpanzees serves to distinguish social position.

12. _____ Chimpanzees can recognize each other by their calls.

13. _____ Washoe has learned to speak.

14. _____ Washoe's mistakes in using language seem to indicate that chimp language learning proceeds similarly to the language learning of the human child.

Exercise 2

Check (✓) those statements with which you think the author would agree.

1. _____ Prehistoric man was similar to the modern chimpanzee in several ways.

2. _____ Chimpanzees, like humans, may have varying abilities.

3. _____ Chimpanzee society has different social ranks.

4. _____ Issues of morality seem to enter into chimpanzee behavior.

5. _____ Physical contact plays an important part in the security of chimpanzees throughout their lives.

(*Continued on page 236.*)

6. _____ Man is the only animal with an awareness of Self.

7. _____ The chimp has reached the height of his development.

8. _____ The similarities between humans and chimpanzees prove that man is not unique.

VOCABULARY FROM CONTEXT

Both the ideas and the vocabulary in the sentences below are taken from "In the Shadow of Man." Use the context provided to determine the meanings of the italicized words. Give a definition, synonym, or description of each italicized vocabulary item.

1. _____ Chimpanzees in the wild use simple objects as tools, but in laboratory situations they can use more *sophisticated* items.

2. _____ A chimpanzee is born with the ability to handle objects, but the actual tool-using patterns are not *innate*; the infants learn them by observing their elders.

3. _____ Some people believe that one's *posture* tells us a lot about one's self-confidence. They claim that people who stand up straight are generally more self-confident than people who stand bent over.

4. _____ The baby chimp *hurled* himself to the ground, screaming and crying, until his mother picked him up.

5. _____ Humans may sometimes feel reassured by touching and *stroking* a dog or some other pet in moments of emotional crisis.

6. _____ When a chimp is angry, he may raise his arms rapidly and wave them wildly. These *gestures* are similar to those of an angry human.

7. _____ Most troubles can be avoided, but death and taxes are *inevitable*.

8. _____ Whereas humans are able to offer help unselfishly, chimpanzees do not seem to help each other for purely *altruistic* reasons.

9. _____ A chimp gets reassurance from touching another chimp just as a person *derives* comfort from touching another person.

10. _____ Some chimps are very independent and appear to be the superior members of a group; others seem to be ruled by the leaders and are quite *submissive*.

11. _____ For chimpanzees, the use of tools is learned behavior which is limited to familiar tasks. They have not demonstrated an ability to use tools *spontaneously* to solve new problems.

12. _____ Hungry chimpanzees have demonstrated their intelligence by using sticks to *probe* for insects in narrow spaces.

STEMS AND AFFIXES

The words in the left column are taken from "In the Shadow of Man." Using your knowledge of stems and affixes, match each word on the left with its synonym or definition on the right. The number in parentheses indicates the paragraph in which the word can be found.

1. _____ dissimilar (1)   a. unable to be solved

2. _____ prehistoric (2)   b. in a lower or inferior class

3. _____ manipulate (4)   c. unlike; different

4. _____ insoluble (4)   d. to free or relieve from trouble

5. _____ reassure (10)   e. occurring before written history

6. _____ unburden (11)   f. to control by skilled use of the hands

7. _____ overjoyed (12)   g. to give confidence or assurance again

8. _____ endearment (13)   h. delighted; filled with joy

9. _____ unease (16)   i. restless; without ease or comfort

10. _____ subordinate (16)   j. a loving word; an expression of affection

FIGURATIVE LANGUAGE AND IDIOMS

In the paragraph indicated by the number in parentheses find the word or phrase that best fits the meaning given. Your teacher may want to read these aloud as you quickly scan the paragraph to find the answer.

1. (4)   Which word means *without an external cause; arising out of the individual*?

2. (12) What phrase means *to begin to cry suddenly*?

3. (13) What phrase in sentence four means *became violently angry*?

4. (13) What phrase in sentence five means *scolded; spoke angrily with*?

5. (14) What phrase in sentence one means *to find similarities*?

6. (14) What phrase means *is knocked down*?

DISCUSSION - COMPOSITION

Each of the quotations below is taken from "In the Shadow of Man." They are intended to focus your attention on specific aspects of the author's point of view.

Quotation 1

It would appear, then, that man and chimp either have evolved gestures and postures along a most remarkable parallel or that we share with the chimpanzees an ancestor in the dim and very distant past; an ancestor, moreover, who communicated with his kind by means of kissing and embracing, touching and patting and holding hands.

What are the two possibilities suggested to explain the similarities between human and chimpanzee behavior? Do you agree with either of these explanations? Why or why not?

Quotation 2

Yes, man definitely overshadows the chimpanzee. The chimpanzee is, nevertheless, a creature of immense significance to the understanding of man.

Do you think that we can reach an understanding of the human race by studying animals?

Quotation 3

Recently it has been proved that the chimpanzee is capable of communicating with people in quite a sophisticated manner.

Is it important that humans attempt to communicate with animals? Why? What animals other than chimpanzees can man communicate with? What kind of information can animals convey to people?

Quotation 4

> In human societies much greeting behavior has become ritualized. A man who smiles when greeting a friend, or who inclines his head when passing an acquaintance in the street, is not necessarily acknowledging that the other has a superior social status. . . . Often, though, human greetings still do serve to clarify the relative social status of the individuals concerned, particularly on formal occasions.

What greetings are you familiar with that indicate social rank? What differences are there in the way you greet your teacher, your parents, and your best friend? What special greetings are used on formal occasions?

Quotation 5

The author concludes her essay with the following thought:

> Just as he is overshadowed by us, so the chimpanzee overshadows all other animals. He has the ability to solve quite complex problems, he can use and make tools for a variety of purposes, his social structure and methods of communication with his fellows are elaborate, and he shows the beginnings of self-awareness. Who knows what the chimpanzee will be like forty million years hence?

What does the author suggest about the chimpanzee's potential for development? Do you believe that chimpanzees will continue to develop? Do you think that chimpanzees will ever have the same abilities as humans?

VOCABULARY REVIEW

Place the appropriate word or phrase from the following list in each of the blanks below. Do not use any word or phrase more than once.

flew into a tantrum	submissive	altruism
draw parallels	sophisticated	inevitable
burst into tears	posture	hurled
spontaneously	gestured	derived
innate	probes	stroking

1. Unlike the simple machines of the early 1900's, today's automobiles are quite _____.

2. "Have a seat," said the professor kindly as she _____ toward a chair.

3. People today are fond of saying that only two things are _____: death and taxes.

4. Some scientists believe that the ability to learn a language is _____ rather than learned.

5. The little girl picked up a stone and _____ it at the postman.

(*Continued on page 240.*)

6. The children were so saddened by the death of their pet that they _____.

7. _____ is encouraged by many religions. Some even suggest that a certain percent of one's income be given to the poor.

8. My mother always advised me, "Be firm but not aggressive; be polite but not _____."

9. When the little boy was told to go to bed, he _____. His mother had to carry him, kicking and screaming, into the house.

10. A good scientist _____ into all aspects of a problem in order to find solutions.

11. Children are often told to stand up straight so that when they grow up they will have good _____.

12. A person who is truly kind does thoughtful things for others _____, without having to be asked or reminded.

13. The political situation is so different in the two countries that it is foolish to try to _____ between them.

14. The children loved their pet dog and would spend hours _____ it and talking to it.

15. The ritualized greetings used today are probably _____ from the primitive gestures of prehistoric human beings.

LONGER READING: Social Science

If you were living in a place where the language, customs, and way of life were very different from your own, how would you feel? What aspects would you enjoy? Would you ever feel homesick? What are the causes of homesickness? If you did feel homesick, what could you do about it?

Is the way you live very different from the way your grandparents lived when they were your age?

Was their life very different from their grandparents' lives? What kind of world do you think your grandchildren will be living in? Would you like to live in that world?

Alvin Toffler examines these ideas in the following selection, the first chapter of his book *Future Shock*.* Toffler identifies a new disease which he believes will soon affect millions of people. He calls the disease future shock. He compares it to the more familiar phenomenon of culture shock, the psychological problems suffered by people who live in a culture very different from their own. As you read "The 800th Lifetime," look for the symptoms of future shock. How are they different from the symptoms of culture shock? What causes future shock? Does Toffler think this new disease can be "cured"?

It will be helpful to do Vocabulary from Context exercise 1 on page 246 and Dictionary Study on page 248 before you begin reading.

The 800th Lifetime

1   In the time between now and the twenty-first century, millions of ordinary, psychologically normal people will face a sudden confrontation with the future. Many of the citizens of the world's richest and most technologically advanced nations will find it increasingly painful to keep up with the incessant demand for change that characterizes our time. For them, the future will have arrived too soon.

2   This book is about change and how we adapt to it. It is about those who seem to thrive on change, as well as those multitudes of others who resist it or seek flight from it. It is about our capacity to adapt. It is about the future and the shock that its arrival brings.

3   Western society for the past 300 years has been caught up in a storm of change. This storm, far from abating, now appears to be gathering force. Change moves through the highly industrialized countries with waves of ever accelerating speed and unprecedented impact. It brings with it all sorts of curious social phenomena—from psychedelic churches and "free universities" to science cities in the Arctic and wife-swap clubs in California.

4   It breeds odd personalities, too: children who at twelve are no longer childlike; adults who at fifty are children of twelve. There are rich men who playact poverty, computer programmers who turn on with LSD. There are married priests and atheist ministers and Jewish Zen Buddhists. A strange new society is apparently developing in our midst. Is there a way to understand it, to shape its development?

5   Much that now seems incomprehensible would be far less so if we took a fresh look at today's rapid rate of change, for the acceleration of change does not merely affect industries or nations. It is a force that reaches deep into our personal lives, compels us to act out new roles, and confronts us with the danger of a new and

---

*Adapted from *Future Shock* by Alvin Toffler. Copyright © 1970 by Alvin Toffler. Reprinted by permission of Random House, Inc.

powerfully upsetting psychological disease. This new disease can be called "future shock," and a knowledge of its sources and symptoms helps explain many things that otherwise resist rational analysis.

The Unprepared Visitor

6   The parallel term "culture shock" has already appeared in the popular vocabulary. Culture shock is the effect that immersion in a strange culture has on the unprepared visitor. Peace Corps volunteers suffer from it in Borneo or Brazil. Marco Polo probably suffered from it in Cathay. Culture shock is what happens when a traveler suddenly finds himself in a place where yes may mean no, where a "fixed price" is negotiable, where laughter may signify anger. It is what happens when the familiar psychological cues that help an individual to function in society are suddenly withdrawn and replaced by new ones that are strange or incomprehensible.

7   The culture shock phenomenon explains much of the bewilderment, frustration, and disorientation that plagues people in their dealings with other societies. It causes a breakdown in communication, a misreading of reality, an inability to cope. Yet culture shock is relatively mild in comparison with the much more serious malady, future shock. Future shock is the frightening disorientation brought on by the premature arrival of the future. It may well be the most important disease of tomorrow.

8   Future shock will not be found in *Index Medicus* or in any listing of psychological abnormalities. Yet, unless intelligent steps are taken to combat it, millions of human beings will find themselves increasingly disoriented, progressively incompetent to deal rationally with their environments. The problems already apparent in contemporary life are merely a foretaste of what may lie ahead unless we come to understand and treat this disease.

9   Future shock is a time phenomenon, a product of the greatly accelerated rate of change in society. It arises from the imposition of a new culture on an old one. It is culture shock in one's own society. But its impact is far worse. For most Peace Corps volunteers, in fact most travelers, have the comforting knowledge that the culture they left behind will be there to return to. The victim of future shock does not.

10   Take an individual out of his own culture and set him down suddenly in an environment sharply different from his own, with a different set of cues to react to— different conceptions of time, space, work, love, religion, sex, and everything else— then cut him off from any hope of return to a more familiar social environment, and the dislocation he suffers is doubly severe. Moreover, if this new culture is itself in constant turmoil, and if—worse yet—its values are incessantly changing, the sense of disorientation will be still further increased. Given few clues as to what kind of behavior is rational under the radically new circumstances, the victim may well become a hazard to himself and to others.

11   Now imagine not merely an individual but an entire society, an entire generation— including its weakest, least intelligent, and most irrational members—suddenly transported into this new world. The result is mass disorientation, future shock on a large scale.

12   This is the prospect that we now face. Change is crashing down upon us and most people are hopelessly unprepared to cope with it.

Break With The Past

13   Is all this exaggerated? I think not. It has become commonplace to say that what we are now living through is a "second industrial revolution." This phrase is sup-

posed to impress us with the speed and significance of the change around us. But in addition to being simplistic, it is misleading. For what is occurring now is, in all likelihood, bigger, deeper, and more important than the industrial revolution. Indeed, a growing body of reputable opinion asserts that the present movement represents nothing less than the second great divide in human history, comparable in magnitude only with that first great break in historic continuity, the shift from barbarism to civilization.

14   One of the most striking statements of this theme has come from Kenneth Boulding, an eminent economist and imaginative social thinker. In justifying his view that the present moment represents a turning point in human history, Boulding observes that "as far as many statistical series related to activities of mankind are concerned, the date that divides human history into two equal parts is well within living memory." In effect, our century represents The Great Median Strip running down the center of human history. Thus he asserts, "The world of today . . . is as different from the world in which I was born as that world was from Julius Caesar's. I was born in the middle of human history to date, roughly. Almost as much has happened since I was born as happened before."

15   This startling statement can be illustrated in a number of ways. It has been observed, for example, that if the last 50,000 years of man's existence were divided into lifetimes of approximately sixty-two years each, there have been about 800 such lifetimes. Of these 800, fully 650 were spent in caves.

16   Only during the last seventy lifetimes has it been possible to communicate effectively from one lifetime to another in the way that writing made it possible to do. Only during the last six lifetimes did masses of men ever see a printed word. Only during the last four has it been possible to measure time with any precision. Only in the last two has anyone anywhere used an electric motor. And the overwhelming majority of all the material goods we use in daily life today have been developed within the present, the 800th, lifetime.

17   The 800th lifetime marks a sharp break with all past human experience because during this lifetime man's relationship to resources has reversed itself. This is most evident in the field of economic development. Within a single lifetime, agriculture, the original basis of civilization, has lost its dominance in nation after nation. Today in a dozen major countries agriculture employs fewer than 15 percent of the economically active population. In the United States, whose farms feed 200,000,000 Americans plus the equivalent of another 160,000,000 people around the world, this figure is already below 6 percent and it is still shrinking rapidly.

18   Moreover, if agriculture is the first stage of economic development and industrialism the second, we can now see that still another stage—the third—has suddenly been reached. In about 1956 the United States became the first major power in which more than 50 percent of the non-farm labor ceased to wear the blue collar of factory or manual labor. Blue-collar workers were outnumbered by those in the so-called white-collar occupations—in retail trade, administration, communications, research, education, and other service categories. Within the same lifetime a society for the first time in human history not only escaped the domination of agriculture, but managed within a few brief decades to escape the domination of manual labor as well. The world's first service economy had been born.

19   Since then, one after another of the technologically advanced countries have moved in the same direction. Today, in those nations in which agriculture is down to the 15 percent level or below, white collars already outnumber blue in Sweden, Britain, Belgium, Canada, and the Netherlands. Ten thousand years for agriculture. A century or two for industrialism. And now, opening before us—super-industrialism.

20   This lifetime is also different from all others because of the astonishing expansion

of the scope of change. Clearly, there have been other lifetimes in which great upheavals occurred. Wars, plagues, earthquakes, and famine hit many earlier societies. But these shocks and upheavals were contained within the borders of one or a group of neighboring societies. It took generations, even centuries, for their impact to spread beyond these borders.

21   In our lifetime the boundaries have burst. Today the system of social ties is so tightly woven that the consequences of contemporary events are felt instantaneously around the world. A war in Vietnam alters basic political alliances in Peking, Moscow, and Washington, touches off protests in Stockholm, affects financial transactions in Zurich, triggers secret diplomatic events in Algiers.

22   But the final, qualitative difference between this and all previous lifetimes is the one most easily overlooked. For we have not merely extended the scope of change, we have radically changed its pace. We have in our time released a totally new social force—a wave of change so accelerated that it influences our sense of time, revolutionizes the pace of daily life, and affects the very way we "feel" the world around us. We no longer "feel" life as people did in the past. And this is the ultimate difference, the distinction that separates the truly contemporary person from all others. For this acceleration lies behind the impermanence—the transience—that influences our consciousness radically affecting the way we relate to other people, to things, to the entire universe of ideas, art and values.

23   To understand what is happening to us as we move into the age of super-industrialism, we must analyze the processes of acceleration and confront the concept of transience. If acceleration is a new social force, transience is its psychological counterpart, and without an understanding of the role it plays in contemporary human behavior, all our theories of personality, all our psychology, must be considered pre-modern. Psychology without the concept of transience cannot take account of precisely those phenomena that are peculiarly contemporary.

24   By violently expanding the scope of change, and by accelerating its pace, we have broken irretrievably with the past. We have cut ourselves off from the old ways of thinking, of feeling, of adapting. This is the major characteristic of the 800th lifetime. And it is this that calls into question man's capacity for adaptation—how will he do in this new society? Can he adapt to its demands? And if not, can he change these demands?

25   Before even attempting to answer such questions, we must focus on the twin forces of acceleration and transience. We must learn how they change the structure of existence, forming our lives and psyches into new and unfamiliar shapes. We must understand how—and why—they confront us, for the first time, with the explosive potential of future shock.

COMPREHENSION

Indicate if each statement below is true (T) or false (F) according to your understanding of the passage. Use information in the passage and inferences which can be drawn from the passage to make your decisions. You should be able to do this exercise without referring to the selection.

1. _____ Toffler predicts that future shock will not strike until the next century.

2. _____ Life changes at a faster rate now than it did in the past.

3. _____ Change is a powerful force which affects individuals and whole societies.

4. _____ Future shock is more serious than culture shock.

5. _____ A victim of future shock is unable to adjust to the world around him.

6. _____ Culture shock is future shock in one's own society.

7. _____ Toffler feels that the 800th lifetime marks a turning point in history.

8. _____ The basic cause of future shock is epochal disasters such as storms, famine, and war.

9. _____ Before we can cure future shock, we must understand the rate and scope of change.

10. _____ Toffler is opposed to change.

READING FOR DETAILS

Indicate if each statement below is true (T) or false (F) according to your understanding of the passage. Use information in the passage and inferences which can be drawn from the passage to make your decisions. You may need to refer to the selection to answer these questions. Be prepared to support your answers with portions of the text.

1. _____ The effects of the rapid acceleration of change cannot yet be seen in Western society.

2. _____ A knowledge of the causes and symptoms of future shock helps explain many aspects of contemporary life that otherwise could not be explained.

3. _____ One cause of future shock is the acceleration of change.

4. _____ Toffler believes that the phrase "second industrial revolution" accurately describes the current period of history.

5. _____ In several technologically advanced nations, more than 50 percent of the non-farm labor is involved in white-collar occupations.

6. _____ In a super-industrialized country, most of the labor force works in factories.

7. _____ Transience is a psychological force which plays an important role in human behavior.

8. _____ Toffler feels that acceleration is a stronger force than transience.

(*Continued on page 246.*)

9. _____ In order to cure future shock, we will have to slow the forces of acceleration and transience.

VOCABULARY FROM CONTEXT

Exercise 1

Both the ideas and vocabulary in the sentences below are taken from "The 800th Lifetime." Use the context provided to determine the meanings of the italicized words. Give a definition, synonym, or description of each italicized vocabulary item.

1. _____ According to Toffler, citizens of the industrialized world will have a sudden encounter with the forces of change. This *confrontation* will cause serious problems if preparations are not made.

2. _____ Some people have no difficulty making the necessary changes in their way of life when they move to a foreign country; others are not able to *adapt* as easily to a new environment.

3. _____ Several generations ago, the world seemed to run in an orderly way. Now, however, everything is in a state of *turmoil*.

4. _____ Our environment is continuously changing, and, even more disturbing, our values are changing just as *incessantly* as our environment.

5. _____ The storm of change, far from *abating*, now seems to be growing stronger.

6. _____ Many famous psychologists are trying to understand the problems modern people suffer from, but even these *eminent* scholars are confused about what causes them.

7. _____ In the past, changes in our world occurred slowly; however, since the industrial revolution, the rate of change has been steadily *accelerating*.

8. _____ The consequences of *epochal* events such as wars and great scientific discoveries are not confined to a small geographical area as they were in the past.

9. _____ Some people seem to *thrive* on change—the more their environment changes, the happier and more productive they become.

10. _____ In order to strengthen his arguments, Toffler quotes *reputable* social scientists who agree with him. He hopes that, by quoting respected scholars, his arguments will be accepted by most readers.

11. _____   Toffler feels that much that now seems *incomprehensible* would be easier to understand if we examined the racing rate of change.

12. _____   Until recently we had underestimated the *scope* of the problem of future shock. The size of the problem is even greater than we had imagined. We didn't realize how many areas would be affected by the rapid rate of change.

13. _____   Some people can deal reasonably and intelligently with the rapid changes in society, while others are not able to behave as *rationally* when confronted with the same changes.

14. _____   When you visit a foreign country, many of the familiar psychological signals that help an individual to function in society are suddenly *withdrawn* and replaced by new ones.

15. _____   Being introduced to someone may be a signal to bow in one country while in another country it is a *cue* to shake hands.

16. _____   In many countries, trying to get a salesman to lower his price is a common practice. However, in the United States, most prices are not *negotiable*.

17. _____   Many travelers feel *disoriented* when they wake up in the middle of the night while visiting a foreign country, but it usually only takes a minute for them to remember where they are and why they are there.

18. _____   Culture shock is a mild disease in comparison with the serious *malady* future shock.

19. _____   Unless we learn to fight future shock, millions of people will find themselves *incompetent* to deal with their environments.

20. _____   Just as coughing and a sore throat are indications of physical illness, a sense of disorientation and an inability to sleep are *symptoms* of the psychological illness, culture shock.

21. _____   The lack of permanence—the *transience*—in our environment and our lives affects the way we behave.

22. _____   Toffler says that "acceleration" is a social force which has a psychological equivalent. His term for the psychological *counterpart* of acceleration is "transience."

Exercise 2

This exercise should be done after you have finished reading "The 800th Lifetime." The exercise is designed to determine how well you have been able to use context clues to guess the meaning of unfamiliar vocabulary in "The 800th Lifetime." Give a definition, synonym, or description of each of the words or phrases below. The number in parentheses indicates the paragraph in which the word can be found. Your teacher may want to read these aloud as you quickly scan the paragraph to find the answer.

1. (8)   combat _____

2. (9)   impact _____

3. (10) cut him off from _____

4. (12) prospect_____

5. (20) upheaval_____

6. (24) irretrievably _____

FIGURATIVE LANGUAGE AND IDIOMS

In the paragraph indicated by the number in parentheses, find the word or phrase that best fits the meaning given. Your teacher may want to read these aloud as you quickly scan the paragraph to find the answer.

1. (7)   What phrase means *caused by* ?

2. (14) What phrase in the second sentence means *a time when important changes occur*?

DICTIONARY STUDY

Many words have more than one meaning. When you use the dictionary to discover the meaning of an unfamiliar word or phrase, you need to use the context to determine which definition is appropriate. Use the portions of the dictionary page* (opposite) to select the best definition for each of the italicized words below.

1. The culture shock phenomenon accounts for much of the bewilderment, frustration, and disorientation that *plagues* Americans in their dealings with other societies.

2. The feeling that something is wrong with society *haunts* many people today.

3. Professor Boulding says that he was born in *roughly* the middle of human history because almost as much has happened since he was born as happened before.

4. A war in Vietnam *touches off* protests in Stockholm, affects financial transactions in Zurich, *triggers* secret diplomatic moves in Algiers.

---

*Reprinted with permission from *Webster's New World Dictionary*, College Edition, copyright © 1966 by The World Publishing Company.

haunt (hônt, hänt), *v.t.* [ME. *haunten, hanten;* OFr. *hanter*, to frequent, resort to], 1. to visit (a place) often or continually; frequent. 2. to annoy or pester (a person) by constant visiting, following, etc. 3. to appear or recur frequently to; obsess: as, memories *haunted* her. 4. to be associated with; fill the atmosphere of; pervade: as, memories of former gaiety *haunt* the house. *Haunt* is often used with a ghost, spirit, etc. as its stated or implied subject. *n.* 1. *a)* a place often visited or stayed in: as, a saloon that was the *haunt* of criminals. *b)* a lair or feeding place of animals. 2. (*also* hant), [Dial.], a ghost.

haunt·ed (hôn′tid, hän′tid), *adj.* [pp. of *haunt*], supposedly frequented by ghosts: as, a *haunted* house.

haunt·ing (hôn′tiŋ, hän′tiŋ), *adj.* [ppr. of *haunt*], often recurring to the mind; not easily forgotten: as, a *haunting* tune.

plague (plāg; *chiefly dial.*, pleg), *n.* [ME. & OFr. *plage;* L. *plaga;* Gr. *plēgē*, a blow, misfortune], 1. anything that afflicts or troubles; calamity; scourge. 2. divine punishment. 3. any contagious epidemic disease that is deadly; specifically, the bubonic plague. 4. [Colloq.], a nuisance; annoyance. *v.t.* [PLAGUED (plāgd; *chiefly dial.*, plegd), PLAGUING], 1. to afflict with a plague. 2. to vex; harass; trouble; torment. —*SYN.* see **annoy.**

rough (ruf), *adj.* [ME. *ruh, rugh;* AS. *ruh;* akin to G. *rauh;* IE. **reuk* < base **reu-*, to tear, tear out (cf. ROTTEN); prob. basic sense "hairy, woolly"], 1. not smooth or level; having bumps, projections, etc.; uneven: as, a *rough* surface, *rough* country. 2. shaggy: as, an animal with a *rough* coat. 3. characterized by violent action, motion, agitation, disturbance, or irregularity; specifically, *a)* stormy; tempestuous: as, *rough* weather. *b)* boisterous, disorderly, or riotous: as, *rough* play. 4. harsh; rude; surly; unmannerly; not gentle or mild: as, *rough* manners, a *rough* temper. 5. sounding harsh; discordant; jarring. 6. tasting harsh, sharp, or astringent: as, *rough* wine. 7. coarse, as texture, cloth, food, etc. 8. coarse in manner, tastes, etc.; lacking refinement or culture: as, *rough* men. 9. lacking refinements and luxuries or comforts and conveniences: as, the *rough* life of the pioneers. 10. not refined, polished, or prepared; natural, crude, unwrought, etc.: as, *rough* jewels. 11. not finished, elaborated, perfected, etc.: as, a *rough* sketch; hence, 12. not carefully or thoroughly worked out; without claim to be exact, complete, or detailed; approximate: as, a *rough* estimate. 13. needing strength instead of skill, intelligence, etc.: as, *rough* labor. 14. [Colloq.], difficult, severe, or disagreeable: as, they had a *rough* time of it. 15. in *phonetics*, pronounced with an aspirate; having the sound of *h*. *n.* 1. rough ground. 2. rough material or condition. 3. the rough part, aspect, etc. of something. 4. [Chiefly British], a rough person; rowdy; tough; ruffian. 5. in *golf*, any part of the course where grass, weeds, etc. are allowed to grow uncut, forming a hazard or obstacle. *adv.* in a rough manner; roughly. *v.t.* 1. to make rough; roughen. 2. to handle or treat roughly; specifically, in *football*, etc., to subject (an opponent) to intentional and unnecessary roughness (often with *up*). 3. to make, fashion, sketch, shape, or cut roughly (usually with *in* or *out*): as, *rough* out a scheme. 4. to apply some preparatory or preliminary process or treatment to. *v.i.* 1. to become rough. 2. to behave roughly.

in the rough, in a rough or crude state.

rough it, to live without customary comforts and conveniences, as in camping.

SYN.—**rough** applies to any surface covered with projections, points, ridges, bumps, etc. (*rough* skin, ground, etc.); **harsh** applies to anything disagreeably rough to the touch (a *harsh* texture); that is **uneven** which is not uniform in height, breadth, etc. (an *uneven* floor, hem, etc.); **rugged** implies a roughness of surface in which the sharp, irregular projections are obstacles to travel (*rugged* country) or a roughness of countenance suggestive of strength (a *rugged* jaw); **jagged** suggests uneven, sharp-pointed projections or notches along an edge, as of broken glass, ragged cloth, etc. Most of these words have extended uses suggested by their basic meanings (*rough* weather, *harsh* sounds, an *uneven* performance, a *rugged* life).—*ANT.* smooth.

rough·age (ruf′ij), *n.* [see -AGE], rough material; coarse substance; specifically, coarse food or fodder, as bran, straw, vegetable peel, etc., containing a relatively high proportion of cellulose and other indigestible constituents and serving in the diet as a stimulus to peristalsis.

rough-and-read·y (ruf′′n-red′i), *adj.* 1. rough, or crude, rude, unpolished, etc., but effective enough: as, *rough-and-ready* methods. 2. characterized by rough vigor and prompt action rather than refinement, formality, or nicety: as, a *rough-and-ready* fellow.

rough-and-tum·ble (ruf′′n-tum′b'l), *adj.* violent and disorderly, with no concern for rules: as, a *rough-and-tumble* fight. *n.* a fight or struggle of this kind.

rough breathing, [transl. of L. *spiritus asper*], in *Greek grammar*, the mark (ʽ) placed over initial vowels or ρ (rho) to indicate a preceding *h* sound, or aspirate.

rough·cast (ruf′kast′, ruf′käst′), *n.* 1. a coarse plaster for covering outside surfaces, as walls. 2. a rough pattern or form, or crudely made model. *v.t.* [ROUGHCAST, ROUGHCASTING], 1. to cover (walls, etc.) with roughcast. 2. to make or shape in a rough form.

rough-cut (ruf′kut′), *adj.* cut into small, chopped irregular pieces: said of tobacco: opposed to *fine-cut*.

rough-dry (ruf′drī′), *v.t.* [ROUGH-DRIED (-drīd′), ROUGH-DRYING], to dry (washed laundry) without ironing: also **roughdry.** *adj.* washed and dried but not ironed.

rough·en (ruf′′n), *v.t. & v.i.* to make or become rough.

rough-hew (ruf′hū′), *v.t.* [ROUGH-HEWED (-hūd′), ROUGH-HEWED or ROUGH-HEWN (-hūn′), ROUGH-HEWING], 1. to hew (timber, stone, etc.) roughly, or without finishing or smoothing. 2. to form roughly; give crude shape or outline to. Also **roughhew.**

rough·house (ruf′hous′), *n.* [Slang], rough, boisterous, or rowdy play, fighting, etc., especially indoors. *v.t.* [Slang], to treat (a person) roughly and boisterously, usually in fun. *v.i.* [Slang], to take part in roughhouse.

rough·ish (ruf′ish), *adj.* somewhat rough.

rough·ly (ruf′li), *adv.* 1. in a rough manner. 2. approximately.

rough·neck (ruf′nek′), *n.* [Slang], a person whose actions and manners are rough and crude; rowdy.

rough·rid·er (ruf′rīd′ẽr), *n.* 1. a person who breaks horses so that they can be ridden. 2. a person who does much hard, rough riding. 3. [R-], a member of a volunteer cavalry regiment organized by Theodore Roosevelt and Leonard Wood for service in the Spanish-American War (1898): also **Rough Rider.**

rough·shod (ruf′shod′), *adj.* shod with horseshoes that have calks, or metal points, to prevent slipping.

ride roughshod over, to treat in a harsh, arrogant, inconsiderate manner; domineer over.

touch (tuch), *v.t.* [ME. *touchen;* OFr. *tochier, tuchier* (Fr. *toucher*); LL. **toccare* < **tok*, light blow; of echoic origin; cf. TOCCATA], 1. to put the hand, finger, or other part of the body on, so as to feel; perceive by the sense of feeling. 2. to bring (something) into contact with (something else): as, he *touched* the paper with his pencil, he *touched* a lighted match to the kindling. 3. formerly, to lay the hand on (a person with scrofula), as some kings, in order to effect a miraculous cure. 4. to be or come into contact with. 5. to adjoin; border on. 6. to strike lightly. 7. to affect through contact; have a physical effect on: as, water won't *touch* these grease spots. 8. to injure slightly: as, frost *touched* the plants. 9. to test by a touchstone or something similar. 10. to stamp (tested metal). 11. to strike the keys of, pluck the strings of, etc. (a musical instrument). 12. to play (a few notes, an air, etc.) on a musical instrument. 13. to draw, change the color of, etc. (the details of a painting, etc.) by using a brush or pencil. 14. to give a light tint, aspect, etc. to: used chiefly in the past participle, as, clouds *touched* with pink. 15. to stop at in passing, as a ship. 16. to lay hands on; handle; use. 17. to mishandle; molest; affect so as to injure. 18. to taste or partake of: usually used in the negative, as, he didn't *touch* his supper. 19. to come up to; reach; attain. 20. to compare with; equal; rival: usually in the negative, as, my cooking can't *touch* yours. 21. to take or make use of without permission or wrongly; misappropriate. 22. to deal with; refer to; mention, especially in a light or passing way. 23. to have to do with; affect; concern: as, a subject that *touches* our welfare. 24. to taint slightly, as in morals. 25. to cause to be slightly ill mentally: usually in *touched in the head*, somewhat demented. 26. to arouse an emotion in, especially one of sympathy, gratitude, etc.; hence, 27. to provoke; irritate; sting: as, it *touched* me to the quick. 28. [Slang], to ask for, or get by asking, a loan or gift of money from. 29. in *geometry*, to be tangent to. *v.i.* 1. to touch a person or thing (especially in sense 3). 2. to be or come in contact. 3. in *geometry*, to be tangent. *n.* 1. a touching or being touched; specifically, *a)* a light tap, stroke, etc. *b)* a delicate stroke made with a brush in painting, etc. 2. the sense by which physical objects are felt; tactile sense. 3. a sensation caused by this, especially one characteristic of a particular substance; tactile quality; feel. 4. an impression received as if by touching; a mental response; slight emotion. 5. a mental capacity analogous to the sense of touch; mental or moral sensitivity. 6. an effect of being touched; specifically, *a)* a mark, impression, etc. left by touching. *b)* a subtle change or addition in a painting, story, or other work. 7. a very small amount, degree, etc.; specifically, *a)* a trace, tinge, etc., especially a characteristic one: as, a *touch* of humor. *b)* a slight attack: as, a *touch* of the flu. 8. *a)* touchstone. *b)* the quality of gold, silver, etc. as determined by touchstone. *c)* an official stamp indicating this. 9. any test or criterion. 10. [Slang], *a)* the act of asking for, or getting in this way, a gift or loan of money. *b)* money so acquired. 11. in *music*, *a)* the manner in which a performer strikes the keys of a keyboard instrument: as, a delicate *touch*. *b)* the manner in which the action of a piano, etc. responds to the fingers: as, a piano with a heavy *touch*. *c)* in bell ringing, a set of changes less than a peal. 12. in *rugby*, the area outside the sidelines. —*SYN.* see **affect.**

in touch with, 1. in communication or contact with. 2. responsive or sensitive to.

out of touch with, no longer well-informed on or in close communication with.

touch at, to stop briefly at (a port, etc.): said of ships and travelers.

touch off, 1. to represent accurately or aptly. 2. to make explode; fire. 3. to motivate or initiate.

touch on (or **upon**), 1. to come near to; come close to; verge on. 2. to pertain to. 3. to treat (a topic) slightly or in passing; merely mention.

touch up, 1. to stimulate or rouse, as by touching. 2. to improve or finish (a painting, literary work, etc.) by minor changes or additions.

touch-and-go (tuch′ən-gō′), *adj.* 1. hasty, rapid, casual, etc. 2. uncertain; risky; precarious.

touch and go, 1. a hasty or casual act. 2. an uncertain or dangerous situation.

trig·ger (trig′ẽr), *n.* [earlier *tricker;* D. *trekker* < *trekken*, to draw, pull; cf. TREK, TRICK], 1. a small lever or part which when pulled or pressed releases a catch, spring, etc. 2. in firearms, a small lever which when pressed back by the finger releases the firing hammer. *v.t.* [Colloq.], to initiate (an action); set off: as, the fights *triggered* a riot.

quick on the trigger, [Colloq.], 1. quick to fire a gun; hence, 2. quick to act, understand, etc.; alert.

DISCUSSION - COMPOSITION

The quotations below are intended to focus your attention on issues relating to future shock.

Quotation 1
Rene Dubos is another author interested in the kind of life twentieth-century man leads. In an article titled "The New Pessimism," Dubos discusses the effects of technology on our lives. He points out an interesting contradiction: technology is supposed to improve our lives, but in fact it causes many new problems almost as troublesome as the problems it is supposed to solve.

> We are creating new problems in the very process of solving those which plagued mankind in the past. . . . Social and technological achievements have spread economic affluence, increased comfort, accelerated transportation, and controlled certain forms of disease. But the material satisfactions thus made possible have not added much to happiness or to the significance of life. . . . The age of affluence, technological marvels, and medical miracles is paradoxically the age of chronic ailments, of anxiety, and even of despair.

Do you agree with Dubos? What are some problems that technology causes for society and for individuals? What do Dubos' ideas mean to a country that is beginning to industrialize? To a country that is already highly industrialized?

Quotation 2
In later chapters of *Future Shock*, Toffler considers the problem of how to fight future shock. He argues against the idea that there is no cure for the disease.

> Most of the problems affecting us, including future shock, stem not from natural forces but from man-made processes that are at least potentially subject to our control.

Do you agree that it is possible for us to solve most of the problems that face us? Consider what causes future shock, are these causes man-made? How do you think we should try to control them?

Quotation 3
Consider the following quote from Dr. John L. Fuller, a senior scientist at a biomedical research center in the United States:

> Some people achieve a certain sense of serenity, even in the midst of turmoil because they have found ways to get just the "right" amount of change in their lives.

Can you give some examples of people whose lives are always changing yet who seem to enjoy it? What ways do you think they have found to control the changes in their lives? What is the right amount of change for you? How do you control the amount of change in your life?

Quotation 4

Toffler feels that a powerful way for a person to cope with the threat of overstimulation caused by change is to establish "personal stability zones," for example, long-lasting relationships that are carefully maintained in spite of all kinds of other changes. The following adapted quote describes a man who has found ways to get the "right" amount of change in his life by building stability zones.

> The case involves a man who has changed jobs at a rapid rate, has moved his family thirteen times in eighteen years, travels extensively, rents cars, uses throw-away products, prides himself on leading the neighborhood in trying out new gadgets, and generally lives in a restless whirl of transience, newness and diversity. However, a second look reveals significant stability zones in his life: a good, tightly woven relationship with his wife of nineteen years; continuing ties with his parents; old college friends interspersed with new acquaintances.

What are this man's stability zones? If he felt that there were too many changes in his life, how could he create other stability zones? What are your personal stability zones? Which of the stability zones that exist in your life now may not exist in the future? How would you create new stability zones when old ones no longer exist?

VOCABULARY REVIEW

Exercise 1

Choose a synonym for each of the italicized words below from the following list. Write your answer in the space provided.

roughly   incessant
cue   transience
incompetently   haunted
trigger

1. _____   The *continuous* noise of the cars going by Jill's hotel room kept her awake all night.

2. _____   The police warned the governor not to say anything that might *touch off* a protest.

3. _____   The dimming of the lights in the auditorium was the *signal* for the orchestra to begin playing.

4. _____   The *impermanence* of life is a universal literary theme.

5. _____   *Approximately* 100,000 people attended the last football game of the season.

6. _____   Herbert was *plagued* by memories of his unhappy childhood.

Exercise 2
Place the appropriate word or phrase from the following list in each of the blanks below. Do not use any word or phrase more than once.

negotiate	symptoms	reputable	abate
counterpart	scope	confronts	incompetent
malady	adapt	incessantly	accelerate
disoriented	thrive	rational	cue
turmoil	plagued	turning point	withdrew

1. Paul thought he had sold his car, but the woman who said she would buy it _____ her offer.

2. When Mrs. Wilson stood up, Jack realized that her action was his _____ to leave.

3. Our house was in a state of _____ while Mother was out of town attending a conference.

4. When you enter onto a superhighway from a smaller road, you must _____ quickly until your car is going as fast as the others on the highway.

5. Bad luck has _____ Mr. Avery throughout his entire life.

6. The discovery of a vaccine to prevent smallpox was an important _____ in the history of medicine.

7. Beverly Robinson was unable to get much work done today because the other people in the office talked _____.

8. The French economic advisor wanted to meet with his _____ in the British government so they could discuss rising oil prices.

9. Ever since Walter returned from his trip, he has been suffering from a strange _____ which his doctors are unable to identify.

10. Albert would like to sell his house for $60,000, but you can probably _____ for a lower price.

11. In the summer, Steve puts his house plants outside on the porch. They _____ on the fresh air and sunlight they get there.

12. Many people from warm climates who move to places like the northern United States find it difficult to _____ to the cold winters there.

13. When Mr. Porter lost his first three business deals, I thought he was just unlucky. However, when he continued to lose money, I decided he was _____.

14. It is dangerous to go out in a small boat when the wind is blowing very hard. A wise sailor waits until the winds _____.

Unit 15
Longer Reading

15. It is difficult to discuss emotional topics like politics in a(n) _____ manner.

16. Many people have been sick with the flu this month. If you have any of the _____ of the disease, call your doctor immediately.

17. When visiting a strange city, one should carry a map because it is easy to become _____.

18. Harry was confident of success when he agreed to take the job. He soon realized, however, that he had underestimated the _____ of the problems he would confront.

19. Although she refused to give the name of the person she had talked to, the newspaper reporter said she got her information from a _____ source.

20. Most of us avoid change whenever possible, but Anthony _____ each new situation with eagerness.

253

Appendix

Below is a list of the stems and affixes which appear in *Reader's Choice*. The number in parentheses indicates the unit in which an item appears.

Prefixes:

(5) a-, an-	not, without, lacking
(3) ante-	before
(5) bene-	well
(5) bi-	two
(9) by-	aside or apart from the common, secondary
(3) circum-	around
(1) com-, con-, col-, cor-, co-	together, with
(3) contra-, anti-	against
(9) de-	down from, away
(9) dia-	through, across
(9) epi-	upon, over, outer
(9) hyper-	above, beyond
(9) hypo-	under, beneath, down
(1) in-, im-	in, into, on
(1) in-, im-, il-, ir-	not
(3) inter-	between
(3) intro-, intra-	within
(1) micro-	small
(5) mis-	wrong, unfavorable
(5) mono-	one, alone
(7) multi-	many
(7) peri-	around
(5) poly-	many
(3) post-	after
(7) pre-	before
(1) re-, retro-	backward, back, behind
(7) semi-	half
(3) sub-, suc-, suf-, sug-, sup-, sus-	under
(3) super-	above, over
(5) syn-, sym-, syl-	with, together
(3) trans-	across
(7) tri-	three

Prefixes (*cont.*)	(7) ultra-	beyond, excessive, extreme
	(7) uni-	one

Stems:

(5)	-anthro-, -anthropo-	man
(5)	-arch-	first, chief
(7)	-aster-, -astro-, -stellar-	star
(1)	-audi-, -audit-	hear
(7)	-auto-	self
(7)	-bio-	life
(9)	-capit-	head
(3)	-ced-	go, move, yield
(1)	-chron-	time
(9)	-corp-	body
(7)	-cycle-	circle
(9)	-derm-	skin
(1)	-dic-, -dict-	say, speak
(3)	-duc-	lead
(5)	-fact-, -fect-	make, do
(3)	-flect-	bend
(5)	-gam-	marriage
(9)	-geo-	earth
(1)	-graph-, -gram-	write, writing
(5)	-hetero-	different, other
(5)	-homo-	same
(9)	-hydr-, -hydro-	water, liquid
(9)	-lith-	stone
(1)	-log-, -ology-	speech, word, study
(5)	-man-, -manu-	hand
(7)	-mega-	great
(1)	-metr-, -meter-	measure
(3)	-mit-, -miss-	send
(5)	-morph-	form
(7)	-mort-	death
(5)	-onym-, -nomen-	name
(9)	-ortho-	straight, correct
(5)	-pathy-	feeling, suffering
(7)	-phil-	love

Stems (*cont.*)		
(1) -phon-	sound	
(9) -pod-, -ped-	foot	
(7) -polis-	city	
(3) -port-	carry	
(7) -psych-	mind	
(1) -scop-	see, look at	
(1) -scope-	instrument for seeing or observing	
(1) -scrib-, -script-	write	
(3) -sequ-, -secut-	follow	
(1) -spect-	look at	
(3) -spir-	breathe	
(7) -soph-	wise	
(3) -tele-	far	
(5) -theo-, -the-	god	
(9) -therm-, -thermo-	heat	
(3) -vene-, -vent-	come	
(9) -ver-	true	
(3) -voc-	call	

Suffixes:

(3) -able, -ible, -ble	capable of, fit for	
(9) -ate	to make	
(1) -er, -or	the one who	
(9) -fy	to make	
(5) -ic, -al	relating to , having the nature of	
(5) -ism, -ist	action or practice, state or condition	
(7) -ist	one who	
(9) -ize	to make	
(5) -oid	like, resembling	
(3) -ous, -ious, -ose	full of, of the nature of	
(1) -tion, -ation	condition, the act of	

Answer Key

Reader's Choice is a reading skills textbook; the purpose of the tasks in the book is to provide students with the opportunity to practice and improve their reading skills. For this reason, the processes involved in arriving at an answer are often more important than the answer itself. It is expected that students will not use the Answer Key until they have completed the exercises and are prepared to defend their answers. If a student's answer does not agree with the Key, it is important for the student to return to the exercise to discover the source of the error. No answer is provided in instances where the students have been asked to express their own opinions or when there is not one best answer.

UNIT 1

NONPROSE READING: Menu

Exercise 1 (page 1)

1. Cocktails
2. Beverages
3. Desserts
4. Weight Watchers' Special
5. Answers are listed by section.
   Special Sandwiches: ham and cheese delight;
   Special Daily Econo Dinners: breaded pork cutlets, pork chop sandwich;
   Omelettes: ham (and cheese) omelettes;
   For Your Late Breakfast Pleasure: ham, bacon, sausage;
   Plain Sandwiches: grilled ham and cheese, Canadian bacon;
   Steak and Chops: pork chops
6. no
7. $2.35 (without tax)
8. Side Orders
9. For Your Late Breakfast Pleasure, Omelettes
10. $1.55 (without tax)
11. Yes; tipping is permitted unless otherwise stated.

Exercise 2 (pages 1-2)

1. F
2. F
3. T
4. F
5. F
6. F
7. T

WORD STUDY: Context Clues

Exercise 2 (page 5)

1. to pounce: to jump
2. to mildew: to mold; to rot
3. egret: a type of bird
4. to inveigh against: to talk loudly against; to attack verbally; to protest
5. to slither: to move like a snake; to slide

6. to pelt: to hit
7. kinesics: the study of body motion
8. gregarious: sociable; friendly
9. ravenous: extremely hungry
10. to salvage: to save

WORD STUDY: Dictionary Usage

Exercise 2 (page 8)

1. no
2. five
3. glu*tam*ic
4. paw, for
5. glottises
6. glued
7. gloweringly
8. glossography
9. Benjamin Peter Gloxin
10. French and Greek
11. no
12. four; although synonyms, their meanings are not exactly the same
13. 1714
14. 26,000
15. Answers include such things as the following: definitions; synonyms; parts of speech; pronunciation (syllabification and stress); alternate pronunciations; spelling and alternate spellings; if verb—principal parts; if noun—plural form; usage labels (archaic, obsolete, regional, etc.); origin of word (etymology); derived words; information about famous people; information about geographical places.

WORD STUDY: Stems and Affixes

Exercise 1 (pages 10-11)

1. a. 4
   b. 1
   c. 2
   d. 3
2. in, into

3. for example: inactive, inadequate, incapable, invisible, insane, insincere, inconvenient
4. yes; to write in a hurried or careless manner
5. no; it is derived from Latin *color*
6. writings which are carved into the wall
7. to predict: to foretell; to say that something will happen before it does (*pre*: before; *dict*: say)
8. for example: co-worker, coauthors, copilot
9. Word analysis indicates that *conspirators* means ones who breathe together (*con*: together; *spir*: breathe; *ors*: ones who). According to the dictionary, conspirators are people who join in a secret agreement, especially in order to commit an unlawful act. The meanings of the word parts have become more general; "breathing together" is related to the idea of "planning and working together quietly or in secret."

Exercise 2 (page 11)

1. b	6. d	11. b	16. d
2. c	7. e	12. a	17. c
3. d	8. b	13. e	18. a
4. e	9. a	14. c	19. e
5. a	10. c	15. d	20. b

SCANNING

Exercise 1 (page 12)

1. Religious Information pp. 341-358
2. Population, Nations of the World pp. 529-618
3. Calendars pp. 237-252
4. Maps (Color) pp. 517-528

Exercise 2 (page 14)

1. Angel 3,212 ft.
2. Highest fall, Angel 2,648 ft.
3. Urubupunga, Alto 40 ft.
4. 984 ft. Cusiana
5. 2
6. 6
7. 1

Exercise 3 (page 16)

1. Theater, Children's Theater, Community Theater
2. Nightlife, Discotheque
3. Sunday, Wednesday, Friday
4. yes; Hyatt Regency
5. James Tatum Trio
6. Detroit Symphony, Oakway Symphony
7. We don't know.

Exercise 4 (page 18)

1. 2 minutes, 26 seconds
2. 1,440 taps per minute, 24 taps per second

3. 8, 513—set by Theodore Roosevelt
4. longer than 8 months and 4 days (modern record); longer than 33 years and 3 months (ancient record)
5. 8 hours 5 minutes; no resting on other foot, no sticks
   12 hours 15 minutes; 5 minute rest period every hour
6. 128 coins (127 coins, 1 U.S. silver dollar)

PARAGRAPH READING: Main Idea (pages 21-25)

Paragraph 1: b
Paragraph 2: b
Paragraph 3: b
Paragraph 4: d
Paragraph 5: c

UNIT 2

**READING SELECTION 1: Technical Prose
"Crowded Earth—Billions More Coming"**

Comprehension (pages 26-28)

1. F	10. F
2. T	11. T
3. F	12. T
4. T	13. T
5. T	14. F
6. F	15. F
7. T	16. F
8. T	17. T
9. F	18. F

19. decline in infant mortality; increased life spans
20. greater likelihood of violence and upheaval
21. It is based on the 1972 rate of increase. Factors include medical advances, birth control education, natural disasters, etc.

**READING SELECTION 2: Mystery
"The Midnight Visitor"**

Comprehension Clues (page 31)

1. T
2. F
3. T
4. T
5. T

Max will not return because he jumped onto a balcony which did not exist.

READING SELECTION 3: Conversation
"Toledo: A Problem of Menus"

Comprehension (pages 35-36)

1. T
2. The tourist menu offers a good meal at a low price.
3. T
4. T
5. Michener was refused the tourist menu because he had not asked for it when he sat down.
6. T
7. T
8. T
9. a. The tourist menu did not include partridge.
   b. It only offered three dishes.
   c. It did not include the special wine.
10. F
11. following in order without interruption; consecutively; successively
    synonyms: running; straight
12. T
13. The man wore a tweed suit.
14. raunchy: offending; gamy; rotten
15. It was spoiled, rotten.
16. Well-hung partridge is partridge which has been left to hang without refrigeration before being cooked.
17. F
18. He didn't want the man to make a fool of himself.
19. inedible: unable to be eaten
20. This question is intended for discussion.

Vocabulary from Context (pages 36-37)

1. à la carte: with a separate price for each item on the menu
2. surcharge: an additional charge
3. adamant: firm, inflexible, determined; unwilling to change one's mind
4. rotten: spoiled; decomposed; tainted; bad
5. abuses: insulting or coarse language
   also: mistreatment, injuries
6. to reprimand: to criticize formally or severely; to scold
7. gravely: seriously
8. objectionable: offending; disagreeable
9. enticing: pleasing; tempting
   gamy: having a strong smell like that of cooked game; slightly tainted
11. raunchy: ugly, unpleasant; rotten

12. to console: to comfort; to cheer (a person) up after a disappointment
13. gingerly: carefully; cautiously; timidly; delicately

UNIT 3

NONPROSE READING: Newspaper Advertisements
(pages 38-40)

1. Lost and Found
2. Business Services
3. Wanted to Rent
4. Roommates
5. 800-4300
6. December 1
7. 2 ads under For Rent (Studio; Efficiency); 1 ad under Sublet (To Sublet)
8. Early Hour Wake-Up Service
9. Jon or Pat
10. 800-6157, 800-6906
11. Bob
12. Babysitter—My Home
13. 800-9846, 800-7487
14. 800-0557; Friday
15. no
16. There is a one-bedroom, modern, furnished apartment for rent. It costs $210.00 per month and has air conditioning. It is available after Christmas.
17. Moving: Must sell before Jan. 31. TV b/w, A/C, misc. clothing, used refrig., artif. Xmas tree, elec. typewriter (avail. after Jan. 20). Call Bob, 800-7351 bef. 9 p.m.

WORD STUDY: Stems and Affixes

Exercise 1 (pages 41-42)

1. c
2. a
3. b
4. c
5. c
6. telephone: an instrument that reproduces sound that comes from far away (*tele*: far; *phon*: sound)
   telegram: a written message sent far away (*tele*: far; *gram*: written)
   television: an instrument that produces a picture of something that is far away (*tele*: far)
7. when he or she wants to take a picture of something far away

8. support: to hold up physically or emotionally (*sup*: under; *port*: carry)
9. Interstate commerce is business between different states. Intrastate commerce is business within one state.
10. supersonic: faster than the speed of sound (*super*: above; *son*: sound)
11. a structure built to carry (lead) water from one place to another
12. He is going bald; his hairline is moving back.

Exercise 2 (page 43)

1. e	6. b	11. c	16. c
2. b	7. d	12. a	17. d
3. a	8. e	13. e	18. a
4. d	9. c	14. b	19. b
5. c	10. a	15. d	20. e

WORD STUDY: Dictionary Usage (pages 44-46)

1. a. 1. adjective
     2. weak; exhausted
   b. 1. noun
     2. break
2. consecutively
3. b
4. b
5. a
6. c
7. a
8. a. runner: 8
   b. runway: 6
   c. runes: 1
9. b
10. b
11. ruralist
12. a. 1
    b. 1

SENTENCE STUDY: Comprehension (pages 49-50)

1. c	6. d
2. b	7. c
3. b	8. a
4. d	9. c
5. a	

PARAGRAPH READING: Main Idea (pages 51-54)

Paragraph 1: c
Paragraph 2: d
Paragraph 3: d
Paragraph 4: a
Paragraph 5: c

UNIT 4

READING SELECTION 1: Newspaper Article
"World's Nonsmokers Take Up Fight for Cleaner Air"

Skimming (page 55)

Smoking is becoming less acceptable. Among the actions nations are taking to curb smoking are:
   restricting smoking in public places
   restricting prosmoking scenes on television and films
   raising the price of cigarettes
   removing cigarette vending machines
   introducing antismoking education
   restricting tobacco advertising
   making life insurance cheaper for nonsmokers

Scanning (page 57)

1. 30
2. a. increase b. increase c. increasing
3. They are seeking new markets in developing countries in order to gain new smokers.
4. Yes; Great Britain has a "forceful antismoking and nonsmokers' program."
5. The number of U.S. nonsmokers is rising.
6. They hope to cut cigarette consumption to the 1920 level and to create a generation of nonsmokers by the year 2000.
7. They are increasingly concerned about the "health effects of smoking."
8. The campaign has had "only limited success."

Vocabulary from Context (page 57)

1. hazard: danger
2. campaigns: programs; a series of organized, planned actions for a particular purpose
3. to eliminate: to remove; to omit; to get rid of
4. to ban: to prevent; to make illegal; to eliminate, prohibit, forbid
5. to restrict: to keep within limits; to hold down; to limit
6. to curb: to control, limit, restrict, restrain
7. consumption: smoking; use of goods or services

Vocabulary Review (page 57)

1. campaign
2. consume
3. health

READING SELECTION 2: Newspaper Questionnaire

Vocabulary (page 61)

attempt

READING SELECTION 3: Magazine Article
"Graveyard of the Atlantic"

Comprehension

Exercise 1 (page 65)

1. T
2. F
3. F
4. F
5. T
6. F
7. F

Exercise 2 (page 65)

1. 1,000
2. "curious glowing streaks of 'white water'"
3. 1973
4. ghost ship: a ship with no people aboard
5. Unique features include the swift Gulf Stream Current, underwater canyons, violent weather patterns, and the fact that compass needles point true north rather than magnetic north in the triangle.
6. Since all maps and charts are based on magnetic north, a sailor who forgets that in the triangle compass needles point true north, will find himself off course.
7. This question is intended for discussion.
8. This question is intended for discussion.

Vocabulary from Context (pages 66-67)

1. unique: exceptional; odd; unusual; one of a kind
2. treacherous: unreliable; unpredictable; changeable; dangerous
3. freak: unusual; oddly different from what is normal; queer; abnormal
4. impassable: not able to be traveled through; not navigable
5. to vanish: to disappear
6. cargo: the load of articles carried by a ship; freight
7. malfunction: failure to function, perform, or work as it should
8. evidence: signs; indications; information
9. to attribute: to think of as produced by or resulting from
10. extraterrestrial: from outer space; not of this universe or planet
11. weird: strange; unusual; odd; queer; mysterious; eerie
12. eerie: weird; frightening; strange; unusual

READING SELECTION 4: Narrative
"Bootle-Bumtrinket"

Comprehension (pages 71-72)

1. He wanted to go to the archipelago to catch animal life.
2. a boat
3. Mother: generous, has more money than the rest of the family; Margo: likes to shop; Larry: literary
4. T
5. F
6. T
7. adamant: firm, inflexible, determined; unwilling to change one's mind
8. F
9. F
10. F
11. the color
12. launch: cause a newly built boat to slide from the land into the water; set afloat
13. T
14. F
15. The boat turned turtle. to turn turtle: to turn over
16. F
17. F
18. F
19. Clydeside is a place where boats are built.
20. incensed: angry
21. After Larry had finished working on *Bootle-Bumtrinket*, it had a very short mast.

Vocabulary from Context (page 72)

1. tortured
2. archipelago
3. to tackle
4. blasphemy
5. to salvage

UNIT 5

WORD STUDY: Context Clues (page 76)

1. hazy: not clear
2. to anticipate: to guess in advance; to think of ahead of time; to foresee
3. massive: large; heavy; clumsy
4. vague: not specific; not clear; imprecise
5. to appease: to satisfy
6. to provoke: to cause
7. to manifest: to show; to demonstrate
8. toll: total; count; extent of loss
9. wretched: poor; terrible; miserable
10. mammoth: large

WORD STUDY: Stems and Affixes

Exercise 1 (pages 78-79)

1. a
2. d
3. c
4. a
5. d
6. b
7. d
8. b
9. c
10. Originally, *manufacture* meant to make by hand (*manu*: hand; *fact*: make). Now, products that are manufactured are often made by machine. Originally, *manuscripts* were books written by hand (*manu*: hand; *script*: write). Today, a manuscript is a document which is either hand-written or typed, but not printed: it is a document in prepublication form.

Exercise 2 (page 79)

1. f	7. a	13. b	19. b
2. b	8. e	14. e	20. c
3. a	9. d	15. a	21. a
4. d	10. f	16. c	22. e
5. c	11. c	17. f	23. d
6. e	12. b	18. d	24. f

SENTENCE STUDY: Comprehension (pages 80-81)

1. d	6. c
2. c	7. a
3. c	8. b
4. d	9. a
5. b	

PARAGRAPH READING: Restatement and Inference (pages 83-85)

Paragraph 1: b, d, e
Paragraph 2: b, d, e
Paragraph 3: a, c
Paragraph 4: b, d, e
Paragraph 5: a, b, e

UNIT 6

READING SELECTION 1: Magazine Article
"Conjugal Prep"

Comprehension (page 87)

1. F
2. T
3. housing, insurance, and child care
4. T
5. nine weeks; ten years
6. renting an apartment, having a baby, paying medical and other bills
7. a mother-in-law moves in, death, imprisonment
8. Some have found the experience "chastening to their real-life marital plans."
9. This question is intended for discussion.
10. This question is intended for discussion.

Vocabulary from Context (page 88)

1. mock: not real; imitation; false
2. to drown out: to cover (up) a sound
3. to giggle: to laugh nervously
4. adjustment: a change (made in order to fit a new situation)
5. to expose: to allow to be seen or experienced
6. nitty-gritty: basic; fundamental
7. trials and tribulations: problems
8. to strain: to weaken by force; to put pressure on
9. alimony: money paid to a former wife or husband
10. unsettling: disturbing
11. to endorse: to give support or approval

READING SELECTION 2: Narrative
Adaptation from *Cheaper by the Dozen*

Comprehension (pages 96-97)

1. F	6. F	11. F	16. T
2. T	7. T	12. F	17. F
3. F	8. T	13. F	18. T
4. T	9. T	14. F	19. T
5. T	10. T	15. F	20. T

Vocabulary from Context

Exercise 1 (page 97)

1. litter: the total number of animals born at one time of one mother
2. whistle: a shrill musical sound made by forcing air through the teeth
3. regimentation: rigid organization by which tasks are assigned
4. aptitude: special ability, talent; quickness to learn
5. (on the) verge: on the edge; about to do something
6. hysterical: wild; emotionally uncontrolled
7. nuisance: a bother; an act, condition, thing, or person causing trouble
8. incentive: encouragement; reward that makes one work or achieve; motive; stimulus

9. voluntary: of one's own will; without being forced to do something
10. ludicrous: extremely funny; ridiculous; silly; absurd

Exercise 2 (page 98)

1. offspring: children
2. tender: young
3. slashed: cut
4. sweep: clean (a floor with a broom)
5. mimicked: copied; imitated
6. abstained: didn't vote

Figurative Language and Idioms (page 98)

1. "practiced what he preached"
2. "no telling"
3. "eat (me) out of house and home"
4. "fits (her) like a glove"
5. "deal him in"
6. "pulled (my) leg"

Dictionary Study (page 99)

1. off: (*adj*. 6.) not up to the usual level, standard, etc.: as, an *off* season
2. bedlam: (*n*. 4.) noise and confusion; uproar also: (*n*. 3.) any noisy, confused place or situation
3. allowances: (*n*. 3.) an amount of money, food, etc. given regularly to a child, dependent, soldier, etc.
4. to tickle: (*v.t.* 2.) to amuse; delight: as, the story *tickled* him.
5. straight face: [from the adjective straight-faced] showing no amusement or emotion
6. spit and image: [Colloq.] perfect likeness; exact image
7. offhand: (*adv*.) without prior preparation or study; at once; extemporaneously

READING SELECTION 3: Magazine Article
"Sonar for the Blind"

Comprehension

Exercise 1 (pages 103-4)

1. They are unable to see and they are likely to be slow in intellectual development.
2. F
3. Dennis used clicking sounds to create echoes.
4. F
5. T
6. F
7. F
8. T

9. They help him distinguish objects on the right from those on the left.
10. a
11. c
12. c
13. The child covers his eyes to make another "disappear"; then he uncovers his eyes and shouts, "peek-a-boo!"
14. T

Exercise 2 (page 104)

1, 3, 4

Vocabulary from Context (page 104)

1. handicap: disadvantage; hindrance; a difficulty that holds one back
2. to lag: to fall behind
3. echo: the repetition of a sound produced by reflection of sound waves off a surface
4. to orient: to locate
5. pitch: the frequency (number of repetitions in a period of time) of vibrations of sound waves; higher frequency = higher pitch
6. to cope: to fight successfully; to be a match for; to manage; to handle

UNIT 7

NONPROSE READING: Poetry

Comprehension Clues (page 108)

"Living Tenderly": a turtle
1. rounded
2. a short snake
3. F
4. T
5. F

"Southbound on the Freeway": a highway with motorists and a police car
1. The tourist is parked in the air.
2. They are made of metal and glass.
   a. Their feet are round.
   b. They have four eyes; the two in back are red.
3. the road on which they travel
4. a. They have a fifth turning red eye on top.
   b. The others go slowly when it is around.
5. a large roadway

"By Morning": snow
1. fresh, daintily, airily
2. transparent
3. a covering
4. They become like fumbling sheep.
5. snow

WORD STUDY: Context Clues (page 109)

1. attributes: qualities; talents; abilities
2. to confer: to grant; to give to
3. plump: fat; chubby
4. pedantic: bookish; boring; giving attention to small, unimportant, scholarly details
5. aloof: above; apart from
6. to refrain: to hold back; to control oneself
7. ineffectual: not effective; not producing the intended effect
8. marigolds: a (type of) flower
9. drab: uninteresting; dull; cheerless; lacking in color or brightness
10. skin/cortex/membrane: outside cover of a body or organ; boundary

WORD STUDY: Stems and Affixes

Exercise 1 (pages 110-11)

1. b   5. b
2. c   6. b
3. d   7. c
4. d   8. a
9. An astronaut is a person who sails (travels) to the stars (outer space). (*astro*: star)
10. All the clothes look the same.
11. birth rate

Exercise 2 (page 112)

1. f	7. e	13. f	19. c
2. e	8. c	14. b	20. d
3. a	9. d	15. c	21. e
4. d	10. a	16. a	22. a
5. b	11. b	17. d	23. f
6. c	12. f	18. e	24. b

SENTENCE STUDY: Restatement and Inference (pages 114-16)

1. c, e	6. d
2. b, c, e	7. b, c
3. b, e	8. b, d, e
4. b, c	9. a, c, d
5. b, d	10. b, e

PARAGRAPH ANALYSIS: Reading for Full Understanding

Paragraph 1 (pages 120-21)

1. a	4. c
2. d	5. a
3. a	6. d

Paragraph 2 (page 122)

1. c	3. b
2. c	4. c

Paragraph 3 (pages 123-24)

1. d	5. b
2. d	6. b
3. a	7. a
4. c	8. a

Paragraph 4 (pages 125-26)

1. c	5. c
2. b	6. a
3. c	7. c
4. a	

Paragraph 5 (page 127)

1. d	3. d
2. a	4. a

UNIT 8

READING SELECTION 1: Magazine Article "Why We Laugh"

Comprehension

Exercise 1 (page 128)

1. T	6. F	11. T
2. T	7. F	12. F
3. T	8. T	13. T
4. T	9. T	14. F
5. F	10. T	

Exercise 2 (page 130)

1. 3 (4)	4. 8
2. 4	5. 1
3. 12	6. 2

(Other answers are possible for these questions.)

Critical Reading

Exercise 1 (page 130)

1. Bergson: essayist
2. Grotjahn: psychiatrist
3. Levine: professor of psychology
4. Plato: philosopher

Exercise 2 (page 131)

1. Freud
2. author
3. author
4. Grotjahn
5. author
6. author

Vocabulary from Context

Exercise 1 (pages 131-32)

1. anxiety: uneasiness; worry; nervousness, tension
2. to resent: to feel displeasure; to feel injured or offended
3. conscious: aware; knowing what one is doing and why
4. tension: nervousness; anxiety; mental or physical strain
5. to disguise: to hide; to cover up; to make unrecognizable
6. aggressive: attacking; bold; energetic; active
7. butt: the object of joking or criticism; target
8. target: the object of verbal attack or criticism; butt
9. to master: to control; to conquer; to overcome
10. factor: any circumstance or condition that brings about a result; a cause; an element
11. crucial: of extreme importance; decisive; critical; main
12. to suppress: to keep from appearing or being known; to hide; to repress
13. to repress: to prevent unconscious ideas from reaching the level of consciousness; to supress
14. drive: basic impulse or urge; desire; pressure
15. to discharge: to release; to get rid of; to emit; to relieve oneself of a burden
16. to trigger: to initiate an action; to cause a psychological process to begin
17. cue: a stimulus that triggers a behavior; a trigger
18. crisis: an emergency; a crucial or decisive situation whose outcome decides whether possible bad consequences will follow
19. guilty: having done wrong; feeling responsible for wrong doing
20. integral: essential; basic; necessary for completeness

Exercise 2 (page 133)

1. to intersperse: to put among things; to interrupt
   to avert: to avoid; to miss; to prevent
2. to inhibit: to suppress; to hide
3. foible: weakness; fault; minor flaw in character
4. to ogle: to keep looking at with fondness or desire
   dowdy: not neat or fashionable

Vocabulary Review (page 133)

1. cue
2. trigger
3. resent
4. conscious
5. aggression

READING SELECTION 2: Narrative
"An Attack on the Family"

Comprehension

Exercise 1 (page 136)

1. F
2. T
3. When he switched on the torch, they would walk away. Also, the family would not allow him to bring scorpions into the house to study.
4. T
5. The babies clung to the mother's back.
6. F
7. when Larry went to light a match after dinner
8. Margo was trying to throw water on the scorpions but missed.
9. F
10. F
11. T
12. The author carried them outside on a saucer.
13. T

Exercise 2 (page 137)

1. Roger is a dog.
2. Lugaretzia is not a member of the family; she is probably a servant.
3. five: Mother (f), Larry (m), author (m), Leslie (m), Margo (f)
4. Leslie
5. Larry
6. Margo
7. Mother
8. the author
9. This question is intended for discussion.

Vocabulary from Context

Exercise 1 (pages 137-38)

1. glimpses: brief, quick views; passing looks
2. enraptured (with/by): fascinated; enchanted; entranced; filled with pleasure
3. rage: extreme anger
4. bewildered: confused
5. plea: a request; appeal; statement of begging
6. courtship: the process or period of time during which one person attempts to win the love of another
7. to crouch: to bow low with the arms and legs drawn close to the body; to bend low; to squat
8. in vain: without effect; fruitlessly

Exercise 2 (page 138)

1. trial
2. to smuggle
3. doom
4. chaos, pandemonium
5. order

Exercise 3 (page 139)

1. assaults: attacks; invasions
2. clinging: holding on to
3. manoeuvred: managed or planned skillfully; manipulated; moved
4. maintain: argue; affirm; declare to be true
5. hoisted: pulled; lifted
6. scuttled: ran or moved quickly, as away from danger
7. peered: looked closely and searchingly, as in order to see more clearly
8. hurled: threw
9. drenched: made wet all over; saturated with water
10. swarmed: moved around in large numbers; completely covered something
11. screeching: screaming
12. reluctance: hesitation; unwillingness; a feeling of not wanting to do something

**READING SELECTION 3: Short Story
"The Lottery"**

Comprehension

Exercise 1 (page 146)

1. T
2. F
3. F
4. T
5. F
6. F
7. T
8. F
9. T

Exercise 2 (page 146)

1. T
2. F
3. T
4. T
5. T
6. F
7. F

Drawing Inferences (page 147)

1. Answers might include such things as the following:
   People were nervous.
   Tessie didn't want to win the lottery.
2. Answers might include such things as the following:
   Normal Lottery
   a. The whole village was present.
   b. Tessie's arrival was good-humored.
   c. Mr. Summers conducted square dances, teen clubs, and the lottery.
   d. The slips of paper and the initial ritual of the lottery seemed typical.
   Strange Lottery
   a. Piles of rocks were prepared.
   b. People hesitated to volunteer to hold the box.
   c. Some villages had already stopped having a lottery.
   d. Mr. Warner considered such villages barbaric.
   e. A girl whispered, "I hope it's not Nancy."
   f. Tessie didn't want to win; she wanted to include her married children in the second drawing.
   Double Meaning
   a. There was no place to leave the box during the year.
   b. The Watson boy blinked his eyes "nervously."
   c. There were continual references to tension, nervousness, and humorless grins.
   d. Mrs. Dunbar said to "get ready to run tell Dad."
3. They had to take part so that everyone would be responsible, so that everyone would have to take part next year.
4. Mr. Warner felt that giving up the lottery would bring bad luck and would be uncivilized. He represents the older, more conservative members of a society who resist change.
5. Tessie wanted more people to be included in the final drawing so that her chances of "winning" would be reduced.
6. *Changes in the Lottery*
   a. The original paraphernalia had been lost.
   b. The box had changed.
   c. Slips of paper had replaced wooden chips.
   d. There used to be a recital and ritual salute.
   Unchanged Elements of the Lottery
   a. The list of names was checked in the same way.
   b. The black box was made with wood from the original box.
   c. There were two drawings and the result of the lottery had remained the same.

Vocabulary from Context

Exercise 1 (page 148)

1. ritual: any formal, customary observance or procedure; ceremony; rite
2. paraphernalia: equipment; any collection of things used in some activity

3. drawing: a lottery; the act of choosing a winner in a lottery
4. gravely: seriously; soberly; somberly; solemnly
5. soberly: seriously; gravely; solemnly; sedately
6. murmur: a low, indistinct, continuous sound
7. to discard: to throw away, abandon, or get rid of something which is no longer useful
8. to disengage: to release oneself; to get loose; to leave

Exercise 2 (page 148)

1. boisterous
2. reprimands
3. gossip
4. fussing
5. interminably

Exercise 3 (page 149)

1. to devote: to give
2. stirred up: moved; shook; displaced
3. to fade off: to slowly disappear or end; to die out
4. shabbier: older; more broken down; worn out; showing more wear
5. to lapse: to fall away; to slip from memory; to return to former ways
6. craned: raised or moved
7. tapped: hit lightly
8. consulted: looked at; checked; referred to; sought information from

UNIT 9

NONPROSE READING: Train Schedule (page 151)

1. three; the St. Clair, the Blue Water, the Wolverine; they offer daily service
2. between Niles, Michigan, and Chicago, Illinois; 2:15 P.M.
3. the Blue Water
4. There is no direct route between Lansing and Ann Arbor.
5. Sarnia to Toronto: 174 miles
   Windsor to Toronto: 223 miles
6. Chicago to Niles: 89 miles; 1 hr., 55 min.
7. the St. Clair
8. No; tickets are not available at Lapeer for some or all trains. No; no penalty is charged if no agent is on duty at train time.
9. the Wolverine (13 hr., 25 min.)
10. a. The Wolverine is faster than the St. Clair (13 hr., 25 min., to 17 hr., 35 min.).

b. Both trains take you to Detroit only. Apparently you must get to the Windsor (Canada) station by bus, taxi, etc., to connect with another train.
c. time between trains:
   the St. Clair: 7 hr., 45 min.
   the Wolverine: 3 hr., 30 min.
d. the St. Clair

Most people would probably take the Wolverine.

WORD STUDY: Stems and Affixes

Exercise 1 (page 153)

1. hydroelectric (plant): a plant which uses water power to produce electricity
2. thermometer: an instrument that measures heat and indicates temperature
3. hyperactive: overactive; too active; abnormally active
4. to verify: to make sure it is true; to confirm
5. pedals: the parts of the bicycle moved by the feet to make the wheels turn
6. dehydration: loss of water from the body
7. tripod: a three-legged stand used to hold a camera
8. hypersensitive: overly sensitive; too easily hurt
9. hypodermic: a needle used to inject substances under the skin
10. orthodontics: a type of dentistry concerned with straightening teeth
11. deported: made (him) leave the country
12. per capita: individual; for each person
13. dermatologist: a doctor who treats skin diseases
14. geothermal: heat of the earth
15. bipedal: walked on two feet

Exercise 2 (page 154)

1. d	7. e	13. b	19. b
2. a	8. f	14. a	20. a
3. e	9. d	15. c	21. c
4. c	10. b	16. f	22. e
5. b	11. a	17. d	23. f
6. f	12. c	18. e	24. d

SENTENCE STUDY: Comprehension
(pages 155-56)

1. d	6. a
2. b	7. b
3. a	8. d
4. c	9. b
5. c	

PARAGRAPH READING: Restatement and Inference
(pages 157-59)

Paragraph 1: e
Paragraph 2: a, b, c, d
Paragraph 3: b
Paragraph 4: a (c)
Paragraph 5: a, d

UNIT 10

READING SELECTION 1: Satire
"Pockety Women Unite?"

Comprehension

Exercise 1 (page 162)

1. They hold better positions because they are men; cultural traditions and social conditioning have worked together to give them a special place in the world order.
2. 9
3. none
4. There is a positive correlation between pockets and power.
5. Pockets hold all the equipment necessary for running the world; they are necessary for efficiency, order, confidence.
6. It is difficult to organize one's belongings in a purse; a purse makes one appear to be disorganized.
7. Women should form a pocket lobby and march on the New York garment district. Women should give men gifts of pocketless shirts and men's handbags.

Exercise 2 (page 162)

This exercise is intended to encourage discussion and to force students to come to a better understanding of the purpose of the article. Students can potentially defend all seven items.

Vocabulary from Context (page 163)

1. status: position; rank; standing
2. prestige: power to command admiration; distinction based on achievement; reputation; standing in the community
3. correlation: a close or natural relation; a correspondence
4. purse: a handbag, pocketbook; a bag in which money and personal belongings are carried
5. to attain: to gain through effort; to achieve; to come to, arrive at; to reach; to get

Dictionary Study (page 164)

1. match: (*n. 1a.*) a person, group, or thing able to cope with or oppose another as an equal in power, size, etc.
2. tip: (second entry, *n. 2.*) a piece of information given secretly or confidentially in an attempt to be helpful: as, he gave me a *tip* on the race. also: (*n. 3.*) a suggestion, hint, warning, etc.
3. lobbyist: (*n.*) a person who tries to get legislators to introduce or vote for measures favorable to a special interest that he represents. [a person who attempts to change a group's opinions]

READING SELECTION 2: Feature Article
"Japanese Style in Decision-Making"

Comprehension

Exercise 1 (page 167)

1. J	6. US
2. US	7. US
3. J	8. J
4. US	9. US
5. US	

Exercise 2 (page 167)

1. In Japan the most important thing is what organization you work for; in the United States one's position in a company defines one's professional identity.
2. See paragraphs 10 and 11, page 165, for explanations of the "I to you" and "you to you" approaches.
   See paragraph 16, page 165, for an explanation of Western versus Japanese decision-making.
3. a. The Japanese try to formulate a rather broad direction.
   b. Westerners like to take time for in-depth planning.
4. Employees stay at work after hours, until the job is completed.
5. The author is Yoshio Terasawa, President of Nomura Securities International, Inc. The article was adapted from a speech before the Commonwealth Club of San Francisco.

Vocabulary from Context

Exercise 1 (pages 168-69)

1. to formulate: to form; to express in a systematic way
2. reliance: dependence

3. adroit: skillful; clever
4. confrontation: a face-to-face meeting, as of antagonists, competitors, or enemies
5. harmony: agreement of feeling, action, ideas, interests, etc.; peaceful or friendly relations
6. consensus: agreement finger in opinion; agreement among all parties
7. mutual: done, felt, etc., by two or more people for each other; reciprocal
8. literate: able to read and write; educated
9. articulate: able to express oneself clearly
10. stability: resistance to change; permanence
11. mobility: movement; change
12. exasperated: angered; irritated; frustrated; annoyed
13. deadline: a time limit
14. dedication: seriousness; loyalty; faithfulness; devotion to some duty
15. unanimous: showing complete agreement; united in opinion
16. homogeneous: composed of similar elements or parts; similar; identical; uniform
17. inflexible: not flexible; rigid; not adjustable to change; not capable of modification
18. unilateral: done or undertaken by one side only; not reciprocal
19. firm: company; business

Exercise 2 (page 169)

1. vocational: professional; relating to one's job
2. forthrightly: directly
3. densely: with many people in a small area; with the parts crowded together
4. consult: to seek information
5. impact: effect; influence
6. converted: changed

Figurative Language and Idioms (page 170)

1. "coming to grips with"
2. "for a living"
3. "sounding out"
4. "keeping (your) finger on the pulse"
5. "falls through"
6. "paper logjam"
7. "pitch in"

Vocabulary Review

Exercise 1 (page 170)

1. adroit
2. articulate
3. transactions
4. exasperated
5. deadlines
6. dedicated
7. reliance
8. formulate

Exercise 2 (page 171)

1. unilaterally
2. confrontation
3. heterogeneous
4. mobility
5. inflexible
6. unilateral

READING SELECTION 3: Short Story
"The Chaser"

Comprehension (page 174)

1. F
2. F
3. a glove-cleaner or a life-cleaner
4. poison
5. T
6. She is sociable, fond of parties, and not interested in Alan.
7. Diana will want nothing but solitude and Alan; she will be jealous; Alan will be her sole interest in life; she will want to know all that he does; she will forgive him anything but will never divorce him.
8. T
9. The first drink is the love potion; the unpleasant "taste" is the fact that Diana will be so possessive; the chaser will be the poison (the glove-cleaner).
10. People who bought the love potion always came back for the $5,000 mixture.

Drawing Inferences (pages 174-75)

1. Alan thinks the old man is describing love. The old man knows he is describing a terrible situation.
2. Alan thinks it is wonderful that his wife will never divorce him. The old man knows that some day Alan may want his wife to give him a divorce and she will refuse.
3. Alan thinks customers come back, as they do to any store, because they have found something there before that they needed; they come back of their own free will. The old man knows that if he "obliges" his customers with the love potion, they *must* come back.
4. Alan thinks the old man means goodbye. The old man means, "until I see you again"; he knows that Alan will return.

271

Vocabulary from Context

Exercise 1 (page 175)

1. poison: a substance, usually a drug, causing death or severe injury
2. imperceptible: not able to be perceived; unnoticeable
3. sufficient: enough
4. confidential: trusting; entrusted with private or secret matters
5. to oblige: to satisfy, please, help someone; to do a favor for; to perform a service
6. solitude: to be alone; isolation
7. jealous: demanding exclusive loyalty; resentfully suspicious of competitors; envious; distrustful; suspicious

Exercise 2 (page 176)

1. dim
2. stock
3. apprehensively
4. oblige
5. sirens
6. grounds

Exercise 3 (page 176)

1. peered: looked at closely and searchingly in order to see more clearly
2. potion: a drink, especially a medicine or poison
3. slip a little: make a mistake; fall into error; be unfaithful to his wife
4. dear: expensive
5. better off: wealthier; richer

UNIT 11

NONPROSE READING: Road Map

Introduction

Exercise 1 (page 177)

2. a. K-10
3. W. Trinity Lane and Whites Creek Pike
4. a. Bowling Green is about 25 miles/40 kilometers from the Ky.-Tenn. border.
   b. Route 31W is a Federal highway while route 65 is an Interstate highway.
   [*All* Interstate highways are multi-lane, divided, controlled access roads. In contrast, Federal highways have widely varying characteristics. For instance, although some Federal highways are divided, 31W is not.]
5. 66 miles (106 kilometers)

Exercise 2 (page 178)

1. e	4. c
2. b	5. d
3. a	6. c

Map Reading

Exercise 1 (pages 178-79)

1. T	7. T
2. F	8. F
3. T	9. T
4. F	10. T
5. T	11. F
6. T	

Exercise 2 (page 179)

1. yes; 50 miles per hour/80 kilometers per hour
2. Answers might include such routes as the following:
   31W or 65 ⟶ 101 ⟶ 259 ⟶ 70
   or (31W) → 65 ⟶ 70
   You can spend the night at the Park.
3. Answers might include such routes as the following:

   70S (Dam) ⟨ 70 or 42 ⟶ 40 / 70 ⟶ 96 ⟩ ⟶

   231 (Park) ⟶ 40 or 41 (Nashville)

WORD STUDY: Context Clues (page 183)

1. precariously: dangerously; uncertainly
2. to trudge: to walk tiredly, slowly
3. turmoil: confusion
4. grooming: personal cleaning; the act of making neat and tidy
5. matrimony: marriage
6. probe: a long slender instrument used for delicate exploration
7. to convene: to call together; to start
8. to ingest: to eat; to take inside
9. autocratic: dictatorial; undemocratic; tyrannical; domineering
10. limnology: fresh water biology

SENTENCE STUDY: Restatement and Inference
(pages 184-87)

1. d	6. a, c
2. a, b	7. b, c, d, e
3. a, b, c, e	8. d, e
4. a	9. b
5. c	10. a, d

PARAGRAPH ANALYSIS: Reading for Full Understanding

Paragraph 1 (page 188)

1. a   4. c
2. b   5. c
3. a

Paragraph 2 (page 189)

1. c   3. b
2. b   4. d

Paragraph 3 (page 190)

1. b   4. b
2. c   5. d
3. c

Paragraph 4 (page 191)

1. b   3. c
2. c   4. b

Paragraph 5 (pages 192-93)

1. c   5. a
2. b   6. c
3. a   7. b
4. c

UNIT 12

READING SELECTION 1: Textbook
"The Sacred 'Rac' "

Comprehension (page 196)

1. the Asu
2. They live on the American continent north of the Tarahumara of Mexico.
3. T
4. The cost is so high because of the long period of training the specialist must undergo and the difficulty of obtaining the right selection of magic charms.
5. T
6. It may be used as a beast of burden.
7. The Asu must build more paths for the rac; the Asu must pay high taxes; some Asu must move their homes.
8. F
9. The rac kills thousands of the Asu a year.
10. T
11. car

Drawing Inferences (page 196)

She feels that individuals and societies are foolish to sacrifice so much for cars. People often notice problems of other cultures more easily than those of their own culture. The author hopes that people in the United States will be able to examine the effect of the car on their society more realistically if they do not realize immediately that they are reading about themselves.

Vocabulary from Context (page 197)

1. preoccupied: absorbed in one's thoughts; unable to concentrate
2. temperament: disposition; emotional or psychological characteristics; frame of mind
3. prestigious: admired; important; distinguished; of a high rank
4. to treat: to give medical care to
5. ailing: sick
6. puberty rites: ceremonies that mark adulthood
7. to petition: to make a formal request; to ask; to beg
8. detrimental: damaging; harmful; injurious
9. to regard: to consider or think of as being something

READING SELECTION 2: Narrative
"The Talking Flowers"

Comprehension (page 201)

1. F   7. T
2. F   8. F
3. F   9. F
4. F   10. T
5. T   11. T
6. T

Reading for Details

Exercise 1 (page 201)

1, 3, 4, 6, 7
(Other choices are possible; impressions of Mrs. Kralefsky will vary from reader to reader.)

Exercise 2 (page 202)

1, 3, 4

Exercise 3 (page 202)

1. Mrs. Kralefsky's hair
2. Mrs. Kralefsky's room
3. the wrinkles on Mrs. Kralefsky's face
4. Mrs. Kralefsky's room
5. Mrs. Kralefsky's hair

Vocabulary from Context

Exercise 1 (page 203)

1. embarrassing: causing to feel self-consious; confused and ill at ease
2. startled: suprised
3. astonished: surprised; amazed
4. gingerly: carefully
5. intrigued: fascinated
6. vanity: excessively high regard for something about oneself; cause for self-esteem; love of self
7. to thrive: to flourish; to be successful; to grow vigorously or luxuriantly; to improve physically
8. flattered: made to feel pleased or honored

Exercise 2 (page 204)

1. finicky
2. eccentric
3. belligerent

Exercise 3 (page 204)

1. lavatories: bathrooms
2. to adopt: to use; to take and use as one's own
3. ushered: led
4. propped up: supported
5. auburn: reddish brown
6. languid: slow; without vigor, spirit, energy
7. touched: slightly crazy; queer
8. plucked: picked
9. pick-me-up: something that makes one feel better

READING SELECTION 3: Essay
"The City"

Comprehension

Exercise 1 (page 208)

1, 2, 3, 6, 8, 10

Exercise 2 (pages 208-9)

1. F	8. F
2. O author	9. F
3. F	10. 0 generations of American theory; those responsible for the Homestead Act
4. O Frenchman	
5. O others	
6. F	11. F
7. O Jefferson	12. O rural Americans

Vocabulary from Context

Exercise 1 (pages 209-10)

1. suspect: viewed with mistrust; believed to be bad, wrong, harmful, questionable

2. priority: value, rank; the right to come first; precedence
3. absurd: ridiculous; silly
4. to subsidize: to grant money to, as the government granting money to a private enterprise; to support
5. predicament: a troublesome or difficult situation
6. integral: essential; basic; necessary for completeness
7. corrupt: spoiled; evil; bad; morally unsound; departing from the normal standard
8. despot: oppressor; dictator; tyrant; autocrat

Exercise 2 (page 210)

1. dispersion
2. fend (for)
3. renovation

Exercise 3 (page 211)

1. to trace: to find the source of something by following its development from the latest to the earliest time
2. flocking: coming in large numbers
3. antipathy: a definite dislike
4. pastoral: rural
5. charting: planning; plotting; mapping
6. waves: arrivals of large groups of people
7. ethnic: of or pertaining to nationalities
8. to bar: to stop; to prevent
9. fled: left; ran away from
10. subtle: indirect; difficult to understand, solve, or detect; clever; skillful

UNIT 13

LONGER READING: Suspense
"The Dusty Drawer"

Comprehension (pages 222-24)

1. The answers to this question depend on the reader's perception of people and events. Students can potentially defend Tritt and/or Logan as answers to all items except a and e (we know from paragraphs 2 and 11 that Tritt is fat).
2. b, d, f, e, a, c
3. Tritt was a teller.
4. Logan was a professor of botany at a local university.

5. T	10. c	15. F	20. c
6. b	11. T	16. T	21. T
7. a	12. d	17. c	22. T
8. F	13. T	18. c	23. a
9. d	14. T	19. T	

Vocabulary from Context (pages 225-26)

1. obsequious: being excessively willing to serve or obey; extremely submissive; acting like a servant
2. to compel: to force
3. grimy: extremely dirty and greasy
4. to restrain: to hold back; to control
5. indulgently: patiently; kindly
6. version: an account showing a particular point of view; a particular form or variation of something
7. futility: uselessness; hopelessness
8. vengeance: injuring someone in return for an injury he has caused you; the return of one injury for another
9. cluttered: messy; confused, disorganized; filled with junk
10. hallucination: a product of the imagination; the apparent perception of sights, sounds, etc., that are not actually present
11. incredulous: unbelieving; doubtful; unwilling or unable to believe; skeptical
12. indignant: angry; scornful, especially when one has been improperly or unjustly treated
13. flustered: upset; confused; nervous
14. to jeopardize: to endanger; to put into danger

Figurative Language and Idioms (page 226)

1. "going a long, long way"
2. "get away with it"
3. "I'll get you"
4. "I can't stand to be had"
5. "pin (the robbery) on"
6. "polished off"
7. "a stick-up"

Dictionary Study (page 227)

1. to reflect: (*v.i.* 4.) to think seriously; contemplate; ponder (with *on* or *upon*) Note: the answer is misleading. Many people would consider *reflect* in this sentence to be a transitive verb. However, there is not an appropriate definition in the dictionary entry under *v.t.* An example of *reflect* used in an obviously intransitive sense is the following: After hearing that he had lost his job, John just sat for several minutes and *reflected*.
2. to stumble: (*v.i.* 5.) to come by chance; happen: as, I *stumbled* across a clue.
3. grip: (*n.* 5.) the power of understanding; mental grasp
4. to stake: (*v.t.* 5.) to risk or hazard; gamble; bet: as, he *staked* his winnings on the next hand.

Vocabulary Review

Exercise 1 (page 228)

1. obsequiousness
2. go a long way
3. restraint
4. flustered
5. hallucinations
6. grime
7. get away with it
8. vengeance
9. grip
10. version
11. futile
12. compelled
13. clutter
14. reflect
15. incredulous
16. indulgent
17. indignantly
18. jeopardize

Exercise 2 (page 229)

1. obsequious
2. incredulously
3. futility
4. vengeance
5. indulgent
6. grime
7. jeopardize

UNIT 14

LONGER READING: Anthropology
"In the Shadow of Man"

Comprehension

Exercise 1 (page 235)

1. T
2. F
3. F
4. F
5. T
6. T
7. F
8. F
9. T
10. F
11. T
12. T
13. F
14. T

Exercise 2 (pages 235-36)

1, 2, 3, 5, 6

Vocabulary from Context (pages 236-37)

1. sophisticated: complex; complicated
2. innate: possessed from birth; inborn; not learned
3. posture: the position of the body; carriage; bearing
4. to hurl: to throw with force; to move vigorously
5. to stroke: to caress; to rub lightly with the hand
6. gesture: movement of the body or part of the body to express ideas, emotions, etc.
7. inevitable: something which cannot be avoided or prevented
8. altruistic: unselfishly concerned for another person
9. to derive: to get or receive (from a source); to trace from or to a source; to originate

10. submissive: humble; compliant; yielding to others
11. spontaneously: naturally; voluntarily; freely
12. to probe: to search; to explore with an instrument; to investigate with great thoroughness

Stems and Affixes (page 237)

1. c   6. d
2. e   7. h
3. f   8. j
4. a   9. i
5. g   10. b

Figurative Language and Idioms (page 238)

1. "spontaneously"   4. "told (him) off"
2. "to burst into tears"   5. "to draw parallels"
3. "flew into a tantrum"   6. "bowled over"

Vocabulary Review (pages 239-40)

1. sophisticated   9. flew into a tantrum
2. gestured   10. probes
3. inevitable   11. posture
4. innate   12. spontaneously
5. hurled   13. draw parallels
6. burst into tears   14. stroking
7. Altruism   15. derived
8. submissive

UNIT 15

**LONGER READING: Social Science
"The 800th Lifetime"**

Comprehension (page 245)

1. F   6. F
2. T   7. T
3. T   8. F
4. T   9. T
5. T   10. F

Reading for Details (pages 245-46)

1. F   6. F
2. T   7. T
3. T   8. F
4. F   9. F
5. T

Vocabulary from Context

Exercise 1 (pages 246-47)

1. confrontation: a meeting; an encounter

2. to adapt: to change (oneself) so that one's behavior, attitudes, etc., will conform to new or changed circumstances; to make suitable, especially by changing
3. turmoil: confusion; disturbance; commotion
4. incessantly: continuously; constantly
5. to abate: to decrease in force or intensity
6. eminent: famous; distinguished; outstanding; prominent
7. to accelerate: to increase in speed
8. epochal: important or memorable; marking the beginning of an important period in the history of something
9. to thrive: to be successful; to flourish
10. reputable: respected; honorable; trustworthy; well thought of
11. incomprehensible: impossible to understand
12. scope: the area or field within which any activity occurs; the size, range, extent of an action
13. rationally: logically; reasonably
14. to withdraw: to take away; to remove from use; to retract
15. cue: sign; signal
16. negotiable: reached by discussion or debate; bargainable; not fixed
17. disoriented: confused; lost, in the sense of time, place, or identity
18. malady: disease; illness
19. incompetent: not able to do a job satisfactorily; lacking the necessary qualifications or abilities
20. symptom: a condition accompanying or resulting from a disease; an indication
21. transience: impermanence; temporariness; the condition of passing quickly
22. counterpart: having the same function or characteristics; equivalent

Exercise 2 (page 248)

1. to combat: to fight
2. impact: effect
3. cut him off from: separate him from
4. prospect: what is expected; probable outcome
5. upheaval: a sudden, violent change or disturbance
6. irretrievably: completely; in a way that can't be recovered

Figurative Language and Idioms (page 248)

1. "brought on by"
2. "a turning point"

Dictionary Study (page 248)

1. to plague: (*v.t.* 2.) to vex; harass; trouble; torment
2. to haunt: (*v.t.* 3.) to appear or recur frequently; to obsess: as, memories *haunted* her.
   also: (*v.t.* 2.) to annoy or pester (a person) by constant visiting, following, etc.
3. roughly (*adv.* 2.) approximately
4. to touch off: (3.) to motivate or initiate
   to trigger: (*v.t.* [Colloq.]) to initiate (an action); set off: as, the fights *triggered* a riot.

Vocabulary Review

Exercise 1 (page 251)

1. incessant
2. trigger
3. cue
4. transience
5. roughly
6. haunted

Exercise 2 (pages 252-53)

1. withdrew
2. cue
3. turmoil
4. accelerate
5. plagued
6. turning point
7. incessantly
8. counterpart
9. malady
10. negotiate
11. thrive
12. adapt
13. incompetent
14. abate
15. rational
16. symptoms
17. disoriented
18. scope
19. reputable
20. confronts